COMPOSITION AND LITERATURE

A Rhetoric for Critical Writing

ROSANNA GRASSI and PETER DeBLOIS

Syracuse University

PRENTICE-HALL, INC., Englewood Cliffs, N. J. 07632

Library of Congress Cataloging in Publication Data

GRASSI, ROSANNA.
  Composition and literature.

  Includes index.
  1. English language—Rhetoric.   2. Literature—
Study and teaching.   3. Criticism.   I. DeBlois,
Peter.   II. Title.
PE1479.C7G68   1984   808'.0668   83-13834
ISBN 0-13-163428-3

Editorial/production supervision and interior design: Virginia Rubens
Cover design: George Cornell
Manufacturing buyer: Harry P. Baisley

Printed in the United States of America

10   9   8   7   6   5

ISBN 0-13-163428-3

Prentice-Hall International, Inc., *London*
Prentice-Hall of Australia Pty. Limited, *Sydney*
Editora Prentice-Hall do Brasil, Ltda., *Rio de Janeiro*
Prentice-Hall Canada Inc., *Toronto*
Prentice-Hall of India Private Limited, *New Delhi*
Prentice-Hall of Japan, Inc., *Tokyo*
Prentice-Hall of Southeast Asia Pte. Ltd., *Singapore*
Whitehall Books Limited, *Wellington, New Zealand*

CONTENTS

PREFACE

TO THE INSTRUCTOR

English teachers have long wanted a text that smoothes the transition from writing courses to literature courses. Such a text should assume neither complete mastery of basic composition skills nor perfected techniques of critical reading and writing. We have written *Composition and Literature* realizing that, while literature courses usually involve writing, these courses serve different purposes at different institutions or even within the same institution. For some, improvement of writing may be a major aim of the literature course and an integral part of class coverage. In other courses, there may be little or no time to review the basics of essay writing, even though some students still need such attention after completing required writing courses.

We hope this text can be useful in both situations. We see it as a bridge between the general freshman composition course and courses in the intensive study of literature. *Composition and Literature* might be used as the core rhetoric for a literature class, reinforcing compositional skills and applying them to the specific discipline of literary study. Or the text might be used as a reference for students who are not yet independent writers about literature. In either case, the text helps expand the writer's repertoire of skills for crafting the *critical* essay, from the large-scale concerns of invention and generating a thesis to such matters as paragraph construction and incorporating evidence.

We assume that *Composition and Literature* will probably be used with an anthology of literature, so we did not try to be comprehensive in choosing literary works for the Appendix. The two stories and ten poems are the basis for sample student writing that, we hope, is representative when illustrating weaknesses and believable when illustrating strengths. It would, of course, be helpful for the student to be familiar with these works when reading the text.

Also, we expect that some of our writing exercises may be more appropriate than others for different courses and students. The exercises are easily adaptable to works outside the Appendix, namely works your students are studying.

Lastly, while Chapter 1 should probably be covered early, the other chapters might be rearranged to suit a particular curriculum; they are fairly independent in their coverage. While we do not have separate chapters on different literary genres, you will notice that many chapters are divided into sections on fiction, drama, and poetry, with the view that common literary elements are the more compelling structural principle. Knowing how complex literary study is, we tread a middle ground between oversimplifying for clarity's sake and presenting the various possible critical approaches to literature. We anticipate that our audience will be beginning writers and students of literature. Hopefully we have not aimed too high or too low.

Our view throughout is that a complete and rewarding reading experience depends on good critical writing. While composition and literature are frequently separate courses at many schools, we hope that intermingling them in this text will help strengthen both and provide students with the tools to become more sensitive readers and more thoughtful, organized, and responsive writers, not just in one class but throughout their college years.

TO THE STUDENT

Writing about literature is a complex task, but the result is a richer reading experience. Critical writing involves reading with perception, not only the literal words on the page, but the implied emotions and thoughts which are subtly woven into the literal meaning. It involves not only understanding the works of literature, but responding to them. Your thoughts about an author's ideas might form the basis for an exploration in an essay. Writing about literature also involves the skills of crafting a critical essay. You first have the opportunity to explore the literary work and your reactions, and then you have the responsibility of organizing and supporting your thoughts in a convincing manner for your own audience—your instructor and perhaps your classmates.

We hope that *Composition and Literature* will aid you in applying what you know already about different kinds of writing to writing an essay about literature. We have tried not to oversimplify a complex task, and yet we could not cover in one book all the possible kinds of critical approaches to literature which you may discover. All we hope to do is to make a start and to join you for the beginning of what we hope will be a lifetime love of reading and writing.

ACKNOWLEDGMENTS

A project such as ours owes ideas and inspiration to many students, teachers, colleagues, and friends. We especially value the encouragement and suggestions of Douglas R. Butturff, Ph.D., Thomas Hahn of the University of Rochester, Richard Harp of the University of Nevada at Las Vegas, Kathryn Hohlwein of California State University at Sacramento, Henry E. Jacobs of the University of Alabama, Carol MacKay of the University of Texas at Austin, Carolyn B. Matalene of the University of South Carolina, John S. Ramsey of the State University of New York College at Fredonia, and Laura M. Zaidman of South Georgia College. We also appreciate the help given us by the first-rate staff at Prentice-Hall—Lisa Femmel and Bill Oliver in the early stages, Phil Miller and Virginia Rubens through to the end. The good friends, colleagues, and family who endured the years of our composing throes and still kept wassail with us are Randall Brune, Paula DeBlois, Rosalyn and Donald DeBlois, Anne Fazekas, Bette Gaines, Anna and Cosmo Grassi, Joseph La Fay, and Franklin Wilbur. We are especially grateful to Joyce Bell and Cindy Purtell, who typed the manuscript with unflagging good cheer. And to each other, credit, blame, and thanks.

ROSANNA GRASSI and PETER DeBLOIS

chapter I

THE NATURE
OF CRITICAL INSIGHT

Samuel Taylor Coleridge, the English Romantic poet, says that a poet "brings the whole soul of man into activity," and, we might add, so do a short story writer, a novelist, and a playwright. Coleridge is saying that the reader becomes actively involved with a literary work in a special way and is not simply a passive receiver of words. In a sense, each reader has to *remake* the poem, story, or play with each reading. "But," you might say, "the author wrote the work, so all the reader has to do is read it." And what does the reader's participation have to do with critical writing?

We should explain from the start that *critical* reading and writing are not negative activities. Criticism can and often does praise, but what is more important than saying something is good or bad is understanding why and how the reader responds to it in a certain way. Notice that we said "why and how the reader responds" rather than "why and how the work affects the reader." There is a great deal of difference, and it has to do with the nature of critical insight.

WHO, WHAT, WHERE AND WHEN, HOW, WHY

To get at the nature of critical insight, let's compare and contrast the similar activities of reading literature, listening to music, and looking at a painting. All these activities can be examined under the familiar headings of the journalistic questions: Who? What? Where and When? How? Why?[1] More precisely, we can ask:

1. *Who* are you when you read literature, listen to music, or look at a painting?
2. *What* is the subject of your attention in these activities?
3. *Where and when* do these activities take place?
4. *How* do you achieve critical insight?
5. *Why* is critical insight valuable?

Who?

Who are you when you read literature, listen to music, or look at a painting? The answer is more complex than you might imagine. Who you are as a reader, a listener, or a viewer depends on all the experiences you bring to the particular activity and, more importantly, on which experiences you consciously or unconsciously select to influence your activity. As a reader of literature, you are affected by a whole range of previous reading experiences. You might ask yourself whether you have enjoyed literature before, or whether you have perhaps been frustrated by difficult works or insensitive teachers. In particular, have you previously read works of a similar type (a sonnet or a historical novel, for example) or works by the same author? As a music listener or museum goer, much the same applies: you like a certain composer, performer, or painter because of previous experiences. Perhaps school-sponsored activities have been too structured, and the kind of artistic experiences you enjoy you've discovered on your own or with friends. Or perhaps you would never have known about a particular artist without the guidance of a special teacher. Whatever the case, what we bring to an imaginative work largely influences how we experience it.

What?

What is the subject of the reader's attention? The literary work, of course—the sequence of words, sentences, lines, paragraphs, stanzas, chapters, scenes, acts, and other components and divisions—in short, the *text*. But think about it. What is a book without a reader? We really can't make any claims other than about its physical and chemical properties, and even then we would need a scientific observer to interpret the sensory data. Look back at the beginning of this paragraph, and you'll notice the phrase, "the *subject* of the reader's attention." We chose the word *subject* carefully because it implies the idea of something happening "inside" the reader. The word *object* would have implied a detached independent existence for the literary work, which does not adequately cover the author's or the reader's contributions. The critical reader-writer needs to think of the text as providing the opportunity for a particular set of *experiences*.

The "what" of listening to music is similar. We don't listen to a score, the musical notation on paper; rather, we listen to a performance. The

---

[1]In Chapter 2, we'll discuss the five journalistic questions as a method of thinking about literature, a method that critic Kenneth Burke calls "the Pentad."

composer must receive primary credit for the harmony, rhythm, tonal color, and structure, but for these musical elements to be realized, there must be a performance, a heard performance. We don't need a performer when we look at a painting, but we do need something more than just canvas and paint. We need the "felt" painting, whether gazed at long with puzzlement, fascination, or understanding, or passed by quickly with disinterest or disgust. It's no accident that we speak of the different forms of art with the same language, often blending the senses. We consider the movement of colors, the tension in a poetic line, the sounds of color, and so on as we try to get hold of and understand our responses, and how it is that the artifact becomes a work, working on us.

The important point is that in all the imaginative activities we've been discussing, we cannot speak of the subject of critical insight without considering the artistic consumer—the reader, the listener, and the viewer. We certainly should not ignore the shaping influence of the artistic work; indeed, we must constantly find our responses *rooted in the work*. But equally, we should not ignore the interaction with a human being—that is, with ourselves—that the work enables. To understand that interaction is the goal of critical insight.

Where and When?

Where and when do these imaginative activities take place? Place, time, and the general "scene" are important factors in critical insight, affecting not only the completeness of the experience but the pleasure we take and even our purpose. It is possible to read *War and Peace* in a noisy bar, but not with the degree of attention necessary to appreciate the complex relationships among Tolstoy's panoramic cast of characters. On the other hand, a noisy bar might be just the place to enjoy country blues or jazz-rock, though you wouldn't expect to hear a Schubert quartet there. DaVinci's "Mona Lisa" hanging on the fence around a construction site? Hardly, but you often find there the ingenious fresco of a budding local artist, a work with perhaps no less dedication than that of the Florentine master. It's no accident that libraries and museums are quiet places or that coughing in a concert hall is taboo. Serious works of art ask for special places and quiet time for concentration.

How?

How do we achieve critical insight and then write about it? That is the subject of this book, and so the discussion here is a brief overview. Louise Rosenblatt, a teacher and critical theorist, has developed a very useful idea called "evoking" a work of art, a process that consists of

- recognizing the purpose of a particular reading
- reacting to the text's features: formal divisions such as lines, stanzas, chapters, scenes, and acts; and literary elements such as characterization, setting, and imagery
- forming a sense of the work's overall plan and meaning

- forming expectations about meaning, character behavior, train of events, and style
- finding expectations confirmed or denied
- reconsidering or reaffirming the original sense of the overall plan, possibly rereading parts or all of the work
- and coming to a personal understanding of the work, an understanding which may be modified over a short or long period of time depending on the reader's personal growth, further reading, or contact with other readers.[2]

We'll discuss specific techniques you can use to sharpen your critical insight during this process in the next chapter. But before that, we need to answer the central question, Why?

Why?

Why should we bother at all with critical reading and writing? One answer is practical. Many of the skills developed in reading and writing about literature can be applied to other subjects, disciplines, and professions. You're probably using this text in a course with varying emphases on improving writing skills and appreciating literature. While you may never again write about literary works, you will most likely have many professional opportunities to summarize, draw inferences from, account for, speculate about, or evaluate the written thoughts of others—in technical reports, budget analyses, diagnoses, legal briefs, personality profiles, policy recommendations, and so on. Reading and writing critically about literature develop the skills of reading closely, analyzing the writer's choices, thinking and feeling from different points of view, and making judgments.

Another answer to the question of why we want to develop the skill of critical insight is to understand ourselves better. If you recall that the text, the musical score, and the painting are nothing in themselves but physical objects, you'll realize that it is your own responses prompted by and grounded in those objects that are the focus of critical insight. Yes, we want to know how the artist crafted the artifact, and yes, we must look closely to understand, but we must always come back to the effects engendered in us, to the work that is remade and synthesized into the experience we recognize as insight.

Now that we have given a brief overview of critical insight, we can look more closely at its two components in literary study: critical reading and critical writing.

CRITICAL READING

The basis of all good writing about literature is careful reading. Good readers will adjust their approach to the material being read and their purpose for reading. You wouldn't read the whole encyclopedia just to

---

[2]Louise Rosenblatt, *The Reader, the Text, the Poem: The Transactional Theory of the Literary Work* (Carbondale: Southern Illinois University Press, 1978), p. 54.

find out about communication among dolphins. Nor would you read the whole sports section to find out how your favorite baseball player did in last night's game. You might read closely an important chapter in your earth science text on which you are going to be tested. You also might skim less important chapters, just in case you were quizzed on these too. You might read leisurely through a mystery novel which you picked up for pleasure, maybe even turn to the last chapter and decide not to finish the middle. However, you would have to read a novel, the subject of your critical essay, from beginning to end.

Our concern in this text is not with reading just for pleasure, though we hope that by becoming a better critical reader, you will increase your pleasure in this type of reading also. For the purposes of this text, however, we'll assume that you're reading literature to write about it.

Reading literature analytically is different from reading textbooks or expository essays, such as those found in magazines and journals. The main purpose of textbooks or expository prose is to inform and, sometimes, to entertain; by contrast, the author who writes a work of literature—a short story, play, or poem—may have many purposes in mind: to inform, to entertain, to provide opportunities for personal insight and feeling, to please with form and sound, or, in short, to create an artistic statement. Unlike a textbook or an expository essay, a work of literature usually implies as much as it states. Part of the reader's appreciation comes from an ability to read literature on more than a literal level and to notice its artistry. A good reader will adjust the reading approach to the author's purpose.

As we suggested in the previous section, reading a poem, a play, or a story is more akin to looking at a painting than it is to reading a textbook. A literary work deserves to be pondered. Just as you cannot merely glance at a fine painting or listen casually to a serious piece of music and fully appreciate or understand it, so you cannot skim through a good story, play, or poem and truly see the artistry and meaning. Yes, you might know the subject or the plot, but that superficial experience of the work would be like glancing at Vincent Van Gogh's painting "Starry Night" and just seeing a picture of a town at night (see page 6).

You might miss the flaming trees in the foreground, the swirling light around the stars and the moon, the rolling clouds and hills. Certainly you would miss the wild brush strokes and forego the impression made by the small, sleepy town surrounded by nature in motion, and the contrasts made by the dark land and the bursts of light in the sky. Would the painting be as memorable or as pleasurable an experience without these details? Probably not.

In order to be able to write critically about literature, you must read the work through—sometimes more than once—with a sensitive eye and a careful ear. In discussing literature and writing critical essays, you'll learn to relate to literature on three different levels: *literal, inferential,* and *evaluative.* First, you must understand the work literally; that is, you must be able to tell what the story, poem, or play is about in your own words. Second, you must be able to draw appropriate inferences from the work—to extract a theme, though it may not be stated; to draw conclusions about characters that are implied, but remain unsaid; to notice the mood or feeling com-

Vincent van Gogh, *The Starry Night* (1889). Oil on canvas, 29 × 36¼ in. Collection, The Museum of Modern Art, New York. Acquired through the Lillie P. Bliss Bequest.

municated indirectly by a setting. You must notice details which fit together, patterns which will serve as the basis for your conclusions. Last—and you cannot read effectively on this level unless you have a firm grasp of the first two—you may be asked to evaluate a work, to judge its artistic merits and shortcomings.

The critical essays which we'll be looking at and those which you'll be writing will focus, for the most part, on the second level of reading, the inferential. You'll need to demonstrate in your essays not only that you understand the literal meaning of the work but that you're able to draw appropriate conclusions about character, setting, theme, imagery, tone, point of view, and other literary elements. The third level, the evaluative stage of reading, we'll leave for later in your literary studies, though you may be asked in some courses to evaluate literary works or to review performances of plays or movies.

You should be aware of these three levels of reading—literal, inferential, and evaluative—and be able to distinguish them in your responses to literature. You should recognize that in recounting or summarizing a work, you're relating to the work only on a literal level. You should know that when you're drawing a conclusion (an inference) which is suggested by the work and, therefore, needs to be supported by details from the work (literal details), you're on the right level for writing a critical essay. If you find yourself drawing inaccurate inferences, you should take one step back and return to the literal level—what the work actually says—to check your understanding. If you find yourself saying, "This is a good poem," or "This is a poorly written story," you are evaluating the work and must show not only a thorough understanding of it, but also how it fits criteria you identify.

Reading Tactics That Work

Reading a literary work for the purpose of writing a critical essay differs from your usual reading. The following steps can help you prepare for this special kind of writing. Of course, you may vary the steps as you get comfortable and better acquainted with critical writing.

1. Preview.   Previewing is preparing to read. It should take you only a few minutes and may yield information which will enable you to read with more understanding and perception. When previewing, you should *take note of the title* of the work and the subtitle, if there is one. What expectations does the title cause you to have? What expectations does the title of a poem such as "The Love Song of J. Alfred Prufrock" raise? Sometimes a title is very important; sometimes it is not important. (Later, as you read, you'll ask, "Have my expectations been fulfilled? If not, is there a reason why the author raised these expectations?")

You should also *note the author* of the work. Have you read anything else by him? What do you know about her? You should *note the publication date* or the dates the author lived. It might help you to understand Wilfred Owen's war poems more fully, for example, if you knew that he was writing about the time of World War I. *Read any background material or introductory notes* provided in your text. *Take note of the stage directions, the scenery notes, and the cast of characters* when you're preparing to read a play. *Take note of the table of contents of a novel; note how the work is divided.* Leaf through a short story to see if it is segmented; note how many sections there are. *Take a look at the typography of a poem.* How is it laid out on the page? Is it written in stanzas? Are the lines and divisions fairly regular?

Skim any poem you are about to read for unfamiliar vocabulary. It's harder to decipher the meaning of unfamiliar words from their context in a poem than in a prose work because poetry frequently uses language in novel ways. Unless you're familiar with the words, you're likely to miss the full meaning. Sometimes even familiar words are used in unfamiliar ways in poems and should be looked up in a dictionary to see if there are any alternate meanings. In fact, when you refer to a dictionary to clarify a poet's diction, you should look not only at all the denotative (literal) meanings of the word(s), but also at any connotative meanings (positive or negative implied meanings). You should also check the history or derivation of the word, which may shed some light on why the poet chose it.

After you've made these preparations, you're ready to begin to read.

2. *Read the work thoroughly, making notes.* You must read a work of literature from beginning to end at least once, even if you intend to write about only a portion of the work. You cannot appreciate the full meaning of any part until you've seen the whole. Can you imagine writing an essay on the Mona Lisa's smile without having looked at the whole painting? Similarly, you cannot write intelligently about the effectiveness of a part of a story without studying the whole story.

As you read, take note of any striking features. Remember, a work of literature is an artifact; it is the result of many careful choices made by the author. A character's name is not accidental; it was chosen. The setting is not arbitrary; it also was chosen. Get used to asking yourself such questions as, why did the author pick this name? this time of day? this place? If you own the book, underline phrases you see repeated. Mark an important turning of events. Circle a pattern of images. If the relationships between characters seem very complex, as in Emily Brontë's *Wuthering Heights,* you might make yourself a crude family tree to help you keep track of who is who. If a work is segmented, take a minute at the end of each chapter, scene, or stanza to jot down a phrase or sentence summarizing what the section was about. Looking back over these summary notes, you'll be able to discover patterns that unify the work. But most important, don't be afraid to make the work your own by reacting to what you read. Your written notes express the early stages of your developing insight.

3. *Question.* After reading the work, you'll be able to decide what you want to write about. Perhaps your instructor has provided you with a list of suggested topics. Now would be the time to consider them carefully and choose one. If your instructor has left the topic open, you might try to generate your own topic, using the prewriting methods covered in Chapter 2. You might also consider analyzing one of the various literary elements that are covered in this text—character, setting, theme, point of view, structure, imagery, or tone. You may need to limit your topic to one aspect of a literary element; for example, in a three-page essay, it would probably be sufficient to discuss just one character in a novel.

After you have a topic, whether it was assigned by your instructor or chosen by you, you should formulate some questions to help you explore it in a meaningful way. (Refer to the section in Chapter 2 on formulating questions or to the prewriting sections in the chapters on character, setting, theme, and so on.)

4. *Review the work with a purpose.* Having chosen a topic and formulated some questions, you should return to the work with your questions in mind and reread it. You may not have to reread the entire work from beginning to end, but you should try to answer your questions accurately and fully. Write down your answers and any new ideas or questions that may be generated by your review of the work.

Now you're ready to begin finding your focus and assembling your ideas.

• EXERCISES

1.1 Practice the first two steps—Preview/Read and Make Notes—on the story in the Appendix, "The Country Husband." Write out your previewing steps. Summarize each section of the story in a sentence; write out any other comments or notes.

1.2 Copy one of the poems in the Appendix and apply steps one and two as in Exercise 1.1. Make your notes directly on the written copy of the poem.

1.3 Choose one story or poem from the Appendix and practice all four steps: preview, read and take notes, question, review.

Reading Poetry and Drama

Most poems and plays are meant to be read out loud.   Sound adds a whole new dimension to our appreciation of these genres. Sometimes lines which seem obscure on the written page are made clear by the intonations of a voice. Don't be timid about reading out loud to see how a poem sounds or having someone read it to you. Listening to recordings of poems and plays can also add to your enjoyment and understanding.

While we suggest rereading a work before you write about it, poems, in particular, frequently should be read many times. A poem can unfold new meaning with each reading if you'll create the opportunities for this to happen.

CRITICAL WRITING

If we can read literary works on literal, inferential, and evaluative levels, we can also write on those levels, depending on our purposes. Purpose in critical writing is determined by the relationships among the major parts of the traditional communication triangle.

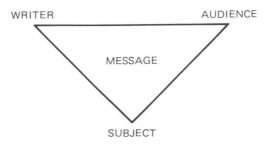

Writer

As the writer of a critical essay, you have read a literary work and have something to say about it. You may play a number of roles: the student who is fulfilling an assignment, either in or out of class; the researcher who looks for biographical or historical clues to shed light on some aspect of the work; the reviewer who profiles and evaluates the work in a local newspaper or literary magazine. By the time you start writing in any of these situations, you may have a fairly well formed idea of what you want to say, but more often than not you'll be unsure, at a loss, and fumbling for words. And this is perfectly all right! Many things can inhibit writing and create the classic "writer's block"—fear of failure and negative judgment (low grades), not knowing how to start and plan the essay, immediate physical distractions, extreme self-consciousness from the pressure of other courses or personal problems, and not understanding obscurities in the literary work itself. The terror of the blank page has haunted many a professional as well. However, one way experienced writers keep the terror under control is by not losing sight of the total picture of the communication triangle—audience, subject, and message—a picture which you're developing now.

Whatever roles you play as a writer, your basic activity is *writing,* and we want to stress that you can discover what to say *by writing,* with special free form and closed form writing done before the first word of the first paragraph. We'll discuss these "prewriting" techniques in the next chapter, but for now we cannot emphasize strongly enough that critical insight comes *from,* and not before, *writing.*

Audience

Audience analysis, the ability to anticipate your reader's needs and expectations, is one of the most basic writing skills, though it is frequently ignored by inexperienced writers. The audience for your critical essay in most cases will be a teacher, but it might also be fellow classmates, a prospective publisher of your essay, and, if you're fortunate, the readers of that publication. While some readers of critical essays will not have read the literary work and thus will need some background material, most of the time your audience will be familiar with the work and, consequently, will be more interested in your own particular insights than in a simple paraphrase or rehash of the plot. This, in fact, is the expectation that the writers of the sample essays in this text have of their audience. Keeping your audience's foreknowledge and expectations in front of you at all times is essential for effective critical writing.

Subject

The subject of a critical essay is rarely the entire literary work. Usually you'll be writing about one or more aspects, or literary elements, of the work that can be covered thoroughly in a relatively short space. Your major concern in this part of the communication triangle is with the essay "topic," a word that is interchangeable with "subject." As we mentioned in the critical reading section, there are three possible subject or topic situations: (1) the topic is "open," and you must discover one that is both interesting and manageable; (2) you must choose one from a number of designated topics; or (3) you must write on an assigned topic. Thorough topic analysis, like audience analysis, is essential for effective critical writing. Often, there is room for selecting and narrowing even within an assigned topic, and once you have a topic worth exploring, you need to have skill in sticking to it and not wandering off on tangents. The first part of Chapter 2 presents detailed topic strategies for selecting, narrowing, and staying with a topic.

Message

This is the essay itself, what you have to say about the selected literary element(s) and how you say it. Like any expository or argumentative essay, a critical essay needs a point—a thrust, a main idea, a thesis—to focus your reader's attention and to lead your reader through the middle paragraphs to the conclusion. We discuss the special skills of trying out tentative theses and committing yourself to one in Chapter 9.

As a piece of writing, an artifact in its own right, your essay needs organization, clarity of thought and literary perception, paragraph coherence and unity, appropriate style (or voice), and technical control of grammar and mechanics. All of these features come together in a good essay, so it will not help to have an obsessive concern for one over the other. Each compositional element works with the others to express your insight on the subject, and all the elements deserve your attention, particularly in the later stages of writing and rewriting. You may, however, discover with your instructor's help that you need to give extra attention to a particular compositional element; independent study or work with a tutor or a writing lab can help polish weak aspects of your "delivery," but you should always keep in mind that all these elements work together in the finished essay and that their success in communicating your ideas to a reader can be one of the most satisfying intellectual achievements.

Composition texts often distinguish between writing as a *product* and writing as a *process*. The writing product is what you present to your audience: the essay you offer in hope that it will recreate your experience of and insight into the literary work. The finished product is your best shot and the end result of all your decisions; it should be something you are proud to claim as your own. The writing process is all the things you do to create the product. The major mistake most writers make is trying to put their message into a final product too early. When a writer ignores or casually rushes through the early exploratory stages of writing, what the ancients called "invention," he or she risks superficial coverage of the subject and a shallow level of critical insight. In Chapter 2, we'll show you how to use the inventional techniques of prewriting that help fill that bothersome, even terrifying, blank page.

• EXERCISES

1.4 If you have ever experienced writer's block, make a list of those circumstances and/or personal habits that helped create the block, and then discuss what you could do to minimize or eliminate blocks in the future. You'll find it amusing and relieving to share your list with others in the class. (If you've never had writer's block, be prepared to tell the class how you avoid it.)

1.5   Write up a brief profile of every conceivable reader of your critical essays. Consider what each probably knows about literature, what each expects of your essay, and what image you want readers to have of you. Be honest!

1.6   Describe, in writing, your own writing process. When you write an assigned essay, what place(s) and time(s) do you use? What physical and emotional sensations do you have? Do you write straight through from beginning to end, or are there stops and starts? Do you use any special planning techniques? How many, if any, rough drafts do you make? What are the greatest strengths and weaknesses of your personal writing habits?

1.7   Read the two critical essays below. How would you assess each writer's picture of the communication triangle? More specifically, how complete is each writer's understanding of himself or herself as a writer, and of the audience, the subject, and the message?

> In "To the Stone-Cutters," Robinson Jeffers examines the longevity of poetry. By the symbolism of stone, he creates a comparison between poets and stone-cutters as well as between poems and sculptures. The speaker begins by questioning the worth of poetry through the imagery of comparison but finally reaches some consolation by reflecting on the enduring pleasure that art provides.
>
> If the comparison is true, then by showing the vulnerability of stone, "knowing rock splits, records fall down, / . . . scale in the thaws, wear in the rain," Jeffers shows poetry's impermanence. Poets too are "foredefeated / Challengers of oblivion," having failed to achieve genuine immortality. Such metaphors as "build his monument," "blotted out, the blithe earth die," and "die blind and blacken to the heart" show the similarity of the two kinds of creation.
>
> In spite of the regret about destructive time, Jeffers is able to conclude on a note of hope: "Yet stones have stood for a thousand years, and pained thoughts found / The honey of peace in old poems." These lines suggest serenity through time, and that no matter how outdated or worn works of art might be, they can still give pleasure, whether we look at an ancient stone monument or read an old poem.
>
> Thus, we can see that Jeffers salvages something positive about the endurance of art through the onslaught of time. Even though stone and poems will wear, they may also survive total destruction and continue providing enjoyment. Jeffers has quite effectively connected the doomed, yet redeemable, crafts of stone-cutting and writing poetry.

> We all know that the use of imagery in a poem is to acquire a mental picture of the author's ideas. Using figurative language like metaphors and similes allows us to get a better understanding while at the same time allowing the author to use fewer words, which is why the poem is so short. In this poem, you can see that Jeffers uses the visual image of stone-cutters to show a futile accomplishment.
>
> Comparing the two artisans, the poet and the stone-cutter, gives us a metaphor in order to sense the image of defeat. Each artist uses his own element to express himself. The poet uses his mind and paper while the stone-

cutter uses his brute strength and marble to exhibit his art. In the first line the word "foredefeated" shows that the stone-cutter is forever doomed. Poets are too.

Yet after all, the poet builds his monument with a mocking gesture: he must know something that the stone-cutter doesn't, probably that books have more chance of lasting indoors than sculptures prone to the weather. You've probably had creations that you wanted to last and worried that they would be destroyed by time or neglect. Well, that's the situation in this poem.

chapter 2

PREWRITING:
THE EARLY STAGES

The chief problem for any writer is getting words down on paper. We discussed the habits and conditions that create writer's block in the last chapter. Now we want to suggest some practical techniques for getting words on paper in the early stages of writing a critical essay. One caution, however: it's very easy to get bogged down in such practical techniques and forget the final goal of the writing process—a successful finished essay.

The following diagram illustrates the linear process of many writers:

THINK ⟶ OUTLINE ⟶ WRITE

On the surface, this might seem to be a useful procedure; in fact, in some writing situations, such as an in-class theme, an exam, a press story, or a report with a deadline, an even more streamlined model might appear necessary. But this model ignores a basic fact: writing is a complex activity. Researchers still do not know precisely how the brain processes all its information to make the choices that result in composition. But we do know that the think-outline-write model oversimplifies the skills involved, and, more importantly, it doesn't work well for the inexperienced writer who has to fill in some rather large gaps. We think the diagram on the next page more accurately shows the procedure for effective critical writing.

THE COMPOSING PROCESS

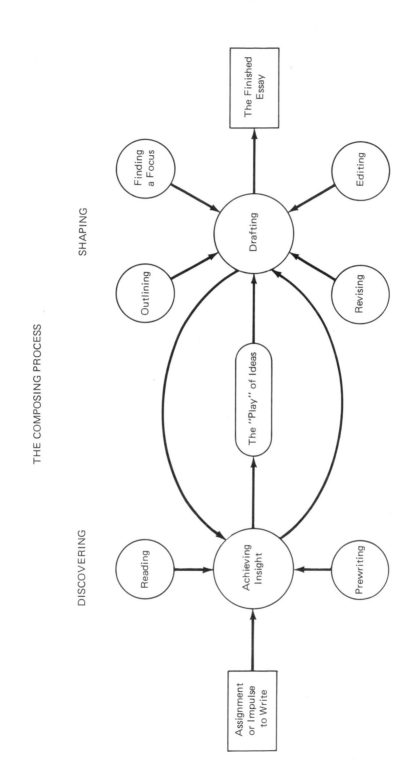

DISCOVERING

SHAPING

Assignment or Impulse to Write

Reading

Prewriting

Achieving Insight

The "Play" of Ideas

Outlining

Finding a Focus

Revising

Editing

Drafting

The Finished Essay

This diagram-model has two important features. First, the key components are labeled with verbs or verb phrases which point to actions, things the writer *does*. The second feature of the diagram is the sequences and directions of activity implied by the arrows. Recall that in the think-outline-write model the arrows go in just one direction—toward writing. By contrast, in the "Discovering" cluster of this model, activity begins when the writer feels an impulse to write, whether in response to an assignment or a personal interest, and moves into the key discovery activities. You might achieve the major insight for your essay in the "Discovering" sequence while reading the literary work, or you might not reach an insight until you had generated many ideas using prewriting methods.

In the other cluster, "Shaping," the activities ultimately lead toward the finished essay, but the arrows pivoting around the "play" of ideas suggest that one might return to reading and prewriting while in the drafting stage. The first draft might prove inadequate because of an incomplete understanding of a literary element, such as setting; the writer would then reread key passages and perhaps try a different prewriting technique. The point we want to make is that all writing involves the central activities of *discovering* and *shaping*, and neither one stops when the other begins. Part II of the text covers the shaping skills. Our concern here is to help you discover.

How do we discover ideas for critical writing? We may draw on the literary work, all we've previously read, what we've heard in class, what we might specifically research for a topic, and what we've experienced in life. Depending on the circumstances of a particular writing situation, we might have an incredibly vast array of resources to tap—or quite limited opportunities and little time. A skilled writer knows what the opportunities are and how to budget time and energy. A nineteenth-century rhetoric text states that in learning how to write, "no one can pump water from a well that is dry." Part of your skill as a writer is to dig the wells and prime the pump. The discovery activities of *prewriting* give you all the basic tools.

We can break prewriting down into informal and formal methods. The informal methods are used mostly during and immediately after the impulse to write, and the formal methods are used when the writer gets closer to shaping the essay.

INFORMAL METHODS OF PREWRITING

Keeping a Journal

There is an important difference between a journal and a diary. A diary is a recording of daily events and experiences for later rereading and reliving. A journal is a series of reflections—thoughts and feelings—that come to the writer, possibly based on events or experiences, but not with the steady ordering by calendar dates that structures a diary. A person who wants to keep in shape may jog, swim, bicycle, or play racquetball regularly; similarly a writer who wants to stay "limbered up" and comfortable with words writes daily in a journal. You may already have had some experience with keeping a journal, on your own or in another course. It's one of the best ways of getting into writing as a regular habit.

One of the greatest journal writers was Leonardo da Vinci, who developed the highly idiosyncratic practice of writing his notebooks from right to left in a reverse mirror script. In the following two excerpts on scientific and symbolic associations with animals, you can see how he uses the journal to express wide-ranging reflections.

Flying Machine

A bird is an instrument working according to mathematical law, which instrument it is within the capacity of man to reproduce with all its movements. . . . We may therefore say that such an instrument constructed by man is lacking in nothing except the life of the bird, and this life needs be supplied from that of man.

Crocodile—Hypocrisy

This animal seizes a man and instantly kills him; and after he is dead it mourns for him with a piteous voice and many tears, and having ended its lament it cruelly devours him. It is thus with the hypocrite, whose face is bathed with tears over every slight thing, showing himself thus to have the heart of a tiger; he rejoices in his heart over another's misfortunes with a face bedewed with tears.

The experiences of one's immediate world are the usual subjects of journal entries, as the following excerpt from Thoreau's private journal of 1858 (not the published *Walden*) illustrates.

I have lately been surveying the Walden woods so extensively and minutely that I now see it mapped in my mind's eye—as, indeed, on paper—as so many men's woodlots, and am aware when I walk there that I am at a given moment passing from such a one's woodlot to such another's. I fear this particular dry knowledge [of the wood's ownership] may affect my imagination and fancy, that it will not be easy to see much wildness and native vigor there as formerly.

The styles of the above journal entries may appear formal, but they come from their writers' times. A journal should be in its writer's own personal voice without filtering.

A *literary journal* has as its subject matter the writer's responses to literary works, and we recommend it highly as a device for recording first and subsequent impressions, not only to focus attention but to provide possible material to draw on later for critical essays. Your literary journal should be kept in a separate, bound notebook, one you can carry around with the literary texts. There are two fruitful times for making journal entries: (a) while you're reading the work, you might note any prominent features, comment on what's happening, or ask questions; and (b) after you've finished the work, you can note your first complete reactions and answer questions you raised earlier. An interesting and productive variation on (b) is to make journal entries on the same work for several days or weeks after finishing the work to see how your reactions change, if at all. You might reread the work on several occasions and write down your reactions, noting how your understanding evolves. This technique is especially effective with poetry.

Here are a number of journal entries on John Cheever's story "The Country Husband" (in Appendix).

> Francis Weed sure has it rough. Plane crash and a family fight all in one day. If I'd been in a plane crash, I would have told my story over and over and wanted everyone to listen, and know they almost lost me. Maybe Francis is too calm about the crash and should have made a bigger stink about it. Why does he put up with family?
>
> I liked the section about the French maid who walked out of the town naked during WW II. Interesting but it didn't belong with the rest of the story with Shady Hill and modern suburbia. Must be a reason.
>
> Beautiful when Francis told off Mrs. Wrightson, the nosy biddy of Shady Hill.
>
> Francis shouldn't have hit Julia. Wonder if they fought before; probably not, because Julia would have walked out sooner. But he's dependent on her; she keeps his life together—does laundry, dinner, looks after kids. She's no pushy feminist but has feelings and finally stands up for herself. He doesn't realize how much he needs her.
>
> Wasn't fair of Francis to keep Clayton Thomas from getting a job. Jealous because he has Anne Murchison, the babysitter, and Francis doesn't. Clayton may be smelly but he deserves a chance; Julia and Trace Beardon think he's all right. Pretty cheap of Francis to bad-mouth him.
>
> I can't figure the ending out. Was it right or wrong of Francis to go to the psychiatrist? He doesn't seem any better off for it. Sure, he goes back to his woodwork and Shady Hill is the same as ever, but is he happy? And what's the image of kings in golden suits riding elephants supposed to mean? Maybe Francis wants to be like them but knows he can't. Maybe he doesn't know.

Notice how the writer uses a comfortable personal voice and doesn't hesitate to indicate uncertainty. Remember, you don't have to worry about form, grammar, punctuation, spelling, or word choice. Focus on your own literary responses, whether positive or negative, pleasing or painful, and express them as they come to you.

- **EXERCISES**

   2.1   Start keeping a literary journal. Your instructor may or may not want to see it periodically, but whatever the case, make your entries honest expressions of how literary works affect you—what questions and doubts you have, what you find believable, what you think causes things to happen, why the author chooses to say things in certain ways, and so on.

2.2 Start a series of journal entries on Karl Shapiro's poem "Auto Wreck" (in Appendix). Reread the poem and write on it every day for at least a week. Does your focus or interest change during the period? Do you come to any greater understanding or appreciation of the poem? Do you come to like the poem any more or less?

Freewriting

The technique of freewriting is used to get words on paper in an accelerated fashion. It's often recommended when a writer has a severe case of writer's block, but even the most experienced writers find it very productive in the early stages of composition. The basic technique is simply to put pen or pencil to paper and force yourself to write nonstop for a period of ten minutes or more. Sound impossible? Think you couldn't possibly have enough to say (write) for ten minutes? OK, then for ten minutes, write, "I can't think of anything to say." We guarantee you'll find something to say if only to relieve the boredom of repetition. Here is part of a student's ten minute freewriting exercise which began this way.

I've got nothing to say I've got nothing to say I've got nothing to say nothing to say What's this for anyway? A new gimmick my composition teacher thought up to torture us? Maybe he can't think of anything to teach today so he's getting us to fill the time up. Couldn't get away with this kind of fluffy writing in history class. Culpepper hates anything that doesn't sound polished like right from the encyclopedia. Couldn't freewrite on a job application—have to be perfect and sharp for the bossman. Interviews with Xerox and IBM next week, hope my resumé clicked with them. Maybe bosses do all the freewriting. Technical reports sharp and to the point. Math is easier, formulas, numbers, no words messing it up. Only 5 minutes! Rotten time. Desk has really dumb graffiti—"Architects make better lovers." Why, because they make plans? drawings?

For someone who had nothing to say, a little over halfway through the exercise, this writer has said quite a bit, from reflections on the purpose of freewriting to the kinds of writing expected in another class and professional writing situations, the contrasting nature of mathematical expression, and the amorous ability of architects. That's quite a lot of material, certainly more than enough seed ideas for a simple essay that might spin out from any one of the casual reflections.

You might also think that there's a good deal of junk in the above excerpt, especially if the writer were preparing for an essay on images of good and evil in *Moby Dick*. Junk is one of the inevitable side products of freewriting; you always produce more than you can use, but that's the advantage as well. How do you know what you can use for a particular essay until you have some material to choose from? Freewriting is one method, admittedly crude, of generating words you can sift through, both to discover focus and to support the focus once you find it.

For critical writing, you can refine the technique into *focused freewriting* in which the ten-minute period (or longer) zeroes in on a particular literary work or some aspect of a work, as in the example that follows on D. H. Lawrence's poem "Snake" (in Appendix).

> Snake, Garden of Eden symbol of evil tempted Adam and Eve. Disappeared mysteriously into bowels of earth. Devil, king. Graceful not caring, does not bother the man, notices him and doesn't hurry. Man is sorry for throwing log, stupid and cowardly. Snake is proud, beautiful gold poisonous not brown but not innocent either. Etna volcano smoking reminds of hell but snake is not totally evil: natural like cattle needing water to sip. Narrator hears voices of education telling him to kill the snake but doesn't know how to react. Misses the snake when it's gone but he gets mad when it starts to leave, he wants to keep it around for some reason, says it's a king in exile a lord of life. Why should a snake be a lord, maybe in the underworld, maybe the man wants to see what the underworld is like. An animal's and the man's territory; the snake is an invader but the man makes it into some kind of symbol but not the old simple symbol of evil in the Bible, something more.

Freewriting often runs on, with fragmentary ideas piling up and leading on to others whose connections only the writer could decipher. The technique lets you tap directly and without inhibition your conscious and unconscious responses to a work. Much of the results may have little bearing on a particular assigned topic, but you may also find fertile possibilities for insight in freewriting.

- **EXERCISE**

   2.3   Using a literary work you've read recently, do a ten-minute freewriting exercise, expressing anything and everything the work stimulates; look over your writing and answer these questions: What did you say that wasn't immediately apparent or conscious when you finished reading? What possible writing topics can you see in the freewriting?

Brainstorming

Brainstorming is a *group activity* which, like freewriting, aims at rapid-fire production of words and ideas on some particular topic. One member of the group is designated the "scribe," or recorder, and on a blackboard, overhead projector, or paper (but preferably some medium that the others can see easily) jots down all the words and phrases that people offer. The important thing is to avoid complete sentences or drawn-out explanations. The goal is quick, staccato, stream-of-consciousness, free associations stimulated by the topic—in other words, mental thunder and lightning, and all that your group can precipitate over a relatively short period of time.

We have reproduced the worksheet of a group that brainstormed on Howard Nemerov's poem "The Vacuum" (in Appendix). Notice how the members build on each other's contributions while not worrying about logical connections. (The numbers indicate the order in which things were said.)

1. old lady is a vacuum cleaner
2. musty old houses
3. dust and dirty work never done
4. husbands never clean house
5. flip switch, housewife slavery
6. wages for housewives
7. cleaning bag like a lung
8. cancer working in a mine
9. nine-to-five cocktails
10. vacuum is alive
11. monster movie matinee
12. devour the husband
13. no children, no love, just work
14. husband misses the noise
15. 3 paragraphs/stanzas, 5 lines each
16. only one rhyme
17. personification, meta-phors,similes
18. what are "woolen mice"?
19. is Nemerov Russian? Polish?
20. vacuum cleaners behind the Iron Curtain?
21. machines dominate us, do all the work
22. no pride in work, American auto workers
23. technology gives control or takes away?

What can you do with such a brainstormed list? Just as with keeping a journal and freewriting, brainstorming aims at loosening up the mind, cracking the shell that surrounds what each of us has to say and so often never lets out to ourselves let alone others. What you do with the results of brainstorming depends on your immediate circumstances and opportunities. Your instructor may assign small groups to brainstorm the same topic or different topics and later to report back to the whole class in order to start a discussion. Or the instructor may have groups use the technique in preparation for an in-class writing exercise. Still another use might be on your own to initiate a brainstorming exercise with a group of friends or classmates to prepare for a group report or simply to share ideas for an upcoming essay. There are many possibilities. The common denominator is what some educators call "collaborative learning," which means stimulating and sharing your thoughts with others by a bit of creative pushing and pulling.

- ● **EXERCISES**

  2.4 Take the brainstormed list on "The Vacuum," and see how many groups of thematically related items you can find. How could you label the groups and turn them into essay topics?

  2.5 Form a group of three to five students in your class, and brainstorm on William Carlos Williams' "The Widow's Lament in Springtime" (in Appendix). Choose a recorder among the members, and work for ten minutes, members saying whatever comes to mind in no fixed order. After brainstorming, work together as a group to find the thematic clusters in the list you produce. Develop at least five good essay topics from the thematic clusters, and report to the class.

  The Prewriting Portfolio

  Now that we've discussed informal prewriting methods, you may be asking, "What do I do with all this stuff?" We hope that you've started a literary journal in a separate notebook. As you prepare for a particular writing assignment, you'll find a *prewriting portfolio* quite useful. You could set aside several pages of your journal for notes and prewriting exercises directed at the particular topic. You could also start compiling a portfolio in a separate file or folder, in which you would record on individual sheets of paper or notecards the results of various discovery activities. The more you collect by way of prewriting, the more you'll be able to sift through and tie together in your rough draft. Igor Stravinsky, the twentieth-century composer, used to jot down short phrases of music and tape them on the music rest of his piano for later use. Think of the numerous sketches an artist makes before brushing the first dabs of paint on a canvas, or the schematic drawings an engineer must make to guide the scale modeler in designing a more aerodynamically efficient automobile. The writer too needs to build up the tangible written beginnings, the material of prewriting, that can later be shaped into the draft of an essay.

FORMAL METHODS OF PREWRITING

A writer can use the informal methods of prewriting to find a topic and to generate ideas when the topic is clear. The *formal methods* of prewriting may be used the same way. As you prepare to write critically about one or more literary elements, you will probably experience one of the following conditions:

1. having a chaotic jumble of unconnected ideas;
2. having one or two promising ideas; or
3. having no ideas at all.

The third condition is unlikely if you've written substantially using the informal methods. Whatever the conditions, the formal prewriting methods can help you *organize* the first, *expand* the second, and *fill* the third. We would like to emphasize that you need not use all of the formal methods. One may be sufficient and comfortable. If not, try another. The important point is that at this stage of composing the critical essay, you need some technique to bring your ideas closer to the first draft.

Just as with keeping a journal, freewriting, and brainstorming, the formal methods are designed to help you generate material for the essay. The difference is that they allow for a more complete and patterned probing of the literary work than the less structured informal methods. The writing that you produce with the formal methods (and add to your growing portfolio), while not necessarily duplicating the final insights of the finished essay, will contain many of the ideas, and even words and sentences, you can use in the essay itself.

You may find the formal methods strange or gimmicky at first, but once you become comfortable with them, they'll go a long way toward overcoming writer's block. You shouldn't feel compelled to memorize and use all of these methods slavishly. We want to show how the methods work and to have you experiment with them on your own to see which work best for you. You may find that the pentad yields more useful ideas for you over a period of time, or that the focal points are simpler to use than the thought patterns, and that's fine! Read through the discussion and illustration of the three methods, practice and try them in real writing situations (in this course and others), and see which are worth building into your repertoire of writing habits. That's basically what we're doing in this text: helping add to your repertoire of skills so that you'll be a more effective and competent writer.

One thing you'll discover as we go through the formal prewriting methods is that they all seem to cover the same ground but in different ways. Certain terms or steps in one method echo those of another. What you'll be finding is the consistent way the mind works. In spite of the brain's incredible complexity and capacity for memory and new discovery, its workings can be understood as a limited number of key operations, and it's these operations that the formal methods try to capture in usable procedures.

Thought Patterns

How do we understand—the motion of the wind, the French Revolution, a mother's behavior toward a child, capillary action in a leaf, a poem? We order our experience with categories of thought, ways of grouping facts, remembrances, observations, feelings, and conclusions. Sometimes the thought patterns are already explained by an author or a speaker; at other times, the thinker, the receiver of language, must complete or supply all of the organization. We can understand this organizing capacity as made up of four basic patterns: classification, definition, comparison, and analysis.

Classification.   We understand a "thing" (an idea, a person, a place, an object, an event) by fitting it into appropriate groups or classes and, if this "thing" or concept is large enough, by seeing what classes are within it. Human beings *belong to* the larger class of vertebrate mammals. Human beings, according to some anthropologists, *consist of* the smaller classes of Mongoloid, Negroid, and Caucasoid. The important feature of classification is discovering a basis for grouping. The vertebrate group is based on a single physiological trait: having a backbone. The Mongoloid, Negroid, and Caucasoid groups are based on a complex of tendencies, including geographic origin, skin color, facial bone structure, and hair texture. The usefulness of a classification depends on how reliable the basis for classifying is. Witness the trouble and charges of racism created by the anthropological classifications.

Classification is also a useful thought pattern for developing literary understanding. We use the very large classifications of poetry, fiction, and drama to label *genre*, or literary type. The basis for these large classifications is obscure, but it probably has something to do with different types of performance (singing, telling a story, and acting a story). Anyone who has read literature realizes that the genres are not very useful—poems can tell stories, plays can be written in poetic form, and fiction can have a poetic style—and so a variety of subclassifications have evolved. For example, under poetry we have classifications based on stanza and rhyme patterns (sonnet, terza rima, villanelle, ode, and so on); rhetorical purpose (epic, elegy, mock heroic, and pastoral); and so on. These formal classifications have arisen over centuries as readers of literature have tried to organize their experiences of so many different forms and purposes. Even though critics rarely agree on the bases for classifications, the effort to find a common set of terms for our experience continues.

In addition to classifications of form, we can classify types of characters, images, settings, and other literary elements by asking the question, "What kinds of _____ does the author use to _____ ?" For example, "What kinds of *images* does Lawrence use to *develop the scene* in 'Snake' (in Appendix)?" You'd first want to identify a basis for classifying, and one basis might be images of *sense*. You'd then identify images of sight (the details of the well and wall, the snake's color and movement when coming to the well, drinking, and returning to the earth); touch (the hot Sicilian day, the imagined feeling when the snake returns to the underworld); sound (the stillness of the day and the snake's silent drinking contrasted with the voices of education and the clatter of the log that the speaker throws at the snake); and smell ("the strange-scented shade" near the well suggesting mystery). You then might want to note those images that seem to combine senses, such as the smoking volcano (sight, touch, sound, and smell) and the snake's easing its shoulders back into the fissure (sight and touch). Classification allows you to reorganize your experience of a work's diverse elements.

- **EXERCISE**

  2.6 Identify a basis for classification, and classify all the characters in Cheever's "The Country Husband," first in one large category and then in several smaller ones.

  Definition. Definition is a thought pattern that builds on classification. To answer the question "What does X mean?" we first fit X into a class and then show how it differs from other members of the class, as in the simplified formula, X = class + differentiation. For example:

  | X | = | CLASS | + | DIFFERENTIATION |
  Anxiety is a kind of fear for which one doesn't understand the cause.

  | X | = | CLASS | + | DIFFERENTIATION |
  Baboon grooming is a physical activity with hygienic benefits (removing parasites from the fur and skin) and social benefits (preserving group closeness).

  | X | = | CLASS | + | DIFFERENTIATION |
  An alexandrine is a line of poetry with twelve syllables.

$$\underline{\hspace{2cm}X\hspace{2cm}} = \underline{\hspace{1.5cm}CLASS\hspace{1.5cm}} + \underline{\hspace{2cm}DIFFERENTIATION\hspace{2cm}}$$

Francis Weed is a suburban man who is bored with life's routines and yearns for passionate adventure.

Definitions cannot always be completed in a simple sentence with a simple formula. Often a definition needs to be extended by qualifications and illustrations; indeed, an entire essay might be built around a definition. Consider the paragraph below, which develops the meaning of growing up in Dylan Thomas' "Fern Hill" (in Appendix).

Thomas shows how *growing up* is an ironic *process involving intensely pleasurable experiences that are slipping away forever.* The child knows the immediate pleasures of playing prince and hunter around the farmyard, dreaming of being carried away by owls and awakening safe again at the farm, but the child does not know that these pleasures are only for a short time and that he will never quite be able to recapture these times as an adult. What is remarkable, though, is the vividness with which Thomas recreates the joy of youth while saving the note of sadness and regret until the end. Growing up, he shows, is both joyous and terrible.

In this paragraph, growing up is defined: X is "growing up," class is "process," and differentiation is the rest of the first sentence. The rest of the paragraph expands and qualifies the definition.

As a prewriting technique, definition can be used whenever you come to a word, a term, a theme, a character trait or behavior that you or the reader of your essay might have trouble understanding. As with classification, you need to turn the thought pattern into a question that will fit the work and your essay topic, such as "What does death mean for Granny Weatherall?" The definition you write in your journal or portfolio might concentrate on how the author develops a definition or on how the author's definition fits in with traditional meanings.

- **EXERCISE**

    2.7 Define "lament" as Williams works it out in "The Widow's Lament in Springtime" (in Appendix).

Comparison. As we will mention in discussing metaphor, much of what we learn about the world comes through comparison. Metaphors are a special kind of stylized, imaginative comparison. With the basic thought pattern of comparison, we look for similarities, shared qualities that enable us to bring things together. Perhaps just as important as finding similarities is the implied opposite—*contrast*—finding differences. Both comparison and contrast are necessary skills for classification and definition: we identify classes by labeling groups of things with similar traits; at the same time, we define by looking for the differences that set something off from other members of its class. For example, puppets are like marionettes in that they are manipulated to simulate human or animal behavior, but unlike marionettes, which are operated from above with strings, puppets are operated by hand and finger movements from within the doll's body. (Note how we can *classify* shadow puppets, sock puppets, rod and stick puppets, marionettes, and ventriloquists' dummies.)

We can ask the question, "How do _____ compare and contrast?" of literary elements within a work or between works. As a prewriting technique in critical writing, there is no end to what you can compare and contrast: literary works themselves, by the same author or different authors, written close together in time or separated by centuries; literary styles; characters; uses of imagery; treatments of the same theme by different authors or by the same author in different works—the list is limitless.

Just as classification requires a basis for grouping items, so does comparison require what is called a *common ground* between the items. Common ground is the reason, or place, for bringing two or more subjects together for examination. A botanist would not compare the molecular structure of blue spruce pine needles with that of sugar maple leaves without a reason, such as wanting to understand the different cellular systems for delivering nutrients. A film critic would have to be interested in something like images of working women before writing about *Nine to Five, Norma Rae,* and *Rosie the Riveter* in the same review. And a literary critic would need a focus— such as the effects of setting on Francis Weed—before contrasting Francis' home in Shady Hill with the site of the airplane crash and his memory of the French town in World War II. In fact, the critical writer needs to look for common ground *before* looking for similarities and differences.

One of the most common critical writing assignments is comparison–contrast, a type of essay we'll describe in detail in Chapter 10.

• EXERCISES

2.8   What common ground can you identify for comparing the images of nature in Shakespeare's "That Time of Year" (in Appendix)?

2.9   In a paragraph, compare and contrast how Porter and Cheever treat the theme of disappointment with life in "The Jilting of Granny Weatherall" and "The Country Husband." (This could, of course, become a whole essay.)

Analysis.   Analysis is the thought pattern which aims at understanding how things work. This pattern has two facets: breaking a subject down into *component parts* to see how they work individually and in unison, and establishing *cause and effect* relationships in processes or events. Analyzing components and cause-effect relationships is basic to understanding how and why things happen. No kind of inquiry, scientific, political, social, or artistic, is possible without the skill of analysis, no matter whether the analysis is highly rigorous and determined by accepted procedures or unstructured and random. We can't get away from our basic need to take things apart, constructively or destructively.

Handled properly, the analysis of literature can be constructive. But people often complain about analyzing, citing the old adage, "We murder to dissect." There is some truth to this adage because taking something apart to understand it can destroy it. For example, the only way to examine organisms and their parts in an electron microscope is to kill them before or in the vacuum necessary for extreme magnification. And after reading certain literary criticism, you come away feeling that neither the writer nor the work survived the critic's knife. But such carnage isn't necessary, and we hope you'll develop the attitude that looking closely at a literary work is a healthy way to enrich your experience of it. What we're really talking about is analyzing your own responses. The work will remain intact. *War and Peace* is still read and *King Lear* is still performed despite thousands of successful and not so successful attempts to account for their greatness. You'll protect your own literary responses if you always make *synthesis,* a putting back together with deeper understanding, part of your analyses.

Literary analysis can focus on the whole work or can zoom in on a particular literary element. We can ask, "What are the major components of Donne's poem 'The Canonization'?" The answer would include structure (five stanzas with nine lines in each), a speaker who is complaining to some unknown audience which objects to his love, images of a world that continues unaffected by his love, images of his self-consuming passion and the art that will tell his story, and finally a prayer in which other lovers will ask to repeat the pattern of his love. If we want to understand the sequence and cause of a principal event or condition in a literary work, we ask, "How did this happen, and what caused this?" Or if we know the cause(s), we can ask, "What are the results or effects of this?" The following paragraph was written in response to the assignment, "Analyze the effects of setting on Huck Finn in the first chapter of the novel."

> The setting in the first chapter of *The Adventures of Huckleberry Finn* brings out one of Huck's most important characteristics: his disgust with the civilized world. After telling how the last novel (*Tom Sawyer*) ended, Huck, the narrator, shows what life is like at the Widow Douglas' house. Because he is such a free spirit, he chafes under all the restrictions. He has to wear proper clothes that make him sweat and feel closed in. He comes to supper at the ring of a bell and may not eat until the Widow says a blessing. Huck's description of the Widow's sister, Miss Watson, shows his extreme uncomfortableness in the environment: "[She was] a slim old maid with goggles on . . . and took a set at me now with a spelling book. She worked me middling hard for about an hour. . . . Then for an hour it was deadly dull, and I was fidgety." Throughout the novel, as in the first chapter, Huck is especially sensitive to the effects a place has on him and is most at home on the river.

Notice how this writer uses illustrations and a quotation from the novel while not slipping into simple plot summary. The writer makes regular comments on *how* and *why* the setting affects Huck.

- **EXERCISE**

  2.10   Analyze and discuss the importance of the component parts of Jeffers' "To the Stone-Cutters" (in Appendix).

The four thought patterns—*classification, definition, comparison,* and *analysis*—are procedures based on key mental operations that we use to understand information from the world. They can work as very productive prewriting techniques when each pattern is turned into questions that fit both the literary work and the emerging critical essay. As with the other prewriting methods, you should use the thought patterns to produce *writing* for your portfolio.

The Pentad[1]

Any act, including written works, has five elements that can be turned into prewriting questions to help the critical writer. The writer may want to understand the work's place in literary history or the work in itself, and in both cases, the five elements and the questions they yield cover virtually everything the writer might want to know. Chapters 3 through 8 will adapt the pentad questions to various literary elements as appropriate. The following chart shows the pentad and its parallel questions for the two types of inquiry.

The Pentad	*The Work in Literary History*	*The Work in Itself*
1. **Who**	1. *Who* wrote the work, and what biographical information relates to the work?	1. *Who* are the principal characters? Who is the narrator?
2. **What**	2. *What* is the work (novel, play, etc.)?	2. *What* is the chief event(s) in the work, and what is the theme?
3. **Where and When**	3. *Where and when* was it written?	3. *Where and when* does the chief event(s) occur?
4. **How**	4. *How* was the work first published and received by the public? How does it relate to similar past and future works like it? How does it reflect or go counter to its cultural context?	4. *How* is the chief event(s) accomplished?
5. **Why**	5. *Why* did the author make the choices that resulted in the work, and why has it remained significant or insignificant, or which will it become?	5. *Why* does the chief event happen, and why does the work have the effects it does?

[1]The term was developed by Kenneth Burke in *A Grammar of Motives* (Berkeley: University of California Press, 1969) to describe basic literary structures. We've chosen to use the more familiar journalistic questions over Burke's special terms (act, agent, agency, scene, purpose).

The perspective on the work in literary history will undoubtedly require research, and while writing assignments do occasionally ask for research, the more common critical writing deals with the work itself. In fact, before you can fully appreciate a work's place in literary history, you need to be able to read closely and appreciate it on its own merits.

The skill in using the pentad as a prewriting method lies in your ability to adapt each of the five elements into precisely worded questions that fit the assigned topic or that will allow you to discover a workable topic. Let's imagine that you've been asked to write about Ahab's relationship with the whale in Melville's *Moby Dick*. (Remember that *writing out answers* to these prewriting questions in your portfolio is the goal of the technique.)

The *who* perspective will yield at least two useful questions: first, "Who is Ahab?" Beyond the obvious answer that he's a seasoned captain of the whaling ship *Pequod,* you'll want to note his physical appearance (tall, proud, detached, with a pegleg made of whalebone, a horrid scar running down the side of his face, and a far-off gaze in his eye) as well as his emotional makeup (fiercely determined to reach his goal at all costs and almost mystical in his ability to win the sailors over to his cause). A freewriting exercise focusing on Ahab or a short character sketch could develop your answer. The second question is, "Who (or what) is Moby Dick?" You'd want first to characterize the physical presence of this mighty beast, its great size and strength and unusual color. Then you'd need to search for those passages where Melville attributes motives, feelings, even intelligence to Moby Dick, often through Ahab's own words. If you feel a symbolic dimension is worth exploring, you might see the whale as a force of nature or Nature itself; the dark side of Ahab's self, perhaps a tangible projection of his own making—every man's evil; or even a cosmic embodiment of all Evil. Such speculation can obviously get out of hand, so be sure you can root all your claims in the work itself, regularly making specific references and drawing out relevant quotations for possible later use in your essay.

The *what* perspective on the topic of Ahab's relationship with the whale might be phrased, "What is the nature of their relationship?" From Ahab's point of view, it might be a combination of hate, revenge, fear, and perhaps a recognition of part of himself or his fate, as he pursues Moby Dick with a terrible, destructive determination.

Where and when refer to the novel's setting, so you'd ask, "What roles do the land, the ship, and the ocean play in the development of Ahab's relationship with Moby Dick?" The land is what Ahab must leave to find the whale. The ship is the microcosmic land-world which allows Ahab to invade Moby Dick's world. The sea is the scene of their epic battle and at the end rolls on as it always has, perhaps mocking Ahab's foolishness, or worst of all not caring.

The *how* perspective might look, on the one hand, at "How does Melville portray this relationship?" and, on the other hand, at "How does Ahab nurture his relationship with Moby Dick?" Your answers might cover Ahab's abandoning the *Pequod*'s task of filling its hold with blubber and whale oil, and his battle of wills with Starbuck, the chief mate, who is bound to the ship's original task and philosophically to avoiding the quest for all that Moby Dick represents. You would show in detail how Melville portrays the relationship through Ishmael's narration, what Ahab says and does, and what others say about him and the whale.

Finally, the *why* perspective asks, "Why does Ahab relentlessly pursue Moby Dick, and why does Melville make this his novel's central action?" The seeds of your answers are in your responses to the other pentad questions. Dramatically, it makes for a startling clash to have Ahab's obsessive personality set against the awesome leviathan, and philosophically it raises difficult if not obscure questions about man's place in the universe. This perspective allows you to probe the work for what is traditionally called "theme."

Your answers to the pentad questions on the *Moby Dick* topic might be somewhat different from those above, depending on the closeness of your reading experience and the novel's importance to you at the particular time in your life when you read and write critically about it. The key point is that you use the pentad to lead you through and to organize your literary experience. If you find it difficult to arrive at a thorough answer to one or more of the questions, you might need to rethink or reread parts of the work. Many readers find that having the pentad questions in mind *as they read,* perhaps using them to guide journal entries, enriches and clarifies their reading.

- **EXERCISE**

    2.11   Develop pentad questions and answers for an open topic on Jeffers' "To the Stone-Cutters." After you've written brief answers to the five questions (or sets of questions), design a precise topic for a possible essay. Compare your answers and topic with those of others in the class.

Focal Points[2]

If you had the world's most sophisticated camera, with infinite microscopic and telescopic power, capable of making both still pictures and movie film, able to exist in any environment and to go anywhere at any speed, you would have an infinite number of *focal points,* or views, on the world. But while you'd have vast degrees of focusing power, there would be only three basic kinds of focal points:

Up close—A view of the subject by itself, isolated and distinct from others of its kind or anything else. (Notice the similarity with the thought pattern of Definition and the pentad perspectives of Who and What.)

Inside—This view would use microscopic power to actually enter the subject, see its parts, how it works, and how it changes. (Compare the thought patterns of Process and Cause-Effect Analysis, and the pentad perspectives of How and Why.)

---

[2]This prewriting technique is derived from the varied perspectives of "tagmemics" as developed by Richard Young, Alton Becker, and Kenneth Pike in *Rhetoric: Discovery and Change* (New York: Harcourt Brace Jovanovich, 1970).

Panoramic—This sweeping view would allow you to survey the subject and its environment in an ever-widening context. (Again, compare the thought patterns of Classification and Comparison and the pentad perspectives of Where and When.)

Imagine a cinematic journey beginning with a close-up view of a rock, moving gradually closer to scan the most minute surface features, then entering a microscopic fissure and magnifying the view one hundred times, a thousand times, ten thousand, one hundred thousand, until you begin to see the molecular structure of metallic and nonmetallic chemical elements, atomic particles with electrons spinning around proton and neutron clusters, and ultimately zeroing in on subatomic particles and elementary energy fields. Then you stop and begin reversing the focal direction to return to the original close-up view and beyond that to ever larger panoramic views. You see the stone in a quarry, part of a glacial formation in a geographic region of the state, then a sector of the country, expanding to a global view as your camera leaves earth's atmosphere and enters interplanetary space. You move quickly past the moon and to the outer reaches of the solar system, seeing the earth shrink to nothing as the context expands. Now in interstellar space, focusing on where the earth was and is, you move in light years to the nearest star system and beyond until you begin to see the configuration of the Milky Way galaxy, now moving into intergalactic space with millions of galaxies, and finally to the edge of the universe and whatever if anything lies beyond.

No camera is ever likely to enable such a journey and certainly not in the time it took you to read the above paragraph. But the brain—the instrument that allowed you to make the progressive leaps through the focal points—is ready and available, and it can use the three kinds of focal points as highly generative tools for looking at subjects for critical writing. Obviously you won't want to get as close to or as far away from a literary text as our film recorded the rock, but you can probe your experience of a work and uncover insights with the focal points in ways not possible with the other formal prewriting methods. Let's see how the focal points could work in a critical writing situation.

Instead of having been assigned a topic, you've been asked to develop your own on any aspect of Robinson's "The Mill" (in Appendix) and then to write the essay. As with the other prewriting methods, the first step is to form questions that fit the subject. The paragraphs that follow are the results of one student's application of the three focal points to this poem. (Notice how the writing has the stylistic flavor of freewriting, with fragmentary and run-on thoughts.)

Up close—What features characterize the poem as a static, separate thing? It has three stanzas, eight lines in each, with regular rhyming pattern *ababcdcd* in each stanza. Every other line indented. Kind of a sing-song effect all through. Don't think it fits gruesome subject of a double suicide. Hard words, have to look up: "mealy" and "weir." Difficult phrases and lines, have to reread for meaning: "nothing wrong / In how he went and what he said"; "She knew that she was there at last" (where did she go?) "What else there was would only seem / To say again what he had meant"; "Would not have heeded where she went"; ". . . thought it followed her"; "one way of the few." Second stanza has most hard lines. Images of chill and death: cold tea and dead fire, smell of the past, hanging from a beam, the dark quiet pond where she kills herself.

Inside—How does the poem (and its parts) work? What is the reader's experience going through the poem? Don't know what's happened at first, kind of like a mystery. First stanza she's lonely and remembers his depression. I felt something was wrong then. Goes to the mill looking for him, and I didn't know he'd killed himself until line 15, "what was hanging from a beam." Third stanza was when I realized what she was up to, line 19 and 20 hard at first reading. "one way of the few there were / Would hide her and would leave no mark"—had to read to the end and go back to know she's thinking of suicide methods. She wanted to go out quiet and undiscovered like her husband. But she discovered him, maybe someone will discover her and start a chain reaction of suicides—wipe out the whole town. No, that's not in the poem, stick to what's inside.

Panoramic—How does this poem compare to other poems by Robinson, similar poems by other poets, and how does it fit into the genre of poetry? Remember "Richard Cory" by Robinson? The guy who was so nice and liked by everyone in the town, who goes home and puts a bullet in his head. Robinson seems to like shocking readers with all the dissatisfied people and losers killing themselves. Isn't anybody normal? Maybe a general despair and hopelessness. None of his characters talk to anyone or when they talk no one really listens. This poem is very much like Pound's "The River-Merchant's Wife: a Letter" and Williams' "The Widow's Lament in Springtime." In "RMW" woman stays faithful and lives but in "WLS" the woman thinks about suicide (in a swamp like the "weir" in "The Mill") but you don't know if she'll have the guts like the miller's wife. In "RMW" and "WLS" the women speak the poems, in "The Mill" someone else tells the story—has to because the miller and his wife are both dead. I like it better when the women talk because you can really get inside their feelings. Seems like an old-fashioned poem with the tight stanza and rhyme structure, not very "20th century" (but it was written in 1920!). How would it feel to rewrite it with no rhymes or regular rhythm?

- **EXERCISES**

  2.12   Either alone or in a small group, scan the above material, and come up with at least three good writing topics to share with the rest of the class.

  2.13   Try using the focal points on another work you've read recently, being sure to develop relevant questions, to write out responses, and to scan for and design writing topics you would find worth exploring in an essay.

In-Class Themes and Essay Examinations

How you use your time is crucial on essay exams and in-class themes. This kind of writing can heighten writer's block unless you have good techniques for getting words down on that blank page. In an in-class writing situation, the opportunities for discovering and shaping are greatly restricted, but while you're under pressure, some time taken for prewriting can yield excellent results.

Let's first consider the two basic types of in-class writing you might encounter in a literature course. You might be asked to organize an entire essay on a single topic during a class period, or you might take an examination with several essay questions, each requiring one or more paragraphs but not a full-blown essay response. For both situations, we recommend using 10 to 15 percent of the time available for the particular question for prewriting activities—that is, for determining your focus before you write the first word of your response. Here are three steps to help turn panic into a reasonable procedure.

1. Analyze the topic or question. With this technique, you break the topic down into its component parts and circle any key words that call for certain kinds of development or that focus on certain literary elements. Here's an example of what you can do with a topic:

What does (life mean) for Granny Weatherall, / and how does Porter (reinforce) this meaning (with imagery)?

The topic calls for two kinds of development: *definition* (Granny's understanding of life) and *illustration* (her understanding as expressed in the story's imagery). Of course, if the topic is vague or you are asked to choose your own topic, then you need to create the key words.

2. Select and try a formal prewriting method that fits the topic. Once you've analyzed key words and types of development called for, see which of the formal prewriting methods seems to work well. We stress *formal* methods here because you probably won't have enough time to go through the entire sequence, and the built-in structure of formal methods will help you shape your response better within limited time. In the example above, the thought pattern of *definition* first comes to mind. You could set up the statement, "For Granny, *life* (subject) is _____ (classification) that _____ (differentiation)." You might fill in the blanks this way: "For Granny, life is a struggle that is characterized by frustration in her relationships with those present at her deathbed and with those she has loved in the past."

After you have a definition you're comfortable with, you can move to the second part of the question and show how Porter uses imagery to reinforce the meaning of life for Granny. You could simply search the story for evidence of the senses at work as captured in figurative language, and if you knew the story well, that might be sufficient. If you wanted to make your connection of imagery with Granny's understanding of life more organized, you could apply one of the formal prewriting methods, one whose generative possibilities seemed well suited to the question. Because of the story's shifting perspectives, *focal points* would be a good bet. Turning each of the three perspectives into a relevant question might result in: *Up close*—"What images, if any, of Granny in bed, in the room, reflect her attitude toward life?" *Inside*—"When the narrative is 'inside' Granny's consciousness, what images, if any, reflect her attitude toward life?" *Panoramic*—"What images, if any, show Granny's attitude toward life as she relates to others in her past and present environments?" Notice how each of the questions ties together the search for images with the first part of the assigned topic, the meaning of life for Granny. The real skill is in constructing prewriting questions that *fit*.

3. Form the initial prewriting into a tentative thesis. To best address the question, your thesis (or topic sentence for an extended paragraph response) should make an observation on both parts to show the reader that you are directly engaging the assignment. A possible thesis for our example might be, "Porter uses images of tension and fading light to reinforce Granny's pessimistic view that life is made up of struggle and compromised dreams."

After this step, you're ready to start writing the actual response that you'll turn in. Together, the three steps can be expanded into a first draft for an essay written outside of class. In their streamlined form, however, these steps work quite well for in-class themes and essay exams by giving order to those first few moments after you see the writing topic and the clock starts ticking.

chapter 3

THEME

When people talk about literature, painting, music—indeed any art form—they often begin and end with *theme*. "What's the theme?" "What's it about?" "The author's meaning is. . . ." "That painting says something to me." "The composer develops two distinct themes." "I thought the movie stunk; it didn't have any point." "If there's an idea behind that sculpture, I can't put it into words." It's interesting to note that even with nonverbal art forms, theme always comes down to *words*: we are word-creatures, set apart more than anything by our highly developed language, and we have an almost compulsive need to pile up words and more words as we see meaning and significance everywhere.

Theme, we can say, is the ideas and values that a literary work expresses. But as soon as we make such a definition, we need to add important qualifications. If a critical writer views a literary work purely as a dressed-up collection of ideas and values—themes—then those qualities that make it a work of art are lost, and critical writing would simply be a distilling process to boil away unnecessary elements in order to get down to basic meanings that could be stated "in other words." Milton's *Paradise Lost* would be a statement about man's responsibility to God; Ibsen's *A Doll's House,* an early expression of feminist self-determination; or Hesse's *Siddhartha,* a merging of the Western idea of the isolated self with the Eastern idea of personal identity becoming one with Nature. It's dangerously easy to lose sight of the epic poem, the play, and the novel when they are reduced to thematic statements. Then they exist only as more or less valid political, social, or philosophical claims.

On the other hand, we can't avoid being aware of what a literary work seems to be about, and what it says about that identified subject. This is a central and natural part of the process of "evoking" a work of art, a process we described in Chapter 1. All the while we're reading and later rereading and writing critically, we're forming a sense of the work's overall plan and meaning, finding expectations confirmed or denied, modifying or strengthening our understanding, until we settle on a final understanding or come to an unresolved confusion. Our sense of "aboutness" is an awareness of theme. The pattern of meaning arises from the interaction of all the literary elements and is not stamped on the work, either by the author or the critical reader-writer.

Our understanding of what theme is can be helped by seeing parallels between the critical essay and the literary work.

Essay		Literary Work
Topic	⟵⟶	Subject
Thesis	⟵⟶	Theme

It's easy to confuse "topic" with "thesis," "subject" with "theme." The topic or subject is some aspect of life, perhaps broad, perhaps narrow, that the essay or work examines. The *thesis or theme is a direct or implied statement about the topic–subject.* While we can say that most good essays have a clearly stated thesis (see Chapter 9), we can't say this about literary works. Whether they're good or bad doesn't depend on whether they have a clearly stated or implied theme, or no theme at all. But when a work does have one or more themes, the critical writer needs to distinguish between the work's subject(s) (what it's about) and the work's theme(s) (a statement about the subject).

TYPES OF THEME

Here is a list of subjects and possible themes which you may find helpful in clarifying the difference between the two. You might note that most if not all sets of subjects and themes come under the broad umbrella of "the human condition."

Subject	Possible Themes
1. The Individual in Nature (Notice how many different meanings of "Nature" are implied in the themes.)	1A. Nature is at war with each of us and proves our vulnerability.
	1B. People are out of place in Nature and need technology to survive.
	1C. A human being is in harmony with Nature as the highest point in its evolution.
	1D. People are destroying nature and themselves with uncontrolled technology.

Subject	Possible Themes
2. The Individual in Society	2A. Society and a person's inner nature are always at war.
	2B. Social influences determine a person's final destiny.
	2C. Social influences can only complete inclinations formed by Nature.
	2D. A person's identity is determined by place in society.
	2E. In spite of the pressure to be among people, an individual is essentially alone and frightened.
3. An Individual's Relation to God (the gods)	3A. God is benevolent and will reward human beings for overcoming evil and temptation.
	3B. God mocks the individual and tortures him or her for presuming to be great.
	3C. God is jealous of and constantly thwarts human aspiration to power and knowledge.
	3D. God is indifferent toward human beings and lets them run their undetermined course.
	3E. There is no God in whom people can place their faith or yearning for meaning in the universe.
4. Human Relations	4A. Marriage is a perpetual comedy bound to fail.
	4B. Marriage is a relationship in which each partner is supported and enabled to grow.
	4C. An old man marrying a young woman is destined to be a cuckold (a victim of adultery).
	4D. Parents should not sacrifice all for a better life for their children.
	4E. There are few friends who will make extreme sacrifices.
5. Growth and Initiation	5A. A boy and girl must go through a special trial or series of trials before maturing.
	5B. Manhood or womanhood is often established by an abrupt, random crisis, sometimes at an unusually early age.

Subject	*Possible Themes*
5. Growth and Initiation (cont.)	5C. Aspects of childhood are retained in all of us, sometimes hindering growth, sometimes providing the only joy in later life.
	5D. A person grows only in so far as he or she must face a crisis of confidence or identity.
6. Time	6A. Enjoy life now, for the present moment, because we all die too soon.
	6B. By the time we understand life, there is too little left to live.
7. Death	7A. Death is part of living, giving life its final meaning.
	7B. Death is the ultimate absurd joke on life.
	7C. There is no death, only a different plane or mode of life without physical decay.
	7D. Without love, death often appears to be the only alternative to life.
8. Alienation	8A. An individual is isolated from fellow human beings and foolishly tries to bridge the gaps.
	8B. Through alienation comes self-knowledge.
	8C. Modern culture is defective because it doesn't provide group ties which in primitive cultures make alienation virtually impossible.

These are just a few of the many possible literary subjects and themes. The point to remember is that a subject is not a theme: a subject is some dimension of the human condition examined by the work; a theme is a statement, direct or implied, about the subject.

The themes about the subjects on our list are still fairly general. As a critical writer discussing a particular literary work, you'll need to bring your observations about theme closer to the work. For example, the last theme (7D) listed under the subject Death applies to Robinson's "The Mill" and Williams' "The Widow's Lament in Springtime" (both in the Appendix). The kind of critical statement you could make about theme in the two poems might be:

Both poems show that, without love, death often appears to be the only alternative. The difference is that the miller's wife actually follows out this idea in committing suicide, while the widow merely contemplates death.

The process of coming to understand theme is, first, identifying the work's subject and then fashioning a statement of what claim (theme) the work makes about the subject. It's important to remember that your first sense of subject and theme may not be accurate and that you may need to try several tentative thematic statements while reading and afterward before coming to one that fits the work and your experience of the work. Your prewriting portfolio is the logical place to record these hypotheses.

- **EXERCISES**

   3.1 See how many more possible literary subjects and themes you can add to the earlier list. Also, try stating additional themes under the subjects already listed.

   3.2 Choose five literary works you've read recently (in the Appendix or elsewhere), and make a list identifying their subjects and stating as precisely as possible their themes. (*Note:* There may be more than one subject and theme in a single work.) Then compare your list with those of other students in the class.

THEMATIC TERMS AND ELEMENTS

Form and Content

These two terms have been used with so much confusion as to be practically useless in critical writing. *Form* usually means shape, organization, or structure, but some critics also use it to include anything in a work that isn't an idea, such as word choice, level of diction, syntax, tone, imagery, characterization, sound devices, rhythm, and meter. Whatever is left is called *content*—the thought that is supposedly "behind" the work, the message, the theme. The danger in using these terms so simplistically is the same as in relying exclusively on paraphrases to understand literary works: they can give the impression that the work is merely an idea or ideas with layers of literary varnish brushed on to obscure as much as to reveal the theme. Thus we cite these terms more as a caution than as an encouragement to use them.

Pleasing and Instructing

The confusing division implied by "form and content" can be traced in part to the Roman poet Horace, who said that the two chief functions of poetry are to please and to instruct. In his view, the poet uses all the arts of language to make a moral lesson palatable. Some call this the "sugar pill" theory of literature, implying that theme is the bad-tasting medicine that the literary elements make easier to swallow. Again, this is simplistic and unrealistically breaks up the wholeness of a literary work. While both pleasing and instructing may be functions of a particular work, the critical writer cannot achieve insight simply by saying, "I was pleased by this and instructed by that"; "I enjoyed the imagery of the raft on the Mississippi, and I learned more about treating blacks like brothers in *Huckleberry Finn*." And what about a work with no apparent theme, such as Pound's "The

River-Merchant's Wife: A Letter" (in Appendix)? How can you sift out what pleases and what instructs in this poem? Saying that the poem teaches us about hope or about Oriental marital customs would force something on the poem that's not there.

The reason we've mentioned these two sets of terms—form and content, and pleasing and instructing—with caution and even doubt is that literary works do not fit into comfortable niches, part artistry and part thought. Literary historians are fond of tracing the pendulum swings from one period to another as writers incline now toward textual features and now toward ideas. The next set of terms tries to suggest a range of emphasis on theme in particular works.

Didactic and Impressionistic

Works that are *didactic* tend toward teaching rather than providing pleasure. Notice the key verb "tend," suggesting degrees of emphasis rather than a fixed purpose. The Bible tends to be didactic, as the principal recorded legacy of a major religion. But the Song of Solomon in the Bible, with its lush and sensuous imagery of romantic love, does more to please than to teach. *Impressionistic* works tend to have no clear theme and aim at providing "pure" experiences that are unconnected with ideas or values. An example would be Pound's two-line poem "In a Station of the Metro,"[1] which produces a single themeless metaphor: faces in a subway crowd compared to petals on a wet branch.

> The apparition of these faces in the crowd;
> Petals on a wet, black bough.

It may help to picture a thematic continuum:

Thematic Continuum
(Tendency)

Didactic —————————————————————————— Impressionistic
   1   2   3   4   5

We can place a work roughly on this continuum depending on the relative transparency of its theme(s), and while we shouldn't use the continuum rigidly, it might help to label the five points thus: (1) almost purely didactic; (2) tending toward didacticism; (3) balanced emphasis on theme and literary experience; (4) tending toward experiential over thematic appeal; (5) almost purely impressionistic. If the author seems at great pains to convey ideas, values, and beliefs, the work would be placed near the didactic end. John Bunyan's *Pilgrim's Progress* (1678), a Christian allegory, would come at the extreme didactic end of the continuum. If the author seems less

[1]Ezra Pound, *Personae.* Copyright 1926 by Ezra Pound. Reprinted by permission of New Directions Publishing Corporation.

interested in theme and more interested in recreating a feeling or experience, as in Porter's story "The Jilting of Granny Weatherall," the work would fall near the impressionistic end of the continuum.

- **EXERCISE**

    3.3 At which of the five points of the Thematic Continuum would you place the following works (in Appendix)? Explain your placement. Shapiro's "Auto Wreck"; Shakespeare's "That Time of Year"; Herrick's "To the Virgins, to Make Much of Time"; Williams' "The Widow's Lament in Springtime."

Minor Themes

Few literary works express only one thematic idea. Several ideas may have equal status or may function as *minor themes* in relation to the main theme, much as a novel or play may have a subplot tracing a revealing story about minor characters. Often, a minor theme can highlight and reinforce a major theme, as in Cheever's "The Country Husband" (in Appendix). If we can say the major theme of this story is that modern suburban life is belittling and stultifying, we might say that a complementary minor theme is a person's need to have adventure and romance in life, even if it means fantasizing. The challenge for the critical writer is sorting through themes and determining the major and minor relationships.

READING CRITICALLY FOR THEME

If you want to strengthen your awareness of theme, there are several literary devices that authors may use to express theme, and you need to notice them in your reading.

Direct Statements of Theme by the Narrator

In short stories and novels, the narrator in commenting on characters and events may make direct statements that help identify theme. You need to be careful, though—narrative voice is not always the author's voice and may express views contrary to the general import of the work. In Henry Fielding's great eighteenth-century comic novel *Tom Jones*, the narrator is almost as fully developed as the title hero, with each part of the novel beginning with a chapter in which the narrator comments on past action, events to come, or the anticipated reactions of critics. Even within chapters, Fielding's narrator doesn't hesitate to jump in and add thematic reflections, as in the following passage on one of Squire Allworthy's good traits.

> Men of true Wisdom and Goodness are contented to take Persons and Things as they are, without complaining of their Imperfections, or attempting to amend them. . . . There is, perhaps, no surer Mark of Folly, than an attempt to correct the natural Infirmities of those we love.

Most writers tend not to be nearly so obvious or intrusive as Fielding's narrator, yet if the narrative point of view is not limited, it may express the idea at the heart of the work. In Nathaniel Hawthorne's "Young Goodman Brown," the story of a young seventeenth-century Puritan who discovers (or dreams he discovers) the usually religious people of his town at a night of devil worship deep in the forest, the narrator in describing the young man's hysteria underscores the true horror and theme of the story—the potential for evil within each of us: "On he flew, among the black pines, brandishing his staff with frenzied gestures, now giving vent to an inspiration of horrid blasphemy, and now shouting forth such laughter, as set all the echoes of the forest laughing like demons around him. *The fiend in his own shape is less hideous, than when he rages in the breast of man.*" The sentence we have italicized is the narrator's direct thematic comment on satanic superstition and the recognition of evil in man.

Repetition of Key Thematic Statements or Images

Occasionally, a character or the narrator of a story or the speaker in a poem will repeat an idea or image that directly connects with the work's theme. This technique has its roots in the ancient Greek dramatic role of the chorus, a single character or group of voices which would give refrains or repeat the answers to moral questions raised in the play. An example of the technique can be found in Stephen Crane's story "The Open Boat," which recreates the alternating fear of death and hope of rescue of four men shipwrecked and adrift in a small boat. Several times throughout the story Crane injects a kind of incantation which may be the unspoken fears of the four men or the larger plight of mankind uncertain about meaning in life.

> "If I am going to be drowned—If I am going to be drowned—If I am going to be drowned, why, in the name of the seven mad gods who rule the sea, was I allowed to come thus far and contemplate sand and trees? Was I brought here merely to have my nose dragged away as I was about to nibble the sacred cheese of life?"

Part of the theme underlying this question, repeated several times in the story, is the idea that there is no justice or fairness in man's fate. Thematic repetition of an image often has a twist to it, as in Dylan Thomas' use of the color green in his poem "Fern Hill" (in Appendix). In the early stanzas, green is associated with the freshness of joy of youth: "happy as the grass was green"; "I was green and carefree"; "green and golden I was huntsman and herdsman"; "it was air / And playing, lovely and watery / And fire green as grass." But in the last stanza, green comes to mean vulnerable innocence, doomed to lose the joy of youth with growing up: "Time held me green and dying / Though I sang in my chains like the sea." As a critical reader-writer, you need to watch for repetition because it signals material that the author wants to emphasize, usually related to theme.

Thematic Words and Thoughts of Characters

What characters say and think often conveys theme. Shakespeare's
Hamlet is famous for his soliloquies that reflect doubt about his own worth
and the human condition as in the following: "How weary, stale, flat, and
unprofitable / Seem to me all the uses of this world! / Fie on't, ah, fie, 'tis
an unweeded garden / That grows to seed." Minor characters too can make
statements that express theme. In Cheever's "The Country Husband," Clayton Thomas, the fiancé of Anne Murchison, tells Francis what he thinks
of life in Shady Hill:

> "And all the dovecotes are phony," Clayton said. "And the way people clutter
> up their lives. I've thought about it a lot, and what seems to me to be really
> wrong with Shady Hill is that it doesn't have any future. So much energy is
> spent in perpetuating the place. . . . I think people ought to be able to dream
> big dreams about the future. I think people ought to be able to dream great
> dreams."

That is exactly what Francis does, and Cheever develops heroic dreams as
a major theme in the story. When narrative point of view allows us to get
inside a character's head, we are often close to a work's major theme. In
Ralph Ellison's "King of the Bingo Game," the story of a black man whose
life revolves around the hope of winning a bingo game in a sleazy Harlem
movie house, the man's thoughts on his dependence on the game express
the theme of all people beaten down by chance: "He felt vaguely that his
whole life was determined by the bingo wheel. . . . It had always been there,
even though he had not been aware of it, handing out the unlucky cards
and numbers of his days."[2] In addition to illustrating a character's thematic
thought, this quotation illustrates another literary device—the thematic
symbol.

Symbolic Characters and Images

While it is foolish and damaging to the literary experience to go
hunting for symbols, powerful symbols conveying important themes can
arise with compelling attraction in a work. The critical reader-writer must
balance a trust in personal responses to symbols—people and things that
stand for ideas, feelings, and cultural values—with a constant guard against
forcing the abstract onto the work. This is a precarious balance and is
developed through much reading and discussion with other readers. The
personified vacuum cleaner in Howard Nemerov's poem "The Vacuum"
(in Appendix) is an almost fearful symbol of the speaker's dead wife: "when
my old woman died her soul / Went into that vacuum cleaner, and I can't
bear / To see the bag swell like a belly. . . ." The vacuum cleaner is also a
symbol expressing the theme of human energy and spirit in the face of
life's drudgery: "I know now life is cheap as dirt, / And still the hungry,
angry heart / Hangs on and howls, biting at air." A character too can have

[2]From Ralph Ellison, "King of the Bingo Game." Copyright 1944 by Ralph Ellison.
Reprinted by permission of The William Morris Agency on behalf of the author.

a symbolic dimension connecting with the theme of a work. In Hawthorne's story "The Artist of the Beautiful," Robert Danforth is a blacksmith who stands for brute strength which is in conflict with artistic sensitivity, represented by the artist-watchmaker, Owen Warland, as illustrated in the following dialogue.

> [Danforth said,] "I put more main strength into one blow of my sledge hammer than all that you have expended since you were a 'prentice. Is not that the truth?"
>
> "Very probably," answered the low and slender voice of Owen. "Strength is an earthly monster. I make no pretensions to it. My force, whatever there may be of it, is altogether spiritual."

Such symbolic transparency in characters is less common in modern literature, and some critics are uncomfortable with overly symbolic characters as too contrived.

• EXERCISE

3.4 Make lists of the four literary devices that express theme—direct statements of theme by the narrator, repetition of key thematic statements or images, thematic words and thoughts of characters, and symbolic characters and images—and under each, list those works in the Appendix using the devices. Which works use all of the devices? Which use the fewest or none?

THEME AND THE FORMAL PREWRITING METHODS

When you generate words and ideas for a critical essay with the formal prewriting methods—thought patterns, the pentad, and focal points—certain parts of each method will help your understanding of theme.

Thought Patterns

Classification and *comparison–contrast* are the two thought patterns that relate most closely to theme. Recall from our discussion in Chapter 2 that when we group items, we look for a *principle of classification,* a basis for sorting, such as images of touch or ways characters behave in a crisis. When we compare and contrast, we look for a *common ground* among two or more subjects, that is, a reason for bringing them together for examination, such as the use of nature in two poems. You can make the leap to theme by asking, "What does the author(s) say or believe *about* the principle of classification or the common ground?" For example, we can classify the characters in Pound's "The River-Merchant's Wife: A Letter," Robinson's "The Mill," and Williams' "The Widow's Lament in Springtime" (in Appendix) as three women who experience the loss of their husbands. We can then get at the poems' themes by stating what the poets seem to be saying *about* this kind of experience: Pound seems not to express any strong feeling about the subject beyond showing a woman's hope in spite of a suppressed life; Robinson and Williams express the theme of death becoming the only hope after the loss of a mate. Whether classifying or comparing, it is the "aboutness" attached to literary subjects that defines theme.

The Pentad

Of the five pentad perspectives—Who, What, Where and When, Why and How—Why quite clearly points to theme. *Why* does a character behave in such a way? *Why* does an author create such and such a conflict, and resolve or fail to resolve it in such and such a way? We know why Francis Weed in Cheever's "The Country Husband" becomes infatuated with the babysitter—because his life is empty of romance, a major theme of the story. And we know (or at least can speculate) why Cheever ends the story with Francis' puttering around in his woodshop: because few people have the courage (or foolishness) to break out of their niches and fulfill their starved passions. The Why of the pentad is synonymous with the "about-ness" of theme.

Focal Points

The *panoramic* as distinct from the *inside* or *up close* perspective yields thematic insight when using the focal points method. When you see a character or an idea in context with other characters or ideas, whether in the same work, other works by the same author, or similar works by different authors, you find connections with the world of shared experience. What do Shakespeare's Lear, Othello, and Macbeth have in common beyond their high social and political status and aside from the important differences between their tragedies? They share the ability to look inside at the very end and to understand the human weakness that leads them to risk and lose what is most precious to them. Insight into theme often depends on seeing such connections while not forgetting the essential differences between literary elements.

Paraphrase

Another way to discover theme, which is particularly helpful with poetry, is to paraphrase. A paraphrase is an attempt to restate a work in your own words. It's possible to do a word-for-word paraphrase of a short work or a more general summary-paraphrase of a longer work. Many teachers and critics object strongly to this activity, feeling that it severely restricts and reduces a work's whole impact. One critic, Cleanth Brooks, goes so far as to condemn the "heresy of paraphrase," and in one sense his concern is right. If all a reader does is try to come up with easily understood paraphrases of literary works, the reading experience will be very shallow, and the works will exist only as cryptograms—texts whose features mask meaning and are simply to be uncovered to reveal underlying themes. Yet paraphrasing can be a useful technique for understanding a work so long as the process of criticism doesn't stop there but moves on to looking at *how* the literary elements work together to express theme. Here's a paraphrase of Jeffers' poem "To the Stone-Cutters" (in Appendix):

> You rock-shapers, who try to fight the onslaught of the years, have a pessimistic reward, knowing that none of your creations can stand up to time and weather. Poets make their poems in the same despairing spirit, knowing that nothing lasts forever. But even so, many monuments and poems have endured long and given pleasure to the living.

From such a paraphrase you might fashion a statement of theme such as, "In spite of their inevitable destruction or loss, works of art may last a long time and in the pleasures they give, however limited, make the artist's toil worthy."

SAMPLE ESSAY

It is impossible to write about theme in a vacuum. Theme is a recognition of meaning in a literary work, and it arises from the interacting elements of a work. We'll see in later chapters how literary elements too cannot exist or be written about in a vacuum—they contribute to meaning, to theme. The following is a student essay connecting images with theme in D. H. Lawrence's "Snake" (in Appendix).

IMAGERY AND THEME IN D. H. LAWRENCE'S "SNAKE"

Most people fear what they do not understand. Every minute of consciousness a battle wages in our heads between reality and our subconscious associations. When a fearful association is strong, the mind sees a distorted view of reality and, acting on misinformation, makes an improper decision. D. H. Lawrence recreates this mental battle between reality and subconscious association in his poem "Snake." His use of imagery in the poem defines this back-and-forth struggle in the mind and reinforces the theme that we should perhaps recognize and even accept the unknown, the dark side of the soul.

The snake has been a symbol of evil and has represented the devil since Adam and Eve's time. Neither the speaker nor the reader can shake this association. Lawrence reinforces this main symbol with lowerworld imagery in his poem. Such phrases as "horrid, black hole," "dark door," and "burning bowels of the earth," along with "the blackness," suggest more than the average snake hole and strengthen the symbol of the snake as the devil. The image of Mount Etna smoldering is a symbolic reminder also of the dark regions from which the snake emerges, as well as a reminder of potential evil and destruction. The narrator finally associates the snake with "a king in exile, uncrowned in the underworld" (l. 69). With this simile, the narrator makes clear the implied associations between the snake and the devil throughout the poem and unearths some reasons for man's fear and disdain of this creature.

But as Lawrence uses symbolism to establish the unconscious association of the speaker, so too does he employ a string of similes to establish what he actually sees (reality). Where the symbols are strong in the subconscious, the visual imagery of the poem is just as strong to the eyes and ears and presents a completely different situation from that which the subconscious wants to believe. The snake is seen to have human characteristics in lines 41–48, acting like a tired man who drank too much, and in lines 16 and 17 Lawrence gives the snake gentle qualities in comparing him to a happy, contented cow. What is interesting in this poem is the way the poet uses two different poetic devices, symbolism and visual imagery, in opposition to each other. The mental battle over whether or not to kill the snake is a thematic battle between cultural tradition on the one hand and personal inclination on the other.

This theme of confusion is further heightened by the rhythm and sounds the poem has when read aloud, as in the following examples: "In the deep, strange-scented shade of the great dark carob-tree" (l. 4), and "And trailed his yellow-brown slackness soft-bellied down" (l. 8). These lines are long and slow. They suggest sluggishness and are appropriate on a "hot, hot day" (l. 2) in Italy. In contrast, lines 22–37 are frenzied, and have the energy of one trying to make quick mental decisions. "Was it cowardice . . .?" The abrupt changes between the slow, articulate descriptions of the snake and the quick, choppy mental thoughts mark the battle between reality and subconscious associations. The regret that the speaker feels after a foolish attempt to kill the snake expresses the disappointment people feel after having lost an opportunity to understand themselves and the world better.

Lawrence never resolves the conflict between the world of cultural value and the domain of the snake. What he does say, though, is that we are diminished and belittled by our frightened unwillingness to take a risk and to understand.

chapter 4

CHARACTERIZATION

As a critical writer, you need to keep in mind the important difference between the terms *character* and *characterization*. "Character" is the larger and more ambiguous term; it refers to the many pieces of information that make up our understanding of an individual: personal traits, habits, actions, experiences, thoughts, feelings, beliefs, and relations with others. Of course, a person's character is not composed of "pieces" at all; rather, we explain a person's behavior by identifying those character features that seem to be more important for a particular account. Here is the important distinction: if *character* is the whole personality, then *characterization* is the deliberate selection or invention of features that an author makes to create a character.

It may, of course, serve an author's purpose to control the amount and timing of information that the reader receives about a character. For example, in *Romeo and Juliet* the first glimpse of Romeo that Shakespeare provides is through the eyes of Romeo's father and a cousin, who have seen him walking forlornly in the early morning and, at first light, shutting himself up in his room. Until Romeo himself speaks in the following scene, we have no notion of the cause of his mood, and, for this early moment in the play, we don't need to know. Shakespeare merely wants to show Romeo at a distance, removed from the traditional feud that brings the Capulets and Montagues clashing together in Act I. What is important to note is the principle of *selection* at work, serving Shakespeare's initial purpose of characterizing Romeo through the reports of others. Romeo's distance from his own family keeps him from their violent hatred that would otherwise close his mind to the future prospect of loving Juliet.

If you approach characterization by keeping in mind not only *how* but *why* the author has filtered a character to the reader, you'll begin to understand this important part of the writer's craft.

- **EXERCISE**

   4.1 Try your hand at creating two characters. For the first, use only *physical* description. Focus on the character's facial features, dress, stature, physique, mannerisms, voice, and so on. You might try images or brief comparisons to help convey the character's personality. Try to create a single impression in your study, such as

   an old man who is vigorous and energetic

   a meticulous young woman

   a distracted young man, confused and lost

   a coarse, vulgar person

   a child who has done something wrong

   a teacher who seems to be from another era

   an extremely shy adolescent

   a person who is not feeling well

   For your second study, create a character using *narrative* description, focusing on actions that make a statement, such as

   dishonesty often has unforeseen consequences

   generosity can sometimes be harmful

   humor is sometimes inappropriate

   being carefree can be dangerous

   shyness can mask inner strength

   After writing each of these character studies, discuss what problems you had in creating them, what decisions you had to make, and what results you think you achieved.

THE TERMS OF CHARACTERIZATION

Like any special aspect of a craft, characterization has collected special words and phrases that try to classify our experience of literary characters. The terms can help clarify our discoveries about characters, but if improperly used or applied as quick and easy labels, the terms can obscure meaning and create doubt about the accuracy of critical observation. Let's consider some of the more familiar terms of characterization.

Protagonist / Hero-Heroine / Main Character

The protagonist (from the Greek *proto,* meaning first, and *agonistes,* meaning someone who tries to win a prize or contest) is the main character who struggles and must meet a challenge of some kind in a literary work. We usually call the protagonist a *hero* or *heroine* if that person shows courage or fortitude in the struggle, but these terms might be inappropriate for some main characters. For example, Raskolnikov, the protagonist in Dostoevsky's novel *Crime and Punishment,* kills an old woman to experience what murder is like and alternately accepts and abhors his horrible secret. Would you call him a hero, or see heroic qualities in him? Most readers would probably be uncomfortable with a label so traditionally associated with goodness, strength, and virtue.

Conflict

The conflict pits the protagonist in one or another kind of struggle, possibly against another character, often called the *antagonist;* against natural forces (weather, land, sea, disasters) or supernatural forces (gods, spirits, embodiments of evil and good); against social forces or cultural traditions; or against him- or herself. Literary works often pose a combination of forces in conflict with the main character, as you can see in D. H. Lawrence's poem "Snake" (in Appendix): the speaker must contend with the snake itself as a potential antagonist, the "voice of my education," expressing the cultural tradition of hatred for snakes, and the opposite impulse within himself of wanting to know the snake and feeling honored by its presence at his well. Without something to overcome, without a crisis by which characters are formed or form themselves, without a basic tension, literature and by extension other art forms would bore us. Whether it's Bilbo Baggins' outfoxing old Dragon Smaug in *The Hobbit* by J. R. R. Tolkien or Achilles' epic fight with Hector in Homer's *Iliad,* conflict is what draws us to follow the fates of large and small characters.

Anti-hero

The anti-hero is a protagonist who lacks those qualities that give the stature of a hero. This is certainly the more appropriate term for Raskolnikov. The figure of Satan in Milton's epic poem *Paradise Lost* is also an anti-hero, opposed to God's favor toward the new creatures, man and woman. Even though Satan is the central figure in the early books of the epic, having broad powers and great pride, he is allied with the blackness and chaos of hell and all that is bent on the destruction of mankind. In modern literature, the anti-hero may be a comic or tragic figure who breaks with society and despairs of finding meaning in life or a will to live, such as the narrator in Albert Camus' *The Stranger,* Willy Loman in Arthur Miller's *Death of a Salesman,* or even Francis Weed in Cheever's "The Country Husband."

Minor Characters

Minor characters may simply serve the plot requirements of a narrative, or they may be important spheres revolving around a central character. A minor character might be a *foil* for the main character. A foil is a character who contrasts with another character, highlighting one or more of the other character's traits. In Ernest Hemingway's story "The Short Happy Life of Francis Macomber," Wilson, the hunter-guide, with his supreme self-confidence and male ego, is a foil for Macomber, who faces self-doubt and tries to prove his courage in facing the buffalo. Another type of minor character is the *double,* who mirrors or parallels the main character. The double has a closer relationship to the main character than a foil does, in that the double functions as a kind of echo reflecting an important dimension of the main character. This echo can help the main character and the reader see the dimension in a new light. For example, the young captain in Joseph Conrad's novella *The Secret Sharer* sees in Leggatt, his physical double, rescued from the sea, the self-confidence and ability to act that he himself eventually finds to justify his first command of a ship. Minor characters can be of major importance in assessing a protagonist or an author's overall skill at characterization. Indeed, one of Charles Dickens' claims to fame is his ability to people his novels with an astonishing variety of eccentric minor characters who, strange as they are, hold up a mirror to all facets of human behavior.

Flat and Round Characters

The English novelist E. M. Forster coined these useful terms in *Aspects of the Novel* (1927).[1] *Flat* characters are one-dimensional, almost wholly associated with one idea or trait, and we do not expect them to change or to surprise us. Squire Western in Henry Fielding's eighteenth-century novel *Tom Jones* is a flat character—a crude country squire concerned only for his dogs, livestock, food, land, and a profitable marital connection for his daughter. He doesn't change for the better or worse, and we wouldn't want him to. Authors play on *stereotypes* when they create flat characters, and while stereotypes imply unfair prejudices, they serve a literary purpose when defining certain tendencies in human behavior that the author wants to ridicule or praise. Squire Allworthy, the counter to Squire Western, is another flat character, almost too good to be true.

There is no clean dividing line between flat and *round* characters. When the characterization develops more than one central quality, we speak of "fleshed out" or round characters, whose behavior can be unpredictable. And it is not only main characters who are "round" in Forster's sense; minor characters too can be given depth. Julia Weed, Francis' wife in Cheever's "The Country Husband," is pictured both as a class-conscious suburban housewife and a woman not afraid to tell Francis how much he is dependent on her. She packs a suitcase to leave after he slaps her but decides to stay and "take care of you a little while longer." When using the terms "flat" and "round," it's better to say that a character tends to be developed toward one or the other extreme than to use the terms as fixed classifications.

The terms of characterization, then, can help you experience the characters as literary creations; however, the terms must be used with precision and not as a way of sidestepping the task of reading closely.

[1]E. M. Forster, *Aspects of the Novel.* Copyright 1927, 1954 by E. M. Forster. Paraphrased by permission of Harcourt Brace Jovanovich, Inc.

READING FOR CHARACTERIZATION

There are two situations in which you might consciously read a literary work to assess characterization: (1) you might have been assigned (or be planning) to write about this element when you first start reading, or (2) you might be assigned (or decide) to write on characterization after reading the work and now have to reread selectively to find material to write about. For both cases, the following set of character questions can guide your reading, and your *written* answers can become part of your growing pre-writing portfolio.

1. How would you describe the character in a brief physical and narrative sketch (as you practiced in Exercise 4.1)?
2. Does the character help reveal the meaning of the work?
3. What techniques does the author use to reveal the character? Do they include:
   * what the character says, thinks, and does
   * what others say, think, and do about the character
   * what, specifically, the setting reveals about the character
   * what the narrator tells about the character?
4. Can characters in the work be classified? If so, is there a purpose to the author's including character classifications?
5. Does the character change in any way? If so, how does the change relate to the author's overall purpose?
6. Are any of the characters symbolic?

Let's see how these questions would work with the answers strung together in a running commentary on the protagonist in Williams' "The Widow's Lament in Springtime" (in Appendix). The numbers in parentheses precede answers to each of the six questions listed above.

(1) The widow is grieving over her dead husband to whom she was married for thirty-five years, making her roughly fifty to sixty years old. Even the presence of a son is not enough to help heal her sorrow. Whereas she used to love the beauty of spring, she cares little now. There is no physical description of her in the poem.

(2) The widow is showing the emptiness and desperation of someone who has lost the will to live after losing a loved one.

(3) The widow herself speaks the poem, so all the techniques of characterization are filtered through her. What she says is that nothing in nature gives her joy anymore. The one action she describes is noticing the colors of flowers and turning away from them. She expresses one wish: to fall into the flowers and drown in the marsh. The setting, with its bright colors, sets off in stark contrast the widow's gloom; she even projects her sadness into the setting in the first six lines: "Sorrow is my own yard / where the new grass / flames as it has flamed / often before but not / with the cold fire / that closes round me this year." There are no other characters or a narrator who says, thinks, or does anything about the widow.

(4) Hence, there is no basis for classifying characters.

(5) The character doesn't change her attitude while speaking the poem, but she does reveal the change from her former joy in spring to the numbness she now feels since her husband died. This change may be Williams' central interest though there is nothing to indicate the poet's attitude toward it.

(6) There are probably not any symbolic dimensions to the widow, other than her representing one kind of response to this kind of loss.

● **EXERCISE**

4.2 Try your own hand at creating a character commentary by applying the six questions to Pound's "The River-Merchant's Wife: A Letter" (in Appendix).

Close Reading for Key Character Words

An author creates a character out of words, and you'll need to be sensitive to the key words that cluster in passages that describe a character. Consider the following passage.

> [Olga Ivanovna] sang, played the piano, painted in oils, modelled in clay, acted in amateur theatricals, and all this not just anyhow, but displaying real talent. Whatever she did, whether it was making lanterns for illuminations, dressing up, or simply tying somebody's tie, turned out artistic, graceful, charming. But in nothing did her talents display themselves so vividly as in her ability to strike up lightning friendships and get on intimate terms with celebrated folk. The moment anyone distinguished himself in the very slightest degree, or got himself talked about, she scraped up an acquaintance with him, made friends instantly, and invited him to her house. Every time she made a new acquaintance was a veritable red-letter day for her. She worshipped the famous, she dreamed of them every night. She thirsted for celebrities and could never slake this thirst.
>
> ANTON CHEKHOV, "The Grasshopper"

The key adjectives—"artistic, graceful, charming"; "lightning"; "intimate"; "celebrated"; "red-letter"—adverbs—"vividly"; "instantly"— and verbs— "strike up"; "scraped up"; "worshipped"; "dreamed"; "thirsted"; and "could not slake"—all help shape our impression of Olga as vivacious and creative, but at the same time desperate and quick to grasp at friendships to keep some hold on the world of the famous. The context of the story would permit a clearer understanding of her motives, but a close reading of this passage shows that Chekhov has used many descriptive words to form his main character so that we *see* Olga before finally coming to understand her.

As you read and reread a work in preparation for writing about characterization, look for those words and phrases that contribute most to your developing picture of a character. A useful *prewriting activity* is to make a *list of key character words* to draw on later when you write the middle paragraphs of your essay.

Drawing Inferences from Character Words

"Drawing inferences" means reading between the lines, coming to critical insights that are not stated but implied in the work. When you write about characterization, your own words should be as precise as possible because, in a sense, you are *recreating a character* in your discussion. When an author uses fewer directly descriptive words than, say, Chekhov in creating Olga, you need to draw inferences by applying your own words to a character. To be true to the author's characterization, your own words should not distort, but should reflect the character as embodied in the work.

In the following passage from "The Jilting of Granny Weatherall" (in Appendix), Katherine Anne Porter's narrative takes on Granny's voice as it reflects on George, the fiancé who failed to show on their wedding day, her life after that day, and the nagging fear that perhaps she had missed something in life.

> Yes, she had changed her mind after sixty years and she would like to see George. . . . Find him and be sure to tell him I forgot him. I want him to know I had my husband just the same and my children and my house like any other woman. A good house too and a good husband that I loved and fine children out of him. Better than I hoped for even. Tell him I was given back everything he took away and more. Oh, no, oh, God, no, there was something else besides the house and the man and the children. Oh, surely they were not all? What was it? Something not given back. . . . Her breath crowded down under her ribs and grew into a monstrous frightening shape with cutting edges; it bored up into her head and the agony was unbelievable. . . .

What could you infer about Granny from this passage? Is she vindictive, vain, regretful, uncertain, ignorant, indifferent, arrogant, stubborn, irrational, jealous, modest, treacherous? Some of these words are accurate while others are not. She is certainly not modest, ignorant, or indifferent, and probably not vain. No single trait-word could accurately describe her here. Different traits come to the surface in her semi-conscious musing; initially, for example, she is proud and vindictive, wanting to tell George that she survived and prospered with a family in spite of his jilting her. She has had more without him than she had hoped for with him. But her vindictiveness changes to uncertainty, almost a fearful cry of anguish and regret about the unknown life and family she did not have.

Just as the author needs precise language to create a character, so does the critical writer in discussing a character. As a *prewriting activity,* after having listed key words and phrases that the author uses, try expanding that list with other words that could describe the character. Try making comparisons to recreate essential traits. For example, you might call Granny Weatherall *hallucinating, withering, sharp-tongued, demanding, a tree with the sap going out of it* (notice the play on words Porter creates with Granny's last name). The skill is to draw your inferences in *words*.

Here are thirteen sets of traits that you may find useful in developing a vocabulary of characterization. Though a dictionary or a thesaurus may list some of these characteristics as synonyms, they have shades of meaning that can make a great difference when applied to a character.

1. PROUD   ARROGANT   VAIN
2. TIMID   SHY   MODEST
3. UNSCRUPULOUS   DISHONEST   DISSOLUTE
4. STUBBORN   WILLFUL   BELLIGERENT
5. APATHETIC   ALOOF   INDIFFERENT
6. GENEROUS   MAGNANIMOUS   INDULGENT
7. COARSE   CANDID   RUDE
8. MALICIOUS   TREACHEROUS   VINDICTIVE
9. IRRATIONAL   INSANE   RASH
10. VIRTUOUS   PIOUS   RELIGIOUS
11. JOVIAL   LUDICROUS   CAREFREE
12. JEALOUS   PROTECTIVE   ENVIOUS
13. IGNORANT   UNCERTAIN   DOUBTING

You could make many more sets of traits, in fact, as many as there are individual personalities. Every time you write about a character, you are doing just this. It is important, therefore, to choose trait-words that faithfully convey the character to your reader.

• EXERCISES

4.3   Give a short definition for each word in the above sets, and discuss which words in each set would be positive, negative, or neutral for a character.

4.4   Identify and list the key character words that illustrate Francis Weed in the paragraph beginning, "In the morning, Francis' snow-covered mountain was gone. . . ." (from Cheever's "The Country Husband," in the Appendix).

4.5   Cheever does not provide many descriptive words. If you were writing about Francis Weed, you would need to expand the few key words Cheever uses with interpretive words and phrases of your own. Using the paragraph cited in Exercise 4.4, generate as many words and phrases as you can to describe Francis as he begins to experience heightened feelings.

4.6   For each of the following character selections, (a) identify and list the key character words, (b) expand this list with words, phrases, and comparisons, and (c) draw some conclusions about the characters presented in the following paragraphs. Be prepared to defend your inferences with evidence.

María Concepción walked carefully, keeping to the middle of the white dusty road, where the maguey thorns and the treacherous curved spines of organ cactus had not gathered so profusely. . . . Her straight back outlined itself strongly under her clean bright blue cotton rebozo. Instinctive serenity softened her black eyes, shaped like almonds, set far apart, and tilted a bit endwise. She walked with the free, natural, guarded ease of the primitive woman carrying an unborn child. The shape of her body was easy, the swelling life was not a distortion, but the right inevitable proportions of a woman. She was entirely contented.

KATHERINE ANNE PORTER, "María Concepción"[2]

[Mr. Bounderby] was a rich man: banker, merchant, manufacturer, and what not. A big, loud man, with a stare, and a metallic laugh. A man made out of coarse material, which seemed to have been stretched to make so much of him. A man with a great puffed head and forehead, swelled veins in his temples, and such a strained skin to his face that it seemed to hold his eyes open, and lift his eyebrows up. A man with a pervading appearance on him of being inflated like a balloon, and ready to start. A man who could never sufficiently vaunt himself a self-made man. A man who was always proclaiming, through that brassy speaking-trumpet of a voice of his, his old ignorance and his old poverty.

CHARLES DICKENS, *Hard Times*

(*Just before the passage below, Huck Finn has lied to save Jim's life from a group of men searching for runaway slaves.*)

They went off, and I got aboard the raft, feeling bad and low, because I knowed very well I had done wrong, and I see it warn't no use for me to try to learn to do right; a body that don't get *started* right when he's little, ain't got no show—when the pinch comes there ain't nothing to back him up and keep him to his work, and so he gets beat. Then I thought a minute, and says to myself, hold on,—s'pose you'd a done right and give Jim up; would you felt better than what you do now? No, says I, I'd feel bad—I'd feel just the same way I do now. Well, then, says I, what's the use you learning to do right, when it's troublesome to do right and ain't no trouble to do wrong, and the wages is just the same. I was stuck. I couldn't answer that. So I reckoned I wouldn't bother no more about it, but after this always to do whichever come handiest at the time.

MARK TWAIN, *The Adventures of Huckleberry Finn*

Characterization in Drama

Writing about characterization in plays presents special problems. Unlike fiction or poetry, drama does not usually have a narrator or speaker who can fill in details of a character's background and behavioral traits. The reader of a play is limited primarily to dialogue and occasional stage directions (more prevalent in modern drama). A theatergoer doesn't have the opportunity to reread a complicated interchange during a performance but can take advantage of the interpretive skills of the director, the set and lighting designers, and the actors. Most likely, you'll be writing about dramatic characterization after having *read* a play, so we'll concentrate on the reader's limitations and advantages.

[2]Katherine Anne Porter, "María Concepción." Copyright 1930, 1958 by Katherine Anne Porter. Quoted from *Flowering Judas and Other Stories* by permission of Harcourt Brace Jovanovich, Inc.

How do dialogue and occasional stage directions help the reader of a play understand a character? What a character says when alone or with others often reveals not only personal traits, beliefs, feelings, and ideas, but also action. Dialogue may be the only clue to what a character did in the past or is doing in the present. In the following exchange from Christopher Marlowe's *Doctor Faustus*, Faustus declares his allegiance to Lucifer, the devil, as he stabs his arm for the devil's servant Mephistophilis to sign away his soul in blood in trade for supernatural powers.

> *Faust.* Lo, Mephistophilis, for love of thee
>   Faustus hath cut his arm, and with his proper blood
>   Assures his soul to be great Lucifer's . . .
>   View here the blood that trickles from mine arm
>   And let it be propitious for my wish!
>
> *Meph.* But, Faustus,
>   Write it in manner of a deed of gift.
>
> *Faust.* Aye, so I do. But, Mephistophilis,
>   My blood congeals and I can write no more.
>
> *Meph.* I'll fetch thee fire to dissolve it straight. [Exit]
>
> *Faust.* What might the staying of my blood portend?
>   Is it unwilling I should write this bill?
>
>   (Act II, Scene 1, ll. 53–65)

Here we have dialogue that explains a pivotal action in the play: up to this point, Faustus has dabbled in the black arts and wished for more secret knowledge; now he is playing for keeps—and his eventual damnation. The most important revelation in this section of dialogue is Faustus' puzzlement and, we may infer, his fear when his blood begins to clot and he can't continue writing. As soon as Mephistophilis departs for the remedy of fire to soften the blood, Faustus expresses some doubt, in a special kind of dialogue called *soliloquy* (spoken alone), on what he is about to do, almost as if his life's fluid objects to his horrible deal. Later in the scene, after Faustus has signed the contract, Mephistophilis says in another special kind of dialogue, the *aside* (spoken with others present but only for the speaker's or audience's benefit), "What will not I do to obtain his soul!" As a critical writer, you need to be sensitive to such important uses of dialogue that reveal action, comment on the action, and thereby develop a character.

Stage directions for action and set design are usually not very extensive, so that both director and designer enjoy a good deal of freedom in interpreting the physical presentation of the play. These directions can provide clues—sometimes vague, sometimes quite specific—to help define a character. Tennessee Williams' *The Glass Menagerie* has quite detailed stage directions that directly connect the set to the characters. In the following example, Williams sets Scene Six, as Amanda, the mother, fixes Laura's dress in preparation for her handicapped daughter's first gentleman caller. The family is poor, and there is a desperation to Amanda's sincere efforts to decorate the apartment.

A delicate lemony light is in the Wingfield apartment. Amanda has worked like a Turk in preparation for the gentleman caller. The results are astonishing. The new floor lamp with its rose-silk shade is in place, a colored paper lantern conceals the broken light fixture in the ceiling, new billowing white curtains are at the windows, chintz covers are on chairs and sofa, a pair of new sofa pillows make their initial appearance . . . Laura stands in the middle with lifted arms while Amanda crouches before her, adjusting the hem of the new dress, devout and ritualistic. The dress is colored and designed by memory. The arrangement of Laura's hair is changed; it is softer and more becoming. A fragile, unearthly prettiness has come out in Laura: she is like a piece of translucent glass touched by light, given a momentary radiance, not actual, not lasting.[3]

We might just as well have included this selection in the chapter on setting, but it is closely entwined with the characters of Amanda and Laura; indeed, Williams inserts himself as a narrator with such directions.

As we noted, such detail in stage directions is unusual, even for modern drama, so you'll need to be aware of those details of setting that are provided and to what extent they relate to or express characters. It is dialogue that you must read and listen to in your mind's ear most closely for what characters reveal about themselves and others.

PREWRITING METHODS AND CHARACTERIZATION

We will now apply each of the three formal prewriting strategies—thought patterns, the pentad, and focal points—to characterization. Presumably, you have been making journal entries while reading a particular literary work and have also done some preliminary brainstorming and freewriting. The material you generate with the informal prewriting methods may contain useful ideas, so hold onto it for possible inclusion in your essay.

When characterization is the subject of a critical essay, you need to guard against writing merely a *character sketch,* a simple redrawing or paraphrase of what the author has already said. A *critical discussion* of characterization involves your relating a character to the work's *theme.* Remember that the principal ideas embodied in the work also work themselves out within a character and/or between characters.

Thought Pattern Questions

Our discussion in Chapter 2 identified basic patterns that the mind uses to understand information from the environment: *classification, definition, comparison,* and *analysis.* Turning these patterns and their subparts into questions about a character in a literary work makes an effective prewriting strategy.

[3]Tennessee Williams, *The Glass Menagerie.* Copyright 1945 by Tennessee Williams and Edwina Williams and renewed 1973 by Tennessee Williams. Reprinted by permission of Random House, Inc.

1. *Classification.* Q: What kind of person is Granny Weatherall? A: A senile woman. (Note: You may have to answer the classification question several times, making several classifications, for a complex character.)

2. *Definition.* Q: What is senility in general? for Granny? A: A condition of weakened physical and mental capacities, varying in degree and caused by aging. For Granny, her breathing is constrained and painful, and her hearing and sight are alternately clear and clouded. Her mind operates without the usual controls of time and space.

3. *Comparison.* Q: How is Granny similar to and different from other characters in the story? other elderly persons? A: She is apparently stronger and feistier than those around her, and she is aware of them in ways they cannot imagine. Her imagination appears more supple.

4. *Analysis.* Q: What are the *causes and effects* of Granny's behavior? What *process* of change, if any, does she go through? A: Her fierce independence and memory of how she always worked for herself make her resentful of her family's and the doctor's protectiveness. As her recollection of the jilting raises new and painful questions, she goes through a stage of anxious doubting about her life, and as death approaches, with no answers or signs, she recovers enough anger to will to die.

There are two steps in using the thought pattern strategy. First, you convert the thought pattern into a question related to the character you are discussing (for example, classification: "What kind of person is Granny?") Second, you *write out* your answer by recalling the story, even rereading those passages most helpful in answering the question. Again, we stress writing your answers because the generated material, collected in an essay portfolio, can later become the ideas you work into the paragraphs of a first draft.

- **EXERCISES**

    4.7 Considering the speaker in Dylan Thomas' "Fern Hill" (in Appendix) as a character, convert the thought patterns into relevant questions.

    4.8 Write out your answers based on a close reading of the poem.

Pentad Questions

The five parts of the pentad—Who, What, Where and When, How, and Why—are useful not only for making an overall profile of a literary work but for focusing on a particular element, such as characterization. As with the thought pattern technique, you need to turn the parts of the pentad into useful questions.

1. *Who.* Q: Who or what are the agents (causes) of the principal acts? A: Granny's mind. Whatever George's motives were.

2. *What.* Q: What principal acts (events) associated with Granny Weatherall occur in the story?   A: Shifting in and out of consciousness, from present to past and back. Interacting with Dr. Harry and Cornelia and, at the end, the rest of her family. George's jilting; Granny's blowing out the light—her death.

3. *Where and When.* Q: Where do the principal acts occur?   A: The physical setting is Granny's deathbed; the principal setting, however, is Granny's mind, including her memory and present consciousness as they shift into each other, modified by imagination.

4. *How.* Q: How or by what means are the acts caused?   A: Granny's increasingly flexible, though deteriorating, mind. Her sharp tongue and hearing, when conscious. George's not appearing on and after their wedding day. Granny's independent will combined with anger and desperation when no "sign" is given.

5. *Why.* Q: What is Granny's purpose? Why has Porter so portrayed her?   A: Granny's main desire is to stay alive and get back to the patterns of living and working that have given her life meaning. She also wants George to know that her life has been meaningful without him. Ultimately, when she realizes there is no hope, her purpose is to die. Porter's purpose is to show a very strong person coming to face her death in the interaction of a love of life with doubts about that life's value. (Note: *Why* is the pentad item most closely associated with *theme*.)

- **EXERCISES**

    4.9   Develop pentad questions with a focus on the speaker in Karl Shapiro's "Auto Wreck" (in Appendix).

  4.10   Write out answers to your questions.

  Focal Point Questions

  The three varied perspectives are another way the mind can organize and understand information from the environment. The *up close* perspective considers a subject as an isolated "thing" that does not change and that is distinct from other "things" in the same category. (Notice how the thought pattern of classification precedes this perspective.) The *inside* perspective shows the subject as undergoing a process of change, as having internal features that work toward some purpose. The *panoramic* perspective sees the subject within a larger system or a number of systems.

  Your skill in using the focal points, as with the other prewriting methods, depends on converting the perspectives into questions related to the topic at hand, in this case characterization. The question-answer format here applies perspectives to a character study of Francis Weed.

  1. *Up close.* Q: What features characterize Francis Weed?   A: He is a middle-class family man who commutes to work by train, a war veteran, a survivor of a plane crash, and is infatuated with a baby sitter. He goes to parties but doesn't seem to have any close friends.

2. *Inside*. Q: What process of change does Francis' identity undergo? A: He is increasingly abrupt and hostile with his family and neighbors. His initial feeling for Anne is tied to his romantic memories of Europe, but as he becomes more desperate, he develops a futile self-image that leads him to seek out a psychiatrist and confess his failure as a romantic. Finally, he appears to submerge himself once more in the blunted life of Shady Hill.

3. *Panoramic*. Q: Is there a "system" of traits and motives working in Francis? What larger systems does he fit into? A: Francis as a "system" is alternately pushed and pulled by his environment. To fight the numbing effect of Shady Hill, he tries to spark an affair with Anne, but when his wife threatens to leave and destroy his security, he expresses passionate love for her. In the system of Shady Hill, he contrasts with his neighbors (Mrs. Wrightson) in disdaining their tastelessness and feeling pulled under by "civilized" living in the modern world. In the larger system of literature, Francis compares with all characters who do not fit comfortably into their world and contrasts with those who find their niches comfortable.

• EXERCISES

4.11 Develop focal point questions for Julia Weed, Francis' wife. While she is not the main character, Cheever has provided enough detail to develop her second only to her husband.

4.12 Write out answers to your questions, paying particular attention to those passages where Julia is most fully developed.

SAMPLE ESSAY

Below is a sample student essay on characterization.

A CHARACTER STUDY OF CHEEVER'S FRANCIS WEED

Monotony in middle age often arouses the memory and the emotions. John Cheever, in his story "The Country Husband," deals with the anxieties and desperate fantasies of a man feeling his middle-age doubts about self and home. After nearly dying in a plane crash, Francis Weed, the story's anti-hero, reflects on the lack of substance in his life. Bored and fed up, he needs an escape from the ordinary, controlled suburban lifestyle of Shady Hill and finds it momentarily in a fantasy romance he creates with his children's babysitter. Cheever shows his protagonist briefly fanning the flames of fantasy but then slipping back into the regimentation that initially drives him out.

The airplane crash is the first of a series of events that inspire in Francis a desire to escape his mid-life boredom. He is unable to communicate his frightening brush with death because of stifling arguments with his children and wife. Later, at one of the weekly parties he and Julia attend, Francis' memory, sparked by the Farquarson's maid, drifts back to Paris during World War II and a lovely woman he saw humiliated by an angry mob. But he cannot share this experience for fear of being "unseemly and impolite." "But the encounter left Francis feeling languid; it had opened his memory and senses, and left them dilated." The train of experiences excites his desire for change.

Anne Murchison, the babysitter, represents the opportunity for escape from Shady Hill. With senses "dilated," Francis becomes infatuated with the young girl's beauty and is swept away into a world of fantasy and romance. As he sleeps, "the girl entered his mind, moving with perfect freedom through its shut doors and filling chamber after chamber with her light, her perfume, and the music of her voice. He was crossing the Atlantic with her on the old *Mauretania* and, later, living with her in Paris." The next morning, his fantasy is fueled by the image of a naked woman passing by in an express train. By pursuing the babysitter, he is seeking out his own youth and passion, which he does not find with his wife. Julia tries to root him in the town's superficial concern with appearance and status, neglecting the essential human needs for passion and romance.

Francis' new love gives him a new and unusual energy. "The autumnal loves of middle age are well publicized, and he guessed that he was face to face with one of these, but there was not a trace of autumn in what he felt." With a "bracing sensation of independence," he enjoys the rudeness he shows to stuffy Mrs. Wrightson at the train station. But his escape, his romantic infatuation, is constantly challenged by the reality of his situation. He dwells on the moral and legal risks if he is caught taking advantage of the young girl. His passionate dreams are interrupted when Gertrude, the local stray urchin, barges in while he is making a pass at Anne. And when the Weed family is photographed for their Christmas card, "the heat of the lights made an unfresh smell in the frosty air, and when they were turned off, they lingered on the retina of Francis' eyes." Through such subtle images, Cheever shows how a taint of unwholesomeness and even sensory restriction covers everything "established" in Francis' life.

Francis' final resort to psychotherapy to solve his agonized swinging from impossible fantasy to bland reality is the classic upper-middle-class "cure." Even the doctor's office exudes Shady Hill: "a place arranged with antiques, coffee tables, potted plants, and etchings of snow-covered bridges and geese in flight, although there were no children, no marriage bed . . . in this travesty of a house, where no one had ever spent the night and where the curtained windows looked straight into a dark air shaft." When a policeman mistakes Francis for a homicidal patient, Cheever underscores the absurdity of Francis' position. No, he is not the deviant he is mistaken for. He is not rebellious. He is simply Francis Weed, a country husband, who ultimately represses his basic human need for adventure and adjusts to the framework of Shady Hill. The doctor recommends woodwork, and ironically Francis is last seen in his basement building a coffee table, a necessary appointment for the suburban living room.

The character of Francis Weed is a weak one. His life is controlled finally by conditions outside himself. Though he can make no claim to heroic stature, we can surely sympathize with his abortive effort, however desperate and pitiful, to break out. Cheever develops him through a series of events that lead him first away from and then back to his monotonous life in Shady Hill. His neighbors, the Babcocks, periodically escape by prancing about in the nude, but Francis is a puppet strung to the town, forever dancing to its tune, perhaps occasionally out of step, but destined to remain a country husband.

chapter 5

IMAGERY
AND SYMBOLISM

And as imagination bodies forth
The forms of things unknown, the poet's pen
Turns them to shapes, and gives to airy nothing
A local habitation and a name.   SHAKESPEARE, *A Midsummer Night's Dream*

Of all the critical terms you'll ever come across, "imagery" is subject to more abuse and confusion than any other. The root word "image," from the Latin *imago,* has a bewildering array of associated meanings: picture, copy, imitation, ghost, idea, shadow, appearance, similarity. When a word can suggest exactness on the one hand and distortion on the other, there's bound to be trouble, so as a critical writer, you need to be especially clear in using this term. Because "symbolism" depends on an understanding of imagery, we'll discuss symbolism later in the chapter.

Imagery is an umbrella term that includes similes, metaphors, and other forms of figurative language. But in its larger, more complete meaning, imagery refers to all references to the senses in a literary work, not just the senses that appear in similes and metaphors. We'll discuss similes, metaphors, and other special uses of imagistic language in the next section of the chapter. Now, however, let's look at how literature makes connections with the five major senses—*sight, taste, touch, smell,* and *hearing*—as well as a sixth, *kinesthesia,* the sense of physical tension and relaxation in the muscles and joints. There are several questions to answer when critically assessing how imagery evokes the senses.

WHICH SENSES ARE USED?

Sight is the most predominant sense in literary imagery. Even when other senses are represented in a work, sight still tends to be the major sense, and it is unusual to find a work that makes few or no specific references to sight. We've purposely included one of these unusual works, Nemerov's

"The Vacuum," in the Appendix. Notice how *hearing* becomes the predominant sense as the poem is framed by references to what the speaker hears. The first line says how quiet the house is after, as we learn later, the speaker's wife has died. The last two lines recreate the human-like howling of the vacuum cleaner after it has been compared with the wife's lingering spirit. When other senses compete with or even suppress the sense of sight, there is usually a reason. In the context of Nemerov's poem, it would be quite natural for the absence of sound to be highlighted in a home where a loved one had recently died. Nemerov works this heightened sense into his poem by showing how the speaker's imagination projects his wife's soul into the silent vacuum cleaner. Normally, though, sight will be the most pervasive sense in literary imagery. It can help your critical analysis of imagery to note both the *types* of senses and the frequency of their appearance in a work. You can then connect these observations with how the presence or absence of imagery affects the reader and serves the author's purposes.

HOW CLEAR ARE THE SENSES?

The sharpness or vagueness with which senses are presented has a direct bearing on the effects an author creates. For example, the bright colors of new flowers in Williams' "The Widow's Lament in Springtime" (in Appendix) show how visually aware the speaker is: "Masses of flowers / load the cherry branches / and color some bushes / yellow and some red." The intensity of even this sight is reduced by the widow's emotional state expressed in the next lines: "but the grief in my heart / is stronger than they / for though they were my joy / formerly, today I notice them / and turned away forgetting." These lines illustrate the importance of seeing imagery in the context of the whole work and not just as isolated references to sense. The isolated image is the vivid colors of the flowers; the image takes on thematic meaning when the pleasure it originally created for the widow is contrasted with her present grief.

Senses may also be presented vaguely, without sharp detail and contrast. In Porter's "The Jilting of Granny Weatherall" (in Appendix), we see the present and past filtering through Granny's failing senses. Granny reflects,

> Plenty of girls get jilted. You were jilted, weren't you? Then stand up to it. Her eyelids wavered and let in streamers of blue-gray light like tissue paper over her eyes. She must get up and pull the shades down or she'd never sleep . . . . Better turn over, hide from the light, sleeping in the light gives you nightmares . . . . Cornelia's voice staggered and bumped like a cart in a bad road. It rounded corners and turned back again and arrived nowhere.

Porter uses the image of tissue to suggest that Granny's sight is blurring. The image of the bumping cart is used to describe Cornelia's voice as it comes unevenly to Granny's ears. Remember, an author's imagery conveys just as much sensory information as he or she feels the reader needs.

Two terms that describe the relative presence or absence of imagery in a work are *concrete* and *abstract*. A concrete work is dense with sensory information while an abstract work is relatively free of imagery, exclusively developed with ideas and concepts. Like the thematic terms *impressionistic* and *didactic*, which we discussed in Chapter 3, concrete and abstract suggest a range rather than a fixed quantity of imagery. A poem such as Pound's "In a Station of the Metro" (p. 40) is considered highly concrete, while Herrick's "To the Virgins" (in Appendix) is fairly concrete in the first two stanzas but abstract in the last two. While authors may not always be right in deciding how much and what kind of imagery is needed, we can't fault an author or a work simply because there is very little or a great deal of imagery. What the critical writer needs to decide is whether the imagery is *appropriate* to the work and how it affects the reader's experience.

What Is the Focus of the Imagery?

Beyond choosing particular senses and how sharply to present them, an author may fit images together to create a *dominant impression*. Images often cluster around a single idea or feeling. For example, the images in "The Widow's Lament in Springtime" recreate pictures of nature in spring. In contrast, the images in Robinson's "The Mill" are not as focused: there are both domestic images and images of nature in the poem. The imagery in Shakespeare's "That Time of Year" focuses on things that are ending or dying—the end of autumn and a tree's yearly bloom, the end of a day, the end of a fire. After identifying the images, you should then look for a pattern, a category or class into which some or all of the images fit. Then see if you can discover why the author has chosen this particular pattern of images.

Critical writing about imagery is not simply a matter of hunting for and identifying images in a literary work. What we want to know about imagery is how it operates, how it determines the "character" of a work, how it reinforces or conflicts with theme, in short, how it affects the reader. Compare the following paragraphs on imagery in Robinson's "The Mill" (in Appendix):

A.   The imagery in the first stanza presents a domestic scene. The miller's wife is waiting at home; there is cold tea and a dead fire, and she remembers how her husband did not seem to want to go out the door. In the second stanza she goes to the mill, her husband's place of work, where the warm smell of the grain strikes her, and she sees her husband hanging from a beam. In the last stanza, the poet uses images of nature—the black smooth water compared to the night sky—as the miller's wife contemplates suicide.

B.   The poem's imagery contributes to feelings of fear, despair, and the end of life. The life has gone out of the home of the miller and his wife, reflected in the cold tea and dead fire, giving the reader a sense of loneliness. The only warmth in the poem is associated with the "mealy fragrance of the past" in the mill, a place where the miller probably used to find meaning in life, but no longer. His last words are, "There are no millers any more." The image of her husband hanging from the beam seems to haunt and follow the miller's wife, as she too has nothing to live for. The poem's final image is of the place she chooses for her own suicide: a black, swampy pond to cover up her desperate act. This place creates a feeling even more lifeless and cold than the spiritless home both she and her husband have left forever.

Notice how the writer of paragraph A is content to rattle off the key "pictures" in the poem in a kind of imagistic paraphrase, as if merely to prove he or she could spot them. In paragraph B, though, the writer shows a sensitivity to the overall effects of the imagery, not only on the wife but on the *reader* as well. Imagery isn't just tacked on to be picked out, but rather it's an integral part of the characters, the story line, the theme, the whole work. This is what you should aim at in writing about imagery.

• EXERCISES

5.1   Using sensory detail, create images of the following:

> something wasteful
> a loved one's eyes compared to something else
> an animal that reminds you of some human quality
> someone's voice compared to something else

What did you do to make each of the images? What types of words did you use to make the connections and comparisons? Exchange your images for those of another class member, and separately jot down what qualities you feel the other images try to portray. Then discuss each other's interpretations.

5.2   What associations come to mind when you think of

soft	empty husks of locusts	green	flashing
red	tourniquets	night	shining
wings	flower	golden	lamb
rocking	streams	chains	

Turn to Shapiro's "Auto Wreck" and Thomas' "Fern Hill" in the Appendix. Which of your associations are applicable to the respective poems?

5.3   Referring to the picture on page 77, what prominent images do you note? What associations does each image call up? What do you think the point of the picture is, and how is the point made?

5.4   Images are often used to represent an intangible concept, such as time. What images are used to represent time in Thomas' "Fern Hill," Shakespeare's "That Time of Year," and Herrick's "To the Virgins, To Make Much of Time"? What images would you use to represent death? What widely shared cultural (artistic or advertising) images can you write down in five minutes?

5.5 The six selections that follow range from scientific to poetic writing. For each
one, apply the three imagery questions—Which senses are used? How clear
are the senses? What is the focus of the imagery?—to answer the larger
question, "Is the imagery effective?"

1.   Darkness is more productive of sublime ideas than light. . . . Extreme
light, by overcoming the organs of sight, obliterates all objects, so as in its
effect exactly to resemble darkness. After looking for some time at the sun,
two black spots . . . seem to dance before our eyes. Thus are two ideas (lightness and darkness), as opposite as can be imagined, reconciled in the extremes
of both; and both, in spite of their opposite nature, brought to concur in
producing the sublime.

ISAAC NEWTON, *Opticks*

2.   Marie-Antoinette, in this her utter abandonment, and hour of extreme
need, is not wanting to herself, the imperial woman. . . . The tricolor streamers on the housetops occupied her attention, in the Streets du Roule and
Saint-Honore; she also noticed the inscriptions on the house-fronts. On reach-
ing the Place de la Revolution, her looks turned toward the Jardin National,
the Tuileries; her face at that moment gave signs of lively emotion. She
mounted the scaffold with courage enough; at a quarter past twelve, her head
fell; the Executioner showed it to the people, amid universal long-continued
cries of "Vive la Republique!"

THOMAS CARLYLE, *The French Revolution*

3.   And afterwards we would watch the lonesomeness of the river, and kind
of lazy along, and by-and-by lazy off to sleep . . . . It's lovely to live on a raft.
We had the sky, up there, all speckled with stars, and we used to lay on our
backs . . . and discuss about whether they was made, or only just happened . . . . We used to watch the stars that fell, too, and see them streak
down. Jim allowed they'd got spoiled and was hove out of the nest.

MARK TWAIN, *The Adventures of Huckleberry Finn*

4.   How weary, stale, flat, and unprofitable
Seem to me all the uses of this world!
Fie on't, ah, fie, 'tis an unweeded garden
That grows to seed.

SHAKESPEARE, *Hamlet*

5.   your slightest look easily will unclose me
though i have closed myself as fingers,
you open always petal by petal myself as Spring opens
(touching skilfully,mysteriously)her first rose
e. e. cummings, "somewhere i have never
travelled,gladly beyond"[1]

6. The fog comes
    on little cat feet.

    It sits looking
    over harbor and city
    on silent haunches
    and then moves on.

CARL SANDBURG "Fog"[2]

FIGURATIVE LANGUAGE

If imagery in its larger sense calls our attention to the physical sensations represented in a literary work, then figurative language is the special use of imagery that makes us see *connections* between things that are familiar and unfamiliar. The diagram shows the relationship between imagery and figurative language.

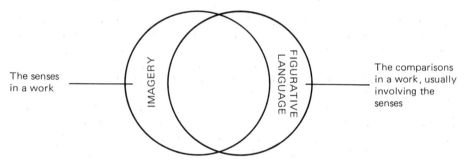

**Connections Between the Familiar
and the Unfamiliar**

Despite the complexities of figurative language, there is a central idea that will help you thread your way through, namely, that connections between the familiar and the unfamiliar usually involve the senses. It may help to get at the nature of figurative language to recall the story of how one of the most famous books of poetry, *Lyrical Ballads* (1798), came to be written. William Wordsworth and Samuel Taylor Coleridge, two young poets in late eighteenth-century England, found that they shared the same ideas about poetry. Like many artists, they wanted to do something "new," so they agreed to write and publish a series of poems that would draw on their individual skills and interests. As Coleridge describes their separate tasks for the book, he actually reveals the two basic components of figurative language: familiarity and unfamiliarity.

It was agreed that my endeavors should be directed to [things] supernatural . . . so as to transfer from our inward nature a human interest and a semblance of truth sufficient to procure for these shadows of imagination that willing suspension of disbelief for the moment, which constitutes poetic

[2]From *Chicago Poems* by Carl Sandburg, copyright 1916 by Holt, Rinehart and Winston, Inc.; copyright 1944 by Carl Sandburg. Reprinted by permission of Harcourt Brace Jovanovich, Inc.

faith. Mr. Wordsworth, on the other hand, was to . . . give the charm of novelty to things of everyday . . . which, in consequence of . . . familiarity . . . we have eyes yet see not, ears that hear not, and hearts that neither feel nor understand.

In short, Coleridge was to make the unfamiliar familiar, and Wordsworth was to make the familiar fresh and new. This is what figurative language does (or tries to do): it enables us to see in new ways things we thought we knew before as well as things we've never imagined. Figurative language may not always work, and you may get tied up in illogical, tired, or dead metaphors, but making connections between dissimilar things (ideas, feelings, and objects) is how we learn. Poets, playwrights, and fiction writers take the method to its most developed possibilities. Let's look at the most common forms of figurative language.

Figures of speech have two parts, one thing being compared to another. The critic I. A. Richards developed two very useful terms to describe these parts: tenor and vehicle. The *tenor* is the main subject or focus of attention; the *vehicle* is the image that "carries" or expands our view of the tenor. For example, in the comparison "Like as the waves make toward the pebbled shore, / So do our minutes hasten to their end," Shakespeare's primary subject, the tenor, is the progress of life toward death. The vehicle with which he develops his subject and holds our interest is the image of waves, one after another, rolling toward a beach.

Simile

A simile is a comparison in which the connection between the tenor and vehicle is made quite obvious with one of four connecting words: *like, as, appear,* and *seem.* The comparison in a simile might be quite logical and believable, or it might be quite illogical and bizarre. The image of the snake in Lawrence's "Snake" (in Appendix) is developed through the poem with similes (underlined):

> He lifted his head from his drinking, as cattle do,
> And looked at me vaguely, as drinking cattle do . . . .
> And lifted his head, dreamily, as one who has drunken . . . .
> And looked around like a god, unseeing, into the air . . . .
> For he seemed to me again like a king,
> Like a king in exile, uncrowned in the underworld,
> Now due to be crowned again.

As we've said before, it's not enough just to be able to identify similes; you need to account for them and their effects in a work, and this means connecting them with *theme.* Lawrence is showing a person (the speaker) confused about the tradition surrounding snakes. The similes show new and unexpected dimensions of the reptile: a gentle cow, a proud god, an exiled king. The similes help us see the snake differently by expanding and even jolting our usual expectations. They may also recall the Christian tradition of the snake as Satan, the fallen angel who rebelled against God, and show Lawrence exploring the possibility of something good and noble in the image traditionally associated with evil.

Occasionally, a simile may be developed at some length, in several stanzas of poetry or paragraphs of prose. Such "extended similes" can be quite intricate and can carry a great amount of compressed meaning. One of the most famous extended similes is from John Donne's "A Valediction: Forbidding Mourning" where the speaker tells his lover that their love can endure a separation because their souls are like the two parts of a compass joined at the top (love is the tenor, a compass the vehicle). The extended simile is introduced by a shorter one comparing the separation to gold beaten thin by a goldsmith. (We've underlined the tenor and vehicle, and boxed the connecting word in each simile.)

> Our two souls therefore, which are one,
>   Though I must go, endure not yet
> A breach, but an expansion,
>   Like gold to airy thinness beat.
>
> If they be two, they are two so
>   As stiff twin compasses are two:
> Thy soul, the fixed foot, makes no show
>   To move, but doth, if the other do;
>
> And though it in the center sit,
>   Yet when the other far doth roam,
> It leans, and hearkens after it,
>   And grows erect, as that comes home.
>
> Such wilt thou be to me, who must,
>   Like th' other foot, obliquely run;
> Thy firmness makes my circle just,
>   And makes me end where I begun.

As you develop your critical sensibility, it's important not to associate imagery and figurative language merely with poetry. Fiction, nonfiction, and drama may also draw on the senses and figurative comparisons, though perhaps not with as much frequency as poetry. In the following selection from Cheever's "The Country Husband" (in Appendix), two similes are used to convey Francis Weed's state of awareness the morning after he realizes he's infatuated with Anne Murchison, the babysitter.

> It was a clear morning; the morning seemed thrown like a gleaming bridge of light over his mixed affairs. His spirits were feverish and high. The image of the girl seemed to put him into a relationship with the world that was mysterious and enthralling. . . . An express train—a night train from Buffalo or Albany—came down the tracks. . . . Then he saw an extraordinary thing; at one of the bedroom windows sat an unclothed woman of exceptional beauty, combing her golden hair. She passed like an apparition through Shady Hill, combing and combing her hair.

Even if "The Country Husband" is the only Cheever story you've read, you probably realize that he does not often use figurative language, making these two instances particularly notable. In terms of the story, there is good reason for their appearance at this point. Francis' life, until his attraction to Anne, has been impoverished of imagination and passion. Now, with his emotions rekindled, two similes close to one another are appropriate complements to his provoked imagination, meshing nicely with Cheever's theme that life in modern suburbia can ironically blend the dull and commonplace with what is rich and visionary.

- **EXERCISE**

  5.6 Identify the similes in Shakespeare's "That Time of Year" (in Appendix), being sure to specify the principal subject (tenor) and what it is being compared with (vehicle). Then discuss how well the similes work in the sonnet, connecting effect with theme.

Metaphor

Similes make quite explicit comparisons that ultimately keep the tenor and vehicle intact and separate. Metaphors make stronger comparisons that often merge the tenor and vehicle. If similes say *A is like B*, metaphors imply that *A is B*. "His words came forth like a rushing torrent" is a simile. "His words were a rushing torrent" is a metaphor. Metaphoric comparisons, though, can't be reduced to a simple formula such as *A (tenor) is B (vehicle)*. The formula won't help us with something like, "The air surged and rolled on with his words." Image-bearing words, the vehicle, are not always connected to the tenor with "is" or a form of the verb "to be." The tenor and vehicle in a metaphor can be woven together in at least three distinct ways.

1. Tenor + form of verb **to be** *+ vehicle.*   (Example: "A shark is an eating machine.") This is the way metaphors are usually described, and many readers never get beyond looking just for this kind, when actually it's the least common. In the example above, "shark" is the tenor, and "eating machine" is the vehicle; tenor and vehicle are connected by "is." Here are several other examples, with "T" indicating the tenor and "V" indicating the vehicle.

> Here, where men sit and hear each other groan . . .
> Where but to think is to be full of sorrow.
>   T   V
>
> JOHN KEATS

(This is a rare example of a metaphor where both parts are non-imagistic, that is, essentially abstract and without references to the senses.)

> I was prince of the apple towns . . . .
> T   V
>
> I was green . . .
> T   V
>
> DYLAN THOMAS

> Sorrow is my own yard.
> T   V
>
> WILLIAM CARLOS WILLIAMS

Granny lay curled down within herself, amazed and watchful, staring at the point of light that was herself; her body was now only
          V   T   T
a deeper mass of shadow in an endless darkness. . . .
            V

                                    KATHERINE ANNE PORTER

One note of caution: not every sentence with a form of the verb *to be* in it
is a metaphor. The primary linking verb *to be* gets quite a workout in most
languages by connecting subjects and objects, and by expanding meaning,
as in, "Shakespeare is a late Renaissance poet," or "Reduced supply is the
greatest cause of inflation." It's only when two *unlike* things are connected
that we have a metaphor.

    2. Tenor + descriptive words, but vehicle not mentioned. (Example:
"The shark eats with mechanical precision.") This is the most common
form of metaphor, as words surrounding the tenor "carry" the image and
make the connection with an unstated vehicle. "Shark" is again the tenor
as in the above example; a machine is the unstated vehicle, expressed by
the vehicle words "mechanical precision." The "vehicle words" (VW) may
be nouns (other than the vehicle itself), verbs, adjectives, or adverbs, as in
the following:

Farewell, Love, and all thy laws forever,
       T
Thy baited hooks shall tangle me no more.
    VW   VW T

                                    THOMAS WYATT

(Here we have the interesting situation of two sets of tenor, vehicle words,
and implied vehicle. The implied vehicles are a fisherman and a fish.)

How dull it is to pause, to make an end,
              T
To rust unburnished [unpolished], not to shine in use!
    VW   VW

                             ALFRED, LORD TENNYSON

(The unstated vehicle is something made of metal, rusting from disuse.)

    **3. Vehicle + descriptive words, but tenor not mentioned at all or long
before.** (Example: "The eating machine sliced through the man's leg with
precision.") This is not as common as the second form of metaphor, but
when it occurs it creates a unique and enriching effect. The connection
between unstated tenor and stated vehicle depends on the context, what
has come before in the work, so that the tenor is echoed without being
specifically identified. In the above example, the unstated tenor is a shark
and is conveyed by the vehicle "eating machine" and the descriptive words
"sliced" and "mechanical precision."
    Two special types of this metaphoric form are *metonymy* and *synecdoche*.

Metonymy (mə-ton´ə-mee) is the use of something associated with the tenor to stand for the tenor, as in "Ten thousand spears marched into battle." The vehicle "spears" represents the unstated tenor "soldiers." **Synecdoche** (si-nek´ -də-kee) is the form of metaphor in which a part is used as the vehicle for the unstated whole (tenor), as in, "His heart was sorrowful." The vehicle is "heart," and the unstated tenor is a man. Here are several examples.

> Beat! beat! drums!—blow! bugles! blow!
> ‾VW‾ ‾V‾ ‾VW‾ ‾V‾ ‾VW‾
> Through the windows—through doors—burst like a ruthless force,
> ‾VW‾ ‾VW‾ ‾V‾
> Into the solemn church, and scatter the congregation.
> ‾VW‾
>
> WALT WHITMAN

(The unstated tenor is war.)

> Those parts of thee that the world's eye doth view
> ‾V‾
> Want nothing that the thought of hearts can mend;
> ‾V‾
> All tongues, the voice of souls, give thee that due.
> ‾V‾
>
> SHAKESPEARE

(Here are three synecdoches standing for those people who will see the speaker's lover and praise his or her attractiveness.)

As we've seen, figurative connections can be made in a variety of ways, with both tenor and vehicle present, or with one or the other absent. In critical writing, depending on your purpose and the assignment, you may want to look closely at the construction of individual metaphors and similes or at the patterns of images set up in a work. For example, after reading Karl Shapiro's "Auto Wreck" (in Appendix), you could approach the poem's figurative language first by listing the poem's major imagistic comparisons, then labeling what kind they are (simile or one of the three types of metaphor), and finally, using the thought pattern of classification, try to group the images into some pattern with a common theme. After each of the key images that follow are line numbers for easy reference to the poem and a classification into type.

> Its quick soft silver bell beating, beating (l. 1)

(Metaphor type 2: the ambulance bell [tenor] is compared with a heart [unstated vehicle] by the vehicle words "beating, beating," recreating the sense of sound.)

> And down the dark one ruby flare
> Pulsing out red light like an artery (ll. 2–3)

(Simile: using sight, touch, and kinesthesia, this figurative image compares the flare [tenor] with a pulsing artery [vehicle].)

> Our throats were tight as tourniquets (l. 22)

(Simile: the condition of the speakers' throats [tenor] is compared with the kinesthetic feeling of tight bandaging to stop the flow of blood [vehicle].)

> Our feet were bound with splints . . . (l. 23)

(Metaphor type 3: in this image, the presence of a form of the verb *to be* does not signal the first type of metaphor. The horror of witnessing the accident [unstated tenor] is conveyed by the image of bound feet [vehicle].)

> Like convalescents intimate and gauche,
> We speak through sickly smiles . . .(ll. 24–25)

(Simile: the speakers–witnesses [tenor] are compared with patients who are recovering and who have developed a shared closeness [vehicle].)

> But we remain, touching a wound
> That opens to our richest horror (ll. 29–30)

(Metaphor type 3: the lasting impression of and the philosophical questions raised by the accident [unstated tenor] are compared with patients' curiosity about their wounds which, upon probing, start bleeding again [vehicle].)

> And cancer, simple as a flower, blooms (l. 35)

(Simile: cancer [tenor] is compared with a blooming flower [vehicle], an ironically positive image but physically accurate because when cancer cells are seen with a microscope they do seem to bloom. The image serves the question, "How can something so beautiful in itself be so deadly?" This creates a deeper metaphor [type 3] in which the unstated tenor is fascination with accidental death.)

> [The accident] Cancels our physics with a sneer (l. 37)

(Metaphor type 2: the accident [tenor] is expressed by the word "this" in the preceding line. The vehicle words "cancel" and "sneer" suggest some person or being with the power to destroy the principles of rational life—"physics." This person or being's power is the unstated vehicle which is being compared with the effect of the accident.)

In looking for patterns or thematic threads running throughout these figurative images, we can say that physical accident and disease predominate as vehicles, with the effect of the accident on the speakers being the consistent tenor. The critical writer needs skill in looking closely at individual images to understand how they work and how they affect the reader, as well as in looking at all the images in a work to discern patterns that develop themes. Your final critical essay will not include a detailed analysis of every image such as we just completed; that activity is part of prewriting about imagery. The final draft would probably be more concerned with image patterns, your observations being supported with specific, representative illustrations of how individual images work.

Personification

From the most primitive to the most civilized person, we have a tendency to see human life everywhere in the world. We "people" the objects and forces of nature with spirits, beings, intentions both beneficial and hostile to human beings, and we build a universe in reference to ourselves. What anthropologists call "anthropomorphism" (seeing everything in terms of human form), literary critics call *personification,* or seeing what is non-human as having human qualities. A variation on this way of seeing is *animation,* that is, giving lifelike qualities (not necessarily human) to something that is lifeless. Personification and animation can be expressed in both similes and metaphors. Here are some examples.

> And now the Storm-blast came, and he
> Was tyrannous and strong;
> He struck with his o'ertaking wings,
> And chased us south along.

SAMUEL TAYLOR COLERIDGE

(Notice how Coleridge has imbedded in the personification of the storm as an overpowering man the metaphoric comparison with a bird of prey.)

> Death's second self [sleep], that seals up all in rest.

SHAKESPEARE

> When the green woods laugh with the voice of joy
> And the dimpling stream runs laughing by . . .
> Come live and be merry.

WILLIAM BLAKE

> Because I could not stop for Death—
> He kindly stopped for me—
> The Carriage held but just Ourselves—
> And Immortality.

EMILY DICKINSON

> [the city of London:]
> Ne'er saw I, never felt, a calm so deep!
> The river glideth at its own sweet will:
> Dear God! the very houses seem asleep;
> And all that mighty heart is lying still!

WILLIAM WORDSWORTH

- **EXERCISES**

    5.7   Identify the images of personification in all the poems in the Appendix.

    5.8   As we did with Shapiro's "Auto Wreck," do an analysis of the figurative imagery in Dylan Thomas' "Fern Hill" (in Appendix). The steps in the process are: (1) list the figurative images; (2) identify each image as a simile or one of the three types of metaphor, including personification; and (3) discuss any patterns of images you discover.

SYMBOLISM

The word *symbol* can be just as confusing and overfull of meaning as the word *image*. The Latin and Greek roots for *symbol* mean "token" or "sign," something that stands for something else. One good way of understanding symbolism is to think metaphorically of *resonance*, the repetition and expansion of sound. When we hear a cello played in a small room, the sound is pleasant enough, but when fifteen cellos joined by a full symphony orchestra play in a large concert hall, the sound resonates throughout. This is something like what a symbol does: it takes something isolated, having a literal meaning in itself, and through tradition and long cultural use, makes it "resonate" with layers of associated meaning. Consider the associations connected with the following visual symbols.

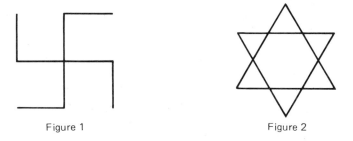

Figure 1   Figure 2

The complexity and power of symbols can be seen if you consider what these two figures mean for each of the groups they represent. Figure 1, the "swastika," is best known as the official emblem of the Nazi party in Germany before, during, and after World War II. For the Nazis, it stood for a rising sense of pride after the humiliation Germany suffered after World War I, the superiority of those with "pure" German-European ethnic backgrounds, and the strength of the German military. For those countries and groups opposed to Germany during World War II, the swastika became a hated symbol for the madness that drove Hitler to try to conquer the world and eradicate minorities, especially Jews. Ironically, this figure among ancient Orientals and American Indians was a good luck symbol. Figure 2, the Star of David, represents the religion of Judaism, the nation of Israel, and the cultural heritage of all Jews. The resonating layers of association include the pride with which Jews see themselves, the historical experience of losing a sacred homeland and then regaining and defending it in the twentieth century, the religious truth of the sacred texts of the Torah, and the obligations of practicing faith and hope in everyday life. Symbols, then, are specific devices which stand for and focus the shared meanings of groups.

Now look at the photograph below. Here we have a number of visual images which operate as symbols on the viewer, all suggesting age and the passing of time: the looming clock tower, the person stooped over using a cane and facing, perhaps contemplating, the great edifice of time, and the ornate roofs and towers of buildings from another age. The photo doesn't specifically point to the values or meanings to be associated with these time-symbols, so, in this case, the viewer has to supply them. On the one hand, we might see the arrangement of symbols as negative—man surrounded, dominated, or even intimidated by time with no hope of outliving these cultural monuments. On the other hand, we might see the presentation of these symbols as positive—the human figure in perspective is just as tall as the clock tower, and, from the photographic angle, towers above the nearby rooftops and lesser towers, perhaps suggesting that man has a stature and grandeur equal to time.

Specific knowledge or information can sometimes fill out our interpretation of symbols. In the photo, for example, how does your interpretation change if you're told that the clock tower is the famous Big Ben

Photo by Nancy W. Stevenson

looming up from Parliament, the seat of British government in London, and, moreover, that the human figure is actually a *statue* of Winston Churchill, the great statesman?

A *symbol* is a natural or manmade object, or a human experience that specifically stands for a concept or a set of values or beliefs. For example, the vacuum cleaner in Nemerov's "The Vacuum" (in Appendix) stands for not only the spirit of the speaker's dead wife but also the emptiness in his house and life. In discussing symbols, we use such verbs as "stands for," "represents," "symbolizes," and "is" to show the direct relationship between the object-experience and the meaning. In modern literature, pure symbols are relatively rare, and what we find more frequently are symbolic associations.

When the object or experience implies rather than stands for a concept or set of values, we have *symbolic associations*. The most common symbolic associations in literature have to do with *time of day* and the *seasonal cycle*. We've all internalized the symbolic connections with times of day and the seasons so well that they sound almost too trite to mention. We associate the setting sun, the west, night, and darkness with fear, melancholy, and death. The east, the light of dawn, and the rising sun have come to mean birth, hope, new beginnings, and happiness. Likewise with the seasons: spring suggests new life, rebirth, youth, love, regeneration, and fertility; summer, the prime of life and growth; autumn, sadness, the approach of death, the final harvest; and winter, the cessation of life, impending darkness, and despair. Of course, experience shows these associations to have their exceptions, but the experiences of generations over the centuries have fixed these connections in our lives so that they evoke fairly consistent shared meanings when used in literary works. To discuss symbolic associations critically, we use such verbs as "suggests," "implies," and "connotes."

While symbols and symbolic associations may have complex, multi-layered meanings, they have just two basic effects: they can *reinforce something* or *create tension with something* going on in the work. When a symbol reinforces, it fits and complements a theme, a character trait, a narrative's direction. In Pound's "The River-Merchant's Wife," the season of autumn with its traditional symbolic associations with sadness, the beginning of endings, the coming of death, reinforces the young wife's anxiety at her husband's long absence:

> The leaves fall early this autumn, in wind.
> The paired butterflies are already yellow with August
> Over the grass in the West garden;
> They hurt me. I grow older.

In addition to the autumnal association, this passage also draws on the symbolic association of the west ("the West garden") with the end of the day and, in this case, love and possibly life.

When a symbol creates tension rather than reinforcement, its associations are in discord and don't fit something going on in the work. Notice how D. H. Lawrence creates conflicting resonances with the traditional symbol of the snake in "Snake" (in Appendix). At first the speaker is conscious of the literal meaning of this particular snake—it is poisonous and capable of killing—and then hears the "voices of my education," which tell him to kill it as an unwelcome representation of the evil underworld. On the other hand, the speaker fights the traditional symbolic meaning and sees the snake alternately as a gentle cow, a proud god, an uncrowned king in exile, someone he'd like to know better. But the traditional symbolic power of the snake (really the speaker's mind) wins out, and the speaker comes to regret having lost his chance with "one of the lords of life." It's the *context* of the work and cultural *tradition* together that determine whether a symbol is working to create tension or to reinforce something.

A danger that critical writers need to avoid is to be constantly looking for symbols in a work. Symbol-hunting for its own sake is risky. If you sense that a symbol or symbolic association is at work, respond to it honestly, but try not to force symbols on a work when they are just not there.

- **EXERCISE**

   5.9 What symbols or symbolic associations are working in Shakespeare's "That Time of Year" and Herrick's "To the Virgins" (both in Appendix)? Do they work to reinforce or to create tension within the contexts of the poems?

PREWRITING ABOUT IMAGERY AND SYMBOLISM

Critical writers may decide or may be asked to write about such literary topics as: Discuss the imagery in work A. What is the relationship between imagery and characterization in work A? Evaluate how effectively imagery expresses the theme(s) of work A. What image patterns does the author create and how do they relate to the theme(s) of work A? Compare and contrast imagery in works A and B. Even when specific problems on imagery are not posed, you may find that building a significant portion of a paper around a discussion of imagery is the only way to deal effectively with certain works. Whatever the assignment or approach you choose, you'll need to be sensitive to your own reactions (and, if the opportunity exists, the reactions of others) to imagery and how it affects the reader.

As with other literary elements, you'll need to live with a work for a while in order to understand and appreciate its imagery. Of course, for in-class, timed critical writing, you'll be relying either on your immediate experience of a new work or on your memory of a work you read previously. But for prepared essays, where you have time to prewrite, draft, revise, and edit, you should try to read through a work several times over a period of time to allow your sense of the imagery to grow. The informal prewriting methods—journal writing, brainstorming, and free writing—can be a rich source of your early reactions to imagery in a work read over a period of time.

- **EXERCISE**

5.10   Try the following experiment. Over the period of a week, record your reactions to a short work you haven't read before, either from the Appendix or from an anthology. Focus the informal prewriting methods you use on imagery and symbolism, and each day for five to seven days, reread the work (but not your prewriting) and try to produce a page of informal writing on the imagery. At the end of the period, read back over your prewriting. Did your reactions change in any way? Were any interpretations strengthened, abandoned, or discovered? Write a short account of the process of understanding the imagery over the period. If there were other students in your class who read the same work, exchange your process accounts and compare each other's results. This kind of activity is an excellent source of writing for your imagery essay portfolio.

Each of the formal prewriting methods can help you generate material for a critical essay on imagery.

Thought Patterns

Classification is the obvious thought pattern that applies to imagery. We can classify the *senses* to which images appeal, as we did to discover the bias toward sound in Nemerov's "The Vacuum." And we can classify the *types of figurative language* (simile, metaphor, personification, symbol). Finally, we can use classification to see *thematic patterns,* as we discovered that the imagery in Shapiro's "Auto Wreck" can be grouped around physical accident and disease. The thought pattern of comparison–contrast is often built into paper topics on two or more works, in which case it's helpful to line up your classifications of senses, types of images, and thematic patterns in a comparison–contrast chart of the works.

The Pentad

The pentad perspectives *what* and *how,* when turned into the specific imagery questions—What images are used? and How are they constructed?—will yield the same material more precisely covered by the detailed questions under the outlines, "Imagery and the Senses" and "Figurative Language" at the end of this section. The perspective *why,* however, gets deeper into the author's purpose in creating certain images and image patterns, and such an insight can be profitably connected with the reader's experience.

Focal Points

The *up close* perspective allows you to distinguish among types of images (simile, metaphor, and so on). The *inside* perspective examines the structure and inner relationships between the parts (tenor and vehicle) of individual images. The panoramic perspective looks for the patterns established within a work as well as between works by the same author, by different authors, by authors in the same literary period, or by authors in different periods. (Remember, if the formal methods appear to be repetitive, they're covering the same ground but from slightly different points of view, some of which work better for different writers.)

The formal methods of prewriting about imagery and symbolism would include the questions and probes we've already illustrated in this chapter.

Imagery and the Senses

 I. Which senses are used (sight, taste, touch, hearing, smell, and kinesthesia)?

 II. How clear (degrees of concreteness and abstractness) are the senses?

 III. What is the focus of the imagery?

Figurative Language—Special Connections Between Tenor (Subject) and Vehicle (Image Carrier)

 I. What *similes* are used?

 II. What *metaphors* are used?

  A. Type 1 (tenor + form of verb *to be* + vehicle)

  B. Type 2 (tenor + descriptive words, but vehicle not mentioned)

  C. Type 3 (vehicle + descriptive words, but tenor mentioned long before or not at all)

   1. Metonymy—something associated with tenor standing for tenor

   2. Synecdoche—a part (vehicle) stands for the whole (tenor)

  D. Personification

 III. Do any patterns or thematic threads run through the work's images?

 IV. Does the author draw on or create any special *symbols*?

Written answers to these questions would also become material for your prewriting portfolio.

The material you generate from any of the formal prewriting methods can later be scanned for possible reshaping into middle paragraphs for your essay. The following student essay comparing and contrasting imagery in two poems is the result of selecting and reshaping material generated by prewriting methods.

SAMPLE ESSAY

IMAGERY IN "THE WIDOW'S LAMENT IN SPRINGTIME" AND "THE RIVER-MERCHANT'S WIFE: A LETTER"

Most of us have wondered what it would be like if a husband, wife, or friend passed away or just left us and did not return. The thought frightens us, and we choose not to discuss death or unexplained departure. In William Carlos Williams' "The Widow's Lament in Springtime" and Ezra Pound's "The River-Merchant's Wife: A Letter," we see the effects of the loss of a loved one on two women, the speakers of the poems. While their situations are clearly different (Williams' narrator is a widow, and Pound's narrator is awaiting her husband's return), both women use the imagery of nature to convey two degrees of despair as they deal with their losses.

Both poems are fairly concrete with the sense of sight dominating most of the images. The river-merchant's wife begins her letter with images of how she and her husband looked when they played and grew up together in the village of Chokan, she pulling flowers and he playing horse around her. The character of the images in the first three stanzas is happy and shows the innocence and shyness of the girl as she becomes a young and bashful wife. In the final two stanzas, however, the focus of the image changes to one of sadness and anxiety as she wonders when her husband will return. One image of sound, "The monkeys make sorrowful noise overhead" (l. 18), and the rest of sight show how she has projected her sorrow onto nature:

> The leaves fall early this autumn, in wind.
> The paired butterflies are already yellow with August
> Over the grass in the West garden;
> They hurt me. I grow older.   (ll. 22–25)

This passage draws on the symbolic connotations of autumn with the coming of death and sadness and of the West with death. The paired butterflies suggest how she and her husband might approach age together and, therefore, remind her of her loneliness.

The widow, in Williams' poem, does not have any hope of being reunited with her husband, and this may explain why there are no happy, innocent images at the beginning of her lament. She immediately connects her despair with the scene around her in a metaphor: "Sorrow is my own yard / where the new grass / flames as it has flamed / often before but not / with the cold fire / that closes round me this year" (ll. 1–6). The image of flaming grass contrasts with the coldness she feels in her heart because of her husband's death. The river-merchant's wife may be motivated to begin her letter with the pleasant images of youth as a way to lure her husband back, but the widow has no motive other than to pour out what she feels at the moment. The beauty of the plumtree and the cherry branches, which "though they were my joy / formerly," creates a tension with her grief: "I notice them / and turned away forgetting."(ll. 17–19).

The basic difference between the two poems is underscored by the final images. The widow has nothing more to live for, and so the trees with white flowers that her son discovers identify the place where she thinks she might commit suicide, falling into the flowers and the marsh nearby. The beauty she had always responded to is now connected with her desired death. The final image in the river-merchant's wife's letter is also a place, but she connects it with the desired reuniting with her husband, not her death: if he returns down the river Kiang, she will meet him at a point called Cho-fu-Sa. The way she phrases this last sentence almost begs for an answer from him to let her know not only where he will return but when.

Both Williams and Pound show narrators whose despair is reflected in images of the nature around them. There are no value judgments coming from beyond the speakers about whether their grief is misplaced or whether the husbands are worthy of their extreme commitment; there is just the natural human coloring of loneliness in different degrees. Perhaps if the river-merchant's wife receives no answer, the physical world will fully take on her sorrow, as it does for the widow, and she will want to sink into the river Kiang.

chapter 6

SETTING

Setting is where it all happens. All action in life and literature happens somewhere in *place* and *time,* and in literature the features of place and time, whether they're clear or vague, prominent or faint, important to the action or insignificant, constitute setting. Some authors make setting the center of a literary work, even giving it the stature of a character as it interacts with human characters, while other authors may give little or no information about setting and may depend instead on plot, characters, or narrative voice to create the major effects.

To appreciate the range of place and time in a literary work, it helps to focus, first close up and then at a distance, as we do with the prewriting technique of focal points. Let's consider *place* first. Close up, place is all the physical details of a particular scene: color and lighting, style of clothing, furniture, drapes, items on tables and desks, or features of an outdoor terrain, contour of land, presence or absence of vegetation, weather, and so on, in as much detail as the writer chooses to give. Stepping back from a particular scene, we can consider the "place" of an entire work and observe if the action principally occurs in one place or if it shifts frequently; whether things happen mostly indoors or outdoors, in cities and towns or in nature; and whether the setting creates any dominant impression or mood.

We can also consider *time* close up and at a distance in a literary work. In a particular scene, it would include all references to time of day, season of the year, or point in a person's life or a group's association. In the whole work, we can consider the importance of the total time covered as it affects character development, and the historical time and place of the work, especially the relevance of certain values and ideas for the author and the society depicted. In William Faulkner's story "A Rose for Emily," Emily

Grierson and her house, relics from a more genteel era in the South, are described with details of both physical place and historical time to show how out of place they are and how, upon her death, Emily joins the memory of her proper era.

> It was a big, squarish frame house that had once been white, decorated with cupolas and spires and scrolled balconies in the heavily lightsome style of the [eighteen-]seventies, set on what had once been our most select street. But garages and cotton gins had encroached and obliterated even the august names of that neighborhood; only Miss Emily's house was left, lifting its stubborn and coquettish decay above the cotton wagons and the gasoline pumps—an eyesore among eyesores. And now Miss Emily had gone to join the representatives of those august names where they lay in the cedar-bemused cemetery among the ranked and anonymous names of Union and Confederate soldiers who fell at the battle of Jefferson.[1]

You may be tempted to equate *setting* with *imagery,* but there is a distinction. Images help us orient ourselves to a literary work through the senses, and setting certainly incorporates many references to the senses. But it is traditional to speak of *imagery* in poetry and of *setting* in fiction and drama. An image, especially in a poem, can have a separate existence— the poet can create it to stand alone and prominent for a short time, such as the snake being compared to drinking cattle in Lawrence's "Snake" (in Appendix). All the images in a work make up its imagery but do not necessarily function as a setting. A setting is the place of *action,* the where and when which locate what happens in a literary work. In many works, for example, lyrical poems, there is little action. An author may want only to create a pure feeling or mood uncluttered with characters and conflict. Robinson Jeffers' "To the Stone-Cutters" (in Appendix) is such a work— while there is distinctive imagery, we couldn't refer to the stone monuments as a setting. There are poems, though, which are essentially narrative; they tell stories and have definite settings. You'll be safe in applying the term *setting* to imagistic details which create a place and time for action.

THE VOCABULARY OF SETTING

When you write about setting, you'll need to use precise words to capture the place and time of action—*how* the setting affects the reader as well as the characters and the action itself. You'll be writing such sentences as:

> In the scene at Penistone Crags (Emily Brontë's *Wuthering Heights*), Heathcliff and Catherine reinforce their love for each other through a mutual love of the land, finding in themselves the rugged spirit of the moors, the blast of the wind, and the beauty of the flowering heather.

> Raskolnikov's shabby rented room (Feodor Dostoevsky's *Crime and Punishment*) reflects his own neglected and disorganized life, with its yellowed, peel-

---

[1]From *Collected Stories of William Faulkner.* Copyright 1930 and renewed 1958 by William Faulkner. Reprinted by permission of Random House, Inc.

ing wallpaper, three old fragile chairs, the worn overcoat used for a blanket, and the unopened books covered with dust on a stained table.

In developing your eye and ear for setting, you'll need a vocabulary to translate the important details into critical observations. The words you'll use have to do with the *qualities,* often the emotions, created by the setting. In some works, the author will use quality words to create the setting, while in other works, the reader needs to infer the qualities from the context— what goes on before and after the description. There follows a partial list of words that could describe various settings; the clusters describe similar qualities but with different shades of value or feeling.

barren, empty, stark, bleak, sterile	turbulent, stormy, raging
homey, comfortable, cheerful, warm	tense, anxiety-filled
isolated, lonely, desolate, cold	plush, elaborate, exotic, gaudy
threatening, frightening, horrifying	cluttered, stuffy, stifling
historic, antique, legendary, traditional	open, spacious, free, airy
dreary, dark, mournful, sad	chaotic, turbulent, haphazard
peaceful, tranquil, calm	orderly, organized, regimented
romantic, mysterious, sensuous,	exuberant, happy, vibrant
dreamlike	dingy, run-down, worn

As we mentioned, this is a partial list, especially when you consider the vast number of adjectives and adverbs that could contribute to the quality and "character" of a setting.

- **EXERCISE**

    6.1 For each of the following passages, make two lists, one of details and the other of quality words. What other quality words could you use to describe each setting?

    A.   None of them knew the color of the sky. Their eyes glanced level, and were fastened upon the waves that swept toward them. These waves were of the hue of slate, save for the tops, which were of foaming white, and all of the men knew the colors of the sea. The horizon narrowed and widened, and dipped and rose, and at all times its edge was jagged with waves that seemed thrust up in points like rocks.
       Many a man ought to have a bathtub larger than the boat which here rode upon the sea. These waves were most wrongfully and barbarously abrupt and tall, and each froth-top was a problem in small-boat navigation. . . . As each slaty wall of water approached, it shut all else from the view of the men in the boat, and it was not difficult to imagine that this particular wave was the final outburst of the ocean, the last effort of the grim water. There was a terrible grace in the move of the waves, and they came in silence, save for the snarling of crests.

    STEPHEN CRANE, "The Open Boat"

    B.   At rows of blank-looking counters sat rows of blank-looking girls, with blank, white folders in their blank hands, all blankly folding blank paper.
       In one corner stood some huge frame of ponderous iron, with a vertical thing like a piston periodically rising and falling upon a heavy wooden block.

Before it—its tame minister—stood a tall girl, feeding the iron animal with half-quires of rose-hued note-paper which, at every downward dab of the piston-like machine, received in the corner the impress of a wreath of roses. I looked from the rosy paper to the palled cheek, but said nothing. . . .

Not a syllable was breathed. Nothing was heard but the low steady over-ruling hum of iron animals. The human voice was banished from the spot. Machinery—that vaunted slave of humanity—here stood menially served by human beings, who served mutely and cringingly as the slave serves the Sultan. The girls did not so much seem accessory wheels to the general machinery as mere cogs to the wheels.

HERMAN MELVILLE, "The Tartarus of Maids"

THE USE OF SETTING IN CREATING CONTEXT

We mentioned above that sometimes the reader has to infer the qualities or significance of a setting from what comes before and after, the context. But more often, the setting itself establishes the context. As the frame of action—the where and when—setting can:

- *reinforce character development* by either paralleling it (as the aging Miss Emily and her house do in the example on page 85) or contrasting with it (as the romantic side of Francis Weed and his comfortable suburban home do in "The Country Husband");
- *reinforce thematic development,* as the idea of industrial inhumanity gains special credence through the factory setting in passage B of Exercise 6.1;
- *create mood* (*that is, emotional atmosphere*) that facilitates both character and thematic development as physical details become charged with feelings that color a scene or an entire work.

Two of the uses of setting can be seen in the following passage.

During the whole of a dull, dark, and soundless day in the autumn of the year, when the clouds hung oppressively low in the heavens, I had been passing alone, on horseback, through a singularly dreary tract of country, and at length found myself, as the shades of the evening drew on, within view of the melancholy House of Usher. . . . I looked upon the scene before me—upon the mere house, and the simple landscape features of the do-main—upon the bleak walls—upon the vacant eye-like windows—upon a few rank sedges—and upon a few white trunks of decayed trees—with an utter depression of soul which I can compare to no earthly sensation more properly than to the after-dream of the reveller upon opium—the bitter lapse into every-day life—the hideous dropping off of the veil.

EDGAR ALLAN POE, "The Fall of the House of Usher"

Poe, one of the great masters of mood, here uses a series of quality words (the adjectives and adverbs we have underlined) that create a context of gloom. Because the passage comes at the very beginning of the tale, it "sets up" the emotional frame in which the speaker will narrate the mental and physical decay of Roderick Usher, the main character.

Two special uses of setting should also be noted: to create ironic and symbolic effects. *Irony* is a complex literary term, but in general it describes an effect of unexpected or surprising contrast. A setting can be ironic when it seems "out of place" with someone or something happening in a work. For example, in another Poe story, "The Cask of Amontillado," a joyous Italian carnival and the parti-colored jester's costume with cap and bells worn by Fortunato contrast ironically with the damp catacombs and the depraved plan of the narrator to bury Fortunato alive. As a *symbol,* an element of setting or the entire setting can stand for a set of ideas or values. In Hawthorne's "Young Goodman Brown," the woods come to symbolize the dark side of man and the potential of evil in everyone, while the town symbolizes civilization, which momentarily controls the hidden dimension.

• EXERCISES

6.2 The following paragraph gives random details about the setting of a carnival one evening. The description as given doesn't create a mood or tone; it's essentially neutral. Rewrite the paragraph to create an emotional context (either positive or negative) for the setting. Select only those details that suit your purpose, and slant your description so that the reader will have either a positive or a negative reaction to the carnival. Don't state the emotion you're trying to create; imply it with quality words attached to the details you select. (You can add to the details, too.)

It was 8:30 p.m. on April 25th at the carnival. Rain was falling. There had been two inches of precipitation that day. Everything was wet. There were many umbrellas and puddles. In the air, the smell of beer, franks, urine, cotton candy, pizza, taffy, and manure could be detected. Loud voices and music could be heard. There were thousands of different colored lights; some were blinking. People were standing or walking. Toys could be seen in booths. There was a ferris wheel and a carousel. Many people were selling foods, rides, and games. There was a gypsy fortune-teller, and a man trying to guess people's weights and ages. Some people were begging. A child was crying. The wind came from the north at about 15 to 20 miles per hour. The temperature was 60°. There were about 1500 people there, mostly adults, some intoxicated; some were smiling; some were gambling; some were very wet. There was a funhouse with a large gorilla mouth for an entrance.

6.3 Go back to Exercise 6.1. Identify the mood created by the setting in each selection. Which words in particular convey the mood?

6.4 Describe a room that conveys the personality of a character associated with it. Exchange your description with someone else's, and describe the character that goes with the setting.

6.5 Robinson's "The Mill" (in Appendix) is a narrative poem that tells a story, using images to create a frame for the action. In your own words, describe the setting. Then discuss how Robinson makes the "qualities" fit the story.

Since setting helps create context in a literary work, as the setting changes, the mood or dominant impression may likewise yield to something quite different. A good example of a work with shifting contexts and settings is Mark Twain's *The Adventures of Huckleberry Finn,* in which much of the action alternates between the Mississippi River and the shore. All of Huck's and Jim's troubles are associated with the shore: the Widow Douglas (Huck's guardian and Jim's owner); Huck's father, Pap; and all those who try to find Huck and Jim once they make their escape on the river. The land means mystery and danger, as Huck finds out many times, while the river means freedom—for Huck, moving away from the strictures of civilization; for Jim, moving toward the free states. At a point in the novel when Huck and Jim have been separated after a steamboat rams their raft, Huck rejoins Jim on the raft and tricks him into thinking the real catastrophe was only a dream. In the passage that follows, Huck relates how Jim interprets the "dream" in terms of the two contrasting settings. (*Note:* "towheads" are sandbars near the shore, overgrown with cottonwood trees.)

> The lot of towheads was troubles we was going to get into with quarrelsome people and all kinds of mean folks, but if we minded our own business and didn't talk back and aggravate them, we would pull through and get out of the fog and into the big clear river, which was the free states, and wouldn't have no more trouble.
>
> It had clouded up pretty dark just after I got on to the raft, but it was clearing up again now.

With Jim's simple interpretation of things associated with the land and the meaning of the river, Huck's own mind clears, for the moment, and Twain connects this with a lifting of the fog.

The critical reader-writer needs to be cautious about interpreting a setting "symbolically." Not all shifts in setting have as clear a significance as the shift between shore and river in *Huckleberry Finn*. But people do behave and feel differently in different places and times, and if shifts do affect a story's direction, then you would surely want to understand how this happens—how the author manipulates setting to create consistent or contrasting impressions.

- **EXERCISE**

  6.6 Which different settings does Cheever use in "The Country Husband" (in Appendix), and how do they affect the development of character and theme?

SETTING IN DRAMA

Setting is especially important to the reading as well as to the production of a play. The reader must imagine the setting, sometimes with very skimpy information from the playwright. For an actual theater production, the set design, lighting, and costuming are essential vehicles for the dramatic experience, and this explains why the team of playwright, director, and the various designers must work well. The situation in drama is different from that of other literary forms because, even though the dramatist can give quite specific stage directions, the actual creation of the set depends heavily on the interpretation of the production team. It's not surprising to find quite startling differences among set designs for different productions of the same play.

You may be asked to write about the importance of setting in plays you read or see produced. In the first situation, that of a critical reader, you'll be relying on information the playwright gives and on your own imagination. As a playgoer, you'll be responding to how others have imagined and created the setting. As in writing about setting in any literary work, your tasks will be to discuss how characters interact with the setting, in a particular scene or the entire play, and to assess how effective the given setting is. The first task is analytical, the second evaluative. Here are examples of both kinds of critical comment on the little collection of glass animals in Tennessee Williams' *The Glass Menagerie*.

> (*Analytical*) Laura Wingfield is never far away from her glass collection, which quite clearly stands for her own fragility. When Jim, her gentleman caller, breaks the unicorn, her giving it to him as a souvenir is a giving away of herself. It is something special on the one hand, but on the other, it is all she dares to give.

> (*Evaluative*) The glass collection, so obviously symbolic of Laura, is a heavy-handed use of setting. We are constantly reminded by what characters say and by the stage directions that the tiny, fragile animals are a reflection of the over-protected, unworldly Laura. The reader and the audience are likely to squirm when Laura tells Jim that the unicorn he breaks is less "freakish" and more like normal horses without its horn.

Whether you build your essay around essentially analytical or evaluative comments will depend on the purpose of the topic or assignment. Good analysis, an ability to read closely and note significant details, is necessary in all critical writing. Of course, evaluation and personal opinion may be either encouraged or discouraged in the directions for a particular assignment. Some instructors ask students to write "reviews" of plays, in which evaluation becomes the focus. If you're not certain of the options in a given assignment, be sure to ask.

- **EXERCISES**

    6.7 Write a brief *analysis* of the setting in a play, film, or television show you've seen recently. Do not evaluate or make any judgments, but simply describe how the setting functions and how the characters interact with it, if at all.

    6.8 Now write a brief evaluative *review* of the setting in the same play, film, or television show. Make sure that your opinions are based on detailed analytical "close-seeing." (Remember, criticism isn't simply what you dislike but also what you like, and *why*.)

PREWRITING ABOUT SETTING

You may be writing about setting as the central topic of a critical essay, or you may be making observations about how setting affects theme or characterization. As we mentioned in Chapter 2, the value of the informal prewriting methods—journal entries, free writing, and brainstorming—is to get out on paper in an unstructured way your first reactions to a literary experience. If you don't find any ideas about setting in whatever spontaneous methods you use, try "directed" free writing, zeroing in just on setting to see what you can generate.

The formal prewriting methods can be adapted to setting by turning them into focused questions. As we've shown before, the different methods will often yield the same material because they probe the same subject, in this case setting, from slightly different perspectives. We'll use the setting in Porter's "The Jilting of Granny Weatherall" ("JGW") throughout our illustrations to show how each method could be used. As always, the *written* answers to the questions you construct would become part of your prewriting portfolio for later use in writing the first draft of your essay.

Thought Pattern Questions

Of the four thought patterns—definition, classification, analysis (process and cause-effect), and comparison–contrast—the last three work nicely with setting.

For *classification,* two large categories are already built into the concept of setting: place and time. We can ask: is there just one place and time, or are there several in "JGW"? There are two general "places" in the story. First, there is the world of Granny's sensations, her mind and body approaching death, and the shifting back and forth from clarity to vagueness. Second, there are places of action in the story: the bedroom in Cornelia's house where she lies dying, and rooms in her own home, the pantry and the attic with the letters from her husband and the man who jilted her. There are also multiple times in the story. In the present when she is dying, Granny is 80 years old. There are at least three other time settings which she remembers: when she was 60, the children all grown, and she first felt no longer needed; when she was a young mother and the children all needed her; and when she was about 20 and was jilted at the altar.

For *analysis (process and cause-effect),* we can ask: does Granny (or anyone else) affect the setting? Does the setting affect Granny? When she was needed as a young wife and mother, she made her home into a safe and comfortable place for her family. Now, as she lies dying in Cornelia's house, the bedroom seems to be closing in and obscuring her fading senses. In fact, the rooms in her home become metaphoric equivalents of her mind: "While she was rummaging around she found death in her mind and it felt clammy and unfamiliar."

For *comparison–contrast,* we can construct two types of questions. If different settings in a work are distinct enough, we can ask: what are the different effects of the different settings on Granny? Her home and its rooms meant something to her so long as a family was there, depending on her. Now she's in a room she can't control, in Cornelia's house, waiting to die. To compare and contrast settings in different works, we could ask such a question as: what do their homes mean to Granny Weatherall and Francis Weed? While Granny's home is fulfilling so long as she has her family, Francis' home does have a family, but home is the place where no one listens to him or appreciates his need for romance.

Pentad Questions

The obvious part of this method related to setting is the scenic *Where and When?* In itself, it asks the two most general and logical questions, and while you could generate some useful material from your written response, the pentad can be used to probe setting in a more productive way. The thing to do is make questions *directed at setting* out of the other four parts of the pentad.

> *Who?* Who in the work either has an effect on the setting or is affected by setting?
>
> *What?* What events in the literary work are affected by where and when they occur?
>
> *How?* How does any feature of the setting play a part in any major action?
>
> *Why?* Why does the author use the particular setting(s)?

Focal Point Questions

With the "zoom lens" feature of this method, we can look at setting from several vantage points.

Up close: This perspective would examine the importance of setting (or even a single object) in relation to the characters in a particular scene with such a question as: how does Cornelia's bedroom play a part in the story's action?

Inside: This perspective looks at a particular place to see if it has a life or dynamics of its own, asking: what goes on in this place that doesn't depend on the human characters? In the case of "JGW," everything in the house seems to depend on Granny, or at least her consciousness.

Panoramic: This perspective could ask: how does this setting compare with settings in other works by the same author or in works with similar themes by different authors? The topic or assignment would have to allow or encourage this type of comparison for any generated ideas to be useful later in writing the draft.

● **EXERCISE**

6.9 Using all three formal prewriting methods, examine and generate as much material as you can on setting in Cheever's "The Country Husband." Decide which methods were most productive for you, and compare your material with that of others in your class to see how they've used the methods. Then, in small groups, plan the thesis and outline for an essay you might write on setting in the story.

Following is a sample student essay written on setting in "The Country Husband."

SAMPLE ESSAY

THE USES OF SETTING IN "THE COUNTRY HUSBAND"

A character may fit well into a setting or may seem out of place, depending on how he or she feels supported or frustrated by the "place." Setting can reinforce or contrast with our impression of a character and also the theme developed around a character. Both effects are true of Shady Hill, the suburban setting of John Cheever's "The Country Husband." At times, Francis Weed seems to fit right in with the quiet, manicured lawns and houses of his upper-middle-class environment, but at other times, he is stifled by its unromantic low-key life style. At those other times, he remembers and yearns for more exciting places, and tries to live like a great lover who would never be caught dead in Shady Hill. Cheever uses setting to show how Francis Weed, modern suburban man, can belong to his world and feel overwhelmed by it at the same time.

Francis is constantly bouncing back and forth between imagined settings, on the one hand, where his sense of adventure is heightened, and the real setting of Shady Hill and the commuter's world, on the other hand, where his romantic imagination is regularly frustrated and ignored. In the story's opening scene, the plane crash is described with the vivid language of terror and shock: "All but the children saw in their minds the spreading wings of the Angel of Death. . . . The loud groaning of the hydraulic valves swallowed up the pilot's song, and there was a shrieking high in the air, like automobile brakes." But when Francis tries to tell his friend Trace about the crash, the time and place are wrong, and he is like a writer who cannot create a setting: "Trace listened to the story, but how could he get excited? Francis had no powers that would let him re-create a brush with death—particularly in the atmosphere of a commuting train, journeying through a sunny countryside where already, in the slum gardens, there were signs of harvest."

Francis' home in Shady Hill is the setting where most of the action occurs, and like the commuter train, it too is no place for the romantic imagination or the story of the crash. He comes home to fighting children, a daughter who reads *True Romance* (no doubt to escape), and a tired wife who feels her youth and beauty have been lost looking after a family of ingrates. All the little details that Cheever injects into Francis' home and the neighborhood show the characters trying to overcome boredom with excitement: Mr. Nixon shouting at squirrels as if they were medieval villains ("Avaunt and quit my sight!"); the dog, Jupiter, whose "retrieving instincts and his high spirits were out of place in Shady Hill"; the playing of Beethoven's "Moonlight Sonata" out of tempo and with excessive emotion; the image of naked Mr. Babcock pursuing the naked Mrs. Babcock across the terrace; and so on. It is as if everyone in Shady Hill, not just Francis, has developed special ways of overcoming the social and psychological restraints imposed by the setting.

One of Francis' methods is to let day- and night-dreaming take him to other settings where he can let out the hero-lover inside himself. At the Farquarson's party, he recognizes the maid as a woman who was run out of a French town during the War for living with a German officer. As Francis remembers the scene of the woman's public punishment, the language shows a degree of sensitivity out of place in Shady Hill: "It was a cool morning in the fall. The sky was overcast, and poured down onto the dirt crossroads a very discouraging light. They were on high land and could see how like one another the shapes of the clouds and the hills were as they stretched off toward the sea." Cheever uses this first remembered setting to heighten Francis' need for romance, as later that night he falls in love with Anne, the babysitter. When Francis dreams about Anne, his mind moves them both away from Shady Hill to an ocean liner heading for Europe, then to Paris where they live together, and finally to an image of himself as a solitary skier in a challenging landscape: "Down the mountain he swung, matching his speed against the contours of a slope that had been formed in the first ice age, seeking with ardor some simplicity of feeling and circumstance."

The major effect of the two types of setting—remembered or imagined romantic scenes and deadening Shady Hill—is to sharpen Francis' senses and his appetite for fantasy. The change is most apparent the morning after his dream and beginning infatuation with Anne. Waiting for the morning train, he is especially attuned to the setting around him, which he would normally give no passing notice.

> It was a clear morning; the morning seemed thrown like a gleaming bridge of light over his mixed affairs. His spirits were feverish and high. The image of the girl seemed to put him into a relationship to the world that was mysterious and enthralling. Cars were beginning to fill up the parking lot, and he noticed that those that had driven down from the high land above Shady Hill were white with hoarfrost. This first clear sign of autumn thrilled him.

Cheever never lets Francis' shifts in setting and emotion get very far before the dull Shady Hill world intrudes, as in the above-mentioned scene when fussy Mrs. Wrightson breaks the spell with her running on about the right curtains for her living room.

The effect of setting on Francis at the end of the story seems purposely unclear. The reader is left to ask if Francis will always be slipping out of and back into the setting of Shady Hill. Is his happiness with woodworking in the cellar a permanent therapy for his love for Anne or for romance in general? Probably not, when you consider how Cheever injects one last Francis-type image into the final sentence: "Then it is dark; it is a night where kings in golden suits ride elephants over the mountains."

chapter 7

STRUCTURE

When we ask why things happen in a certain order, or why things seem to be so disordered in a work, we're interested in literary structure. Structure is not just the isolated parts of something; it's *the relationship of the parts to each other and to the whole.* The key word is "relationship," how things work together. If you put all the parts of a high-performance, formula racing engine on a garage floor, you don't have structure. You have a mess, or at least a jigsaw puzzle that will take a master mechanic to assemble. When it's all together and working in a car, then you have structure. Structure in a literary work isn't as easy to see as in a racing engine, but the same principle applies: parts work together to make a whole.

The basic pattern that most of us refer to when talking about literary structure is *beginning–middle–end, introduction–body–conclusion,* or *rising action–climax–falling action.* These terms are widely applied to just about any creation that occurs over time: college essays, stories, poems, plays, music, jokes, recipes, speeches, and so on. Just as with a bridge or a building, the language of structure has to do with support. "Does it *hold together* well?" "Does one part *fit* another?" "Are any parts especially *weak* or *strong*?" "Does it *fall apart* after a certain point?" And just as we don't know how sturdy the structure of a bridge is until we use it, so we can't say much about the structure of a literary work until we experience it—that is, until we read it. The engineer, architect, and writer all design structure, but it's *use* that tests structure.

Critical writers are often uncomfortable when asked to discuss literary structure, perhaps because they feel there's something wrong with breaking a story or a poem down into parts to see how the parts work. We're not uncomfortable slicing up a leaf stem in botany class, but we sometimes squirm if an exam question asks for an analysis of stanza form in a Shake-spearean sonnet. Actually, it's healthy to be suspicious of literary analysis if the end result is that the reader gets so caught up with looking at small parts that the work becomes fragmented and no longer gives pleasure as a whole. What's the value of Hemingway's *The Old Man and the Sea* if we think of it only as a series of close encounters between a man and a great marlin? We can get all the fish stories we want in monthly issues of *Field and Stream,* some even more exciting than Hemingway's. It's how those close encounters work together to create a structure of meaning that makes the novel special and enduring, and worthy of critical discussion.

The good thing about critical analysis of a literary work is that it can end with synthesis—putting things back together. You can't do that with the leaf stem in botany class; once you've sliced, pulverized, and boiled it, it won't hold a leaf anymore. The Shakespearean sonnet, though, will survive and can be put back together after its stanzas have been studied in relation to each other. As a critical writer, you should always be aiming at synthesis, whether your topic is structure, imagery, or any of the literary elements. Your own response to a work, relived and reassembled, counts; without that, the results of your critical writing will be unfinished and unsatisfying.

HOW TO FIND STRUCTURE

Authors use a variety of ways to segment or signal the structural divisions of a literary work. In fiction, there may be numbered or unnumbered sections consisting of several paragraphs or pages (there are four unnum-bered sections in Cheever's "The Country Husband"). In longer works, there may be chapters and numbered parts containing several chapters. In drama, there are usually acts and scenes within the acts. And in poetry, there may be stanzas and numbered sections, rhyme and rhythm patterns, as well as special word formations (rhetorical figures) to identify divisions. All of these ways that authors use to set off parts of their works we can call *textual cues*—specific, planned patterns that create quickly identifiable parts.

Many works, however, don't have textual cues to identify structure and may move from beginning to end with no obvious breaks. In such works, the reader has to rely on a sense of things happening in a certain order for a certain purpose to appreciate the "structure of meaning." Im-portant shifts in ideas, moods or feelings, character development, place and time, and events, are thus called *reader's cues*. We develop the skill of recognizing these cues by being aware of *changes* in a work, such as

- stages of a character's growing maturity and self-knowledge
- a new place or time for action
- an important change in images
- a shift in narrators (point of view)
- a shift in emotions from negative to positive or positive to negative

- one key action coming to an end and another beginning
- a "subplot" (secondary story) interweaving with the main story
- introduction of a new idea or theme

These are all reader's cues signalling change, the signposts of a work's structural parts. We'll discuss reader's cues specific to fiction, drama, and poetry later in this chapter.

Reader's cues are clearly not as obvious as textual cues and require a careful reading in order to note the shifts. Let's look at a work with no textual cues to discover its structure. William Carlos Williams' "The Widow's Lament in Springtime" (in Appendix) is a poem with 28 lines, no stanzas, and no rhyme patterns. How can we talk about this poem's structure? We could look for a sequence of images or a development of tone. For example, lines 1–6 contrast the widow's cold feeling of sorrow (tone) with an image of the "flaming" grass in her yard. Lines 7–8 factually state how long she was married, and lines 9–10 factually describe a plumtree (image). Lines 11–19 contrast bright cherry flowers (image) with the strength of her grief (tone) and explain that the flowers no longer please the widow as they used to. Lines 20–24 factually tell of her son's report of white flowering trees near the woods (image). And lines 25–28 express her desire to die in the marsh near the flowers. Throughout, she alternates between expressions of despair and beautiful images of spring. We can say that the poem's structure is a series of ironic contrasts between what would normally have given joy and what she really feels because of her husband's death. The *changes,* the shifting back and forth from positive images to negative feelings, create the structure.

- **EXERCISE**

    7.1 Robinson Jeffers' "To the Stone-Cutters" (in Appendix) is another work that has no obvious textual cues to indicate structure. After reading the poem several times, refer to the list of reader's cues above, decide which cue(s) helps you discover the "parts" of the poem, and write a brief discussion of how the parts work together to fulfill a purpose.

Now we'll consider in more detail the two main skills for discovering structure: identifying parts and discovering their relationships.

Identifying Parts

A useful technique for identifying a work's structure is to make an *outline* of its major parts. An outline can be a paraphrase in that it says in your own words what the work says or implies. Its purpose, however, is not to follow the work word for word but rather to summarize what "happens" or "goes on" in each important section. The sections can be chapters, stanzas, segments indicated by the author (textual cues), or segments you identify such as units of ideas or actions (reader's cues). If there are no obvious textual or reader's cues, you can always outline on the basis of paragraph or sentence units. The structural outline can become an important part of your prewriting portfolio, whether you're planning a paper specifically on structure or simply gathering material for an open-ended topic. The outline is not the work's structure; it is a tool to identify parts. You have to go beyond the outline to discover relationships between the parts.

In order to be useful, a structural outline should be concise enough to give an overview of the work's structure, yet detailed enough to give you something to say about each part. Two levels of outlining—Roman numerals for major divisions (from textual and reader's cues) and capital letters for describing what each part does—should be sufficient for most poems and stories. Here's a structural outline of Robinson's "The Mill" (in Appendix).

    I. First stanza (ll. 1–8)
        A. Describes how the wife waited for the miller, how it seemed a long time
        B. Gives the miller's last words about the lack of millers
   II. Second stanza (ll. 9–16)
        A. Describes the wife's vague fear and then her discovery of her dead husband
        B. States the indifference of the dead miller to where his wife goes now
  III. Third stanza (ll. 17–24)
        A. Describes the wife's desire to choose a method of suicide that will leave no trace of her
        B. Describes the swamp pond at night that would serve her purpose

We can see a narrative progression that alternates between the wife's and the miller's problems and the solutions they choose. Now that we've identified the parts, we have to do something more—we have to describe how they work together, what their relationship is.

Discovering and Describing Relationships

Because we experience literary works over *time*, the effects of structure accumulate. We may not fully appreciate an individual part or section until we've read the next part or the entire work. The beginning of a work may take on greater significance when we see how a character turns out in the middle or at the end. For example, in Chapter 3 of Charles Dickens' *Great Expectations,* young Pip agrees to bring food and clothes to an escaped convict in hiding. The event tells us something about the boy's generosity and bravery but seems to have no greater significance. However, near the very end of the novel—in Chapter 39—we learn that a mysterious stranger who has been anonymously providing Pip with money for an education and an independent life all along is none other than the grateful convict he helped as a young lad. This structural relationship which spans many chapters creates surprise and revelation.

In order to discover and describe relationships between parts, we need a set of terms to cover *structural effects on the reader*. The parts of a work experienced in their complete sequence can have two basic effects: they can *reinforce* each other or *contrast* with each other.

Reinforcing Effects

1. All parts lead to a logical conclusion, some parts causing others to happen and contributing to an overall effect.
2. One or more parts interrupt others. As with a flashback, these fill in a gap or provide helpful background.

Contrasting Effect

1. One or more parts create an unexpected but effective turn of events or change in effect, perhaps with irony. The contrast can be between characters, settings, moods, or themes.

Whether the parts of a work reinforce or contrast with each other, the critical writer needs to relate these basic effects to the author's purpose in the work—developing a thematic idea, expressing an emotion, or creating a "pure" sensory experience. We can now specify three tasks in writing about structure:

1. Identifying the parts (outlining from textual and reader's cues).
2. Discovering and describing the relationships between parts that either reinforce or contrast.
3. Relating structural effects to author's purpose.

Now we can complete our structural analysis of Robinson's "The Mill." In looking at the outline of the poem, we can see that its three stanzas all reinforce each other by going along in time from when the miller and his wife are alive to when the miller is dead and his wife is about to kill herself. We don't at first understand the miller's declaration in the first stanza that "There are no millers any more." But the words do fit in once we discover the miller's suicide in the second stanza—presumably he didn't fit in to a world where the old technology of milling grain has been replaced with a new technology. The parts of the poem altogether set up a logical structure: the miller's wife waits alone, the miller has killed himself because he sees no place for millers in the world, the wife discovers her husband hanging in the mill and goes off to find some less conspicuous place for her own death, most likely because she too now sees no place for herself in the world. This poetic narrative is the tragedy of two people who choose not to live when their main reasons for living are taken away.

The important thing to remember is that structural *analysis* should go hand in hand with structural *synthesis*. It's not enough just to identify the parts; the critical writer must also discuss their relationships in terms of the work's larger purpose or effect. The poem develops its theme first by showing the miller's problem and solution (stanzas 1 and 2) and then reinforces the theme by showing the parallel problem and solution of the miller's wife (stanzas 1, 2, and 3).

• EXERCISE

7.2 Referring to Cheever's "The Country Husband" (in Appendix),

(a) identify the major parts by making a structural outline,

(b) describe the relationships between the parts, and

(c) relate the structural effects to Cheever's purpose.

STRUCTURE IN FICTION AND DRAMA

Although fiction (short stories and novels) and drama are very different literary forms, they share important features that shape plot. *Plot* is the term that has come to mean structure in works that tell stories. *Plot development* suggests a movement of events from one point to another, toward a happy or comic ending, a tragic ending, a cliffhanging or an ambiguous ending. Continuing this metaphor of movement, the reader is carried along by shifts and changes in key literary elements. The critical writer needs to note and account for the effects of these changes which make up a work's plot development.

A useful method for understanding structure in fiction and drama is to make questions out of the textual and reader's cues, such as, "How does each chapter, act, scene, etc. affect plot development?" "Are there stages of a character's maturity or self-knowledge that affect plot development?" "How do changes in place and time (setting) affect plot development?" "Do any patterns of conflict emerge that affect plot?" "Does a particular section introduce any new ideas or themes?" Ultimately, any of the literary elements that undergo change have an effect on plot development. In the remainder of this section, we'll show how to apply such questions to the structure of the first act of Shakespeare's *Hamlet*.

Textual Cues

What easily recognizable cues does Shakespeare provide to indicate structure? Changes in place and time are divided into five scenes in Act I:

I.i. Castle battlements in Elsinore, Denmark, from midnight to dawn

I.ii. The royal court, the morning after scene i

I.iii. The royal court, just after scene ii

I.iv. Castle battlements, just before midnight

I.v. Castle battlements, just after scene iv

Reader's Cues

What major actions occur in each scene of Act I? This question calls for a paraphrase-outline:

I.i.   The soldiers Bernardo and Marcellus report to Horatio, Hamlet's friend, of two previous nightly appearances of a ghost. Then the ghost appears to all three in the image of the dead king, Hamlet's father. They agree to tell Hamlet.

I.ii.   At court, the new king (Hamlet's uncle, Claudius) and his new wife (Hamlet's mother, Gertrude) ask Hamlet to remain with them instead of returning to school. Then, when all others leave, Hamlet expresses his disgust with the hasty marriage of his mother and uncle in a soliloquy (a speech made with no other characters present). Horatio arrives to tell Hamlet of his father's ghost, and Hamlet, his suspicions aroused, agrees to watch with Horatio and the soldiers that night.

I.iii.   Polonius, counselor to the king, gives his son, Laertes, who is returning to school in Paris, advice on keeping a modest, frugal, and wise lifestyle. He also lectures his daughter, Ophelia, about not taking seriously Hamlet's recent advances.

I.iv.   On the castle battlements that night, Hamlet, Horatio, and Marcellus see the terrifying ghost, which beckons to Hamlet to follow him.

I.v.   With Hamlet removed from the others, the ghost reveals how Claudius murdered him for the crown and for his wife. He charges Hamlet not to let the king's spirit wander unavenged. The ghost leaves, and Hamlet vows a single-minded commitment to avenge the murder. Rejoining his friends, he swears them to secrecy, as he curses the fate that has singled him out to bring justice to Denmark.

What shifts in emotion are there?   Scene i is essentially mysterious and frightening. Scene ii initially shows Hamlet's coolness toward Claudius and Gertrude; the soliloquy uncovers the heat of his disgust, and finally the report of his father's ghost creates anxiety and suspicion. When speaking to those he trusts, Hamlet shows good humor and wit, but for the most part he is clearly disturbed. Coming right in the middle of Act I, scene iii provides a comic break and introduces the parallel or subplot surrounding Polonius and his family. The emotions of scenes iv and v closely interweave as the fear and mystery of scene i return, yielding to the determined wrath of the ghost, the now-confirmed anger of Hamlet, and his first expressed regret that all of the responsibility for righting things has descended on him.

How do stages of a character's maturity or self-knowledge affect the plot? The answer to this question might closely parallel the shifts in emotion (Hamlet's) in the five scenes of Act I. While we probably wouldn't say that Hamlet matures greatly by the end of scene v, we could say that he certainly comes to understand his world better, that there can be spirits, that his uncle murdered his father, and that he alone, with this knowledge, must do something.

What themes and ideas are introduced?   Because it's the beginning of the play, Act I introduces, progressively in the structure, several major themes. Scene ii touches on the nature of relationships between members of a family—a son, a dead father, and a mother recently married to the dead father's brother. Scene ii also raises the problem of what to do about feelings that can't be directly expressed or acted on. The basically comic scene iii, through Polonius' well-meaning but pompous advice to his son and daughter, introduces the theme of how difficult, even absurd, it may be to live by rigid precepts and rules, a theme that becomes more important later in the play when Hamlet can't act on what he believes is his duty. And scene v presents the theme of responsibility, of acting on a just cause, and how heavy a weight that can be.

The *written* answers to these text and reader cue questions become part of the prewriting portfolio and, as you can see, would provide the critical writer with many ideas for shaping an essay on structure. At the end of this chapter, we present a sample essay on the structure in Act I of *Hamlet* to show the finished results of this prewriting activity.

STRUCTURE IN POETRY

Just like stories and plays, poems "happen" over the time we read them. The time is shorter for most poems, though there are poems longer than some novels (Homer's *Iliad,* Milton's *Paradise Lost*), and some readers can dwell on a ten-line poem longer than it takes to read a book-length play. Poetry is usually much more highly concentrated, compressed, and "charged" than fiction and drama. Of course, there is poetic prose in some fiction, and some plays are written in verse, so let's acknowledge obvious exceptions from the start. But because poems tend to be more compressed, poetic structure occurs over a shorter space, both in time and on the page, and compression can help the reader identify structure. Poets also have evolved a host of special techniques for structuring poems. Poems need to be read carefully, closely, and with a sensitivity to the various structuring techniques that operate. Remember, though, you don't want the dismembered poem lying scattered on the floor, like the racing engine, after you've read and analyzed it. When you know how it works, well or poorly, *synthesize*—put it back together by relating the parts to the total reading experience. The critical writing you do can be the bridge between a first, confused or uncertain reading and that fulfilling pleasure that comes from an informed reading.

The Process of Reading for Structure

In order to describe the structure of a poem, first read the poem through one or more times until you're comfortable with its meaning. As you read, try to note any patterns or repetition. These patterns can operate at the levels of individual words, lines, stanzas, or even larger divisions of the poem. We can group the kinds of patterns under two large headings: sound and shape, and meaning.

Patterns of Sound and Shape	**Patterns of Meaning**
Rhyme	Rhetorical Purpose
Alliteration, Assonance, and Consonance	description
	narration
Rhythm and Meter	exposition
Stanzas	argumentation
	Order of Images and Symbols

Patterns of Sound and Shape

Rhyme. Rhyme is the repetition of the major vowel sound in rhymed words, such as "no / blow," "bite / light," and "appeal / steal." *Exact* or *true rhymes* also repeat the consonant sound following the vowel, as in the last two pairs just given. *Slant* or *half rhymes* are close but not true rhymes, as in "does / doze." The most familiar and easy to spot rhymes are *end rhymes*, those that come at the ends of lines. But rhyming words can also appear within the same line or between lines; these are called *internal rhymes*. The following four lines by Sir Philip Sidney illustrate both end and internal rhymes. The internal rhymes (in this case some are slant and some exact) are circled and connected. Note the use of small letters to show the repetition of end rhymes: *a* designates all end words rhyming with "*dust*"; *b*, all end words rhyming with "*things*." A new end sound following these lines, not rhyming with "dust" or "thing," would be designated *c* and so on. The rhyme pattern described by these letters is called *rhyme scheme*, in this case *abab*.

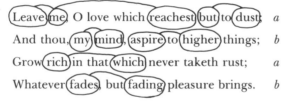

Leave me, O love which reachest but to dust;   *a*

And thou, my mind, aspire to higher things;   *b*

Grow rich in that which never taketh rust;   *a*

Whatever fades, but fading pleasure brings.   *b*

Rhymed words can have significance beyond the mere repetition of sound. The poet may carefully select important words to be rhymed. For example, "dust / rust" in Sidney's poem are nouns that describe decay in the physical world, which he contrasts with the "higher things" of the mind. A poet may also select rhyming sounds that have a certain character fitting the meaning or intended effect, such as "brick / kick / stick" for a hard, harsh sound, or "fair / air / hair" for a soft sound. But *be cautioned!* Critical writers often get carried away making preposterous claims for effects not present or intended. In the Sidney selection, there is no significance at all to the "things / brings" rhyme; the two words simply fit the established rhyme pattern. More often than not, a rhyme is a rhyme, is *just* a rhyme. However, if a pattern of pleasant or unpleasant rhyming sounds seems to fit a poem's meaning, then by all means mention that in your discussion. But don't go forcing significance on the poem's sounds.

Alliteration, assonance, and consonance. These are three kinds of sound repetition that occur within and between lines. *Alliteration,* the most common of the three, is the repetition of consonant sounds at the beginning of words, such as "*b*reath / *b*loat / *b*argain." *Consonance* is the repetition of consonant sounds at the middle or end of words, as in Howard Nemerov's "The vacuum cleaner . . . / Its bag lim*p* as a sto*pp*ed lung. . . ." *Assonance* is the repetition of vowel sounds in words that do not rhyme, as in the first line of Karl Shapiro's "Auto Wreck": "*I*ts qu*i*ck soft s*i*lver bell beat*i*ng, beat*i*ng" (notice too the alliteration of "*s*oft / *s*ilver" and "*b*ell / *b*eating / *b*eating"). As with rhyme, the critical writer should be careful not to force interpretations on these special repetitions of sound unless the patterns fit meaning or create an appropriate effect. In Shapiro's line, the assonance of the short "i" effectively duplicates the ring of the bell that an ambulance (of the 1940s—see publication date) would make.

These three types of sound repetition have the effect of connecting words. The words may *reinforce* each other ("beast / blood") or may *contrast* with each other ("fiery / frost"). Whatever relationship is established, sound repetition used by a master at the craft can be central to the pleasure of reading lines like the following from D. H. Lawrence's "Snake," in which the soft "s" sound complements the quiet action of sipping.

> He sipped with his straight mouth,
> Softly drank through his straight gums, into his slack long body,
> Silently.

• EXERCISES

7.3 In the selection below, from Shelley's "Adonais," mark the rhyme pattern with small letters to the right of each line, circle the initial consonant of any instances of alliteration, underline once any consonance, and underline twice any assonance. (If you own this book, you can mark on this page; otherwise, copy the lines, double-spaced, and mark that sheet.) Note: Shelley's poem is an *elegy,* a poem lamenting the death of his friend, the poet John Keats.

> Ah woe is me! Winter is come and gone,
> But grief returns with the revolving year;
> The airs and streams renew their joyous tone;
> The ants, the bees, the swallows reappear;
> Fresh leaves and flowers deck the dead Seasons' bier,*
> The amorous birds now pair in every brake,†
> And build their mossy homes in field and brere‡
> And the green lizard, and the golden snake,
> Like unimprisoned flames, out of their trance awake.

> *funeral stand
> †thicket
> ‡briar

7.4 In one paragraph, discuss how the rhyme and other sound patterns relate to each other in the stanza above. Do they set up reinforcements or contrasts, and how do they relate to the overall effect and purpose of the stanza?

Rhythm and meter.   Much that we pay attention to depends on beats and pulses, the rhythms of life. Sometimes we want them to be regular and predictable, as with heartbeats or the vibrations of a tuning fork. Other times we like rhythms to be irregular or to vary an already established regular beat, such as the complex syncopations of a jazz performance. At the root of rhythm is a pleasure, both physical and intellectual, that finds expression in simple toe-tapping, dancing, singing, and just spotting a pattern. In poetry as in speech, rhythm depends on the way words are pronounced with accents, or stresses, on some syllables, and no accents or softer stresses on other syllables. For one-syllable words, though, *normal pronunciation* doesn't help determine stress, so we have to rely on *meaning.* Notice how meaning determines how the word "her" is stressed in the following sentences.

> The President shook her hand.
> The President shook her hand, not the ambassador's hand.

In the first sentence, "hand" would have a greater stress than "her," but in the second sentence "her" takes the greater stress to set up the necessary contrast with "ambassador's."

When the rhythm in a poem falls into a more or less regular pattern of stressed and unstressed syllables, we call it *meter,* from the Greek word for "measure," and we measure the pattern by seeing how the stressed (–) and unstressed (◡) syllables are grouped. The process of *scanning,* or *scansion,* begins with marking the stresses in several (or all of) the lines. (The examples below are taken from poems by Edgar Allan Poe.)

> Oh, lady bright! can it be right—
>
> This window open to the night?

The next step is to identify the predominant *foot,* usually a sequence of one stressed and one or more unstressed syllables, marking each foot off with a slash (/). To discover a meter, we

1. mark accents in multisyllable words according to pronunciation ("window");
2. determine whether one-syllable words receive a stress or not according to their importance in the line ("the night").

In the Poe selection, the predominant foot is one unstressed syllable and one stressed syllable, with four of these feet in each line.

> Oh, la/dy bright! / can it / be right—
>
> This win/dow o/pen to / the night?

The meter is named by the type of predominant foot and the number of feet, the line length, in a typical line of the poem. Below are the basic types of feet and line lengths.

Metrical Feet		Line Lengths	
Name	**Pattern**	**Name**	**Length**
iamb (iambic)	/˘ –/	monometer	one foot
trochee (trochaic)	/– ˘/	dimeter	two feet
anapest (anapestic)	/˘ ˘ –/	trimeter	three feet
dactyl (dactylic)	/– ˘ ˘/	tetrameter	four feet
spondee (spondaic)	/– –/	pentameter	five feet
pyrrhic (pyrrhic)	/˘ ˘/	hexameter	six feet
amphibrach (amphibrachic)	/˘ – ˘/	heptameter	seven feet
amphimacer (amphimacic)	/– ˘ –/	octameter	eight feet

Using these charts, we can see that the Poe selection, containing iambic feet, four to a line, would be called "iambic tetrameter."

No poem could sustain our interest and toleration with perfectly regular meter, so poets use *metrical variation* for a variety of reasons: to more closely duplicate the naturally varied rhythms of human speech, to emphasize key words, to imitate some nonspeech rhythm such as that of waves or machines, or to surprise. In a different poem but with the same basic iambic tetrameter pattern, Poe uses a powerful spondee (/– –/) to open the first line.

> Lo! Death / has reared / himself / a throne.

The spondee combines an ancient attention-getting word, "Lo" (meaning "look here" or "there") with the equally stressed "Death" to create a strong double accent appropriate for this opening ceremonious tone.

Variation can also occur through the tension set up between normal pronunciation and meter. In yet another poem using iambic tetrameter (Poe's favorite), we can feel this tension centered on the word "romance."

> Romance / who loves / to nod / and sing
>
> With drow/sy head / and fold/ed wing.

Normal pronunciation puts the stress in "romance" on the first syllable and thus makes the word a trochiac (– ˘) foot, but the predominant foot in the line is iambic (˘ –).

The type of metrical variation closest to speech—with no regularly repeated pattern of stresses and irregular line lengths—is called *free verse*, a meter most characteristic of modern poetry. Free verse does, however, use other devices of repetition, such as sound and sentence structure, as you can see in the following passage from Walt Whitman's "Song of Myself."

> Now I will do nothing but listen,
> To accrue what I hear into this song, to let sounds contribute toward it.
>
> I hear bravuras of birds, bustle of growing wheat, gossip of flames,
>   clack of sticks cooking my meals,
> I hear the sound I love, the sound of the human voice,
> I hear all sounds running together, combined, fused or following,
> Sounds of the city and sounds out of the city, sounds of the day and night.

The repeated structures of exact words ("I hear . . . ," "I hear . . . ," "I hear . . . ," "the sound of . . . ," "sounds of . . . ," "sounds of . . .") and the pattern /noun/ + "of" + /noun/ builds a list of grammatically parallel images showing the expanse of the poet's vision and experience. Note also the alliteration throughout.

- **EXERCISE**

  7.5 Scan the following examples by identifying the meter (predominant foot and line length), and note any instances of metrical variation.

  A. No sleep. The sultriness pervades the air
      And binds the brain—a dense oppression, such
      As tawny tigers feel in matted shades,
      Vexing their blood and making apt for ravage.
      HERMAN MELVILLE

  B. He loves to sit and hear me sing,
      Then laughing, sports and plays with me;
      Then stretches out my golden wing,
      And mocks my loss of liberty.
      WILLIAM BLAKE

  C. Things are cruel and blind; their strength detains and deforms;
      And the wearying wings of the mind still beat up the stream of
          their storms.
      Still, as one swimming upstream, they strike out blind in the blast,
      In thunders of vision and dream, and lightnings of future and past.
      ALGERNON CHARLES SWINBURNE

  7.6 Scan the following poems in the Appendix: Herrick's "To the Virgins . . . ," Robinson's "The Mill," and Shakespeare's "That Time of Year."

Stanzas. Stanzas are groups of lines, usually set off by a space, that may be very carefully structured by traditional patterns of rhyme and meter or that may be tailored to a particular poem. Below are definitions of several of the most common stanzas, in ascending order of length.

Couplet: two lines rhymed, usually iambic pentameter or tetrameter. "Closed couplets" contain a complete sentence or thought and come to a strong pause or complete stop at the end. "Open couplets" carry over to the first line of the next couplet.

Triplet or tercet: three lines rhyming consecutively (triplet) or interlocking with the rhyme of the next stanza (terza rima: *aba bcb cdc*, etc.), with no specific meter.

Quatrain: four lines with or without special rhyme and metrical pattern. Possible rhyme patterns are *abab, abcb, abba,* or unrhymed; meters may be iambic pentameter or tetrameter for all four lines or alternating iambic tetrameter and trimeter. Quatrains are by far the most popular stanza in poetry, having numerous possibilities for balance and imbalance, reinforcement and contrast in the two pairs of lines.

Cinquain: five lines with no determined meter and rhyme, except for the highly structured (and popular) limerick, in which lines 1, 2, and 5 are anapestic trimeter, and lines 3 and 4 are anapestic dimeter, all of which rhyme *aabba* and swing along to their happy (or lusty) ending.

Sixain, sestet, or sestina: six lines, usually iambic pentameter or tetrameter, with such possible rhyme schemes as *ababcc* (really a quatrain and a couplet) and *ababab.*

Septet: sometimes called "rhyme royal" or "Chaucerian stanza," seven lines of iambic pentameter, rhyming *ababbcc,* and not very common.

Octave or octet: eight lines, usually iambic tetrameter or pentameter. The numerous possible rhyme patterns include *abababcc* (the popular "Ottava rima"), *abaaabab, ababcdcd, abcddefe, abbaabba,* and *abbacddc.* As you can see, the octave can be two joined quatrains, allowing for varying structural possibilities.

Spenserian stanza: nine lines rhyming *ababbcbcc,* the first eight being iambic pentameter and the last iambic hexameter. Invented by Edmund Spenser for his sixteenth-century allegory *The Faerie Queene,* this stanza has attracted several major poets including Keats and Shelley, who has used it in "Adonais" (see page 104).

Sonnet: The sonnet is not actually a stanza. It's a special type of poem with several different, specialized stanza forms, which has been quite popular in the history of poetry. The *Italian* or *Petrarchan* sonnet, named for the fourteenth-century Italian poet who perfected the form, has two parts: the octave, or first eight lines, which rhymes *abbaabba,* and the sestet, the last six lines, which may rhyme *cdecde* or *cdcdcd.* The *English* or *Shakespearean* sonnet consists of three quatrains, usually rhyming *abab cdcd efef,* and a closing couplet, *gg.* In this text, George Meredith's "Lucifer in Starlight," in exercise 7.7, is a Petrarchan sonnet, and Shakespeare's "That Time of Year" (in Appendix) is Shakespearean.

Stanzas are patterns of shape that make a bridge to patterns of meaning. Stanzas may contain one or more complete ideas or emotions; they may contain one or more complete syntactic units (clause or sentence); or they may contain only parts of ideas, emotions, and syntactic units, running together with and depending on other, adjacent stanzas to make sense.

The critical writer is concerned with how stanzas structure the reading of the poem: do they segment the poem with nearly perfect regularity, or does the poem's meaning flow through the major parts without strong pauses or stops at the points of division? And, as with the smaller devices of sound, how do the larger shapes relate to one another? Do they create similarity and reinforcement or difference and contrast?

• **EXERCISE**

7.7 Read Shakespeare's sonnet "That Time of Year" (in Appendix), and write a paragraph discussing the relationships of the three quatrains and the closing couplet. Then write a discussion contrasting the four-part structure of the Shakespearean sonnet with the two-part structure (octave and sestet) of George Meredith's Petrarchan sonnet "Lucifer in Starlight."

> On a starred night Prince Lucifer uprose.
> Tired of his dark dominion, swung the fiend
> Above the rolling ball, in cloud part screened,
> Where sinners hugged their specter of repose.
> Poor prey to his hot fit of pride were those.
> And now upon his western wing he leaned,
> Now his huge bulk o'er Afric's sands careened,
> Now the black planet shadowed Arctic snows.
> Soaring through wider zones that pricked his scars
> With memory of the old revolt from Awe,
> He reached a middle height, and at the stars,
> Which are the brain of heaven, he looked, and sank.
> Around the ancient track marched, rank on rank,
> The army of unalterable law.

Patterns of Meaning

How Does a Poem Mean?, the title of a well-known book by poet John Ciardi, asks a question about poetic meaning. It's more important to know *how* a poem means—how we come to understand through experiencing the poem—than *what* a poem means—a fixed paraphrase of its theme or expressed emotion. If poets only wanted to get ideas and feelings across, they might only write essays and give speeches. The fact is, though, poems do get ideas and feelings across, and we "receive" meaning by reconstructing it, more or less the way the poet wants us to, in a certain order. One of the most important ways that poets organize meaning is in terms of *rhetorical purpose,* the way a poem affects the audience.

Rhetorical purpose. We traditionally classify the purposes of communication into four large categories as follows.

> *Description:* A descriptive structure portrays the physical characteristics of an object, person, setting, or isolated action. It usually consists of a series of details and qualities added to a subject.

Narration: A narrative structure describes a complete, complex action or tells a story. It usually includes characters, conflicts, turning points, climaxes, resolutions, or no resolutions, and the order of events may move forward chronologically, backward in flashbacks, or unpredictably.

Exposition: An expository structure may explain an idea or procedure, or it may express an emotion. It may begin with a stated idea or emotion and develop it through one or more examples; or it may begin with one or more examples and conclude with a generalization. It may also simply present examples and leave the generalization unsaid.

Argumentation: An argumentative structure expresses an opinion, argues and proves a point, or tries to convince by appeals to emotion. It usually has a main proposition or thesis and may have various proofs or reasons, with examples of benefits and consequences, refutations of opponents' arguments, and/or emotional attacks and appeals to sentiment.

Few pieces of writing fit completely into a single category. The purposes usually interweave: to narrate, you often have to describe; to argue requires explaining ideas. The four purposes, however, are useful for naming *tendencies,* and even poems that have complex, mixed rhetorical purposes may be structured by one overriding purpose or may have parts developed essentially by one purpose.[1]

We've already discussed how narrative structure works in a poem, "The Mill." Let's see how description and exposition can work together in a poem. In Shapiro's "Auto Wreck" (in Appendix), the first 24 lines are descriptive, a series of details that fill out the scene of the ambulance arriving at the accident, picking up the victims, leaving, and the physical effect of the scene on the spectators-speakers. At line 25, the poem's structure becomes expository as the speaker expresses the crowd's feelings and interpretations of the significance of the accident. So even though there are four irregular stanzas (patterns of shape), there are two basic rhetorical purposes (patterns of meaning)—*describing* the scene and *expressing* the crowd's grasping for meaning in the horror—that structure the poem.

You may find patterns of shape (stanzas) meshing perfectly with patterns of meaning, but that's not always the case. A fine example where different patterns do mesh perfectly is Robert Herrick's "To the Virgins, to Make Much of Time" (in Appendix). In this *carpe diem* ("seize the day," live for now) poem, we have an essentially argumentative structure which is developed using description and exposition. The first two stanzas use descriptive images to illustrate the idea that things in nature have only a short time to thrive and fulfill their purposes: rosebuds that will die and the sun that will set. The third stanza is a more purely expository statement that life is much better in youth, when there is excess energy, than in old

[1]One example of an apparently pure rhetorical purpose in a poem is Ezra Pound's "In a Station of the Metro" (page 40). Here we have a poem structured by a single descriptive metaphor: the first line presents the tenor, faces in a crowd, and the second line presents the vehicle, flower petals. One might be tempted to reach for an expository or argumentative pattern of meaning, perhaps the vitality of humanity set against the dinginess of a city. That would be stretching, and poems do invite stretching, but the poem itself is simply structured by the comparative description.

age when things get "worse." All leads to the fourth and final stanza which begins with the word "then" and states the poem's thesis to young women, namely, that they should not reject passion because, presumably, like the rose and the sun, their days are numbered. Thus this poem's structure meshes the patterns of shape (four stanzas) with the patterns of meaning (an argument consisting of two descriptive illustrations, one expository reason, and a thesis).

- **EXERCISE**

    7.8   What are the relationships between patterns of shape and patterns of meaning in Pound's "The River-Merchant's Wife: A Letter" (in Appendix)?

Order of images and symbols.   Another important pattern of meaning is created by the order of key images and symbols in a poem. Our experience of a poem is influenced by the qualities of sensory details and figurative language, encountered over time, as they build to a dominant impression, or through the clashing of conflicting images that create surprise or even anxiety in the reader. Consider the order of images surrounding the snake in Lawrence's "Snake" (in Appendix). Our first impression coincides with our traditional reaction to a reptile; then the poet compares him to peaceful cattle, then to a god, and finally to a king in exile. The order of images is meant to move the reader away from the traditional negative image of snakes to one that explores the positive side of the dark forces that snakes have always symbolized. The structure allows a movement from one point of view to another.

- **EXERCISE**

    7.9   Discuss the order of images and symbols in Shakespeare's "That Time of Year" (in Appendix). How would you describe the "movement" of images from beginning to end? Does the reader arrive at some different point because of the juxtaposed images?

In poetry, then, the reader's experience is structured by patterns of sound, shape, and meaning. The critical writer needs to be aware of how these devices work on him or her during the reading experience. Prewriting guided by the kinds of questions we've asked in this section will allow you to record your experience and draw it out on paper in rough form. The prewriting record of your poetic encounters will eventually become the finished critical essay.

- **EXERCISE**

    7.10   Using the prewriting guides (outlining and identifying textual and reader's cues), write a complete structural *analysis and synthesis* of your reading experience of Thomas' "Fern Hill" (in Appendix), covering all significant patterns of sound, shape, and meaning. To see how analysis and synthesis work together in a critical essay, read the sample essay that follows.

SAMPLE ESSAY

This sample essay on structure in Act I of Shakespeare's *Hamlet* is shaped around the identification of textual and reader's cues discussed earlier in this chapter.

STRUCTURE AND ILLUMINATION IN ACT I OF *HAMLET*

"The time is out of joint. O cursed spite / That ever I was born to set it right!" With these words, the fifth and final scene of *Hamlet,* Act I, ends with the protagonist expressing what we all feel when faced with something we would rather not do. Hamlet's chore is especially hard: he must avenge the murder of his father at the hand of his uncle and bring justice to Elsinore. The way Shakespeare moves the reader (or playgoer) to Hamlet's crisis of knowledge and responsibility at the end of Act I is a fascinating study of dramatic structuring. What begins as a simple ghost story develops into a powerful conflict between the dead, the living, and the voices of Hamlet's inner self.

The most obvious structural device Shakespeare uses in Act I is the five scenes occupying two locations, the castle battlements of Elsinore (scenes i, iv, and v) and the royal court (scenes ii and iii), during the time frame of one full day, from just after midnight to the same time the following morning. Shakespeare wants to raise dramatic curiosity as he raises Hamlet's fear and anxiety.

Before he even introduces his hero, Shakespeare uses scene i to reveal the ghost, who resembles Hamlet's dead father. At the end of this scene, the reader, like Hamlet's friends, wants to know what the ghost is and why it has appeared. Hamlet is the key, but instead of resolving the mystery by jumping to the next night, the playwright shows us Hamlet in the world of the court. Scene ii has three sections: the new king (Hamlet's uncle, Claudius) and his new wife (Hamlet's mother, Gertrude) trying to persuade Hamlet to remain with them and not return to school; then Hamlet alone in a soliloquy expressing how repulsed he is at his mother's hasty marriage so soon after his father's death; and finally Horatio's report of the ghost's appearance and Hamlet's aroused suspicions. Scene ii also leaves the reader anxious for the inevitable encounter between Hamlet and the ghost, but Shakespeare holds off for another scene, iii, which momentarily breaks up the rising suspense. Scene iv brings the reader back to the castle battlements for the awaited encounter; when the ghost appears, Hamlet is appropriately stunned and willingly goes off alone with the ghost to learn its secret. Scene v finally reveals all the elements that will set up the rest of the play—the murder of Hamlet's father and the ghost's charge that Hamlet avenge the foul deed. The scene ends with Hamlet's cursing the fate that has singled him out for such a great responsibility, and the reader is now prepared to see Hamlet perform his task.

The structure of Act I can also be traced in the shifting emotions of the characters. Mystery and fear run through the soldiers and Hamlet's friends in the first scene, as Horatio says, "This bodes some strange eruption to our state . . . / but soft, behold, lo where it comes again! / I'll cross it though it blast me.—Stay, illusion." In the second, Claudius and Gertrude's concern ("we with wisest sorrow think on him") for Hamlet's ongoing grief mingle with Hamlet's repressed disgust, which is suspended by his uneasiness and suspicion after learning of the ghost resembling his father ("All is not well. / . . . Sit still, my soul."). The third scene interrupts the rising emotions of the first two scenes with Polonius' good-natured concerns for Laertes' return to Paris and Ophelia's emotional turmoil over Hamlet. Scenes iv and v return to the fear and mystery of scene i ("What may this mean / That thou, dead corpse . . . / Revisits thus the glimpses of the moon, / Making night hideous . . .?") and progress into the wrath of the ghost and the anger of Hamlet ("Yes, by heaven! / O most pernicious woman! / O villain, villain, smiling, damned villain!"). Act I ends on the note of Hamlet's anguished cry over his duty.

Emotions are not the only structuring device in Act I. The reader is also introduced to several major topics throughout the five scenes. Scenes ii and iii bring up the nature of relationships between members of a family (a son, his responsibility to a dead father, and his attitudes toward his mother and uncle; a father [Polonius] and his advice to a son and daughter). Scene ii also conveys the dilemma of suppressed emotions and what to do about them; Hamlet must resolve his anger toward his mother and uncle. Scene iii raises the question of how much a life can be based on rigid principles (Polonius' advice to Laertes). And scene v presents the theme of responsibility for acting on what one believes to be right and how heavy a burden such responsibility can be.

We can, therefore, see several levels of structure in Act I. The reader's experience is ordered by obvious shifts in place and time, but more importantly by the progression and interruption of emotions, and by the distinctive themes introduced. These devices of structure enable the reader to move with Hamlet through suspicion and fear to an understanding of his world and his need to do something about it.

chapter 8

POINT OF VIEW
AND TONE

Point of view in literature refers to the angle or perspective from which a work is "told." We commonly think of a *speaker* of poems and a *narrator* of stories; in drama, a play isn't so much told as conveyed by the speeches and actions of characters representing a variety of viewpoints. Point of view is an extremely important literary element because through it the author determines not only *what* the reader perceives but *how*. Just as the prewriting technique of focal points helps the critical writer use point of view to examine the subject of an essay, so the creative writer uses one or more of these perspectives—up close, inside, panoramic—to draw in the reader.

THE USES OF POINT OF VIEW

The key to understanding point of view is the distinction between the author on the one hand and the speaker-narrator on the other. Even though an author may choose to express him- or herself through the "teller," the two should be kept distinct, because more often than not the speaker-narrator is a device for getting across a slightly or radically different point of view from the author's own. For example, in Herman Melville's story "Bartleby, the Scrivener," the narrator is Bartleby's employer, a lawyer who sees Bartleby every day and is exasperated by his stated preference not to do anything. Ultimately, the narrator can't decide what to do with this strange person, and though Melville may have been acutely aware of moral obligation in this case, the narrator can only show desperation: "Bartleby was one of those beings of whom nothing is ascertainable. . . . What my own astonished eyes saw of Bartleby, *that* is all I know of him . . . . What shall I do? . . . What shall I do? what ought I to do? what does conscience say I *should* do with this man, or rather ghost? Rid myself of him, I must; go, he shall. But how?"

Persona

A term that has come to be associated with the speaker-narrator is *persona*, from the Latin word for "mask," suggesting that the author uses a shield or filter to keep the literary work from becoming a completely transparent self-portrait or confession. The special persona a writer chooses for point of view may explore or hide an aspect of the writer's own personality, express an idea or feeling that the writer wouldn't express in private life, or create an attitude totally opposite from the writer's own. So, when you are writing about point of view, try to get in the habit of saying, "The speaker-narrator says or implies . . . ," rather than, "The author says. . . . "

Narrative Stance

Authors use point of view to create relationships between the speaker-narrator and the reader, the characters, and the subject or theme of the work. This "stance" we can imagine falling somewhere along a scale, depending on the speaker-narrator's attitude and involvement in the work.

STANCE SCALE

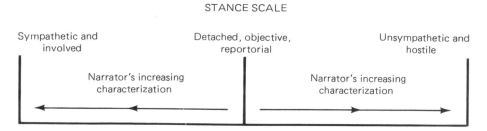

Notice that as the narrator becomes more or less sympathetic, moving away from the center of neutral detachment, he or she becomes fleshed out as an actual character who participates in the action of the work. The young wife in Pound's "The River-Merchant's Wife: A Letter" (in Appendix) is an example of a sympathetic, involved speaker who is also a main character. She describes her childhood, courtship, and marriage with a respectful commitment, though we can imagine a deep loneliness running beneath the surface of the words she addresses to her absent husband. We can contrast the river-merchant's wife with the detached, objective speaker of Robinson's "The Mill" (in Appendix), who simply reports the tragedy of the miller and his wife, seeming to have little voice as a character and no personal involvement with the characters. Unsympathetic, hostile speaker-narrators are not common in literature, and their hostility is usually directed toward themselves or other characters. An example is one of the speakers in John Dryden's "MacFlecknoe," a seventeenth-century satire on a pompous playwright named Shadwell. The speaker is MacFlecknoe, the reigning dunce of literature, and in one of the many double barbs he throws at himself and his subject, he says, "Shadwell alone my perfect image bears, / Mature in dullness from his tender years: / Shadwell alone, of all my sons, is he / Who stands confirm'd in full stupidity."

In some literary works, the stance can be mixed; the speaker-narrator's relationship to a character or to the reader may shift. In Porter's "The Jilting of Granny Weatherall," for example, the point of view moves around from that of a detached observer somewhere in the room ("She flicked her wrist neatly out of Doctor Harry's pudgy careful fingers. . . . ") to that of a voice coming from inside Granny's mind, privy to her most private thoughts, Granny's own voice describing herself ("It was good to be strong enough for everything, even if all you made melted and changed and slipped under your hands, so that by the time you finished you almost forgot what you were working for."). A shifting, fluid point of view such as Porter's is more characteristic of modern literature, in which the writer seems to feel reality can only be accurately captured from multiple angles, as in a photograph merging two or more different exposures of the same scene.

- ## EXERCISE

  8.1 Using the Stance Scale, describe the point of view of Williams' "The Widow's Lament in Springtime," Jeffers' "To the Stone-Cutters," Shapiro's "Auto Wreck" (all in Apendix), and a work of fiction you've read recently. What evidence specifically helps you identify the stance?

Types of Narration

In addition to the degree and kind of involvement suggested by the Stance Scale, the critical writer can discuss point of view in terms of *pronouns*—first person ("I, me, my, we, us, ours") or third person ("he, him, his, she, her, hers, they, them, theirs, it, its")—and *knowledge*—limited (only knowing some things) or omniscient (knowing all things or more than one character would know). We'll now discuss each of the possible combinations.

First-person limited.   This type of speaker-narrator is usually a major or minor character, either directly involved in the action or observing at some distance. In Samuel Richardson's epistolary (told in letters) novel *Pamela*, we learn most of the story through the letters of the heroine, a young, poor woman kidnapped by a rich gentleman. The first-person narration of a personal letter directly exposes her feelings and what she knows at any given time: "So here was a trap laid for your poor Pamela! I tremble to think of it! O what a scene of wickedness was here laid down for all my wretched life! Black-hearted wretch! how I hate him!"

A special kind of first-person limited narration is the *unreliable* speaker-narrator, one whom we are not meant to trust fully. Such a narrator might say something the reader knows to be wrong, might make contradictory statements at different points, might exaggerate, or might oversimplify. Such a narrator is Montresor in Edgar Allan Poe's "The Cask of Amontillado," a man proud to the point of planning the murder of his friend Fortunato, who once insulted him. While Montresor relates the facts of the story accurately enough, the reader is not meant to rely on his hints that he is justified in his revenge. In addressing the reader as an intimate friend— "You, who so well know the nature of my soul, will not suppose . . . that I gave utterance to a threat"—Montresor tries to cajole his audience into a special trust which would approve his diabolical plan. With the unreliable narrator, the author counts on the reader to be a collaborator in discovering the truth.

First-person omniscient.　Authors don't often use this narrative type, perhaps because most readers would find a speaker-narrator using "I" and knowing everything (or just about) unbelievable and too godlike, however removed from the action. One famous and certainly justified example is the speaker in John Milton's *Paradise Lost*, who takes on the voice of a poet seeking inspiration from his muse (source of creativity): "What in me is dark / Illumine, what is low raise and support; / That to the highth [sic] of this great Argument / I may assert Eternal Providence, / And justify the ways of God to men." Actually, this speaker realizes his limitations at the start and asks for omniscience, which he presumably receives because the poem continues for 10,565 lines.

Third-person limited.　This type of narrator functions as an observer with limited knowledge, perhaps knowing only the thoughts and feelings of a principal character or none at all. Such a narrator is the one in Herman Melville's "Benito Cereno," reporting and interpreting events mostly from the point of view of Captain Delano who, as reported, is wondering at the strange behavior of another captain, the title character: "The singular alternations of courtesy and ill-breeding in the Spanish captain were unaccountable. . . . he began to regard the stranger's conduct something in the light of an intentional affront, of course the idea of lunacy was virtually vacated. But if not a lunatic, what then?" Later in the story, the motives for Don Benito's curious behavior become clear, but at this point in the story, the narration is limited to what Delano knows and speculates.

Third-person omniscient.　Few narrators are so completely all-knowing that they can predict (or would be willing to predict) events before they happen. The term *omniscient* is usually applied to a speaker-narrator whose understanding goes beneath the surface behavior of virtually all characters, who knows backgrounds, who has a larger sense of the connections of things, and who interprets events and sometimes judges characters. Washington Irving's narrator in the famous sketch "Rip Van Winkle" speaks with an omniscience that shows a knowledge of how things turn out for everyone after Rip returns from his twenty-year sleep.

> To make a long story short, the company broke up, and returned to the more important concerns of the election. Rip's daughter took him home to live with her; she had a snug, well-furnished house, and a stout cheery farmer for a

husband, whom Rip recollected for one of the urchins that used to climb upon his back. As to Rip's son and heir, who was the ditto of himself, seen leaning against the tree, he was employed to work on the farm . . . . and it is a common wish of all henpecked husbands in the neighborhood, when life hangs heavy on their hands, that they might have a quieting draught out of Rip Van Winkle's flagon.

We can now set up a chart to help characterize the point of view in a work by combining attitudes on the Stance Scale and the types of narration.

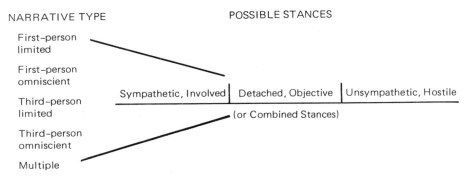

NARRATIVE TYPE   POSSIBLE STANCES

First–person
limited

First–person
omniscient

                    Sympathetic, Involved | Detached, Objective | Unsympathetic, Hostile
Third–person
limited   (or Combined Stances)

Third–person
omniscient

Multiple

This chart shouldn't be used simplistically or rigidly. Multiple narrative types and different stances in the same work show that point of view is not necessarily fixed, and the critical writer should account for the effects such shifts create in a work.

Narrative Comment

Narrative type, focal point, and stance influence the reader's experience. A closely related aspect of point of view is *narrative comment*, the degree to which a speaker-narrator is allowed to say something *about* what is going on. Speaker-narrators can explain, interpret, speculate on, evaluate, and judge, or they may provide none of these services, depending on stance. But to the degree that the narrator has a voice and character, narrative comment directly affects the reader's own interpretation and judgment. Narrative comment can be as subtle as the choice of words and images, as when the narrator in Cheever's "The Country Husband" (in Appendix) describes the effect of Julia's telling the bickering children to wash up for dinner: "This simple announcement, like the war cries of the Scottish chieftains, only refreshes the ferocity of the combatants." The narrative comment here lies in the half-mocking, half-sympathetic contrast of a culturally distant heroic cry with the unheroic clatter that greets Francis Weed on coming home from work. Narrative comment can be much more direct, making the speaker's and/or author's values quite clear, as in this statement about the hero of Hawthorne's "Ethan Brand," who sacrifices his human feeling for knowledge and power over others: "So much for the intellect! But where was the heart? That, indeed, had withered,—had contracted,—had hardened,—had perished! . . . a cold observer, looking on mankind as the subject of his experiment . . . ." One question you need to ask yourself as a critical writer discussing point of view is to what extent narrative comment, when it appears, is helpful or intrusive.

Prewriting About Point of View

Focal points is the logical prewriting technique to generate material for a portfolio on point of view in a particular work. The first question to answer would be, "Is the narration essentially *up close* (looking at characters and events in relative detail but in isolation), *inside* (looking at the dynamics of one or more characters' inner feelings), or from a *panoramic* view (seeing characters and events as related in an overall context)?" A second, important prewriting question is, "Does the narration mix the focal points or is it consistent throughout the work?" To answer these questions you would need to write a brief profile of the speaker-narrator, pinpointing *narrative type* (first-person limited, for example) and *stance* (sympathetic, hostile, or indifferent). Once you've generated a profile of the speaker-narrator, you can develop your prewriting with the following questions:

- How reliable is the speaker-narrator?
- Does the speaker-narrator change or shift perspective, or is he/she consistent throughout?
- Is this particular perspective good for telling the story or speaking the poem? Why or why not?

Remember, written responses to these questions added to your prewriting portfolio become the material for the finished essay.

• EXERCISES

8.2 Using relevant prewriting questions, pinpoint the speaker-narrator (type and stance) in the following passages.

A. It is a truth universally acknowledged, that a single man in possession of a good fortune must be in want of a wife. . . . Mr. Bennet was so odd a mixture of quick parts, sarcastic humor, reserve, and caprice that the existence of three-and-twenty years had been insufficient to make his wife understand his character. *Her* mind was less difficult to develop. She was a woman of mean understanding, little information, and uncertain temper. When she was discontented she fancied herself nervous. The business of her life was to get her daughters married; its solace was visiting and news.

JANE AUSTEN, *Pride and Prejudice*

B. The story had held us, round the fire, sufficiently breathless, but except the obvious remark that it was gruesome, as, on Christmas eve in an old house, a strange tale should essentially be, I remember no comment uttered till someone happened to say that it was the only case he had met in which such a visitation had fallen on a child.

HENRY JAMES, *The Turn of the Screw*

C.   Were I (who to my cost already am
One of those strange, prodigious creatures, man)
A spirit free to choose, for my own share,
What case of flesh and blood I pleased to wear,
I'd be a dog, a monkey, or a bear,
Or anything but that vain animal
Who is so proud of being rational.
                          JOHN WILMOT, "A Satyr Against Reason and Mankind"

D.   The scene made Robin's heart shiver with a sensation of loneliness stronger than he had ever felt in the remotest depths of his native woods; so he turned away and sat down again before the door. There were graves around the church, and now an uneasy thought obtruded into Robin's breast. What if the object of his search, which had been so often and so strangely thwarted, were all the time mouldering in his shroud?
                          NATHANIEL HAWTHORNE, "My Kinsman, Major Molineux"

8.3   Read the early passage describing Francis Weed's return from work in Cheever's "The Country Husband" (in Appendix). Instead of the third-person omniscient narrator Cheever uses, retell the passage using a first-person limited point of view from the perspectives of Francis, Julia, and one of the children, one paragraph each.

TONE

If *point of view* is the angle or perspective from which a literary work is told, then *tone* is the actual attitude or feeling that is expressed by point of view. If we think of tone as something that is directed somewhere, we can speak of two potential *sources*—the author and the speaker-narrator—and three potential *targets*—characters, audience, and theme or a condition of life. In any given work, there are several possible tonal conditions:

1. The speaker-narrator's attitude may be obviously positive, negative, or neutral.
2. The author's and the speaker-narrator's attitudes may conflict. (This usually occurs when the narrator is first-person limited and hostile or unsympathetic.)
3. Attitude may shift or blur.

Tone is an effect that an author may want to be strong or may want to suppress, but whatever an author's intentions, the reader usually detects an undercurrent of feeling or value in a literary text, a kind of emotional stance behind the voice speaking the words. And those features of the text that create tone are the critical writer's concern.

Reading for Tone

The vocabulary of tone.   While reading, we've all experienced the phenomenon of a voice speaking in the mind. The more skilled a reader is, the more developed that reading voice will be in the sense of having a variety of voices that can be fitted to the material being read. As a critical writer, you need to train your inner ear to listen for the qualities of the voices that authors create and that you recreate. In order to write about literary tone, you need a vocabulary to describe the qualities. The list of tonal words that follows is by no means exhaustive yet covers a wide range of attitudes for several different emotions.

formal, majestic, serious, highfalutin, pompous

warm, caring

concerned, sweet, sentimental, syrupy

disapproving, disgusted, scandalized

ironic, mocking, satiric

pleading, begging, prayerful

despairing, helpless, lamenting

angry, enraged

sad, grieving, anguished, tragic

humorous, comic

anxious, frightened, terrified, horrified

thrilled, exhilarated

shocked, surprised

There are important shades of difference between many of these tonal words, so if you're not sure of any, look them up. The greatest facility, though, comes in practice, both in discussions with other readers and in your own writing. You may find that several words describing related emotions are necessary. For example, consider the following passages:

> I have been assured by a very knowing American of my acquaintance in London, that a young healthy child well nursed is at a year old a most delicious, nourishing, and wholesome food, whether stewed, roasted, baked, or boiled. . . .
> JONATHAN SWIFT, "A Modest Proposal"

> O powerful western fallen star!
> O shades of night—O moody, tearful night!
> O great star disappear'd—O the black murk that hides the star!
> O cruel hands that hold me powerless—O helpless soul of me!
> O harsh surrounding cloud that will not free my soul.
> WALT WHITMAN, "When Lilacs Last in the Dooryard Bloom'd"

The selection from Swift *mocks* the "knowing American" by combining the *emphatic seriousness* of the observation about children as a food source with the unstated *horrified disgust* the reader is supposed to feel. Whitman creates a *lamenting, helpless* tone mixed with *fear* and a sense of *loss*.

- **EXERCISES**

   8.4 From the list of tonal words, choose three sets to apply to a short incident you create. In three different paragraphs, describe the incident in three different tones.

   8.5 Draw on the list to help you identify a number of different tones in Lawrence's "Snake" (in Appendix).

Now that we can name tones and tonal effects, we're ready to discuss just what creates tone in a literary work.

Diction and syntax. In part, your profile of a particular speaker-narrator develops from the "level" of style you sense from diction and syntax. *Diction*, the choice of words, has a great deal to do with tone. There are so many optional words authors can use to express the same emotion or to describe the same scene that it's no wonder they do so much rewriting. Actually, using different words to describe the "same" thing can subtly or drastically change its meaning and how it's perceived by the reader. Consider the effects of word choice in the following selections.

> Turning on the lights was nice. The kids got close to her and snorted like young cows waiting by the fence at sundown.

> Lighting the lamps had been beautiful. The children huddled up to her and breathed like little calves waiting at the bars in the twilight.

The second selection is from Porter's "The Jilting of Granny Weatherall" (in Appendix); it has a softer, more gentle tone than the first selection because of the different words: "lighting" instead of "turning on," "beautiful" instead of "nice," "children" for "kids," "little calves" for "young cows," and "twilight" for "sundown."

Diction is often classified as *low, middle,* or *high*—slangy, conversational, or formal, or in Walker Gibson's delightful terms, "tough, sweet, and stuffy." There is no fixed line between these so-called levels of diction, but in terms of word choice, low diction would use primarily single-syllable, easy-to-understand, and slang words; middle would use more multi-syllable words in the vocabulary of the average educated adult; and high would use an even greater number of multi-syllable complex, abstract words not common in everyday usage.

The low, middle, and high categories are not determined by word choice alone. *Syntax*, or the way sentences are constructed, also affects how we hear the speaker-narrator's tone of voice. Short, simple sentences of the subject-verb-direct object form are more characteristic of the low and middle levels of style, while long, complex sentences with embedded clauses and modifiers are associated mostly with high style and occasionally middle style.

- **EXERCISES**

  8.6 Pick three different tones from the list in the preceding section, and by changing the diction (but preserving the structure), rewrite Pound's "In a Station of the Metro" (p. 40).

  8.7 The first five lines of Jeffers' "To the Stone-Cutters" (in Appendix) constitute one fairly long and complex sentence that could be said to be in the high style:

"Stone-cutters fighting time with marble, you foredefeated / Challengers of oblivion / Eat cynical earnings, knowing rock splits, records fall down, / The square-limbed Roman letters / Scale in the thaws, wear in the rain. . . ." By modifying the sentence structure, creating shorter sentences, and changing the diction, rewrite these lines, first in the middle style and then in the low.

Imagery.   The kinds of images used in a literary work can have a strong effect on tone. The connotations, or associated meanings, of the words used to create images often have overtones that express attitude. At the beginning of Geoffrey Chaucer's *The Canterbury Tales*, the speaker creates a pleasant atmosphere of rebirth and renovation with images of spring, a time of year in fourteenth-century England when people would renew themselves by making religious pilgrimages. A paraphrase of Chaucer's Middle English in the first twelve lines might read,

> When April with his sweet showers has saturated the drought of March, and bathed every plant's veins; when the god of wind inspires with his sweet breath the tender buds in every bower and field, and small birds sing that sleep all night with open eye—so does nature touch their hearts—then do people yearn to go on pilgrimages . . . and from every shire of England, they make their way to Canterbury.

The personification of April, the god of wind, and nature, along with such positive words as "sweet showers," "bathed," "sweet breath," "tender buds," "sing," and "hearts" all create a happy tone well fitted to the outset of a journey that will provide fascinating characters and wonderfully entertaining tales.

When the speaker who expresses the images in a work is a carefully drawn character, those images usually convey the tone of a state of mind. In Shakespeare's "That Time of Year" (in Appendix), the speaker talks of his age and impending death. The tone throughout suggests sadness, regret for times that are passed, perhaps even fear; the tone is elicited by the three major images that structure the sonnet:

1. yellow leaves hanging on branches shaking in the cold and ruined churches where birds used to sing,
2. fading sunset and the approaching night that takes it away,
3. fire glowing on the ashes of wood that no longer fuels it.

The speaker purposely creates a melancholy tone and asks the audience, presumably a lover, to note these images and to use them to strengthen a love whose object will soon be gone.

• **EXERCISE**

8.8   What tone(s) does the central image in Nemerov's "The Vacuum" (in Appendix) create, and how do the words describing the image influence the tone?

Changes in Tone

As a critical writer, you need to be sensitive to changes in tone because they signal important shifts in the speaker-narrator's or author's attitude toward a character, some condition of life, or the work's theme. In Shapiro's "Auto Wreck" (in Appendix), there is a subtle but significant change in tone from the initial horror and physical shock of the spectators ("We are deranged . . . . / Our throats were tight as tourniquets") to the closing despair of finding any meaning in the accident (". . . . this invites the occult mind, / Cancels our physics with a sneer, / And spatters all we know of denouement / Across the expedient and wicked stones.").

We usually think of change as a clear movement from one thing to another, as when a feeling of sadness changes to one of joy. But tonal change can also involve the author's intentional blurring of attitude, wherein the "change" occurs in the reader's uncertainty about two or more possible tones. For example, many readers have found the ending to Cheever's "The Country Husband" (in Appendix) to be ambiguous in terms of tone.

> A miserable cat wanders into the garden, sunk in spiritual and physical discomfort. Tied to its head is a small straw hat—a doll's hat—and it is securely buttoned into a doll's dress, from the skirts of which protrudes its long, hairy tail. As it walks, it shakes its feet, as if it had fallen into water.
> "Here, pussy, pussy, pussy!" Julia calls.
> "Here, pussy, here, poor pussy!" But the cat gives her a skeptical look and stumbles away in its skirts. The last to come is Jupiter. He prances through the tomato vines, holding in his generous mouth the remains of an evening slipper. Then it is dark; it is a night where kings in golden suits ride elephants over the mountains.

The closing allusion to the heroic figure of Hannibal crossing the Alps should not surprise the reader. Throughout the story, the narrator has injected references to heroes and heroines of history and classical mythology, with the effect of putting Shady Hill and Francis Weed's romantic yearnings into ironic contrast with epic characters and deeds. But what is the attitude at the end, where Cheever juxtaposes a slipper in a dog's mouth with a night reminiscent of a legendary Carthaginian general? Some readers sense a mocking tone here, highlighting the absurdity of such a connection in modern suburbia, while others sense a more tolerant tone of sympathy for the foibles of Shady Hill. Whatever each reader's impression of the tone, such ambiguity is not a defect; it's part of Cheever's art to leave us unsettled.

Whether tonal change is clear, moving sharply from one different attitude to another, or blurred, your critical assessment should deal with the effect of such changes on the reader's experience and the author's purpose. If experience and purpose complement one another, then the tone is probably working well. If experience and purpose clash, then there may be a problem.

- **EXERCISE**

  8.9 There are a variety of tonal changes in Porter's "The Jilting of Granny Weatherall" (in Appendix). Write a brief discussion which identifies the changes and which evaluates their effectiveness.

  ### Prewriting About Tone

  The thought pattern *classification* is most useful for prewriting about tone. In a simple two-step process, you first list all the words and images in a poem, passage of prose, or dialogue that express attitude and emotion. Second, you group these particular words and images under the appropriate tonal headings. To illustrate, read the following passage from William Wordsworth's "Lines Composed A Few Miles Above Tintern Abbey . . . ," in which he returns to a favorite boyhood place, the river Wye, and speaks to it.

  > how oft—
  > In darkness and amid the many shapes
  > Of joyless daylight; when the fretful stir
  > Unprofitable, and fever of the world,
  > Have hung upon the beatings of my heart . . .
  > O sylvan* Wye! . . . .
  > How often has my spirit turned to thee!
  >   And now, with gleams of half-extinguished thought . . .
  > The picture of my mind revives again . . .
  >   And so I dare to hope.
  >
  >   *woodland

  Here are the key words and images from the passage, grouped by classification into related tonal words.

Despair, Anxiousness, Weariness	*Hope, Expectation, Longing*
darkness	O sylvan Wye!
joyless	my spirit turned
fretful	to thee
unprofitable	gleams of half-
fever	extinguished thought
hung on the beatings	revives
of my heart	hope

  This material would become part of the prewriting portfolio.

- **EXERCISE**

  8.10 Using the two-step classification process, identify and group words and images that express tone in Williams' "The Widow's Lament in Springtime" (in Appendix).

SAMPLE ESSAY

The sample essay that follows deals with point of view and tone in Thomas' "Fern Hill" (in Appendix).

THE HAPPY DYING VOICE IN DYLAN THOMAS' "FERN HILL"

"Fern Hill" is both a celebration of joyous boyhood and a sad reflection on the loss of youth. Dylan Thomas manages a difficult balancing act in expressing believable tones of innocent joy and longing regret for what some of us lose completely and others hold on to. He makes these contrasting attitudes believable by using a first-person speaker whose point of view subtly changes from the self-centered, limited knowledge of a boy to the greater understanding of a mature man.

For the first four stanzas, the tone is pure joy, the delight of a young boy growing up in the country. All of the adjectives describing the emotions and the images of playing express youthful innocence: "I was young and easy" (l. 1), "happy as the grass was green" (l. 2), "honoured . . . I was prince" (l. 6), "I was green and carefree" (l. 10). Even his environment takes on the qualities of beauty and happiness he sees everywhere: "the happy yard" (l. 11), "the calves / Sang to my horn" (ll. 15–16), "it was air / And playing, lovely and watery / And fire green as grass" (ll. 20–22). The feeling expressed by tonal words and images flows freely between speaker and setting.

Throughout the first four stanzas, even though spoken in the past tense from a distant perspective, the voice is that of the boy, often rushing breathless with excitement, as when he exclaims, "All the sun long it was running, it was lovely, the hay / Fields high as the house" (ll. 19–20), and later, "My wishes raced through the house-high hay" (l. 41). In this attitude of unrestrained joy, there is a foundation of safety. The boy's fantastic dream of the farm flying through the night with owls, birds, and flashing horses always returns to normal the next morning: "And then to awake, and the farm, like a wanderer white / With the dew, come back, the cock on his shoulder: it was all / Shining" (ll. 28–30). So long as there is certainty and the farm "comes back" after each night's dream ride, the happiness will last.

But, of course, we know even before being told by the speaker that this state will not last. Hints of the inevitable shift in tone come as early as the first stanza when time is personified as a being who *permits* the boy to feel so free: "Time let me hail and climb" (l. 4), and the second stanza: "Time let me play and be / Golden in the mercy of his means" (ll. 13–14). A gift from such a being does not last, as the speaker first directly says in the fifth stanza, "time allows / In all his tuneful turning so few and such morning songs / Before the children green and golden / Follow him out of grace" (ll. 42–45). This pied piper takes away what he gives. The words and images of the sixth and final stanza express an attitude of regretful loss at the process of aging that works even as the boy revels in the life of the farm. With the insight of age, the speaker loses the farm, and he wakes "to the farm forever fled from the childless land" (l. 51). What saves the poem from despair at the end is knowing that the speaker who has lost the fact of his wonderful youth can still recreate the feel of it in his poem, or song: "Time held me green and dying / Though I sang in my chains like the sea" (ll. 53–54).

Through carefully chosen tonal words and images of joy and loss, Thomas recreates innocence and its passing. Though his speaker looks back nostalgically on his boyhood, his voice can still capture the exuberance without getting too sweet and, now, the sense of regret without complete bitterness.

chapter 9

DISCOVERING A TENTATIVE THESIS

In Part I of this text we discussed the steps that precede the writing of a literary essay. We talked about reading literature and reacting to what you read, and we discussed the purpose behind reading and writing about literature. We also reviewed and practiced a number of ways, both formal and informal, to generate ideas that you might later include in your essay, and, to help you think critically, we defined and explored the roles of various literary elements.

Now in Part II we'll look at the actual crafting of a literary essay. In these chapters we'll discuss what a literary thesis is and how to discover and shape one; how to organize your essay; how to develop your introduction, middle paragraphs, and conclusion using appropriate literary evidence; how to avoid logical pitfalls; and finally how to revise and edit your work to make it as polished as possible.

THE THESIS

It may be called "the controlling idea," "the main idea," "the central idea," "the main point," "the focal point," "the focus," "the direction of your essay," "the thesis statement," or simply "the thesis." Regardless of what it is called, the idea embodied in this central sentence (a thesis cannot be a word or a phrase) is the kernel from which your essay takes form and grows. Like a cell with its own genetic coding, a thesis will direct the shape of your work, suggesting the substance of the middle paragraphs in your essay. The thesis will also raise certain expectations in your readers, who will assume you'll follow your plan through.

Because it's the idea from which the essay grows, the thesis is usually found in the introduction, not in the later parts of the essay. An essay without a thesis will likely seem a random collection of thoughts which the reader then tries, sometimes unsuccessfully, to put together into a meaningful whole. As good writers, we strive to control the expression of our thoughts so that our meaning is clear to our audience; the basis of this control is the thesis.

THE LITERARY THESIS

The literary thesis, like all theses, makes a statement which is not at once obvious to the audience. The statement requires explanation before the reader will understand and be persuaded to accept it. The literary thesis, of course, makes a statement about a work of literature. The intention of the writer is to persuade the reader to accept this statement by presenting and discussing evidence from the story, poem, or play. The thesis should be an assertion, not a question. It frequently focuses on the writer's craft, making clear the purpose of the work and how the author achieves his or her purpose, the interaction of the literary elements in a work, or the analysis of one particular element and how it is used.

While there are many kinds of assertions which a writer can make about literature, we will look at three types of thesis statements which are progressively more complex and challenging. They are (1) the static or simple thesis, (2) the dynamic thesis, and (3) the integrated thesis.[1] Briefly, the *static thesis* focuses on one literary element with the purpose of identifying that element and defining and describing it further. The *dynamic thesis* still focuses on one literary element but shows how it evolves or alters in the course of the work. The *integrated thesis* shows interaction between two or more literary elements for a stated purpose. This last type of thesis requires the writer not only to identify the parts and to see how they work, but also to explain why they work and for what purpose they exist. Let's use a popular literary tale, *Dr. Jekyll and Mr. Hyde* by Robert Louis Stevenson, and develop these three types of thesis statements about it.

As you might recall, the gentle but inquisitive Dr. Jekyll mixes a potion which, when he drinks it, allows his baser, more animalistic nature to come to the surface, and thus he becomes the murderous Mr. Hyde. If we were to describe the character of Dr. Jekyll as we encounter him in any segment of the story, we might say, "Dr. Jekyll is a kind and generous person who values scientific knowledge and discovery." This is a *static thesis*. It isolates Dr. Jekyll and identifies him as a man with certain qualities. The essay which follows from this thesis, we expect, will further describe him and provide evidence of his kindness, generosity, and desire for knowledge.

However, we can see that this static thesis is very limited. It accounts for only part of Dr. Jekyll's personality. It does not try to take into account

---

[1]These terms have been adapted from Richard Young, Alton Becker, and Kenneth Pike, *Rhetoric: Discovery and Change* (New York: Harcourt Brace Jovanovich, 1970), pp. 122–124.

the changes that occur in Dr. Jekyll's personality in the course of the story. A *dynamic thesis* would do just that; it would take into account the changes that occur in Dr. Jekyll's character over a period of time: "The kind, generous, and intellectual Dr. Jekyll is periodically and then finally overpowered by his brutal, animalistic other self, Mr. Hyde." This thesis is more complete than the static thesis, but it does not account for the reason, the meaning behind this change in Dr. Jekyll's character. In forming an *integrated thesis*, we would try to understand the change in Jekyll's character and state a purpose or reason for his transformation, a reason which helps us to understand the whole story: "Through the transformation of the kind, intellectual Dr. Jekyll into the deformed, brutal Mr. Hyde, Stevenson points out the dangers of humans' interfering with nature." Or, "Through the transformation of Dr. Jekyll into Mr. Hyde, Stevenson explores the delicate balance between the kind-hearted intellectual and the brutal animal, the double nature which every human being shares." The change in Dr. Jekyll, therefore, has a purpose; it illustrates an idea—that manipulating nature may have unknown and dangerous consequences, or that human beings are both animalistic and intellectual, a balance which Dr. Jekyll upsets.

The first thesis is not very ambitious; it needs little proof. The second thesis is more ambitious than the first, but the last is the most challenging and perceptive because it goes beyond description in attempting to understand and not just record the changes in Dr. Jekyll's character, connecting this character with an idea, a theme, to see a purpose behind his transformation.

The Static Thesis

When our main point consists of identifying and describing a literary element—such as character, imagery, setting, structure, point of view, or tone (theme will be dealt with in the section on the integrated thesis)—we have a static thesis. Consider the following examples:

1. In Cheever's "The Country Husband" (in Appendix), Francis Weed is a character who is unable to communicate. (Weed is identified as a character with a certain quality.)
2. Robinson Jeffers compares poets to stone-cutters in "To the Stone-Cutters" (in Appendix). (The central metaphor of this poem is identified.)
3. In William Faulkner's "A Rose for Emily," the house is seen as ancient and out of place in the changing Southern neighborhood. (Setting is identified as a house with certain qualities.)
4. "The Mill" (in Appendix) is formally written in eight-line stanzas with rhyme and iambic tetrameter lines. (The structure of the poem is identified.)
5. "The Jilting of Granny Weatherall" (in Appendix) is told from Granny's disoriented point of view. (Point of view is identified and described.)
6. The tone of "The Widow's Lament in Springtime" (in Appendix) is melancholy. (The tone is identified.)

Each of these thesis statements might be developed further through description and evidence. How do we know Francis Weed is unable to communicate, and what do we mean by this assertion? What similarities does Jeffers discuss in his comparison of poets and stone-cutters? What is ancient and out of place about the house in "A Rose for Emily"? What more do we know about the structure of "The Mill"? Can we further describe the meter and the rhyme? How do we know Granny is telling the story, and how does she tell it? How can we further describe the widow's tone?

You can see that once you've answered these questions fully, any additional comments would digress from the thesis. None of these thesis statements would be appropriate for a long essay because the focus of the statements is very limited. Each calls for identification and description— with no discussion of purpose. A common type of static thesis occurs in the character sketch, which may vary in length depending on the number of personality traits the writer decides to discuss. The static thesis particularly suits a literary element that is unusual and, therefore, merits being singled out for description.

The Dynamic Thesis

The dynamic thesis has at its core a change noted in a literary element as the work progresses: the character changes, the setting changes, the tone changes, and so on. This type of thesis is most common in essays which focus on characterization, although it is certainly possible in essays which examine change in imagery, setting, structure, point of view, and tone. Theme is usually consistent throughout a work, so it's unlikely to become the subject of a dynamic thesis. In the following examples, the italicized words signal a dynamic thesis.

1. Francis Weed in "The Country Husband" (in Appendix) *changes from* a man who conforms to the values of Shady Hill *to* one who challenges those values. (character)
2. In Matthew Arnold's "Dover Beach," the sea imagery *dominates the first three stanzas while* the imagery in *the last stanza focuses on* the confused land. (imagery)
3. The house in Edgar Allan Poe's "The Fall of the House of Usher" *deteriorates until* it falls apart in the chaos of the storm at the end. (setting)
4. In Emerson's poem "Hamatreya," the long prose-like lines *yield* to short chant-like lines when the earth speaks. (structure)
5. The point of view in J. D. Salinger's "For Esmé—With Love and Squalor" *shifts from* first-person *to* third-person limited, although the entire story is told by Sergeant X. (point of view)
6. The tone of "The Mill" (in Appendix) *changes from* anxiety and anticipation *to* desperate resignation. (tone)

This type of thesis will require more discussion than the static thesis since more than one part of the literary work must be analyzed. Typically the essay will identify and describe a literary element—character, imagery, setting, point of view, or tone—as it appears at the beginning of the work and as it appears at the end of the work, noting as many changes in between as necessary. The essay that evolves from this type of thesis will probably rely heavily on comparison as a means of organization and as a mode of paragraph development, a technique we'll discuss in Chapters 10 and 12.

The Integrated Thesis

In an integrated thesis, we try to explain the interaction between parts of a literary work. The point made by this type of thesis is not just that the literary elements exist or change, but that they are meaningful in some way and that they help fulfill the author's purpose. In this treatment, we look at character, imagery, setting, structure, point of view, or tone not in themselves, but as a way of understanding the *whole* work.[2] We deliberately left theme out of our discussion of the static thesis because theme, as you recall from Chapter 3, is the purpose of the work. When we talk about theme, we are automatically talking about the whole work. A thesis which focuses on theme, therefore, integrates other literary elements into the discussion since theme is revealed through the interplay of the other elements.

One way to form an integrated thesis is to state the relationship between one or more literary elements and the theme of the work. Consider the following questions:

- What is the author's purpose, and how does he or she achieve this purpose?
- How does character reveal the theme?
- Is there a pattern of images or symbols which forms a thematic focus?
- Does the setting complement the theme?
- How does the structure serve the author's purpose?
- How does the point of view affect the theme?
- Does the tone complement the theme?

If you're able to answer one of these questions in relation to a specific work, then you'll have an integrated thesis.

In addition to relating one or more literary elements to the theme of the work, an integrated thesis can relate two or more literary elements to each other without directly including theme. Consider the following questions:

- How does the setting reveal character? (setting/character)
- Does the setting create a mood which ironically contrasts with the action? (setting/tone/plot)

[2]Alan Purves notes that the discussion of part of a work as a key to understanding the whole work is the link between perception and interpretation (see *Elements of Writing About a Literary Work: A Study of Response to Literature*, NCTE [National Council of Teachers of English] Research Report No. 9 [Urbana, Ill., 1968], p. 31).

- How does point of view affect characterization? (point of view/character)
- How does point of view affect structure? (point of view/structure)
- How does point of view affect tone? (point of view/tone)

There are obviously other combinations, but the ones we've just listed are fairly common. We include a more extensive list of thesis questions at the end of this chapter.

There is still another way to arrive at an integrated thesis; you can convert a static or dynamic thesis into an integrated thesis by including a discussion of the author's purpose. *Why* is this character, setting, or other element portrayed in this manner? *Why* do the images, structure, and so on change? The following thesis statements are revisions of some of those given as examples of static and dynamic statements. A *purpose* or an *effect* of the literary elements has been added (in italics) to each thesis. Note the differences.

1. Robinson Jeffers' "To the Stone-Cutters" (in Appendix):

   Jeffers compares poems to stones and poets to stone-cutters *in an effort to justify the existence of poetry despite its impermanence and to explain poetry's purpose.* (Imagery and theme are connected.)

2. William Faulkner's "A Rose for Emily":

   Miss Emily's character is reflected in her house, a deteriorated structure which was once elegant and which is now sadly out of place. (The purpose of the setting is to tell us about the character.)

3. Edwin Arlington Robinson's "The Mill" (in Appendix):

   The sing-song rhyme and meter of "The Mill" are jarring in *a serious poem which shows the desperation of two characters who choose suicide rather than face a meaningless life.* (Structure, tone, and theme are joined in this thesis.)

4. Katherine Anne Porter's "The Jilting of Granny Weatherall" (in Appendix):

   Because the story is told by Granny, who is disoriented and dying, *it moves freely from reminiscences to hallucinations to physical sensations and reactions to her immediate environment.* (Point of view and structure are connected.)

5. William Carlos Williams' "The Widow's Lament in Springtime" (in Appendix):

   Ironically, through images of spring, Williams creates a melancholy tone, *as the widow is reminded of death and loneliness.* (Tone, imagery, and theme are united in this thesis.)

6. Matthew Arnold's "Dover Beach":

   The imagery changes focus from sea to land *as the narrator turns from a consideration of the world's problems to a consideration of his present plight.* (Imagery is connected to plot and structure.)

7. Edgar Allan Poe's "The Fall of the House of Usher":

   The progressive deterioration of the House of Usher *parallels the mental and physical deterioration of the Usher family.* (Setting and character are connected.)

8. Edwin Arlington Robinson's "The Mill" (in Appendix):

   The tone changes from anxiety and anticipation to desperate resignation *as the wife, who had been waiting for the miller's return, discovers her husband's suicide and then decides to take her own life.* (Tone is seen as paralleling plot.)

9. J. D. Salinger's "For Esmé—With Love and Squalor":

   The point of view shifts from first person to third person even though Sergeant X continues to narrate the story *because he is so psychologically wounded that it becomes painful for him to talk about himself personally.* (Thesis joins point of view and characterization.)

The essays which would result from these thesis statements would be complex, uniting a number of different literary elements. For example, the essay evolving from thesis No. 4 would not only describe Granny's point of view, but would show its effects on the structure of the story. The essay would discuss each of the categories outlined—reminiscences, hallucinations, physical sensations, and reactions to her environment—and show why they are part of Granny's experience at the time of her death and how they are connected to each other as the story is structured. The essay evolving from thesis No. 8 would not only describe the change in tone in "The Mill," but would explain the reasons for this change. The essay would trace the tone through the three stanzas, linking it with the development of the plot in each of the stanzas, as well as showing what words or images carry the tone.

The integrated thesis can serve as the basis for a brief or an extensive discussion of a work. It can bring into focus two or more literary elements at the same time, and it will allow you not only to analyze a work, showing its parts, but to synthesize as well—to fit the parts of the work back together with your interpretation. It is a challenging and creative type of writing, and the most comprehensive of the three types we've reviewed. You may have occasion to use a static or a dynamic thesis, but the integrated thesis is the hallmark of a more complete understanding of literature.

• **EXERCISE**

9.1 Label each of the following thesis statements "static," "dynamic," or "integrated." Identify what literary elements (character, theme, imagery, etc.) are to be discussed. If the thesis is static or dynamic, evaluate it, and decide whether it is appropriate for an essay. Rewrite any static or dynamic thesis statements which are on works included in the Appendix so that the thesis statements integrate more than one literary element.

1. In the poem "Departmental," Robert Frost belittles mankind by personifying the ants, making them reflect the insensitivity of modern human society.

2. The poem "Snake" (in Appendix) contains images of the underworld.

3. The river-merchant's wife changes from a carefree child to an unhappy bride and then to a loving wife. ("The River-Merchant's Wife: A Letter" is in the Appendix.)

4. In "Fern Hill" (in Appendix), garden imagery, reminiscent of the Biblical Garden of Eden, is used to portray the world of the innocent narrator before he is robbed and imprisoned by time.

5. "That Time of Year" (in Appendix) makes use of three images: a tree in autumn, a sunset, and a dying fire.

6. Wilfred Owen deromanticizes war in his poem *"Dulce et Decorum Est"* by dwelling on horrible images of suffering and death.

7. In "The Jilting of Granny Weatherall" (in Appendix), Porter uses Granny's first jilting to foreshadow the second jilting which occurs at Granny's death.

8. The tones of "The Vacuum" (in Appendix) are anger and sadness.

9. In the poem "Christ Climbed Down," Lawrence Ferlinghetti shows how inappropriate materialistic celebrations of Christmas are by the use of contrasting images, repetitive structure, and biting irony.

10. Huckleberry Finn is superstitious, self-reliant, and kind-hearted.

THE TWO-STEP THESIS

The thesis contains only the kernel of an essay, implying but not necessarily stating all the supporting points which will be developed in the middle paragraphs. The thesis is most effective when it is clear and compact, a statement that the audience might hold in mind while reading the essay or might easily refer to, if the need arises. If the thesis is not made clear for your readers, they'll have to "manufacture" one for themselves—from the clues you've dropped or the points you've made in the body of the essay. The writer takes a chance when the thesis isn't clearly and concisely stated, risking many interpretations and misinterpretations of the essay, since the thesis that each reader deduces will depend on the reader's skill and the clarity of the essay's organization. The writer may also frustrate a part of the audience who may not want to put together the point for themselves or who cannot find the link between the ideas in the essay.

For these reasons, the thesis is frequently a *sentence*, not a paragraph, though it may be found in an introductory paragraph. But sometimes our ideas are so complex, or we join so many different ideas in our thesis that to make it one sentence would be awkward. The sentence would be so long and complicated that clarity would be sacrificed. In such circumstances, a two-sentence thesis can be helpful.

The two-sentence thesis is especially suited to a literary essay if you want to include not only your main point, but also the major divisions of your essay. The first sentence would state the main point; the second sentence would list the aspects of the work to be considered in the essay.

Main Point + Major Aspects = Two-Step Thesis

Look at the following examples.

A.   In "The Country Husband" (in Appendix), a near brush with death causes Francis Weed to change his attitude toward Shady Hill. This change is especially evident in his feelings for Anne Murchison and in his treatment of Mrs. Wrightson and Julia.

B.   On "Snake" (in Appendix):   Lawrence's snake is more than a simple animal; it represents at the same time evil, royalty, and a hidden part of man. Lawrence makes these symbolic meanings clear through images of the underworld, through the snake's demeanor, and through the interaction between the narrator and the snake.

In examples A and B above, the first sentence is the thesis; the second sentence contains the major divisions or aspects to be discussed in the essay. You'll notice that the two-step thesis is a mini-outline of your essay. The essay evolving from thesis A would have at least three middle sections: (1) a section discussing Francis' feelings for Anne Murchison, how these feelings are connected to the plane crash, and how they reflect Francis' new attitude; (2) a second section discussing how Francis' treatment of Mrs. Wrightson shows that he has changed and again how this change is related to the plane crash; (3) a third section detailing Francis' relationship to Julia, how it has changed, and how this change is related to the plane crash. The writer of this essay may feel that it's desirable to begin with a discussion of the plane crash to show how and why it affected Francis, and then to proceed to the three areas in which the change is most evident. All these ideas are part of this two-step thesis.

The essay evolving from thesis B might be even more complex. It could evolve into an essay with three to nine middle sections. The three symbolic meanings would each require a section, and each of the three elements in sentence two might be related to one or more of the symbolic meanings. So we might have an essay whose middle sections look like this:

A.   The snake is evil.
    1.   Images of the underworld prove this point.
    2.   The snake's demeanor proves this point.   one to three
    3.   The interaction between narrator and snake proves   paragraphs
        this point.

B. The snake is royal.
   1. Images of the underworld prove this point.
   2. The snake's demeanor proves this point.
   3. The interaction between narrator and snake proves this point.

   one to three paragraphs

C. The snake is a hidden part of man.
   1. Images of the underworld prove this point.
   2. The snake's demeanor proves this point.
   3. The interaction between narrator and snake proves this point.

   one to three paragraphs

Or perhaps the writer intends to relate only one aspect in the second sentence to each symbolic meaning in the first sentence. Then the middle section would look like this:

A. The snake is evil as shown by the images of the underworld.
B. The snake is royal as shown by the snake's demeanor.
C. The snake is a hidden part of man as shown by the interaction between the narrator and the snake.

Such an outline might be developed by only three middle paragraphs, or the writer might expand the treatment depending on the amount of development each point needs.

In brief then, the two-step thesis serves to present not only the main idea, but also the major divisions in the middle section of the essay, and in doing so, the two-step thesis helps structure the body of the essay.

- • **EXERCISE**

  9.2 Create a two-step thesis on "The Jilting of Granny Weatherall" (in the Appendix) or another work suggested by your instructor. Exchange your two-step thesis with that of a classmate. Outline the essay which would logically grow out of your classmate's two-step thesis. Discuss your outline with the author of the thesis.

  9.3 Choose a one-sentence thesis from a previously written essay. Add a second sentence to it. Describe how this second sentence would alter or reinforce the present organization of your middle paragraphs.

THE COMPARATIVE THESIS

Ezra Pound, in a book called *ABC of Reading*, suggests that students of literature should become more like biologists in carefully examining and comparing specimens.[3] There is no doubt that we can learn a great deal through comparison. When we compare two works, we look at them in

---

[3]Ezra Pound, *ABC of Reading*. Copyright 1934 by Ezra Pound. Reprinted by permission of New Directions Publishing Corporation.

light of each other and will notice features which we might have missed if we'd looked at each work independently. For example, when comparing Robinson's "The Mill" (in Appendix) to Williams' "The Widow's Lament in Springtime" (in Appendix), we note obvious differences in form, which might lead us to question which works better. Robinson's poem is highly structured, while Williams' is free verse. We might consider what advantage each poet gains by his choice of form. Also, Williams' poem has a first-person narrator; a third party outside the disaster narrates Robinson's poem; the difference in narration affects the tone of each work. The narrative perspective and its effect might not be as noticeable if the two poems were considered separately. By comparing these works we learn about both poems.

Comparison poses special problems for the critical writer. The number of elements which will have to be united in a thesis will increase twofold. Not only will you have to consider similarities between two or more works, but you will also need to cite some differences; after all, the works are not identical. The task is challenging but worth the time and effort. The following guidelines are intended to help you shape a thesis for an essay comparing two works of literature.

1. *Choose two works which have a significant common ground.* A good comparison is based on well-chosen works which provide a range of important similarities and differences. Imagine trying to compare Thomas' "Fern Hill" (in Appendix) with Robinson's "The Mill" (in Appendix). You'd have a long list of differences, but what would be the point of comparing them? What is their common ground, the reason for bringing them together? You might as well compare turnips to coffins. For a comparison to be meaningful, there should be a good reason for bringing the works together.

2. *Limit the scope of your comparison and choose a focus.* Most likely you won't be able to include every similarity and difference you notice. In order for your essay to be unified and not merely a discussion of random similarities and differences, you need to choose a *major* similarity or a *major* difference as your focus. All other points should be related to this principal focus. In addition, you should adjust the number of points you intend to discuss to suit the scope of your paper. In a short essay, you may only want to touch upon one important similarity and difference; in longer essays, you may include many similarities and differences.

3. *Try to group the points of comparison so that the thesis is not unwieldy.* Not every similarity or difference discussed in the essay needs to be specifically stated in the thesis, but each point should be *implied* in the thesis.

4. *The points you cover should apply to both literary works* or your essay will be unbalanced. If you choose an aspect of one work which the other totally lacks, you can discuss only one work.

5. *Consider a subordinate clause to set off a similarity or a difference from the main point in a single-sentence thesis.* "Although," "while," "despite," and "even though" are useful conjunctions to begin a clause which shows a contrast. (See pages 230-231 for a discussion of subordinate clauses.)

6. *Use the two-step thesis when you have too many ideas for one sentence.* A comparative thesis lends itself to easy division into similarities and differences:

Similarities + Differences = Two-Step Comparative Thesis

Before we look at some examples of comparative thesis statements, let's see how one prewriting technique—brainstorming—can be an invaluable tool in generating ideas for a comparison essay and an aid in finding a thesis. The technique can be applied to comparison topics by making a list of *any* similarities and differences you find in two literary works. The following is the result of a brainstorming exercise on "The Vacuum" (in Appendix) and "The Widow's Lament in Springtime" (in Appendix).

Similarities	*Differences*
1. Narrators of poems have lost a spouse.	4. "Vacuum": male narrator "Widow": female narrator
2. Both narrators feel sad.	5. "Vacuum": images of mechanical vacuum, dirt, house-cleaning "Widow": images of flowers, fire, nature
3. Both are reminded of the dead person by other things.	6. "Vacuum": anger "Widow": no anger, just depression
	7. "Vacuum": narrator goes on living "Widow": narrator wants to die
	8. "Vacuum": long lines "Widow": short lines

After generating as many ideas as possible, select only the points which seem to fit together (given the criteria previously mentioned), and formulate a thesis which adequately conveys these points. There will probably be more than one thesis possible from any brainstorming list.

A well-constructed comparative thesis will virtually organize your essay for you. Let's look at a few examples. (Thesis A was derived from the brainstorming exercise we've just discussed.)

A. Comparison of Nemerov's "The Vacuum" (in Appendix) and Williams' "The Widow's Lament in Springtime" (in Appendix):

> *Thesis*: Although different objects remind the narrators of their grief, they both feel saddened by the loss of a spouse and have difficulty continuing with their own lives.

"The Vacuum" and "The Widow's Lament in Springtime" are logical choices for comparison because their subjects are so similar—the grief experienced by those who lose a loved one, particularly a spouse. This writer has limited the focus to the similarities and differences in the narrators' experiences: the cause of the grief, the objects that remind the narrators of the loss, and the narrators' reactions to the loss. Points 1, 2, 3, 5, 6, and 7 from the brainstorming list are joined in this thesis; however, points 6 and 7 are implied rather than stated in detail. In developing the plan laid out by the thesis, the writer may very well discuss the difference in the endings of the poems: Nemerov's narrator is angry but still has a will to live; Williams' narrator wants to die. This point is implied in a discussion of the narrators' "difficulty continuing with their own lives" mentioned in the thesis. There is no point to cluttering the thesis by specifying a subdivision of a point already mentioned. This thesis also mentions a major difference between the two works in a subordinate clause beginning the sentence. The statement covers three points, though there certainly may be subdivisions which occur in the development of the points. The points seem balanced and applicable to both poems.

B. Comparison of "Not Marble, nor the Gilded Monuments" by William Shakespeare and "To the Stone-Cutters" by Robinson Jeffers (in Appendix):

> *Thesis*: By comparing poems with monuments, each author shows that a poet's work endures over time. However, Shakespeare is more confident than Jeffers that his work will survive.

Both poems are about poetry and are suitable for comparison. The focus of the comparison is the theme—that poems will last a long time. The two other aspects covered relate to this theme: both poets use similar imagery to show a poem's longevity, and both poets feel a different degree of confidence (tone) about the survival of their work. The discussion will be balanced.

Notice how each of the previous thesis statements avoids including points which do not relate to the chosen focus. For example, the structure of the two poems in each case is easily comparable, but unless it can be related to the rest of the discussion, it would be a digression in the essay. None of these writers is able to fit a comparison of structure into the focus, although such a comparison might be possible with other topics.

The next thesis has a problem with focus and balance:

C. Comparison of Pound's "The River-Merchant's Wife: A Letter" (in Appendix) and Williams' "The Widow's Lament in Springtime" (in Appendix):

> *Thesis*: Although both poems are about a woman's loneliness due to the absence of her husband, they differ in that Pound's poem gives us some background, and Pound's narrator has some hope that she will see her husband again, while Williams' narrator has no hope.

The problematic point in this thesis is "Pound's poem gives us some background." After the writer says that Williams' poem gives no background, what is there left to say about Williams' poem? The writer can't compare the childhood or early marraige of Pound's narrator with that of Williams' widow because Williams does not provide us with any details about these parts of the widow's life. The background discussion will involve only one poem. In addition, while the points about loneliness and hope seem to fit together nicely, how does "background" relate to the focus the writer chooses: the loneliness a woman feels due to the absence of her husband? And finally, couldn't the last two points—Pound's narrator has some hope that she will see her husband again, while Williams' narrator has no hope— be stated more concisely? The elaboration should be saved for the development of this point in the middle paragraphs.

The next two thesis statements present even more of a problem than thesis C, which does have a focus (although the writer strays from it). We haven't included the titles of the works on which these essays were written because, as you'll see, it really doesn't matter.

> D. *Thesis*: The purpose of this essay will be to show how the two poets, while dealing with the same subject, use different structures, tones, and images to convey different themes.

> E. *Thesis*: Although the poems are similar in their subjects and their structures, the poems are different in their themes, tones, and images.

Neither of these thesis statements has a focus of comparison. The points are so vague that they can be applied to almost any two literary works. A laundry-list thesis like D or E will likely result in an essay whose points seem randomly chosen. And even if the writer is able to relate all these literary concepts to one idea, the reader will still have to decipher the idea from the middle paragraphs because this type of thesis gives no direction at all.

• EXERCISE

9.4 Make a list of some of the literary works you've read which you think could be profitably compared. Also list your reason(s) for considering each pair. For example, "The Vacuum" by Howard Nemerov and "The Widow's Lament in Springtime" by William Carlos Williams would make a good pair for comparison because they are both about a person whose beloved has died.

9.5 Choose three pairs of works from the list in Exercise 9.4; brainstorm for similarities and differences, and then formulate a comparative thesis for each pair. Review the guidelines on page 138 before you start.

THESIS PROBLEMS

The Vague Thesis

A *vague thesis* can weaken more than a comparative essay. It can be a serious problem in any type of writing. A vague literary thesis is characterized by unspecified key terms which might be applied to any work of literature and which should instead be defined for the specific works under consideration. There are, of course, degrees of vagueness. In general, you should make the key terms in your thesis as specific as the ideas discussed in your essay will allow.

Take the following thesis from an essay on Nemerov's "The Vacuum" (in Appendix):

> *Thesis*: The narrator's *attitude* toward the death of his woman is reflected through the author's use of *imagery*.

There are two key terms left undefined in this thesis—attitude and imagery. The writer should try to specify what attitude is revealed and what images will be discussed. Compare this revision to the original thesis:

> *Thesis*: The narrator's sorrow and anger at his woman's death is revealed through his personification of the vacuum cleaner.

The tone (attitude) and imagery in the revised thesis are not left as generalizations but are taken from the poem. The attitude is sorrow and anger; the imagery is a personified vacuum cleaner.

After you have a thesis, take a clear look at the key terms. If you find any that can be made more specific, do so.

The Factual Thesis

We should briefly mention one other thesis problem: the thesis that is *too limited*. In one sense, the static thesis discussed earlier may fall into this category if it is too narrow to support an entire essay, but of even greater concern are statements that appear as thesis statements but are really statements of fact—plot details. For example, the writer who sets out to show that "Francis Weed in 'The Country Husband' (in Appendix) dreams of having an affair with the babysitter" will soon find there is nothing to prove. There is no need to demonstrate this point; it is stated in the story. The writer is not elaborating on the use of a literary element, or showing a relationship between elements, or discussing the purpose of the work. The same problem occurs in the essay whose thesis is, "The narrator of D. H. Lawrence's 'Snake' (in Appendix) throws a log at the retreating animal." This fact is stated in the poem. It doesn't require an essay to prove it.

Remember, in order to sustain an essay, a thesis must be a point which needs explanation and proof. If it's obvious to the reader, there's no point in writing an essay about it.

• EXERCISE

9.6   Label the following thesis statements *vague*, *narrow*, or *OK*. If the statement is vague, underline the key terms which are too general and rewrite the thesis, making the terms more specific. All the works on which these statements are based are in the Appendix.

   1.   On "Snake": D. H. Lawrence used the snake as a symbol to convey his theme.

   2.   On "The River-Merchant's Wife: A Letter": The narrator and her husband knew each other as children.

   3.   On "The Vacuum": The vacuum is not only a metaphor for the dead woman, but also a symbol of the void the narrator feels because of her absence.

   4.   On "To the Stone-Cutters": Jeffers claims that stone monuments are destroyed by harsh weather.

5. On "The Widow's Lament in Springtime": Vivid images are used which contrast with the widow's feelings.
6. On "The Mill": "The Mill" is structured like a short story which suspensefully begins with anticipation, builds to a climax in the middle stanza, and then ends with a desperate resolution.
7. On "The Country Husband": Certain scenes in the story reveal Francis Weed's newfound desire for life.
8. On "Fern Hill": Thomas employs many images in "Fern Hill" to show how good childhood is.
9. On "That Time of Year": The narrator reflects on the twilight or sunset of the day.
10. On "The Jilting of Granny Weatherall": The structure of the story shows us Granny's state of mind.

FROM PREWRITING TO A THESIS

In Part I of this text, we suggested several activities that might be helpful in generating ideas so that you might find a thesis and construct a well-developed essay. Too frequently, writers will start out by trying to come up with an immediate thesis before exploring their ideas in prewriting activities. The results are often poorly developed, vaguely conceived essays. Now that you have a good idea of what a thesis is, let's turn to your prewriting portfolio and see how you might go about discovering a thesis of your own.

Sometimes in the very act of writing your journal—or freewriting, or using formal prewriting techniques—a thesis will become obvious. You'll simply know what you want to prove. Look, for example, at the following journal entries on the poem "Christ Climbed Down" by Lawrence Ferlinghetti.

April 8

At first reading, the poem stirred up feelings of guilt. Most of the trappings of our modern Christmas celebration are recognizable. The poem contrasts Christ's humble birth and cruel death with the modern materialistic frenzy of our American holiday season.

April 9

Christ's tree (the cross) is bare, as compared with the traditional Christmas tree, which is gaudy and fragile. The second stanza points out not only the overblown tradition of the Christmas tree, but also the artificiality of today's "evergreen." The next stanza further undermines current religious symbols and practices. The Bible is sold instead of given, and by a man in a Cadillac. The Three Kings are spokesmen for booze.

April 10

<u>Structure is important in this poem. The simplicity of the first four lines of</u> <u>each stanza which refer to Christ contrasts with the intricate description in the</u> <u>rest of the stanza, similar to the contrast of Christ's life with our own.</u>

April 11

Santa Claus doesn't fare too well in stanza four. The poem suggests that he has been elevated to sainthood. Yet he is portrayed as an obnoxious fake. Also bearing gifts that are from a very status-conscious department store.

April 12

I thought of the poem as a whole today. There is so much in the poem that one could discuss it for a week. <u>The first stanza introduces the theme, stanzas</u> <u>2–5 elaborate on the theme, and the last stanza makes one wonder what the</u> <u>consequences of the materialism surrounding Christmas will be.</u>

We've underlined three possible thesis statements which are apparent in this writer's journal. Of course, they would have to be reworked slightly to make them more precise and polished, but the thesis ideas are there from the beginning of this writer's explorations of the poem. The thesis which he put together for an essay includes ideas mentioned in the entries for April 8th, 9th, and 11th:

Thesis: In the poem "Christ Climbed Down," Ferlinghetti contrasts Christ's humility with the materialistic frenzy of the modern Christmas holiday by using repetitive and contrasting images and ironic description of our semi-religious traditions.

Certainly the writer will be able to use the other ideas mentioned in his journal to fill out his essay.

Of the three formal prewriting methods illustrated in Part I, thought pattern questions seem to yield more or less complete thesis statements. We'll discuss these patterns and the thesis statements which lead to essays using classification, definition, comparison, and analysis in the next chapter. For now, it will suffice to say that the following thought pattern questions can help you find a thesis for your essay.

What kinds of _____ does the author use to _____ ? (Classification)
What does X mean in this story, play, or poem? (Definition)
How do X and Y compare and contrast? (Comparison)
What are the results or effects of X? (Analysis)
How did X happen or what caused X? (Analysis)

The answers to these questions may be a thesis in the rough that needs only to be reworked slightly.

It's unlikely that the thesis will present itself full-blown in your prewriting activities, so you'll have to review what you've written to discover a focus. It will undoubtedly take some practice for you to recognize patterns, possible topics, and thesis statements. You'll probably be forming your thesis out of meaningful fragments drawn from your prewriting portfolio. We'd like to suggest a few steps to help you begin to organize your thoughts:

1. *Review.* Read through your prewriting portfolio to get an overview of your reactions.
2. *Sift.* Go back and underline parts which seem to have potential for critical writing. Circle important words.
3. *Group ideas.* Try to discover some patterns in your observations. Do you find yourself talking about theme, as the student who wrote the journal entry on "Christ Climbed Down" did? Do you make any observations about character, setting, imagery, point of view, tone, or structure? Are there any other ways you can classify your material? Perhaps there are some recurring words or thoughts.
4. *Label ideas.* Label your underlined thoughts by category—either relating them to specific ideas or to literary elements. You may have many different labels. Make a list of your labels; these are the potential topics from which your essay will evolve. If you've been assigned a topic, you may begin at this point by analyzing the language of the topic for key ideas, such as "discuss the *identity crisis*," and required writing strategies, such as "*compare and contrast.*"
5. *Question.* After deciding on your topic (perhaps you'll want to try more than one), formulate some questions which will help you put your fragmentary thoughts into a thesis statement. Use the list of questions at the end of this section if it helps point you toward a thesis. If you've been assigned a topic, turn the topic into one or more related questions, or you may find some questions in the list at the end of this section which pertain to your topic.
6. *Answer.* After you've sifted through your prewriting material for clues, answer your questions in writing. You might also want to look back at the literary work.
7. *Formulate* a tentative thesis from your answers; refine your thesis so that it's not vague or narrow.

That sounds like a lot of steps, but they can be done quickly and will become automatic for you before long. In fact, steps 2, 3, and 4 can be done almost simultaneously, or as you underline you can label and later group your thoughts. These are suggested activities, and you, of course, should adapt them so that they work for you. The material that doesn't become part of your thesis might help you to develop the middle paragraphs of your essay, so collect all of your early written impressions in your portfolio.

Following is a list of thesis questions for you to draw on after you discover what your general topic is. Indicated in parentheses is the type of thesis the question is likely to yield. Many of the questions overlap one another. Choose only those which are appropriate for your topic.

Character

How would you describe the character? (static thesis)

Does the character reveal the meaning of the work? In what way(s)? (integrated thesis)

What technique does the author use to reveal the character? (integrated thesis)

Can the characters be classified? (static thesis)

Is there a purpose to including two or more character classifications in the work? (integrated thesis)

Does the character change? (dynamic thesis)

How does the character's change relate to the author's overall purpose (theme)? (integrated thesis)

Are any of the characters symbolic? (integrated thesis)

Theme

What idea does the work develop, and how is the idea made clear? (integrated thesis)

What is the purpose of the work, and how is that purpose achieved? (integrated thesis)

Imagery and Symbolism

Can you identify an important image or a pattern of images? (static thesis)

Is there an image or a pattern of images which helps convey the purpose of the work or a central idea? (integrated thesis)

Is there an image or a pattern of images which helps portray a character? (integrated thesis)

Is there an image or a pattern of images which helps convey the tone? (integrated thesis)

Does the imagery change in the course of the work? (dynamic thesis)

Is there a purpose to the change in imagery? (integrated thesis)

Are there any symbols which reveal character? (integrated thesis)

Are there any symbols which reveal the theme? (integrated thesis)

Setting

What is the setting? (static thesis)

Does the setting help convey the theme? (integrated thesis)

Does the setting help portray a character? (integrated thesis)

What mood does the setting create? (static thesis)

Does the setting create a mood which complements or ironically contrasts with the action? (integrated thesis)

Does the setting change? (dynamic thesis)

What is the purpose of the change in setting; how does the change relate to theme or character? (integrated thesis)

Is the setting symbolic? (integrated thesis)

Structure

What is the structure of the work? (static thesis)

How does the structure of the work serve the author's purpose? (integrated thesis)

If the story, play, or poem is not told chronologically, what is the purpose behind the arrangement of events in the work? (integrated thesis)

What is the rationale behind the divisions in a story, play, or poem? (integrated thesis)

How is the conclusion foreshadowed (prepared for) by the author? (integrated thesis)

Point of View

What is the point of view? (static thesis)

What are the advantages and/or disadvantages to the point of view the author chose? (integrated thesis)

How does the point of view affect the theme of the work? (integrated thesis)

How does the point of view affect the characterization in the work? (integrated thesis)

How does the point of view affect the structure of the work? (integrated thesis)

How does the point of view affect the tone of the work? (integrated thesis)

What is the effect of the point of view? (integrated thesis)

Does the point of view change in the work? (dynamic thesis)

What is the purpose for the change in point of view? (integrated thesis)

Tone

What is the tone of the work? (static thesis)

How is the tone conveyed? (integrated thesis)

How does the tone affect the main idea of the work? (integrated thesis)

Does the tone change in the course of the work? (dynamic thesis)

What is the reason for the change in tone? (integrated thesis)

Following is an example of a prewriting exercise which is used to find a thesis according to the steps on page 145. This exercise is on "Snake," which is in the Appendix. You might recognize this freewriting exercise from Chapter 2.

Snake, Garden of Eden, symbol of (evil) tempted Adam   symbol—evil

and Eve. Disappeared mysteriously into (bowels of the)

(earth.) (Devil,) (king,) (Graceful) not caring, does not   setting; devil, king

bother the man, notices him and doesn't hurry. Man
is sorry for throwing log, stupid and cowardly.
Snake is proud, beautiful, gold, poisonous not brown
but not innocent either. Etna volcano smoking reminds
of hell, but snake is not totally evil; natural like
cattle needing water to sip. Narrator hears voices
of education telling him to kill the snake. Doesn't
know how to react. Misses snake when it's gone
but he gets mad when it starts to leave, he wants to
keep it around for some reason, says it's a king
in exile a lord of life. Why should a snake be a lord,
maybe in the underworld, maybe the man wants to see
what the underworld is like. An animal's and the man's
territory; the snake is an invader but the man makes
it into some kind of symbol but not the old simple
symbol of evil in the Bible, something more.

narrator-snake rela-
tionship, contrast

snake—setting
snake—evil
snake—natural

narrator—education

narrator—confused

narrator—snake rela-
tionship

snake—king

snake—symbol

This writer notices three possible *topics* in this freewriting exercise:

- the symbolism and characteristics of the snake
- the narrator's reaction to the snake
- the setting

The following *questions* are formulated from the topics and the list given on pages 146–147:

- What does the snake symbolize?
- Why does the narrator react as he does to the snake?
- What is the purpose of the setting?

Looking back at the poem and the freewriting paragraph, the writer *answers* the questions in order:

- The snake is part evil, part natural animal, part king.
- The narrator is afraid of the snake; snake seems to be in control, yet narrator is attracted by snake's grace and beauty; the narrator is cowardly and petty.
- The setting, especially the volcano and the underworld images, seems to add to the snake's evil character and power.

The writer *formulates* three possible *thesis* statements (others might have also evolved from these responses):

1. The narrator's reactions to the snake show it to be both detestable and admirable, a symbol of evil, power, and beauty.
2. The narrator compared to the snake is cowardly and petty.
3. The images of the underworld and the volcano make the snake seem hellish, powerful, and mysterious.

The answers to the initial questions may need a little refining before they can serve as a thesis upon which to base a rough draft.

• **EXERCISE**

9.7 Take the results of two prewriting methods from your portfolio and follow the steps outlined to shape a thesis: review, sift, group, label, question, answer, and formulate one or more thesis statements.

chapter 10

THE ESSAY: PATTERNS OF ORGANIZATION

The specific comments you make in your essay about character, tone, structure, and so on, will help to prove your thesis by providing evidence and thereby persuading your readers that your views on the story, poem, or play are right. In the course of the essay, you'll undoubtedly need to draw on one or more ways of developing your point—describing, narrating, classifying, defining, illustrating, or comparing—which we'll cover in Chapter 12 on modes of development. However, in this chapter we'll concentrate on the four predominant modes that will help you organize the middle sections, or body, of your work. They are:

Classification
Definition
Comparison–Contrast
Cause-Effect Analysis

The thesis of the essay, that central sentence we discussed in the last chapter, will help you decide whether your essay falls into one of these categories. The outline at the top of the next page shows major organizational and developmental patterns for an essay.

While there are other possibilities and combinations, we're focusing on classification, definition, comparison–contrast, and cause-effect analysis because they are common organizational patterns in literary essays which develop from the more complex thesis statements. You should keep in mind that while these four modes can indicate a structure for the middle

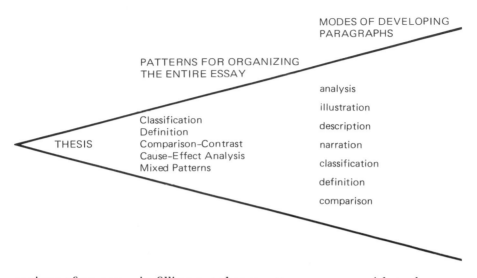

sections of an essay, in filling out that structure you may wish to draw on other rhetorical techniques. In fact, it is rare that we write in just one rhetorical mode. A descriptive essay frequently involves definition and illustration; a comparative essay may draw on classification and analysis, and so on. Most essays are hybrids, so writers need to practice all the rhetorical modes.

When you're trying to shape the essay, you may find it very helpful to do some more *directed* prewriting specifically on the topic you have focused on. The thought pattern questions are particularly helpful in structuring an essay, and we'll refer to them in our discussion of each of the four modes—classification, definition, comparison–contrast, and cause-effect analysis.

CLASSIFICATION

Classification is as common in the study of literature as it is in any other subject. When we classify, we *divide a group of related items according to some basis or principle into a number of distinct subgroups.* We might divide fiction into three categories according to the length of the work:

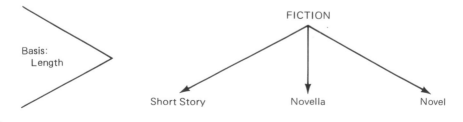

We might divide literature into three types according to the work's form:

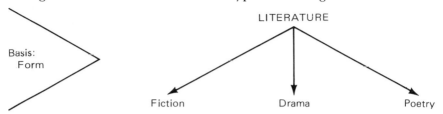

Logically, when we classify items, we must remember to apply the *basis for classification* consistently and not to change it in midstream. We can classify items more than once, but only one basis of classification can be used at a time. For example, works of literature can be classified according to form; then each category may be further divided using a different basis:

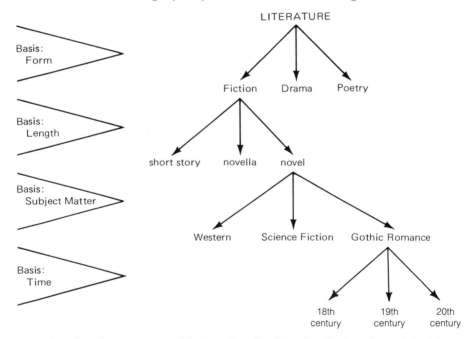

Another important guideline for classification is that the subdivisions should be discrete. This point is not as crucial in studying literature as it would be if we were doing a scientific investigation, but it's still an important consideration. By "discrete" we mean that in strict classification the members of one category or subdivision are excluded from another category or subdivision. For example, the subdivision of Gothic romance above is discrete because the same Gothic romance could not have been completed in both the nineteenth and twentieth centuries. However, the division of literature into fiction, drama, and poetry is not discrete. We know that many plays are written in poetic form, so the categories, still useful to some extent, are not mutually exclusive.

Also, logically *all* of the items under the major heading must fit into one of its subdivisions. Again, in our literature classification "tree" we'd have no place to fit a work of literature like Henry Thoreau's *Walden*, an autobiographical journal which is not fiction, drama, or poetry. In strict classification, such an omission cannot happen. Even though literary classifications tend not to be as clean-cut as scientific classifications, they are still useful, especially when each category is well defined.

Since classification involves dividing a group of related items into subgroups, *you can't classify unless you have a group of items.* Therefore, only certain works will lend themselves to a classification essay. You need a group of characters to divide, or sets of images to categorize, or a variety of settings to sort into types. Unless the literary work has multiple characters, images, or settings, classification won't be possible if you're writing about just one work.

In addition to having the elements to classify, *you need a purpose for classifying.* The activity should not be a random exercise but should be used to explain some aspect of the work. State the *reason* for the classification. For example, if you look back at the discussion of thought patterns in Chapter 2 (p. 24) you'll note a classification of the imagery used in D. H. Lawrence's "Snake" (in Appendix). A diagram of this classification is shown on page 154.

In order to make this classification of sensory images the basis for an essay, we need a purpose. For what reason do all these sensory images exist? The thought pattern question which we need to pose is:

What kinds of X does the author use to Y ?

X in this case is imagery.

What kinds of *images* does the author use to Y ?

We conclude that he uses the sensory images of sight, touch, sound, and smell. What is the purpose of these images? Looking back at the poem, we might see that the images help convey both a positive and a negative feeling about the snake. Or perhaps the images point up a difference between the snake and the narrator or a similarity between the snake and the narrator. However, since so many of the images focus on the snake, let's use the first reason, which will allow us to look at more images than the second reason. The thesis, therefore, that we might propose in answer to the question "What kinds of X does the author use to Y ?" might be:

D. H. Lawrence uses <u>images of smell, sound, touch, and sight</u>
X

<u>to suggest that the snake is both attractive and repulsive to the narrator.</u>
Y

Outlining the Classification Essay

The organization of the middle sections of a classification essay should follow the categories (subdivisions) noted in the thesis. The categories should be ordered in a coherent fashion, from least important to most important

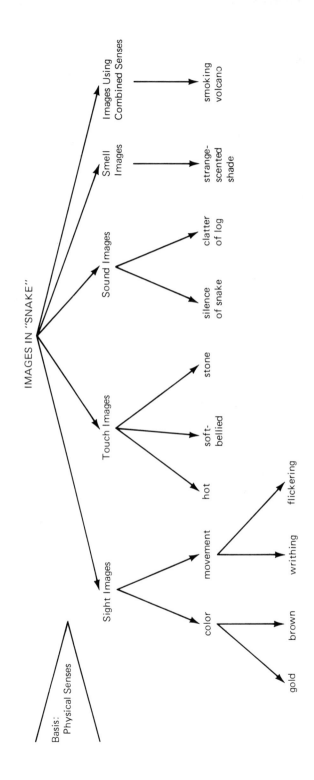

IMAGES IN "SNAKE"

Basis: Physical Senses

Sight Images
- color
  - gold
  - brown
- movement
  - writhing
  - flickering

Touch Images
- hot
- soft-bellied
- stone

Sound Images
- silence of snake
- clatter of log

Smell Images
- strange-scented shade

Images Using Combined Senses
- smoking volcano

154

if no other order is suggested by the topic. The writer should also clearly connect each of the subdivisions to the stated purpose, the "Y" of the thesis. In addition, the introduction should mention both the "X" part of the thesis—the group of items to be divided—and the basis for classification. In general, the outline for a classification essay will look like this:

    I. *Introduction*
       A. Discussion of X and basis for classification.
       B. Thesis: include subcategories of X and reason for classification, Y.

   II. *Middle Section One*
      Discussion of class 1. Define further, explain with examples, and note how it relates to Y.

  III. *Middle Section Two*
      Discussion of class 2. Define further, explain with examples, and note how it relates to Y.

  IV. *Middle Section Three*
      Discussion of class 3. Define further, explain with examples, and note how it relates to Y.

   V. *Conclusion*

Each section might be one or more paragraphs. There can be as many sections as there are classes.

The following is an outline for an essay on "Snake" using the thesis we decided on before:

    I. *Introduction*
       A. Discussion of images in general in "Snake" and basis for classification (division according to physical senses).
       B. Thesis: D. H. Lawrence uses images of smell, sound, touch, and sight to suggest that the snake is both attractive and repulsive to the narrator.

   II. *Middle Section One:* Smell
      The image of smell—strange-scented shade—suggests the snake is attractive.

  III. *Middle Section Two:* Sound
      Images of sound—quietness—suggest the snake is attractive.

  IV. *Middle Section Three:* Touch
      Images of touch—specifically, soft-bellied—suggest the snake is repulsive.

   V. *Middle Section Four:* Sight
       A. Color images suggest the snake is attractive.
       B. Movement images suggest the snake is both attractive and repulsive.

  VI. *Conclusion*

Each section in this outline on "Snake" is related to the thesis in a very repetitious way. A skilled writer, however, will use transitions, varied topic sentences, and synonymous phrases to relate each paragraph to the thesis. Each section would thoroughly deal with its particular class and provide examples of each type of image (some have been suggested).

SAMPLE ESSAY

The following essay on characterization uses classification as the basis for its organization. The minor characters in "The Country Husband" (in Appendix) are classified in order to help us understand the main character, Francis Weed, and his problems. A diagram of the classification looks like this:

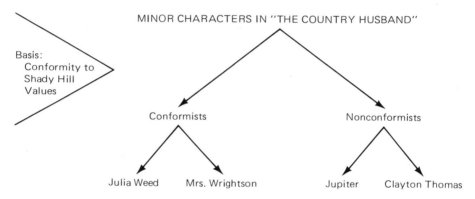

In answer to the thought pattern question, "What kinds of _X_ does the author use to _Y_?" the writer has come up with the following thesis:

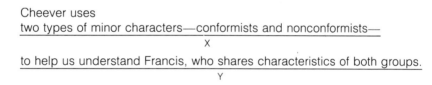

Cheever uses
two types of minor characters—conformists and nonconformists—
X

to help us understand Francis, who shares characteristics of both groups.
Y

BORES AND DREAMERS: THE CHARACTERS OF SHADY HILL

I.   John Cheever populates his story "The Country Husband" with many diverse characters. In most of his characters, Cheever presents two contrasting aspects of Shady Hill: one, its shallowness and superficiality; the other, its imaginative rebelliousness. The shallowness and superficiality are apparent in characters such as Julia and Mrs. Wrightson, who conform to expected social standards. The nonconformists, the rebels of Shady Hill, such as Jupiter and Clayton Thomas, seem to have more interesting lives, even if they are not exactly happy. Cheever uses both these groups of characters to help us understand Francis Weed, the main character, who is both a conformist and a rebel, a man who belongs to neither group fully and who, therefore, has lost his identity in Shady Hill.

II.   Francis' wife, Julia, is a Shady Hill conformist. Her desire to fit in is obsessive. She fears "chaos and loneliness," and she tries to fill her life with parties and other social engagements. She would go out every night of the week if Francis were willing. She has worked hard for their invitations, establishing the Weeds socially in Shady Hill. The price she has to pay is that she has to kowtow to the likes of Mrs. Wrightson and to put her family on public display in their very best clothes, as she does when she arranges the Christmas card photo. She cannot understand Francis' desire to be "sweet and bawdy and dark"; instead, she adapts to the requirements for the Shady Hill social register that they be polite, reserved, and on display.

III.   Julia and other characters adapt to Shady Hill, but Mrs. Wrightson sets the standards of mediocrity for the community. She is the epitome of superficiality. She is Shady Hill's present social director and, one might assume, a person to look up to. Mrs. Wrightson spends three days on the superficial task of adjusting the length of her curtains. She considers her problems important and interesting enough to drag the details out for Francis who she probably assumes will be a polite and reserved Shady Hill listener, given her social power. When Francis is rude to her, she is petty enough to take her revenge by refusing to invite the Weeds to her anniversary party and might also "punish" their daughter by not inviting her to other social events. She is a shallow woman with an exaggerated notion of self-importance.

IV.   At the opposite extreme to these conformists in Shady Hill are the characters who seek adventure. Jupiter, the dog, for example, is a nonconformist hated by the duller members of the Shady Hill community who may one day poison him. Jupiter is bold and free. He seems to do what he pleases and enjoys himself. Francis describes him as proud and intelligent with "high spirits" and eyes that "gleamed with mischief." Jupiter is not obedient to commands, nor restrained in any way. He wrecks parties and gardens and makes off with the steak at barbecues. He is not liked by the conformists of Shady Hill who would probably make him as uncomfortable and miserable as they make the less fortunate cat who is dressed up in doll's clothes.

V.   Another character who not only refuses to conform but totally rejects the values of Shady Hill is Clayton Thomas. Clayton was never really an integral part of Shady Hill because his father died leaving his family incomplete; in a conforming community, apparently, all families must have a mother and a father. Clayton disapproves of the phoniness of Shady Hill, the social excesses at parties, and, most of all, Shady Hill's lack of imagination. He says,

> what seems to me to be really wrong with Shady Hill is that it doesn't have any future. So much energy is spent in perpetuating the place—in keeping out undesirables, and so forth—that the only idea of the future anyone has is just more and more commuting trains and more parties. I don't think that's healthy. I think people ought to be able to dream big dreams about the future. I think people ought to be able to dream great dreams.

He is young and he has a number of dreams: he wants to be a writer, he wants to work in a bank, he wants to improve himself, he wants to marry Anne Murchison, he wants to have a big family. He is ready to leave Shady Hill and begin his dreams. While Francis Weed reacts positively to Jupiter's independent spirit, he reacts very negatively to Clayton, probably because he is jealous. Although Clayton has very little in material possessions, he has all that Francis wants. Clayton can make his dreams come true; he is leaving Shady Hill with Anne Murchison.

VI. Francis Weed's life exhibits both the values of the conformists and those of the nonconformists. His waking life, his daily routine, is very much a part of the conforming sector of Shady Hill. He commutes daily to work and comes home to an evening of parties. He has a lovely house, children, and Julia, his wife, who would not have stayed with him so long if he were not behaving in a fashion suitable to Shady Hill. His fantasy life, however, is nonconforming. He does not dream of bigger and better parties, as Julia probably does; he dreams of exciting skiing escapades, and most of all, of running off to France with the babysitter. Francis' fantasies show his longing to escape from the routine of Shady Hill. He has the dreams Clayton thinks are so important, although one cannot say they are great dreams. Even so they will remain dreams for Francis since he is trapped in Shady Hill and is unable to act on his fantasies. He is a divided man.

VII. There are other minor characters who fit the categories of conformist and nonconformist in this story; all of them serve to highlight qualities in the main character, Francis Weed. Francis, it seems, has come to a personal crisis because he has dared to leave the world of the routine and cross over into dreams of passion which are alien to the conformists. His psychotherapy seems to be a way of bringing him back into the conformist fold. But Francis has partaken of a forbidden fruit in his fantasies, at least as far as Shady Hill is concerned, and it is questionable whether he will be able to forget its taste forever.

• EXERCISE

10.1 The following thesis from an essay on the story "The Jilting of Granny Weatherall" (in Appendix) uses classification:

Porter reveals Granny's strengths and weaknesses through her reactions to her present circumstances and her remembrances of the past.

What is being classified? What is the basis of the classification? What is the purpose of the classification? Can you add a sentence to clarify "strengths and weaknesses"? Make a potential outline for this essay like the one on page 155.

10.2 Classify the images in Thomas' "Fern Hill" (in Appendix) or another assigned poem for a particular purpose. State the basis of your classification. Formulate a thesis using your classification and the thought pattern question: What kinds of _X_ does the author use to _Y_? X in this case is images.

DEFINITION

Definition is closely related to classification. While classification involves breaking down a group of items into subgroups, definition requires that the essential characteristics of *one item* be outlined. In this process, we usually *identify the item to be defined as belonging to a certain group or class and then list the characteristics which differentiate it from the other members of the class.* For example, "To the Stone-Cutters" can be defined as a poem (class) written by Robinson Jeffers (first characteristic) about the value and longevity of poetry (second characteristic), which compares poets to stone-cutters (third characteristic). Labeling "To the Stone-Cutters" a poem tells us *what* it is but does not tell us *how it differs* from all other poems. The three characteristics differentiate this poem from others in the class. (Look back at Chapter 2 under "Thought Patterns" for a more complete explanation of definition.)

Frequently definition is just a small part of an essay. It can be an introductory tactic as discussed in Chapter 11, or it can help develop a point in the middle paragraphs, as we show in Chapter 12. But definition can also be the basis for an entire essay. There are two ways a writer might use definition to structure an essay about literature; both use class and differentiation as the basis of organization, but the emphasis is different in each.

Outlining the Definition Essay:
Class = Literary Tradition

The first type of definition essay involves fitting a literary work or element into a literary class or tradition. For example, essays which set out to prove that "Hamlet is a *tragic hero*," or "Francis Weed is an *anti-hero*," or "Anne Sexton's poem 'The Double Image' is *confessional*," or "Archibald MacLeish's play *JB* is a modern *mystery play*" use definition. These essays will highlight the *similarities* between the works mentioned and the literary class (italicized) they are associated with. What about Hamlet is similar to all tragic heroes? How is Francis Weed like all anti-heroes? What features does "The Double Image" share with literary confessions? What characteristics does *JB* share with the medieval mystery plays? While the characteristics which differentiate the works from these literary traditions must be mentioned, they are not the main part of the essay. If the differentiation is mentioned in the thesis, it is usually in a subordinate clause. ("Although *JB* is a modern play [differentiation], it shares many features with the medieval mystery play [class].") The stress is on the class, not the differentiation. In fact, the thesis frequently mentions only the class: X = Y. X is the work or aspect of the work under consideration. Y is the class or literary tradition.

An essay using definition in this manner can be outlined as follows:

I. *Introduction:* Including thesis: X = Y.
II. *Middle Section One:* The characteristics of Y, the literary tradition.

III. *Middle Section Two:* The characteristics X shares with Y.
Characteristic A
Characteristic B
Characteristic C, etc.
IV. *Middle Section Three:* Differentiation
The difference between X and other members of the class Y.
V. *Conclusion*

Middle section one can be made part of the introduction if it's not too lengthy. Middle section two, the heart of the essay, can be one or more paragraphs depending on the number of similarities and how fully they are developed. Middle section three might be made part of the conclusion, or if you're more comfortable getting the less important details out of the way first, you might discuss the differentiation after your introduction. In any case, this section should be limited because of its subordinate role in the essay.

Outlining the Definition Essay:
Class + Differentiation

The second way that definition is used in an essay about literature is to identify and describe the characteristics of particular literary elements within a work. Description as a method of paragraph development is frequently important in definition essays. (We'll discuss description in Chapter 12.) The static thesis discussed in the last chapter often evolves into an essay using definition. Look at the following examples:

Francis Weed is a character who is unable to communicate, but who has an
          CLASS   DIFFERENTIATION
active fantasy life.

The setting of William Faulkner's "A Rose for Emily" is a house which is
                                                          CLASS
ancient and out of place in a changing neighborhood in a small Southern town.
                              DIFFERENTIATION

The first thesis is the basis of a character sketch. The class Francis belongs to is "character"; his unique qualities (differentiation) are twofold: inability to communicate and active imagination. In the essay which evolves from this thesis, class is not really important; it will be mentioned but is too obvious a point to develop. However, the two points of differentiation will surely require development. The same is true of the Faulkner thesis. That the setting is a house needs to be mentioned, but it is *the qualities of the house*—those aspects which make it different from other houses—that will be developed in an essay.

The form for this thesis is: $X = Y + Z$. X is the element to be defined; Y is the class; Z is the differentiating characteristic. Unlike the first type of definition essay we discussed, the differentiation, and not the class, will be emphasized in this essay. The class may just be mentioned. An outline of the essay would look like this:

I.   *Introduction:* Including thesis: X = Y + Z.
II. *Middle Section One:* First differentiating characteristic (Z) explained.
III. *Middle Section Two:* Second differentiating characteristic (Z) explained.
IV. *Middle Section Three:* Third differentiating characteristic (Z) explained, etc.
V.   *Conclusion*

A more challenging definition essay involves the definition of an idea discussed in a work. Such an essay helps us discover the intended meaning of the work. In discussing thought patterns in Chapter 2, we noted a question which might lead to this type of definition essay:

What does _X_ mean in a particular work?

On page 25 is a prewriting paragraph on the poem "Fern Hill" (in Appendix); here "growing up" is defined as a process (class) involving intensely pleasurable experiences (first characteristic) that are slipping away forever (second characteristic). One might find a different definition of "growing up" in other works. An essay evolving from this thesis would also follow the second organizational pattern mentioned.

SAMPLE ESSAY

Following is an essay which uses the second type of literary definition to organize thoughts on the meaning of death for Granny in Porter's "The Jilting of Granny Weatherall" (in Appendix). Death is defined as an experience (class) with three differentiating characteristics: a loss of physical sensations, a freedom from time, and a disappointing extinction of life.

GRANNY'S EXPERIENCE OF DEATH

I.   Presenting a realistic death is a challenge for any writer. After all, even a writer who has witnessed many deaths can only guess at what the experience is like for the person dying. Presenting the death from the perspective of the one who is dying is even more of a challenge, but one which Katherine Anne Porter faces squarely, choosing to delve directly into a mystery and help the reader experience and understand. Her short story "The Jilting of Granny Weatherall" is structured so that the one telling the story, Granny, is the person who dies. The reader is made to experience the approach of death with the narrator. Porter is successful in her daring attempt, for the reader comes away with a feeling of what death is like for the main character. Death for Granny is an experience which entails a loss of physical sensations, a freedom from time, and finally a disappointing extinction of life.

II. From the very outset of the story, Porter shows how Granny's senses are confused and no longer under her control. Even though Granny claims that "she still had ears," her sense of hearing is not clear. She thinks she is hearing leaves in the wind outside her window; then she decides, "No, somebody was swishing newspapers: no, Cornelia and Doctor Harry were whispering together. She leaped broad awake, thinking they whispered in her ear." Not only does she have difficulty deciphering what the noise is, but she cannot tell how distant it is, whether it is outside or inside, in the next room or near her ear. She notices that she did not hear Cornelia's footsteps before she felt Cornelia's hand on her face. She also thinks she is talking loudly enough to be heard, but it is clear from Cornelia's reaction that she is not. She is losing control of her voice. She also loses control of her sight. "Her eyes closed of themselves." As death approaches, the light dwindles, and Granny identifies light with life: "The blue light from Cornelia's lampshade drew into a tiny point in the center of her brain, it flickered and winked like an eye, quietly it fluttered and dwindled. Granny lay curled down within herself, amazed and watchful, staring at the point of light that was herself." Her life seems to diminish with the light, and her death is signaled by her blowing out the light.

III.   Besides losing control of her senses, Granny seems to be "floating" in time. There are many images of floating in the story. Granny feels like she is floating: "Her bones felt loose and floated around in her skin"; the pillow floats under her; Dr. Harry floats around the bed; the faces of her children seem to drift above her. Corresponding to the physical sensation of floating, Granny's mind floats back and forth between past and present time, between dream and reality. At one point she believes that she is napping and hopes the children will not disturb her, giving the impression that the children are little and not adults. She remembers parts of her past, particularly the jilting. She does not realize that a whole day has elapsed between Dr. Harry's visits; she thinks he comes back every five minutes. She associates her troubled breathing with childbirth and believes that she is once again having a baby. The boundaries of time have been removed, and her experience of death seems to involve a reliving of parts of her life.

IV.   Death at the end appears deliberate, an act which Granny decides to do. She blows out the light herself, although one gets the impression that the dark would have eventually engulfed her. From Granny's desire to see a sign from God and from her obvious disappointment, the reader can conclude that Granny receives no sign, and that her death is simply an extinction, an end of life. She is hoping for the bridegroom's appearance, a reference probably to her savior. But this reference also calls to mind the earlier jilting when darkness covered her once before, and she experienced hell. The implication seems to be that Granny is once more faced with an abyss, but whether it is simply a total darkness, an emptiness, or an actual hell is never made clear.

V.   Porter does not leave the death ambiguous. The experience she describes involves a loss of sensation, confusion, freedom from time, growing darkness, disappointment, and extinction of being. But there are many implications which are left unconfirmed. Is death simply a void? Is Granny experiencing a hell comparable to the aftermath of the jilting by George? Or did she blow out the light too soon and despair needlessly? The reader will never know, for we do not see Granny beyond the grave. Porter finally confronts us with the limits of our knowledge and experience. Death cannot be fully understood by the living.

The writer of this essay has devoted one paragraph to each of the characteristics which make death different from other experiences. Granny's loss of control over her senses is supported in paragraph two with examples of hearing and sight. The sensation of floating is described in paragraph three with examples of Granny's physical feelings, the floating movement of other people, and the floating of time between past and present. Paragraph four focuses on the deliberateness of Granny's dying and her disappointment, drawing on images of light from the story and the parallels made between Granny's death and her jilting. Each paragraph expands upon the characteristics mentioned in the thesis of the essay, and this expansion is summarized in the conclusion.

• EXERCISE

10.3 Using the second type of definition (class + differentiation), formulate a thesis in response to the following questions:

1. What does old age mean for the narrator in Shakespeare's "That Time of Year" (in Appendix)?
2. What is the snake in Lawrence's "Snake" (in Appendix)?
3. How would you define the narrator's experience of youth in Thomas' "Fern Hill" (in Appendix)?

Make an outline for the essays which would evolve from each of these thesis statements.

COMPARISON–CONTRAST

We've already discussed the purpose of comparison and the guidelines for setting up a comparative thesis in Chapter 9. In this chapter we'll assume that you have done some prewriting, have a thesis, and are ready to structure your middle paragraphs.

Outlining the Comparative Essay

There are two basic patterns for structuring a comparison–contrast essay. The first, Pattern I, involves structuring the essay by points of comparison; each point is discussed one at a time, and both literary works are considered under each point. The outline might look like this:

Pattern I

I. *Introduction* (with thesis)

II. *Middle Section One:* First similarity or difference
   A. as seen in work A,
   B. as seen in work B.

   III.   *Middle Section Two:* Second similarity or difference
          A.   as seen in work A,
          B.   as seen in work B.

   IV.   *Middle Section Three:* Third similarity or difference
          A.   as seen in work A,
          B.   as seen in work B.

   V.   *Conclusion*

   Of course, you may have more than three middle sections. Each middle section may be one or more paragraphs depending on how lengthy your discussion of each work is. Also, you might want to discuss similarities first and then differences, or differences first and then similarities. There should be some order to your paragraphs. The important feature to note about this pattern of organization is that for each similarity or difference which you discuss, you bring together both works before proceeding to the next point.
   In the second method of organizing a comparison–contrast essay, Pattern II, you structure the essay according to the works being compared. You first discuss one work fully, touching all the points which are the basis of your comparison. Then you turn to the second work, discuss the same points and show how each item is similar to or different from the first work. In the conclusion, both works are brought together, and the similarities and differences are summarized. An outline for this second method of comparison would look like this:

Pattern II

   I.   *Introduction* (with thesis)

   II.   *Middle Section One:* Literary work A
          A.   First point of discussion,
          B.   Second point of discussion,
          C.   Third point of discussion.

   III.   *Middle Section Two:* Literary work B
          A.   First point of discussion, similarity to or difference from work A pointed out;
          B.   Second point of discussion, similarity to or difference from work A pointed out;
          C.   Third point of discussion, similarity to or difference from work A pointed out.

   IV.   *Conclusion:* Including summary of points discussed in both works

Middle section one consists of a discussion of only one work; however, there may be many paragraphs in this section, perhaps one for each point or group of points. In middle section two, *the second work is considered in relation to the first.* It's not until middle section two that the comparison becomes clear. What were merely points of discussion in middle section one become clear similarities or differences in middle section two. It's very important that the same points covered in section one be covered in section two and that you note how the works compare on each point. If you don't refer to the first work when you're discussing the second, your essay will divide into two distinct parts, and the point of the comparison will have been lost.

You can compare two or more elements (characters, images, settings, structures, tones, or points of view) within one work, as well as elements in different works. In fact, you can compare versions of the same element— a character, for example—at the beginning of one work and at the end of the same work. A dynamic thesis, such as, "The tone of 'The Mill' changes from anticipation and dread to desperate resignation," discussed in Chapter 9, would require such a comparison. Either of the two organizational patterns we've mentioned would work in an essay with a dynamic thesis, but probably the second pattern would be better suited for emphasizing a change occurring over a period of time, as the dynamic thesis does. The first part of the comparison would center on the element as it is seen early in the work; the second half would discuss the element as it appears later in the work.

SAMPLE ESSAYS

Let's look at two sample essays. The first follows Comparison–Contrast Pattern I. We've underlined the topic sentences in the middle paragraphs which begin a discussion of the comparative points using both poems.

STONES AND TONES: A STUDY OF POETRY

I.   Many poems have been written about poetry—what it is, what it is for, why it is read, why it is important. Two of the most famous poems about poetry are William Shakespeare's "Not Marble, Nor the Gilded Monuments" and Robinson Jeffers' "To the Stone-Cutters." Both touch upon the longevity of poetry. Each author shows that the works of poets last a long time by comparing poems with monuments, but Shakespeare is more confident than Jeffers that his poetry will survive.

II.   It is with good reason that both Shakespeare and Jeffers compare poems to stone works in order to point out their longevity. Stone is a very durable material which, though not eternal, can last thousands of years. Witness the Roman ruins which still stand, reminding us of an empire long gone. Shakespeare and Jeffers choose one of the hardest stones, marble, to emphasize the length of time their poems will endure. Shakespeare catalogues the misfortunes that monuments are subject to. They are "besmeared with sluttish time"; they are overturned and burned in war. But his poem, he claims, will escape this fate and live on " 'Gainst death and all-oblivious enmity" (l. 9). Jeffers is less personal in his claim, but he still sees poetry as enduring. Jeffers also notes how "rock splits, records fall down, / The square-limbed Roman letters / Scale in the thaws, wear in the rain" (ll. 3–5). But in defense of monuments and, therefore, of poetry, he notes how "stones have stood for thousands of years . . ." (l. 9), and so poems can expect as long a life.

III.   Jeffers is not as confident as Shakespeare, however, that poetry will survive, which is shown by the very fact that "To the Stone-Cutters" is a defense of poetry, an attempt to prove that it has some value. Shakespeare never questions the value of his work. He claims that he has immortalized his love for all time by writing a poem about her: "your praise shall still find room / Even in the eyes of all posterity / That wear this world out to the ending doom" (ll. 10–12). Till the end of the world, Judgment Day, he claims that she will live "and dwell in lovers' eyes" because of his poem. He calls it a "powerful rhyme," "more bright . . . / Than unswept stone." In fact, Shakespeare sees his poem as better than monuments. Jeffers, on the other hand, does not share his confidence. He equates poets and stone-cutters, poetry and monuments. He calls the creators of such works "foredefeated / Challengers of oblivion" (ll. 1–2). They are cynical, or rather he is cynical, because they and he know their work will be destroyed eventually: "For the man will be blotted out, the blithe earth die, the brave sun / Die blind and blacken to the heart" (ll. 7–8). These occurrences might be seen as comparable to Shakespeare's Judgment Day, probably a long time off. Yet, Jeffers feels defeated by these events while Shakespeare is elated that he can prolong the memory of a person for generations, if not for eternity.

IV.   Jeffers does finally claim some value for poetry, that "pained thoughts found / The honey of peace in old poems" (ll. 9–10), but he is much more skeptical about the value of poetry than Shakespeare, who pits his poems against not *any* monument, but "the gilded monuments / Of princes . . ."(ll. 1–2). Jeffers' skeptical tone seems more appropriate to a modern poem in a time when human limitations are all too obvious, and the day of doom sometimes seems not that far away, but Shakespeare's exuberance is refreshing. His enthusiasm and self-confidence are well founded since we recall his love even today, nearly four hundred years later.

The next essay follows Comparison–Contrast Pattern II. We've underlined those sentences in the second part of the essay which refer to "The Vacuum" (discussed in the first part) and which attempt to relate it to "The Widow's Lament in Springtime" and thus unify the essay. This essay is based on the brainstorming exercise in Chapter 9, page 139.

DEATH AND RECOVERY

I.   "The Vacuum" by Howard Nemerov and "The Widow's Lament in Springtime" by William Carlos Williams are poems narrated by persons who have recently lost a loved one. The narrator of Nemerov's poem seems to be male; he refers to the dead person as "my old woman," a clue to the narrator's sex. The narrator of Williams' poem is obviously female. The kinds of grief experienced by these two people, however, are very similar as both their environments remind them of their loss. It is easy to see how dependent both these narrators were on their mates. Although different objects remind the narrators of their grief, they both are saddened by the loss of their spouses and have difficulty continuing with their own lives.

II.   The narrator of "The Vacuum" is reminded of his "old woman" by the vacuum cleaner which she apparently often used. He so associates her with the vacuum that he personifies the machine, saying that it "sulks" in the corner, that its "lung" has stopped as if it were dead, that its "belly" no longer "swells." The vacuum seems to be "grinning" at his "slovenly life," as if the woman were saying, "See how you can't get along without me." The narrator resents the fact that his woman has died; he has an "angry heart," which is perhaps why he recalls her in such an unflattering manner. She apparently kept his life orderly. "She used to crawl, in the corner and under the stair" (l.12), keeping the house clean. Now his house is a mess, and he rationalizes this mess by claiming that he can't vacuum because his old woman's soul is in the vacuum cleaner.

III.   While a reader may be tempted to look down on the narrator's "slovenly life," it would be unfair to ignore his suffering. His messy physical surroundings can be seen as a symbol of the emotional mess he is in. He misses his woman, and not only her housekeeping. The quietness of the house bothers him, and he feels an inner vacuum, an emptiness which also may have prompted him to see his woman as a vacuum cleaner. He now feels that "life is cheap as [the] dirt" which surrounds him. And while he "hangs on" and goes on with his life, his heart "howls," a sign of pain, and is "biting at air," a futile act. His life has lost its value.

IV.   The widow of Williams' poem is also reminded of her dead husband, not by a mechanical object, but by the flowers of spring. The husband is not personified, but rather the flowers are reminders of the previous springs which the widow spent with her husband and the happiness she experienced while he was alive. Ironically, these happy reminders are now the source of her grief. The widow is surrounded by sorrow; it has become as familiar to her as her "own yard" and "closes round" her as "cold fire." The new life which "flames" like the grass in spring ironically reminds her of death; the paradox of the "cold fire" brings to mind this death-life irony.

V.   Just as the narrator of "The Vacuum" is surrounded by dirt, so is the widow surrounded by flowers, but they make her no more happy than the dirt makes Nemerov's narrator. Many of the images present flowers of various colors, but the emphasis is not on their beauty or fragrance, but on their weight. The widow sees them as heavy—"Masses of flowers / load the cherry branches" (ll. 11–12)—probably because they weigh her feelings down. But her grief is so intense, it outweighs the flowers and overrides any happiness that they might bring, as the widow claims, "the grief in my heart / is stronger than they" (ll. 15–16).

VI.   There is no hint of anger in the widow's tone, as there is in the narrator of "The Vacuum," only sadness and depression. One gets the impression that she is older than the narrator of "The Vacuum," who can still refer to his youth. The widow had lived with her husband 35 years before he died, which probably accounts for the intensity of her grief. She does not have a desire to go on living. Her desire is to forget. Unlike Nemerov's narrator, who finds himself living despite his sorrow, the widow does not "hang on." She desires to let go, to "sink into the marsh." Nemerov's narrator exclaims,"I've lived this way long enough" (l. 6), showing that he wishes to be rid of the dirt which surrounds him and live in some other fashion. The widow, on the other hand, wishes to succumb to her surroundings, to let nature hide her, to die.

VII.   Both narrators experience intense sorrow at the loss of someone who was central in their lives. Both are naturally reminded of the one who is missing by things in their environment. Williams' narrator, however, seems to have given up. Her son's attempt to cheer her up has failed; she has no desire to relinquish her grief and continue without her husband. Nemerov's narrator will continue to live despite the pain. Although his life is a mess right now, there are signs that he is fed up with wallowing in his physical and emotional debris, and there is hope he may come out of it.

In the thesis of this essay, the writer specifies one difference and three similarities around which the essay is structured: the narrators of both poems are reminded of their loss by objects (similarity); the objects, however, are different (difference); both narrators are grief-stricken (similarity); both narrators have difficulty continuing their own lives (similarity). The first part of the essay (paragraphs two and three) mentions only "The Vacuum," but covers the points mentioned in the thesis. The second part (paragraphs four through six) points out how "The Widow's Lament in Springtime" covers the same points but is also different from "The Vacuum."

• EXERCISES

10.4   Outline each of the sample essays as they are written. Then, make a second outline for the essay entitled, "Stones and Tones," using Comparison–Contrast Pattern II. Make a second outline for the essay entitled, "Death and Recovery," using Comparison–Contrast Pattern I.

10.5   Choose two works suitable for comparison, brainstorm for similarities and differences, formulate a thesis, and write *two* outlines for a comparison–contrast essay, one using Pattern I, the other using Pattern II.

10.6   Choose a comparison essay you have already written. If it follows organizational Pattern I, rewrite it using Pattern II. If it originally follows organizational Pattern II, rewrite it using Pattern I.

CAUSE-EFFECT ANALYSIS

The final organizational pattern we'll consider is cause-effect analysis. You'll recall that when we analyze, we divide a subject into its parts in an attempt to understand the workings of the whole. One type of analysis that is useful when discussing literature divides the subject into causes and effects (see

Chapter 2 for additional discussion of cause-effect analysis as a thought pattern). Consider the following analytical questions on works you'll find in the Appendix: What causes Francis Weed of "The Country Husband" to seek the psychiatrist's help? What causes Granny to be disappointed at her death in "The Jilting of Granny Weatherall"? What causes the widow's intense grief in "The Widow's Lament in Springtime"? What causes the miller and his wife to commit suicide in "The Mill"? What causes the narrator of "Snake" to throw a log at the animal? What effect does the passing of time have on the narrator of "Fern Hill"? What effect does the passing of time have on the narrator of "That Time of Year"? What effect does the passing of time have on poetry in "To the Stone-Cutters"? What effect does her husband's prolonged absence have on the river-merchant's wife in "The River-Merchant's Wife: A Letter"? What effect does the death of his "old woman" have on the narrator of "The Vacuum"? Almost any literary work presents the opportunity for cause-effect analysis.

Outlining the Cause-Effect Essay

You probably noticed from the list of questions above that there are two types of prewriting questions which can help generate a cause-effect thesis:

> What causes X?
> What effect does Y have on Z?

In order to answer the first question, you need to isolate a specific effect—Francis' visit to the psychiatrist, Granny's disappointment at her death, the widow's grief, the suicides of the miller and his wife, the narrator throwing a log at the snake—for which you're searching for a cause, a motive, a force which effects a change. The cause or causes will be the main part of your thesis and the focus of your essay. An outline for an essay investigating causes might look like this:

Causes

I. *Introduction*

    A. A description of X, the situation for which a cause is needed;

    B. A thesis: A, B, C caused X.

II. *Middle Section One:* Discussion of how A caused X,

III. *Middle Section Two:* Discussion of how B caused X,

IV. *Middle Section Three:* Discussion of how C caused X.

V. *Conclusion*

If X involves a situation which is too lengthy for the introduction, you might make the explanation of X your first middle section. What is important is that you explain the situation for which you're looking for a cause before you present the cause(s).

In order to answer the second type of question—what effect does Y have on Z—you must have identified an important event or force (Y) which makes a difference in a person, place, or thing (Z). The passing of time (Y) causes a change in the narrator (Z) of "Fern Hill" and the narrator (Z) of "That Time of Year." The passing of time (Y) affects poetry (Z) in "To the Stone-Cutters." The prolonged absence of her husband (Y) affects the river-merchant's wife (Z). The death of his old woman (Y) affects the narrator (Z) of "The Vacuum." The *effects* in each of these cases would be the focus of the thesis and the essay. The motivating force, the cause (Y), would have to be discussed either in the introduction or the first middle section so that the reader understands the effects. The organizational pattern of the essay which focuses on effects would be:

Effects

   I. *Introduction*
      A. A discussion of the cause, the motivating force (Y),
      B. The thesis: Y has A, B, C, etc. effects on Z.

   II. *Middle Section One:* Y has effect A on Z.

   III. *Middle Section Two:* Y has effect B on Z.

   IV. *Middle Section Three:* Y has effect C on Z, etc.

   V. *Conclusion*

There are a number of fallacies which can make a cause-effect analysis illogical. We refer you to Chapter 14 and the discussion of the *non sequitur.* In general, it's best to be cautious when claiming that one event causes another. Most likely you'll be discussing *probable* causes or effects, not certain, indisputable causes and effects.

SAMPLE ESSAY

THE NARRATOR'S CONFUSION IN "SNAKE"

I. Picture a hot summer day at noon and a man about to draw some water to quench his thirst. Imagine his being confronted with a poisonous snake who has reached the water before him. What should he do? Should he kill it? Should he scare it? Should he just wait until it goes away? Or should he just get his water anyway and share the trough with the snake? This is the dilemma the narrator faces in D. H. Lawrence's poem "Snake." After waiting awhile, he decides to throw a log at the snake and scares it away, but he quickly regrets his action. It is not just thirst for water which causes the narrator to attack the snake who is retreating anyway, but the fear and confusion he feels in its presence causes him to act irrationally and later to repent of his actions.

II. The narrator does not immediately strike out at the snake. He waits impatiently for awhile. He is forced to stand in line "like a second comer. . . ." He notices the snake's golden beauty and realizes it is also poisonous. It is at this point, after recognizing the snake as a threat, that the narrator hears "the voice of . . . education . . ." which confronts him with a dilemma: "*If you were not afraid, you would kill him!*" (l. 36). But the narrator is afraid, and he admits it: "truly I was afraid, I was most afraid" (l. 37). He has probably been taught to fear snakes with some reason. A poisonous snake is dangerous. But deep in his inner mind he must also associate the snake with evil. He frequently refers to the hellish home of this animal with such images as "the burning bowels" of the earth and the "horrid black hole," bringing evil connotations to mind. This association would also cause him to be repelled by the animal. The snake does cause feelings of revulsion in the narrator, especially as the snake "put his head into the *dreadful* hole" [italics mine]. He feels "a sort of horror" as the snake eases into the black hole. It is after the snake begins his return to the underworld that the narrator strikes.

III.   The narrator cannot kill the snake, "take a stick and break him now, and finish him off" (l. 26), as the voice of education demands, because he likes the snake. At the same time he feels fearful, he also feels "honored" by the snake's visit. And while he feels revulsion as the snake goes into the hole, before and after that moment, he admires the reptile. He compares the snake to a "god," and describes his unhurried graceful movement: he "slowly turned his head, / And slowly, very slowly, as if thrice adream, / Proceeded to draw his slow length curving round / And climb again the broken bank of my wall-face" (ll. 46–49). He notices how his cowardly act, throwing a log at a snake whose "back was turned," causes the snake to convulse in "undignified haste." Upon reflecting on his actions, the narrator scorns himself and once again praises the animal, this time calling him a "king," "one of the lords / Of life" (ll. 69, 71–72).

IV.   It is clear that the snake is more to the narrator than an obstruction to his getting water. It is powerful and dangerous—it scares him. It is beautiful and self-assured—it fascinates him. It is not hard to understand his illogical re-action, lashing out at the retreating animal. He cannot kill it because he finds it at once powerful and beautiful, even if a threat. He cannot leave it alone because his own manhood and self-esteem are challenged. The voices claim, "If you were a man" (l. 25), you would kill him. His hesitation is understandable, but at the same time some action is necessary for him to protect his self-respect. Ironically, however, the action he chooses—throwing a log at the retreating snake—neither proves his manhood, nor allows him to contemplate the snake further. In fact, his action confirms his cowardice. It is a "paltry," "vulgar," and "mean" act by his own admission; he is sorry for his act. Throwing the log is an impulsive act emerging from conflicting feelings which the narrator only begins to understand.

V.   The narrator in "Snake" has a number of alternatives. The one he chooses, while it does not allow him to achieve his goal of understanding the snake, does reflect the confusion he feels in the reptile's presence. The incident provides him not with the opportunity to "talk" with the snake, but with an opportunity to understand himself, the influence of his education, the appreciation he has for natural beauty and force, and the fear he has of the unseen world where the snake lives. It is unfortunate that he only regrets his action and does not analyze it further. Such an investigation might lead him to an understanding of the dark parts of his own mind and existence.

The writer of this essay cites the narrator's conflicting feelings of fear and admiration for the snake as the *causes* of his behavior—throwing the log and later regretting it. Paragraph two establishes the narrator's fear of the snake because of its poisonousness and its association with evil. Paragraph three establishes the narrator's admiration of the snake, which he likens to a god and king. Paragraph four relates these feelings (causes) to the narrator's actions (effects).

● **EXERCISE**

10.7   Propose a thesis and outline an essay (1) on the effects of time on the narrator in "Fern Hill"; (2) on the effects of his old woman's death on the narrator of "The Vacuum"; or (3) on the effects of the car crash on the narrator in "Auto Wreck." All of these works are in the Appendix.

chapter II

WRITING THE INTRODUCTION

Written introductions, like social introductions, are governed by some conventions. In interacting with people, we abide by many subtle rules and rituals, most of which we practice unconsciously. For example, we continually vary the way we introduce ourselves to others by adjusting to the circumstances. We can be so adept at suiting ourselves to the occasion that we hardly consider the methods used. For instance, if you were sick, you would introduce yourself to a doctor by giving not only your name, but your physical complaints and a brief family and medical history. You might introduce yourself to a fellow student in psychology class by giving your name and mentioning that you're in the same class. For introductions between people to be meaningful, they must be *relevant*. To a more or less important degree, they should be *informative* and *interesting* as well. Whether or not your doctor is able to diagnose your problem correctly may depend upon the information you provide. Whether or not an acquaintance chooses to continue the conversation may depend upon how interesting you seem.

An introduction to an essay serves a similar purpose. It forms the reader's first impression of the writer. A good introduction can pique a reader's desire to read further. A poor introduction can turn a reader away or, if the reader has no choice, can lower enthusiasm and interest. Like a skilled host or hostess adapting introductions to the situation and the guests, the writer of a critical essay should strive for an introduction whose content is:

- informative
- relevant and coherent
- interesting

INFORMATIVE CONTENT

The introduction to an essay about literature usually contains at least two essential points of information:

1. the titles and authors of the literary works being considered;
2. the thesis or direction the essay will take in discussing the literary works.

The first point needs no discussion; the second has been covered in detail in Chapter 9. In addition, the introduction gives a sense of the writer's overall experience of the literary work. It may also provide other information when appropriate—background material about the author or the work, for example, or definitions which are not common but which are important to the discussion. We'll discuss these and other methods of introducing an essay later in this chapter.

RELEVANT AND COHERENT CONTENT

Just as you would adjust a social introduction to the situation, an introduction to an essay must be adjusted to the topic. An introduction is relevant when its substance is directly tied to the topic of the essay. An introduction is coherent when it logically moves the reader from the general subject to the particular purpose or thesis of the paper.

For example, if the subject of an essay were "The River-Merchant's Wife: A Letter" (in Appendix) by Ezra Pound, and if the writer intended to show how the narrator, the wife, had grown to love her husband as she matured, an introduction discussing Ezra Pound's political views or mental health would be *irrelevant*. Neither the poem nor the critical essay on the poem is concerned with these subjects. However, an introduction noting Pound's interest in the literature of the Far East, moving toward a consideration of this particular poem and its narrator, might work. An explanation of relevant cultural details pertaining to eighth-century China would also help the reader understand the situation of the narrator in this poem. Yet another way to introduce the narrator's circumstances would be to make a statement about love and marriage today in our culture and how our values differ from those of previous cultures, particularly eighth-century China.

Besides considering the relevance of an introduction, you must consider its coherence. You should look very carefully at the connections—transitions—made from the introductory statements to the work under discussion to the thesis of the essay. There must be a logical link making the thesis seem the next step in focusing the paper. Consider, for example, the following outline of the last suggested introduction for the essay on "The River-Merchant's Wife" (in Appendix) mentioned in the previous paragraph:

Step One: Consider twentieth-century marital freedom; women can marry whenever and whomever they wish, freedom supposedly insuring happiness.

Step Two: Consider the attitude of contemporary Americans toward arranged. marriages—while freedom of choice may not guarantee happiness, lack of freedom, it is assumed, leaves little hope of happiness.

Step Three: "The River-Merchant's Wife: A Letter" presents an arranged marriage in a very different culture.

Step Four: Thesis: Contrary to modern expectations, the river-merchant's wife has grown to love her husband as she has matured, which she makes evident in the way she tells her story.

The outline for this introduction progresses from general to more specific statements. If any one of the steps were missing, the gap created would raise questions about the relevance and coherence of the introduction. The links, which may seem obvious, must be drawn out in the introduction if the paragraph is to be coherent.

The *length* of the introduction must also be appropriate. A 500-word essay should probably not have a 250-word introduction, nor should a 1000-word essay have a 50-word introduction. The introduction should be proportionate to the rest of the essay. It may be a single paragraph, several paragraphs, or a whole chapter in a book, depending on the length of the entire essay. You should adjust the length of the introduction so that it's appropriate for your essay.

INTERESTING CONTENT

This aspect of the introduction is the most difficult to discuss. There are no prescribed methods guaranteeing an interesting introduction, though perhaps a few guidelines would be helpful:

1. Be specific; boredom follows on the heels of vagueness.
2. Direct your introduction; don't let it ramble.
3. Try not to say what you are going to do; just do it. The reader does not need to be told, for example, that in your essay you will compare Shakespeare's characters, Hamlet and Macbeth. That you are comparing these characters should be obvious in your essay.
4. Avoid artificial means of getting attention. While advertisers continually bombard us with images totally unrelated to their products to get attention, if you consider the effect of such tactics, you have to question their wisdom. Consumers may well be disappointed, confused, or annoyed to find their attention diverted by a promise of adventure or love only to find deodorant or cigarettes. Remember: your introduction should relate to the subject and thesis of your paper. If intrigue and adventure are not part of your topic, they are better left for another essay.

- **EXERCISE**

11.1   Evaluate the following introductions. Rate them using the scale below. Jot down the reasons for your evaluation.

	Not At All	Somewhat	Satisfactory	Good
Informative	1	2	3	4
Relevant and Coherent	1	2	3	4
Interesting	1	2	3	4

A.   The following introduction is from a 1000-word essay entitled, "The Tragic Clown as Unscrupulous Savior," on Ken Kesey's novel *One Flew Over the Cuckoo's Nest*.

Clowns, fools, jesters, buffoons have been making people laugh and cry for centuries. They have never been taken too seriously, and in the opinion of those who measure popular tastes, today's audience has become too sophisticated to be entertained by the antics of the clown. Fellini, for example, in his movie entitled *The Clowns*, while visually celebrating these artists, admits that they are a dying breed. But contemporary literature seems to have adopted what the entertainment world has "outgrown." The literary clown, foreshadowed by such film personalities as Charlie Chaplin and Buster Keaton, is not only entertaining, but can be heroic as well. Randle Patrick McMurphy, for example, in Ken Kesey's *One Flew Over the Cuckoo's Nest,* is one such heroic clown. Through his antics and laughter, he enables Chief Bromden to gain the pride and confidence he needs to escape from the destructive mental institution and the clutches of Big Nurse.

B.   The following introduction is from a 1000-word essay entitled "Beware the Snake" on D. H. Lawrence's "Snake" (in Appendix).

Volcanoes can be dangerous. There are a few active ones left in the world today. Mount St. Helens recently erupted and sent burning ash for miles in its vicinity on the West Coast of the U.S.A. Back in olden times, a volcano named Vesuvius destroyed Pompeii, a town in Italy, with its molten lava. In D. H. Lawrence's poem "Snake," the snake is like the volcano, Mount Etna, because it is dangerous.

C.   The following introduction is from a 500-word essay on the poem, "Christ Climbed Down" by Lawrence Ferlinghetti.

Every year one inevitably overhears people remark how commercial Christmas has become, implying that it was not as commercial in years past. Yet every year these same people celebrate this holiday, which seems to begin on the day after Thanksgiving and end abruptly on December 26th, by spending millions of dollars on decorations, food, greeting cards, and gifts, forgetting the poverty and humility of Christ's birth, life, and death. Lawrence Ferlinghetti tries to remind us of the true meaning of Christmas in his poem "Christ Climbed

Down." With biting irony, he repeatedly contrasts Christ's "bare tree" with our materialistic symbols of Christmas.

D. The following introduction is from a 1000-word essay on "To the Stone-Cutters" by Robinson Jeffers (in Appendix) and "Ozymandias" by Percy Shelley.

In writing about poetry there are several ways of comparing and contrasting poems. A standard way is a basic five-paragraph essay with an introduction and a conclusion. Of the paragraphs in between, one paragraph is comparison and the other contrast. These two poems, "To the Stone-Cutters" and "Ozymandias," are both about how stone seems to wear away with time. In this paper, I will show how, even though the cutters and builders go to great pains to build their statues and monuments, the abuses of time make their work crumble.

E. The following introduction is from a 500-word essay on Shakespeare's "That Time of Year" (in Appendix).

Poetry can be difficult to understand especially if you are not used to reading it. Many times schools don't emphasize poetry before you get to college, and then maybe the students weren't interested even if it was taught. There are many things to learn about poetry, for example, similes, metaphors, personification, and sonnet structure. Shakespeare can be especially hard because he does not write in modern-day English. His poems are famous, however. In "That Time of Year," he shows his greatness by using similes and metaphors.

SUGGESTIONS FOR BEGINNING

Even with the caution about relevance, there are still countless ways to begin an essay about literature. Too often writers will fall into a rut; having discovered one way that works, they are hesitant to try another. In this chapter we list some ways to introduce an essay about literature that have worked for us and our students. Perhaps you can add to this list other introductory tactics that have worked for you. In any case, we hope you'll begin to see the range of possibilities you have as you scan your notes and search for ways to begin. Keeping in mind that your introduction must suit your topic and thesis, you might experiment and create some interesting beginnings.

From Life Experience to Literary Experience

Very often what interests us in a short story, a poem, or a play is how true or real the literary work seems. We can picture any number of situations in real life which are similar to those we read about in literature. Recognizing this similarity, many writers intuitively start their essays by discussing life situations which are comparable to the literary situation, moving from the more general human experience to the experience presented in the story, poem, or play. Such a beginning is especially useful in essays on characterization, although it may also be used when looking at other literary elements as well.

Consider the following introduction to an essay about Margot, the wife, in Ernest Hemingway's short story "The Short Happy Life of Francis Macomber." The writer will attempt to prove that Margot murdered her husband, an ambiguous point in the story.

> Men and women get married for many different reasons. Whether a couple marries for love, money, sex, companionship, or security, their relationship is likely to be tested. Partners may change in time and grow apart from one another. Marriages must frequently overcome sexual problems, infidelity, or plain boredom in order to survive. Ernest Hemingway's story "The Short Happy Life of Francis Macomber" presents a marriage in trouble. Margot Macomber married Francis for money and security. When that security is threatened by Francis' new-found courage, Margot kills him rather than try to adjust to the change.

The writer of this introduction starts with a general discussion of why people marry and what difficulties they face and then moves to a discussion of why Margot married Francis Macomber, what difficulties she faces, and what resolution she chooses.

The next paragraph introduces an essay which compares two poems, "The River-Merchant's Wife: A Letter" (in Appendix) by Ezra Pound and "The Widow's Lament in Springtime" (in Appendix) by William Carlos Williams. The writer begins with a discussion of different degrees of grief and anxiety people feel when separated from a loved one and then turns to the poems about two women experiencing loss and their reactions.

> The absence of a loved one can be a very traumatic experience. Whether the person will return or not, the person left behind usually feels a great void. It takes a considerable amount of strength to cope with the emptiness. A death would certainly be more difficult to deal with than a long, but temporary absence of a loved one. But if the return is uncertain, the one who waits may suffer an intense anxiety as emotionally draining as grief. In the poems "The River-Merchant's Wife: A Letter" by Ezra Pound and "The Widow's Lament in Springtime" by William Carlos Williams, the women-narrators are sad due to the absence of their husbands. While both women experience a loss, their emotional reactions and the intensity of their emotions differ because of their circumstances—the river-merchant may return; the widow's husband is lost forever.

Sometimes you'll come upon a work of literature very unlike anything in real life. Horror stories, science fiction, and fantasy, for example, gain some of their effectiveness by surprising the reader with highly imaginative rather than lifelike experiences. The pattern of introducing a critical essay by moving from life experience to literary experience can be adapted to show how unlike present experience a literary work can be. For example, the following introduction to an essay on Kafka's "Metamorphosis" emphasizes how much more like a nightmare than an actual experience this story is. The essay attempts to show that the character's change from a man to a bug is appropriate. The introduction again moves from life experience to literary experience, pointing out a *difference* rather than a similarity in this case.

> Comparisons between humans, animals, and insects are common in everyday life. When a person feels good, he might say he is "flying high," comparing himself to a bird. When a person has done harm to someone he cares for, he may feel like a "rat," lowly and mean. A person who is always busy might be compared to the tireless bee; a person who is underhanded and sneaky is said to be a "snake," or, if he doesn't deserve even that stature, he might be compared to a worm. While these common comparisons provide quick everyday assessments of people's characters, they are never meant literally. Only in a nightmare might a human change into a lower species. Such is not the case, however, in Franz Kafka's "Metamorphosis." Gregor Samsa wakes up one morning to find he actually has changed into a beetle. His metamorphosis somehow seems appropriate, however, if one considers that Gregor Samsa never allowed himself to be a person, an individual human being. He is rightly portrayed as less than a man.

From General Idea to Author's View

Many works of literature investigate human experience from a metaphysical (beyond the physical) perspective, notably from a philosophical or religious stance. Concepts of time, chance, fate, good, evil, the meaning of life, the reality of death, the existence of God have all been subjects for literary artists. Before dwelling on a particular author's views about death or time, a writer may decide to discuss such concepts more generally in the introduction. If you wish to begin an essay in this way, you must first identify a prominent idea in the work that will be the focus of your thesis. Then you step back from the particular literary work and consider where the author's views fit into a range of opinions on the subject. Introductions which begin by discussing ideas are frequently useful in essays focusing on the theme of a literary work, though such an introduction certainly has other applications. Consider the following introduction to an essay on "Fern Hill" (in Appendix).

> Time is infinite, intangible, and inevitable. Some consider it a curse, others a blessing. Time cripples youths and heals wounds. Everyone shares time but is affected differently by it. In the poem, "Fern Hill," Dylan Thomas portrays time as the agent of the narrator's loss and distress. Benevolent only for a while, time leads the narrator out of childhood and imprisons him in the less happy world of the adult who is aware of age and death.

This introduction begins by generally discussing time before presenting what the writer interprets as Dylan Thomas' statement on time.

Beginning with an Overview

Yet another way to introduce an essay on a work of literature is to give an overview of the work—a brief account of *relevant* and important details. This method is especially useful when you find there are aspects of the work that are related to your topic but which will not be discussed in detail in your essay. You should not, however, narrate those elements of the plot which will be prominent in your later discussion of the work. Your purpose in such an introduction is to give a broad view of the story, play, or poem before narrowing to a thesis. Consider the following paragraph on "The Country Husband" (in Appendix). Notice how the overview is unified by critical observations (underlined) that keep the introduction from slipping into simple plot summary.

> Shady Hill, the setting of John Cheever's story "The Country Husband," seems to be a very quiet, unified community. It has a social life with a social director, Mrs. Wrightson. There are numerous parties and gatherings. Yet interspersed throughout the story one catches glimpses of the outcasts of Shady Hill. There is Jupiter, the dog, who wrecks gardens and disrupts barbecues, and Clayton Thomas, the Shady Hill critic, whose family is missing a "piece," and Gertrude, who is a "stray," seemingly without a home. There is the French maid who suffered greatly during World War II, and the babysitter, Anne Murchison, who lives on the wrong side of town and whose father is a drunkard. These outcasts form the hidden outer fringe of Shady Hill. They are an important part of the story, however, in that they are not without relevance to the main character. Francis Weed in some way relates to all these outcasts. As his name suggests, he himself is an outcast of Shady Hill, not because of his social position, but because of his temperament.

The essay introduced by this paragraph is about Francis Weed and how he does not fit into the Shady Hill society. The characters mentioned in the introduction appear in the essay only briefly, if at all, in the discussion of the main character. They serve as background or a take-off point for a discussion of Francis Weed.

In the following paragraph, the writer gives a brief summary of Granny Weatherall's thoughts as she lies on her deathbed and next chooses from among these thoughts the ones that indicate that she is dying, the focus of the essay. ("The Jilting of Granny Weatherall" is in the Appendix.)

> "The Jilting of Granny Weatherall" by Katherine Anne Porter is a story about an elderly woman lying sick in bed. As she lies there, many thoughts flow through her mind. She thinks about her life, about George, who jilted her at the altar, and about her dead husband, John. She remembers all the hard work she had to do after John died and she was left alone to raise the children. She remembers digging post holes, being a midwife and a nurse, and lighting the candles at night with the children. She thinks about her daughter, Hapsy, who is dead, and about Hapsy's child. The reader is not immediately aware that Granny is about to die since she is a strong woman who, as she notes,

gave up thinking of her own death when she was 60, twenty years before. Granny only realizes that she is dying at the end of the story, but <u>Porter prepares us for Granny's death by the appearance of Hapsy and by her use of light and birth imagery.</u>

Without the underlined portions, this paragraph would fail to express the writer's insight into Porter's crafting of the story.

Beginning with a Quotation

Sometimes writers find that beginning an essay with an appropriate quotation is an interesting way to open a literary discussion. The quotation, of course, should be well chosen. It should be important, pertinent to the subject of the paper, and well integrated into the rest of the introduction. (Note: the usual place for quotations which serve as *evidence* for an assertion is in the body of a literary essay, not in the introduction. The type of quotation you're looking for here is one that will make an interesting, informative, and appropriate opener.) Consider the following paragraph.

"I prefer not to," a phrase echoed throughout Herman Melville's story "Bartleby the Scrivener," would seem to be the words of a polite activist, a passive resister, a person of strong convictions and social sensitivity. The words, however, are applied to nothing important. They are, in fact, the emblem of a pathetically withdrawn man. Bartleby would prefer not to leave his office, would prefer not to proofread, would prefer not to write, would prefer not to eat, indeed would prefer not to live. He is a man who, by his lack of action, challenges the charity and values of other men. Bartleby, by his passivity, affects the other characters in the story and causes a significant change in at least one, the lawyer.

This writer chose the quote, "I prefer not to," to open his essay because it is the only thing Bartleby says in the story; it is repeated often, and it is important. The remainder of the introduction explains the quote, but also provides an overview of the story.

Beginning with a Definition

Sometimes the main point of an essay about literature will involve a term that is not common knowledge or that is used in a particular sense and, therefore, needs to be explained. The introduction is the perfect place to define vague or unusual terms to insure that the reader and the writer have the same meaning in mind when the writer discusses the literary work. However, there is no need to define common literary terms, such as simile, metaphor, setting, character, tone, and so on.

Consider the following examples:

A. Sherwood Anderson's characters are frequently referred to as "grotesques." What they have in common with gargoyles and other monsters is that in some way these characters are distorted human beings. They may be ugly or funny looking, but usually it is their actions that are the most bizarre. Many times they try to be what they are not, making them seem unnatural to others. In Sherwood Anderson's story, "The Egg," the father fits this description. He is a pathetically funny man. Like his deformed chickens, he is distorted. He has attempted to meet his wife's ambitions, and in the process he tries to be what he is not—a successful, good-humored businessman.

B.   Personification is a term used when inanimate objects or nonhuman living beings are given human qualities. For example, if ants were to talk, vegetables sing, or rocks dance, they would be personified. Personification is very often used in poetry. In the poem, "The Vacuum," by Howard Nemerov, the narrator personifies the vacuum cleaner because it reminds him of his dead wife.

The first introduction defines the term *grotesque* as it is applied to characters. Without this definition there might be some confusion about how "grotesque" is used in this essay, since people may differ on what is considered grotesque. Are the character's actions grotesque? Is the character's appearance grotesque? Before considering the main character, the writer of this paragraph answers the question: in what sense are Sherwood Anderson's characters grotesque? The second introduction, on the other hand, includes a needless definition. "Personification" is a commonly used literary term. It does not need to be defined for an audience acquainted with literary study.

Beginning with Background
About the Author or the Work

Another possible way to introduce a critical essay is to mention details about the author's life or the story's background which may be interesting and relevant to the focus of your essay. For example, you might begin a discussion of Nathaniel Hawthorne's "Young Goodman Brown," the story of a young Puritan's discovery of the evil side of human nature, by making reference to Hawthorne's own Puritan ancestry and his interest in questions of good and evil. Or, as in the example that follows, you might begin a discussion of the indifference of nature in Stephen Crane's short story "The Open Boat" by a brief account of Crane's real experience in an open boat on the sea after being shipwrecked.

In early January, 1897, Stephen Crane, a newspaper correspondent, was aboard *The Commodore* leaving Florida, bound for Cuba. He was to report on the Cuban Revolution. After being at sea for less than a day, the ship began to take on water and sank. Crane spent thirty hours in a 10-foot dinghy with the cook, the captain, and the oiler. Many of the other crewmen were in a larger boat; those on rafts were sucked into the sea when the ship went down. Crane survived this horrible experience; the oiler who shared his boat did not. While Crane recorded the facts in his newspaper account,[1] many of his thoughts

---

[1]Stephen Crane, "Stephen Crane's Own Story," *New York Press*, January 7, 1897.

and feelings were left out. They were not lost, however. His short story "The Open Boat" transforms this experience into art. His emphasis in this story is less on the facts of the disaster and more on the terrible indifference of nature to the suffering men.

For an introduction of this type, obviously you will have to do a little research. Be sure to note the source of your information either in the text of your essay or in a footnote. (Check to see if your instructor has a preference.) Also, you must use biographical data cautiously. Be careful about drawing unwarranted connections between the author's life and work. Not all stories or poems have an autobiographical basis, and even when a story or poem does grow out of an actual experience in the author's life, unless the connection is obvious, you must have proof that the work is based on experience.

Beginning with the Literary History or Tradition of the Work

As a student of literature, you've probably noticed already that many stories, poems, and plays are written about similar themes. The *carpe diem* motif, for example, has been popular for centuries. Literally translated this Latin phrase means, "seize the day," or, more loosely translated, "time is fleeting, so take hold of the moment and enjoy life." Essentially this is the theme of Robert Herrick's poem "To the Virgins, to Make Much of Time," published in 1648; of Alfred, Lord Tennyson's poem "Ulysses," published in 1833; of X. J. Kennedy's poem "In a Prominent Bar in Secaucus One Day," published in 1961; of Saul Bellow's novella, *Seize the Day*, published in 1956. The list is long. The more you read, the more connections you will be making among works of literature. A good way to introduce a study of a work of literature is to show how it fits into a particular tradition.

Also, you have probably noticed that authors frequently draw upon previous literature in their works. Anne Sexton, for example, rewrites Grimm's fairytales in her book of poems called *Transformations*. Anthony Hecht parodies Matthew Arnold's poem, "Dover Beach," in his own poem, "Dover Bitch." John Gardener's novel *Grendel* is a reworking of the Old English epic, *Beowulf*. And the list goes on. If you're writing about a work which is a *re-vision* of an earlier work—a parody, for example, or a modernization—or an answer to or a continuation of an earlier work, your discussion might effectively begin by introducing the earlier work and the way the work which you're considering is indebted to this piece. You might also discuss how the work you're considering treats the earlier version.

Consider the following introduction to an essay on Tennyson's poem "Ulysses," which begins with a brief reference to Homer's *The Odyssey* and relates it to Tennyson's poem.

> Ulysses, or Odysseus as he is known in Greek, is the hero of Homer's epic, *The Odyssey*, which recounts his valor in the Trojan Wars, his long and treacherous journey home, and his victory over his wife's suitors upon his return to Ithaca after an absence of twenty years. Homer's hero-king has been the

subject of many works of literature since *The Odyssey* was written over 2000 years ago. One of the most well-known later works about Odysseus is Alfred, Lord Tennyson's poem, "Ulysses," published in 1833. An older Ulysses narrates Tennyson's poem, which begins years after *The Odyssey* ends. The man who, in his previous wanderings, confronted the Cyclops, escaped Circe and the Sirens, and returned home despite the wrath of the god Poseidon is seen in this poem as bored with ruling his kingdom and hungry for adventure even in his old age. Full of zest for living, Ulysses contrasts his present stagnant life with his past glories and decides to sail again in search of adventure and fulfillment.

The writer first notes how Tennyson's poem captures the spirit of the early Odysseus but then sets him in a different time in his life and different circumstances.

Beginning with a Discussion of a Literary Technique

Some writers introduce their discussions of character, setting, point of view, or imagery by exploring the general uses authors make of a particular literary element and then considering the way an author uses the same literary element in the specific work being discussed. This type of introduction is especially valuable if the work to be discussed is unusual in its technique. In discussing characterization in a play like Edward Albee's *The American Dream*, you might note how characters are frequently developed fully in other plays, contrasting this fact with how Albee's characters are deliberately left nameless and undeveloped stereotypes known simply as "Mommy," "Daddy," and "Grandma." If you're discussing structure in Vladimir Nabokov's novel, *Pale Fire*, you might begin by noting the narrative structure of most novels and contrasting this with the way in which Nabokov's novel innovatively combines a poem and extensive commentary on it to reveal the plot. Or if you're discussing imagery in Shakespeare's sonnet, "My Mistress' Eyes Are Nothing Like the Sun," as the writer of the following introduction does, you might note how unusual the imagery is for a love poem.

Men have been writing poems about their loved ones probably since poetry originated. Love poems are frequently filled with comparisons. The loved one is compared to a flower—her rosy cheek or lily-white hand. The lovely lady may be seen as a goddess. Her eyes may be stars; her tresses, raven or golden, but never mousy brown, are always soft to the touch. Indeed, loved ones have come to expect this praise in poetry written about them. It is with wonder then that one reads William Shakespeare's sonnet, "My Mistress' Eyes Are Nothing Like the Sun." His images are just the opposite of what a beloved would expect. He may be making fun of the exaggerations of most love poems, but that is not his only purpose. Shakespeare, through his negative images, shows that the narrator has a realistic picture of his mistress and loves her very truly.

Beginning with a Critical Stance

As you continue studying literature, you'll notice how critics take a number of different approaches when interpreting a work. For example, some will look at literature psychologically—Freudians searching for manifestations of the id, ego, and superego; Jungians looking for archetypal patterns. Feminists might look at literature as an illumination of the female condition, past and present. Marxists will look at the economic and social values exhibited in a work. The critical stance which we've adopted in writing about literature in this text is limited, as are the others. We've been looking at literature as a crafted work with identifiable parts (character, setting, structure, imagery, and so on) which contribute to the whole impression. By looking more closely at each of the parts, you can better appreciate the merit of the whole work, the achievement of the writer, and further develop your critical sensibility.

If you decide to try one of the other approaches to literature (and if your course presents the opportunity), you would have to orient your reader in the introduction to your particular critical approach. In discussing your stance, you might begin by briefly explaining the theories which you'll be applying to the work, or the values by which you intend to judge the work. Reading the essays of professional critics who use these approaches would best prepare you to experiment on your own.

• EXERCISES

11.2 Try to think of two other ways to introduce a literary essay that might also be effective.

11.3 Write an introductory paragraph for an essay on one of the characters in "The Country Husband" (in Appendix) using the first method of development mentioned: begin with a life experience and progress to the literary experience.

11.4 Write an introductory paragraph for an essay on either "The Widow's Lament in Springtime" or "That Time of Year" which begins with a discussion of nature using the second method of development: from general idea to particular expression.

11.5 Write an introductory paragraph giving an overview of a story you choose and leading to your thesis.

11.6 Rewrite an introduction from an essay you have already completed, using a different method of development from the one you originally used. Briefly describe the techniques you used in your first version and in your second.

INTRODUCTIONS TO AVOID

Sometimes wanting to start the essay and get the writing quickly underway, you may not give the introduction the attention it deserves. Having outlined your essay, you might return to it for a way to begin. Frequently the results are either:

1. a simple statement of the main idea or purpose of the essay, or
2. a summary of some or all of the major points of the essay.

While either of these introductory techniques may be appropriate in a rough draft to get you started, after the essay is written, the introduction should be reconsidered and rewritten so that it is fully developed, informative, relevant, coherent, and interesting.

Consider the following examples of poor introductions:

> In the play, *Hamlet*, by William Shakespeare, Hamlet treats Ophelia cruelly because he is obsessed with avenging his father's murder and because, hurt by the actions of his mother, he loses respect for women.

This introduction consists of the main point of the essay. It's not even a developed paragraph and is inappropriate in length even for a short essay. The next introduction is also inappropriate.

> The narrators of the stories "The Tell-Tale Heart" and "The Cask of Amontillado" are both telling of the murders which they have committed. Both of the narrators of these Edgar Allan Poe stories thought out their murders well before they performed them. The murders were planned in such a way that neither narrator expected to be caught. The murders themselves were very similar in several ways. Neither of the narrators told anyone about his plans to commit murder. The plans in both cases were complicated. The narrators both concealed the bodies in places where they probably would not be found for a long time. The two stories are very similar.

As you can see, this essay compares two stories by Edgar Allan Poe, "The Tell-Tale Heart" and "The Cask of Amontillado." You also know all the major points of comparison in the entire essay. There is little incentive to read the paragraphs that follow this introduction since the entire essay is summarized in the first paragraph. There is little left to say which would not be repetitious. The whole introduction needs to be reconsidered and rewritten. Can you condense the points mentioned to form a thesis and suggest an interesting technique for introducing this essay?

In writing the introduction, keep the reader in mind. Think of yourself reading an essay and what you'd expect from a written introduction. Remember that it is the part of the essay in which the reader forms an important first impression of your written work, so it deserves your attention.

chapter 12

MIDDLE PARAGRAPHS: ORGANIZATION AND DEVELOPMENT

The ability to arrange things in an orderly fashion is a common and essential skill which most of us practice daily. We arrange our day into a series of events; we arrange our furniture to suit our needs and please our tastes; we arrange our clothes to protect ourselves from the weather and also to express our personalities; we're all skilled in arrangement to different degrees. Some of us are able to make our arrangements pleasing and meaningful, as well as useful. Artists have to be very sensitive to arrangement, whether it be the musical notes in a score, the images and colors on a canvas, or the bodily movements in a dance. For writers, also, arrangement is part of expression. How our thoughts are sequenced will affect the perception of our meaning. How our thoughts are spatially presented on a page may also affect the reader in subtle ways.

We've all come across books or essays that we wouldn't want to read after just a brief glance at a few pages. Without even considering the content, we may be discouraged by double columns of unrelieved prose, or full pages without any indentations or discernible units. To accommodate the reader, writers arrange their thoughts spatially into paragraphs which appear as distinct units on a page. A paragraph may vary in length according to the width of the page or column. It's not unusual to see one-sentence paragraphs in a newspaper with narrow columns. The average typed page, however, requires several sentences to make a paragraph. Generally, we avoid writing a paragraph which requires a number of pages.

A paragraph, however, is not only a way of providing spatial relief to the reader, to make a page of prose more pleasing to the eye; it's also a unit of thought which helps us divide our ideas into a noticeable sequence, and thus helps the reader to see and remember our plan. The paragraph, therefore, has meaningful as well as aesthetic value in helping to arrange our thoughts.

As a unit of thought, the paragraph can be compared to an essay in that

1. it has one central focus or idea;
2. all the sentences in the paragraph relate to that focus.

The focus of a paragraph is frequently expressed in a special sentence called the *topic sentence*. The topic sentences of paragraphs in an essay have a dual purpose. First, they control the paragraphs in which they occur—the topic sentence, remember, states what the paragraph is about. Second, each topic sentence connects the paragraph to the thesis of the essay, expressing a thought which clearly furthers the main point of the entire essay.

The topic sentence of a paragraph should be limited in scope even more so than the thesis of the essay since it governs a relatively small unit of thought. Unlike an essay which can develop an idea using many paragraphs and pages, a paragraph usually develops its idea in a few sentences. Therefore, the idea expressed in a topic sentence should be clearly defined and suitably narrowed.

While there are variations, most topic sentences occur at the beginning of a paragraph, just as the thesis will occur at the beginning of an essay. As you become a skilled paragraph writer, you may decide to place the topic sentence at other points in the paragraph for a specific effect or reason. For example, a topic sentence placed at the end of a paragraph can act as a conclusion, culminating from the evidence which precedes it. Sometimes topic sentences are not even stated, but the controlling idea of the paragraph is implied in its development.

Since the organizational pattern that begins with the topic sentence is most common to paragraphs in the middle sections of an essay, let's examine this structure. In this pattern the topic sentence is followed by details which support its claim—details which are not just listed but *discussed*. (We'll soon turn to the types of discussion most frequently used to develop the topic sentence.) However, to illustrate graphically what we've said so far, the basic organization of a middle paragraph will follow this pattern:

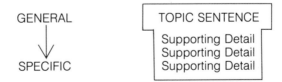

With the supporting details, the discussion becomes more limited, more specific than even the topic sentence. Choosing appropriate supporting details from the literary work and incorporating them in a suitable fashion into the middle paragraphs are important skills when writing about literature and will be the focus of our next chapter on evidence. After you have examined some sample topic sentences, we'll turn to techniques which can be used to develop a paragraph.

- **EXERCISE**

12.1 The following topic sentences are either too vague or too general to be a proper focus for a single paragraph. Underline the vague or general terms and rewrite the sentence using more precise terms, aiming for a limited focus. Remember that the topic sentence governs only a paragraph, not an essay; its focus should be suitably adjusted. All the literary works mentioned are in the Appendix.

1. Francis Weed has some positive characteristics. ("The Country Husband")
2. Many of the images in "Auto Wreck" convey a feeling of urgency.
3. "The Vacuum" and "The River-Merchant's Wife" are different in many ways.
4. "That Time of Year" has a definite structure.
5. "To the Stone-Cutters" changes in tone at the end.
6. The death scene in "The Jilting of Granny Weatherall" has many similarities to the jilting.
7. In "Fern Hill" time is portrayed with images.
8. The setting is important in "Snake."
9. "The Country Husband" has an interesting structure.
10. Shapiro creates a narrator for "Auto Wreck."

METHODS OF DEVELOPMENT

In this section we'll describe seven ways of developing a paragraph which are common in critical writing. Some are already familiar to you from Chapter 10, in which we considered how the structure of the essay is affected by a thesis which calls for classification, definition, comparison–contrast, or cause-effect analysis. We'll also discuss illustration, description, narration, as well as classification, definition, analysis, and comparison as means of developing a paragraph. While we'll describe each method separately, you'll probably have occasion to use more than one in any given paragraph. It's only in textbook illustrations that we have "pure" paragraphs of illustration, comparison, and so on. In actual writing, mixed methods are more common.

We've put illustration and analysis first in our discussion because they are the two most common methods occurring in an essay about literature. Although they are often used together, we'll consider them separately first.

Illustration

To illustrate is to give an example. Within a paragraph, the example would support the point made in the topic sentence. Examples in an essay about literature are drawn from the literary work or works being discussed. Illustration can involve a *series of examples* or *one extended example*.

A *series of examples* is just that, more than one example, usually brief, which support the main point. For example, you might support a topic sentence about the reaction of the speaker to the accident in "Auto Wreck" (in Appendix) by citing and discussing a number of images used to present the speaker's discomfort, that is, examples from the poem.

Topic Sentence	The speaker of "Auto Wreck" is mentally and emotionally disturbed after witnessing the accident.
Supporting Details	1. The speaker says, "We are deranged." 2. Physical symptoms such as their throats are constricted, and they are dazed and can't move. 3. The speaker claims they have a "wound"; they are "convalescents" with "sickly smiles."

Of course, each of these images would be discussed in detail in developing this paragraph, not simply listed.

When using an *extended* example, you would focus on only one scene or image which supports the topic sentence. The example must be substantial enough to warrant a detailed paragraph discussion. Consider the following outline for a paragraph on the poem "Snake" (in Appendix).

Topic Sentence	The setting helps convey the evil and powerful nature of the snake,
Supporting Detail	particularly the image of the smoking volcano because
Discussion	a. it is an active volcano and potentially destructive, as is the poisonous snake; b. it is powerful and causes fear, as does the snake; c. the smokiness reminds one of hell, the underworld; the snake lives in the ground and is associated with the devil.

This paragraph would use one image from the poem, the volcano, as an example to help the reader see how the setting is associated with the nature of the reptile. A discussion of points a, b, and c would fill out the paragraph.

Illustrations are frequently introduced by such phrases as "for example," "for instance," and others. A more complete listing of these transitional phrases can be found in Chapter 14, page 234.

Analysis

The discussion (points a, b, and c) of the image we used as an example in the development of the paragraph on "Snake" is actually a combination of analysis and comparison. Analysis, like illustration, is basic to all critical writing. We've discussed analysis previously as the technique a writer uses when he or she divides a subject into its parts in an attempt to understand the workings of the whole. In this chapter, we'll discuss two different kinds of analysis which are useful when developing paragraphs about literature.

Cause-effect analysis. Cause-effect analysis, discussed previously, can sometimes be a method of organizing and developing a paragraph, as well as an essay. A paragraph using cause-effect analysis can account for the motives of characters, the sources of change, the results of a stimulus or force, and so on. The focus of the paragraph, stated in the topic sentence, can be either the cause or the effect. Cause-effect analysis might be used to develop topic sentences like the following:

1. The flowers intensify the widow's grief in "The Widow's Lament in Springtime."
   CAUSE   EFFECT

2. One of the effects of time on the narrator in "Fern Hill" is the
   CAUSE

   loss of his imaginary world
   EFFECT

The paragraph developed from the first topic sentence would discuss how and why the flowers cause the widow's grief. The paragraph developed from the second topic sentence would discuss the effects of time on the narrator, particularly one effect—the loss of the narrator's imaginative world.

Explication. Explication, sometimes called textual analysis, involves the study of the author's choice of words and diction. It is used frequently as a method of analyzing poetry, though sometimes prose passages also bear close scrutiny. When explicating, you would elaborate on the meaning of the words in a passage, taking note of denotative (literal) as well as connotative (suggested) meanings. Explication is more than paraphrase because a critical writer attempts to uncover the reasons behind the author's choice of words, noting various levels of meaning as well as arrangement and the effect of arrangement on meaning. Explication sometimes involves a discussion of the author's style.

The first task in an explication is to provide the general meaning of the lines. For example, consider the following lines from Thomas' "Fern Hill":

And nothing I cared, at my sky blue trades, that time allows
In all his tuneful turning so few and such morning songs
   Before the children green and golden
      Follow him out of grace. . . .

If we paraphrased these lines, we might say that, as a child, the narrator was carefree, preoccupied with childhood games, and oblivious of the fact that time would allow him to be young only for a short period before the onset of a less desirable state—adulthood. Dylan Thomas' poetry, unlike some other poetry, is very figurative, and so in the very act of paraphrasing, the writer must interpret. (This is not true, for example, of some lines in Williams' "The Widow's Lament in Springtime" where a paraphrase of "Thirtyfive years / I lived with my husband" would be a simple repetition— she lived with her husband for 35 years.)

In addition to providing the general meaning of the passage, an explication—like all analyses—would look more closely at the parts, the words or phrases which make up the selection. Returning to the example from "Fern Hill," a writer explicating these lines might comment on the implications of portraying childhood occupations as "sky blue trades," a fanciful image which links the child with nature. The writer might notice the alliteration in time's "tuneful turning," the very sound of which suggests the "song" mentioned later in that line. The image might call to mind the Pied Piper who also led children to an uncertain fate. An explication of "Fern Hill" might also include a comment on the image of "morning song," a pleasant image that conjures up thoughts of nature and the "youthful" part of the day or, by implication, the youthful part of human life. The colors in the next line convey both youth, "green," and preciousness, "golden." The indentations of the lines seem to indicate a progression as the children follow time "out of grace," or out of their innocent, blessed state.

You see how detailed an explication can be. Depending on the passage, a line or even an image might very well warrant a whole paragraph. You would, of course, include in your explication only those details which relate to your topic sentence. For example, if your topic sentence were "Thomas sees youth as a precious and blessed state," you might want to discuss the reference to the "children green and golden" and "grace," but might not include the "tuneful turning."

The subject of analysis is obviously the literary work, but not the whole work at once. We concentrate on smaller units within the work as outlined by the thesis and, even more so, by the topic sentences. You can see why analysis is linked so frequently to illustration. Illustration provides us with the segment of the work to be analyzed in a specific paragraph.

Description

Description may also be used in presenting examples. When we describe, we give concrete, sensory details which help the reader form an image of the subject of the description. We tell how the subject looks, sounds, feels, smells, and tastes. Good description hinges upon the use of specific nouns, verbs, adjectives, and adverbs, such as the following:

Sight: Color—red, green, yellow, brown, orange
        Light—sunlight, moonlight, firelight, dark, shaded, bright
        Movement—slithered, hopped, flashing, trudge, quickly, slowly
        Shape—roundness, squareness, oval, spherical, pointed

Sound: Tone—whining, shrill, deep, lyrical, pleading
        Volume—whisper, yell, scream, holler, loudly, softly

Smell: pungent, sharp, sweet

Taste: salty, sour, sweet, bland

Touch: soft, rough, sandy, smooth, cool, warm, hot

Besides using specific nouns, verbs, adjectives, and adverbs, you can use comparison or simile to help describe a person, place, or thing. For instance, if you were to describe a fish, you might say:

It looks as silvery as a wet half dollar.	Sight
It sounds as quiet as a bubble bursting.	Sound
It smells like the sea when it's fresh.	Smell
It tastes a little like chicken.	Taste
It feels like a wet bar of soap.	Touch

When using description in a literary essay, chances are you'll be describing a person, place, or thing in the literary work. Accuracy will be important. Your description should coincide with the actual details given by the author. For example, if you were to describe the setting in "Fern Hill" (in Appendix), you might use different adjectives than Thomas does, but the reader should come away with an appreciation of Thomas' farm and apple orchard, not a farm or orchard of your own creation. You couldn't, for example, change the positive images of "holy streams" and "daisies and barley" to "murky rivulets" and "weeds."

In a literary essay, a description of a person, place, or thing usually precedes an analysis of that subject. The description may occur as part of an illustration.

Narration

To narrate is to tell a story, a sequence of events or actions. Narration is used in a literary essay much like description is. It involves retelling in your own words a sequence of actions or an event in a work of literature. A narration again may be a vehicle for an illustration, an example. When we retell part of a work, we want to talk about it, analyze it more closely. The retelling should not exist for its own sake but should support a point made in the topic sentence. For example, if you were to support a topic sentence which claimed that "Francis Weed becomes more aware of the physicalness of things because of the plane crash," you might retell the first scene in "The Country Husband," pointing out how Francis' senses are awakened. (See page 213 for a paragraph that does this.)

Verbs are very important in a narration, and you should be conscious of your use of them. We all have a habit of relying on the verb *to be* in all its forms (*am, are, is, was, were*) instead of using more active, more vigorous verbs. Where action is being portrayed, try to stay away from the passive *to be* verbs. Compare the following versions of a paragraph using a narrative paraphrase of a section of "The Country Husband" to prove how much of a misfit Francis Weed has become. The verbs are underlined, and the narrative portion is italicized.

> A.   By the end of the story, it becomes clear how much of a misfit Francis seems to be. *He is mistaken by the psychiatrist's receptionist and a policeman for a deviant, a potential murderer. It seems he calls the psychiatrist's office for an appointment. He is insistent that he has to come right away. His arrival is marked by his dazed state. He is shocked by his venturing from his loneliness to discuss his private affairs with someone else. Francis is struck by the fact that the doctor's office is very much like a suburban home,* but Francis is far from welcomed. *Francis is greeted as an intruder in this "home." He is awaited by a policeman, and he is frisked before being allowed to see the doctor. The doctor's secretary explains that he was thought to be the patient who is threatening the doctor's life.* But Francis is not that much of a deviant; his crime against society is much smaller: he is in love, which makes him an intensively alive person in a community which thrives on bland routines and social restrictions.

> B.   The end of the story makes clear how much of a misfit Francis has become. *The psychiatrist's receptionist and a policeman mistake him for a deviant, a potential murderer. Francis calls the psychiatrist's office for an appointment insisting that he cannot wait. He arrives at the office in a daze, shocked by his venturing from his loneliness to discuss his private affairs with someone else. Francis notices that the doctor's office looks like a suburban home,* but Francis is far from welcomed. *The policeman who awaits Francis greets him as an intruder in this "home." The policeman frisks Francis before he is allowed to see the doctor. The doctor's secretary explains that they thought he might be the patient who threatened the doctor's life.* But Francis is not that much of a deviant; his crime against society is much smaller: he is in love, which makes him an intensively alive person in a community which thrives on bland routines and social restrictions.

Notice how the many passive verbs in the first paragraph make it wordy and less vivid than the second paragraph, where a sense of action is retained in the simpler verbs. Notice also that in both paragraphs the narration is offered *as proof of Francis' being a misfit* (see the topic sentence); it doesn't exist for its own sake. Also, an analysis follows the narrative, further pointing out its relationship to the topic sentence.

Classification

Classification is rarely the substance of an entire paragraph. More often than not, it *orders* the discussion in the paragraph, dividing the paragraph into two or three parts. Each part then employs description, definition, comparison, and/or illustration. You will remember from Chapter 10 that classification involves dividing a group of items into subgroups according to some principle or basis of division. Just as classification can help structure an entire essay, so also it can help structure a single paragraph (which may or may not be part of a larger classification essay). Take, for example, the following paragraph on "Auto Wreck" (in Appendix) from an essay which profiles the reaction of the speaker and other witnesses to the accident. This paragraph involves classification, illustration, comparison, and analysis. The classification can be diagrammed as follows:

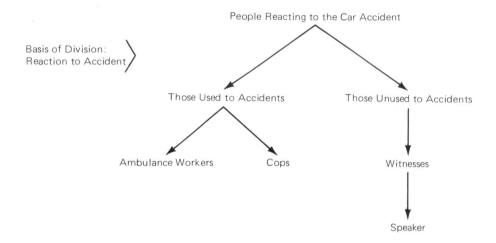

One way Shapiro emphasizes the momentary derangement of those who witness the accident is by contrasting their ineffectiveness and paralysis with the activities of others at the scene. To do this Shapiro presents two types of reactions to the accident. The first two stanzas show the efficiency of those who continually deal with accidents, the ambulance workers and the "cops." The last two stanzas show the reactions of those who are shocked by the accident, the witnesses. Since the speaker is one of the latter group, the emphasis is on his or her perceptions. From the speaker's vantage point, the ambulance workers hardly exist, as the speaker's attention is riveted on the ambulance and the victims. The reader can't help but notice the swiftness and efficiency of the vehicle which travels at "top speed" to the rescue, with doors that "leap" open and are barely closed as the ambulance pulls away with "its terrible cargo." The police also go about their duty methodically, sweeping glass, "making notes," washing away the blood, and hanging lanterns so the wreckage is visible to the endangered traffic. From the speaker's perspective, their actions seem almost callous. They seem to go about their task mindlessly. Shapiro contrasts these actions with the paralysis of the witnesses who are in shock and can do nothing but stand around, gaze, and question. While the others act, the narrator and other witnesses are incapacitated by the accident and search for a reason for an event that is purposeless.

Notice how classification is used in this paragraph to set up the "two types of reactions" at the outset of the paragraph and thus helps structure the paragraph.

Definition

Like classification, definition can be *part* of a middle paragraph. It rarely is the substance of an entire paragraph. More likely, definition in a middle paragraph will involve a phrase or a sentence or two to clarify a difficult point or an unusual term. Remember that a formal definition provides both the class which the subject belongs to and the characteristics which differentiate the subject from other members of the class. But a brief definition used to clarify a term or point of discussion in the middle of an essay need not be so formal. Many times a *synonym*, a more familiar word or term which has approximately the same meaning as the one being defined, will be sufficient. Or perhaps you'll want to use an incomplete definition which points out only those characteristics which are relevant to your discussion of the literary work.

Take, for example, the reference to the "carob-tree" in Lawrence's poem "Snake" (in Appendix)—"the deep, strange-scented shade of the great dark carob-tree." Let's say that you'd like to discuss this image but have never seen, smelled, nor heard of a carob tree, and you suspect that your readers haven't either. What do you do? You provide the necessary details about the carob tree so that both you and the reader understand the image and its significance in this poem. While searching for a definition of this tree, you may come across many details which may not be applicable to the use of this image in the poem. The shape of the leaves and the biological Latin name for the tree, for instance, might be important points of differentiation in a formal definition, but are only of importance to you if they can be applied to the poem. You might discover that the carob tree has sugary black pods, which are edible and contribute to its smell. The shape of these pods has reminded people through the ages of locusts, destructive insects. So the carob tree is also known as the "locust tree." This information might be useful in your discussion of the poem if you see the tree as another natural image which is at once enticing—a sweet-smelling tree which provides food and shade—and repulsive—one whose pods look like locusts. This image might fit well with those of the volcano and the snake, which also have positive and negative qualities. In this case *your* definition of "carob tree" might simply be a tree with sweet edible pods which look like locusts, because these are the features of the tree which will play a part in your discussion of the poem. Your definition should be tailored to suit your purpose in the essay. Not all details will be important; cite only those which are.

Comparison

You may frequently want to use comparison to help make a point in essays whose purpose is not necessarily to compare two elements or works. Remember, when we compare, we discuss the similarities and differences between two things. Like definition, comparison used to help prove a point in a middle paragraph need not be as exhaustive or formal as it would be if the purpose of the whole essay were comparison. Sometimes only one similarity or difference is needed to help you make your point. For example, in an essay discussing the character of Francis Weed ("The Country Husband," in Appendix), you may feel that comparing him to Julia and other Shady Hill characters will help you develop a paragraph proving Francis' isolation. So you may include a sentence or two like the following: "Unlike Julia and many of the other characters of Shady Hill, Francis has a limited tolerance for social gatherings. Julia would go to a party every night, but Francis has limited their outings." The entire paragraph might then be given over to other illustrations of Francis' isolation; the comparison would only be a limited part of the discussion. Look back at the paragraph in the section on classification in this chapter. In showing how the narrator is stunned by the accident in "Auto Wreck," the writer compares the witnesses (including the narrator) to the police and ambulance workers on the scene.

In paragraphs which focus on metaphors and similes, comparison is frequently an important method of development. You really would have difficulty discussing the poets and their work in "To the Stone-Cutters" (in Appendix) without comparing them to the stone-cutters because Jeffers makes the stone-cutters a central metaphor for the poets. In Shakespeare's sonnet "That Time of Year" (in Appendix), it would be pointless to consider the twilight/sunset image or any of the other images without comparing them to the narrator's encroaching old age. It is the nature of metaphor and simile to compare, and so in a discussion of these images, you will inevitably draw out and elaborate on this comparison.

Another way to use comparison in support of a critical point is to create your own analogies or similes. The simile should help clarify your meaning. For example, you might say that the "cops" in "Auto Wreck" (in Appendix) seem *like automatons or robots*, doing their jobs automatically, seemingly without feeling when compared to the speaker. A simile is often a concise and effective way of making a point.

Remember, however, that the similes you create, or the similarities and differences you choose to discuss, should support the critical point embodied in the topic sentence of the paragraph.

- **EXERCISES**

   12.2 Illustration
   Choose two of the topic sentences which you have narrowed in Exercise 12.1. What illustrations from the literary works would you choose to support your point? List them.

   12.3 Explication/Analysis
   Explicate three of the following sets of lines. Look back at the works in the Appendix for help with the context of the passages. Do not simply paraphrase, but focus also on the implied meaning of the words. Use a dictionary if you like.

   1. "Sorrow is my own yard"
   from "The Widow's Lament in Springtime"
   by WILLIAM CARLOS WILLIAMS

2. "It is a night where kings in golden suits ride elephants over the mountains."

from the conclusion of "The Country Husband" by JOHN CHEEVER

3. Oh as I was young and easy in the mercy of his means,
Time held me green and dying
Though I sang in my chains like the sea.

from "Fern Hill" by DYLAN THOMAS

4. "Cornelia's voice staggered and bumped like a cart in a bad road. It
rounded corners and turned back again and arrived nowhere. Granny
stepped up in the cart very lightly and reached for the reins, but a man
sat beside her and she knew him by his hands, driving the cart."

from "The Jilting of Granny Weatherall" by KATHERINE ANNE PORTER

5. In me thou see'st the glowing of such fire,
That on the ashes of his youth doth lie,
As the deathbed whereon it must expire,
Consumed with that which it was nourished by.

from "That Time of Year" by WILLIAM SHAKESPEARE

12.4 Description
Write your own description of a snake. Be as detailed and concrete as possible.
Turn to the Appendix and list the descriptive words which refer to the snake in
Lawrence's poem "Snake." Compare your description with his. What senses
do you use? What senses does he use? What other ways are your descriptions
similar or different? Why do you think he wrote his description the way he did?
What is he trying to emphasize? Why did you write your description the way
you did?

12.5 Description
Using adjectives, nouns, verbs, and adverbs, as well as comparisons, describe
the scene of the accident in the poem "Auto Wreck" (in Appendix). Try not to
rely too heavily on the author's words, but present the scene accurately.

12.6 Description
Describe the structure of the poem "Fern Hill" (in Appendix). Say specifically
how it looks and sounds. Reading it aloud will help you complete this exercise.

12.7 Narration
The following paragraph uses narration to prove that the first stanza in "The
Mill" (in Appendix) anticipates the miller's suicide by giving the reader the
impression that something is seriously wrong, even though the miller's wife
fights this impression. The narration includes and is followed by a brief analysis.
While the paragraph makes a good point, it is wordy because of the overuse
of the passive voice and the verb *to be*. Change as many of these verbs as
possible to active verbs or verbs other than *is* and *are*. You will probably have
to revise the sentences to do this. The verbs are underlined.

The first stanza in "The Mill" conveys the feelings of waning hope and
growing anticipation. The miller's return is awaited by his wife. He is unusually
delayed which is made clear by the tea which is seen as cold and the fire
which is seen as dead. The wife is still hopeful that nothing is wrong, but she
is worried by her husband's manner and words. The full meaning of his words,
" 'There are no millers any more' " (l. 5), is not understood by her. But his odd
behavior is noticed as the miller seems to linger endlessly at the door. The

reader, however, is prepared for the suicide by the miller's action and words and by his wife's uneasiness. That all is not normal is seen immediately by the reader, while the desperate hope that "there might yet be nothing wrong" (l. 3) is held on to by the wife. The reader knows that something terrible is about to happen.

12.8 Definition
Define the following terms and names taken from works in the Appendix. Show how your definition can be worked into a discussion of these works.

1. "*True Romance* magazine" ("The Country Husband")
2. "Jupiter" ("The Country Husband")
3. "Dr. Herzog" ("The Country Husband")
4. "locusts" ("Auto Wreck")
5. "tourniquets" ("Auto Wreck")
6. "convalescents" ("Auto Wreck")
7. "stillbirth" ("Auto Wreck")
8. "windfall" ("Fern Hill")
9. "Adam and maiden" ("Fern Hill")
10. "miller" ("The Mill")

12.9 Comparison
Develop the following topic sentences using comparison and any other methods you find useful. The literary works mentioned are in the Appendix. Indicate the methods you used to develop the paragraph.

1. The widow's reaction to spring has changed since her husband has died. (Compare past and present in "The Widow's Lament in Springtime.")
2. The narrator in Lawrence's poem compares the snake to "a king in exile." (What similarities does the snake have to "a king in exile" in "Snake"?)
3. In portraying the effects of time on the narrator, Shakespeare compares growing old to a tree in late autumn. (What similarities do you see between the image present in the poem and growing old?)
4. In the last stanza, Dylan Thomas shows how the adult narrator has been exiled from childhood. (Show the differences in the narrator's condition in the last stanza of "Fern Hill" and the previous stanzas.)

PARAGRAPH PATTERNS

As we mentioned earlier, each of the seven methods of paragraph development rarely occurs alone in our paragraphs. More likely we'll draw on a number of the methods in developing even one point. While there are numerous combinations of methods possible in one paragraph, it would be very difficult to write a paragraph about literature without using both illustration and analysis. Illustration and analysis are fundamental ways of developing a critical point. The illustration, which is drawn from the literary work, may also include description or narration. The illustration provides evidence from the literary work showing the validity of the topic sentence.

But it's not enough just to present this evidence; the reader must be made to see how the evidence proves the point at hand. Thus a discussion of the evidence is necessary. The discussion usually involves analysis and any other useful methods.

There are two common paragraph patterns using illustration and analysis:

1. the three-tiered paragraph
2. the multi-tiered paragraph

In the three-tiered paragraph, there are three levels of discussion[1]: the first is the topic sentence, the point of the paragraph; this is the broadest part of the discussion. The next is more specific—the example(s) which support the topic sentence. Finally, the third level narrows the discussion down to specific components of the example(s) and how they prove the topic sentence. Thus the three-tiered paragraph becomes progressively narrower as its content becomes more specific.

Some writers like to add a fourth step to this structure, which ends the paragraph on a broader scale by reaffirming the main point. This variation would look slightly different:

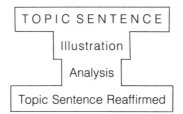

Of course, the topic sentence isn't repeated verbatim, but a variation is introduced which ideally acknowledges the development of the point within the paragraph and makes a transition to the next paragraph.

Let's look at the following example, a paragraph written on the first image in Robert Herrick's poem, "To the Virgins, to Make Much of Time" (in Appendix).

---

[1]In his essay "A Tagmemic Approach to Paragraph Analysis," reprinted in *The Sentence and the Paragraph* (Urbana, Ill.: National Council of Teachers of English, 1966), pp. 33–38, A. L. Becker discusses the three levels of generality in a paragraph, although his paradigm (TRI) ends with illustration as the most specific level.

TOPIC SENTENCE	In the first stanza, Herrick presents the fragility of youth.
ILLUSTRATION	The images of the "rosebuds" and the smiling "flower" establish this point.
ANALYSIS (including some comparison)	The rosebuds are a symbol of the young girls who are picking them. They, like the rosebuds, are young and fresh. They have not yet experienced life fully. They have not yet blossomed. Herrick stresses the shortness of the flower's life and of youth. Roses are certainly radiant, but they do not last long. In personifying the flower—Herrick says it "smiles"—he connects it to the human experience. The young girls, like the flowers, will be radiant for a brief moment, as time, which moves swiftly, takes away their beauty and ushers in death.

The above paragraph could end on a broader note, using the alternate pattern, if the writer concluded with a sentence like:

TOPIC SENTENCE REAFFIRMED	Thus Herrick creates a sense of urgency at the outset of the poem, as he reminds the young women that they, like the flowers, will soon mature, lose their beauty, and die.

This sentence is not an exact repetition of the topic sentence, but it contains the main point, notes the gist of the discussion within the paragraph, and looks forward to the next paragraph in this essay, which continues a discussion of the urgency mentioned in this sentence.

This next paragraph considers the tone or "urgency" as reflected in images of time in Herrick's poem. The pattern of this paragraph, however, is multi-tiered:

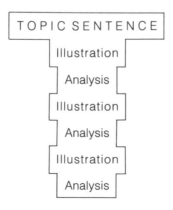

In this paragraph pattern, more than one illustration is used, but the illustrations are discussed one at a time. They are not all presented at the beginning of the paragraph, as in the first pattern. Each of the illustrations refers back to the topic sentence, and each analysis discusses the illustration preceding it. The multi-tiered paragraph may also be concluded with a reaffirmation of the topic sentence, as the three-tiered paragraph can be.

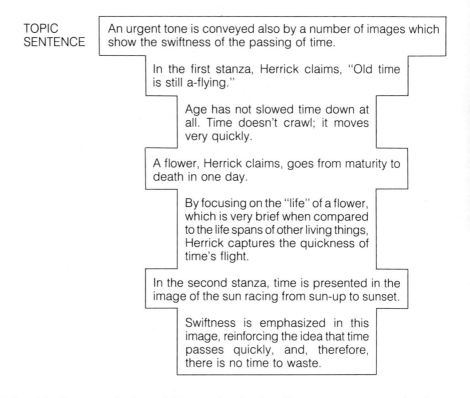

TOPIC SENTENCE — An urgent tone is conveyed also by a number of images which show the swiftness of the passing of time.

In the first stanza, Herrick claims, "Old time is still a-flying."

Age has not slowed time down at all. Time doesn't crawl; it moves very quickly.

A flower, Herrick claims, goes from maturity to death in one day.

By focusing on the "life" of a flower, which is very brief when compared to the life spans of other living things, Herrick captures the quickness of time's flight.

In the second stanza, time is presented in the image of the sun racing from sun-up to sunset.

Swiftness is emphasized in this image, reinforcing the idea that time passes quickly, and, therefore, there is no time to waste.

We've sifted out analysis and illustration in the diagram to try to make the point clearer, but in actual writing, analysis and illustration are frequently combined in the same sentence. The important thing to remember is that you need both illustration and analysis to support your topic sentence fully.

• EXERCISES

12.10 Choose an essay from Chapter 10 and describe the development of the middle paragraphs. Identify the topic sentences, and label the parts of the paragraph: illustration, analysis, description, narration, classification, definition, or comparison. Decide whether each paragraph is a three-tiered paragraph or a multi-tiered paragraph.

12.11 Choose one of your own essays and follow the steps outlined in Exercise 12.10. Are there any illustrations which are not followed by analysis? Are there other ways of developing the paragraphs which you would include in a revision?

12.12 Choose two of the topic sentences which you have narrowed in Exercise 12.1. Develop one according to the three-tiered pattern and the other according to the multi-tiered pattern.

chapter 13

MIDDLE PARAGRAPHS: EVIDENCE

Writers frequently rely upon the fundamental pattern of *assertion and support* in developing their essays. Writing about literature is no different. The assertion is usually an interpretation of the literary work set forth in the thesis and refined in the topic sentences. The assertion may be an evaluation of a character, the tracing of a theme or the effect of a series of images, or perhaps an assessment of the structure of a work and its relation to the theme. The possibilities are numerous; many have been set forth in previous chapters. In this chapter we'll consider specifically what constitutes support or evidence in a literary essay.

When we think of evidence, perhaps a number of standard types come to mind—statistics, testimony of experts, facts. But the courtroom analogy is limited. What have facts to do with fiction? How do we support a literary interpretation? The answer is simple: with the words of the literary work, with the "facts" or incidents in a story, with the images in a poem. Although the answer seems obvious, the application—drawing evidence from a literary work to support a thesis—requires skill and discipline. You're limited to the literary work for evidence and cannot change, nor add to, what is written. You must also have a selective eye and an ear for smooth transitions in choosing quotes and incorporating them into the text of your essay. The following sections in this chapter will discuss the selection and incorporation of evidence in a literary essay and the common problems which you should avoid in supporting your literary interpretations.

THE PRINCIPLE OF SELECTION:
SUMMARY AND SPECIFIC REFERENCE

We're all familiar with the stereotypical husband and wife comic routine where one spouse, usually the wife, is long-winded when responding to a specific question, digressing into a long, wandering story, apparently unrelated to the point at hand. After exasperating her listeners, she finally comes to the point. The audience laughs. The character, seemingly slow-witted and absent-minded, turns out to be intelligent and perceptive. There is a germ of truth or relevance in her story as she finally makes her point.

This comic ploy might be appropriate for TV situation comedies, but telling the whole story from the beginning without omitting a detail is not an effective or efficient way to write a critical essay. The writer doesn't want to try the reader's patience, nor elicit questions such as, "What has this to do with the main point?" The effective literary essay presents evidence *selectively* from the story or poem. The evidence is not lost in a summary, but highlighted. Not every detail in the work of literature will be relevant to the specific interpretation chosen as the thesis for a literary essay, though you must always be fair to the story, poem, or play and not ignore details which seem to contradict your thesis. Contradictory details must be accounted for and acknowledged in an interpretation, but irrelevant details should be omitted.

There is a difference between summarizing the plot of a work and using specific references to support a thesis about a literary work. A book report is a summary, a piece of writing that briefly touches upon the main points of a story in the order in which they are written. A critical essay is an interpretation, a piece of writing that employs *selective* details from a literary work to prove a point.

The following guidelines may help you choose evidence appropriately and selectively:

1. Remember that unless you are doing a review, the audience for whom you are writing has read the story, play, or poem. There is no need to repeat it for the reader's information.
2. It is not necessary to follow the exact chronology of the story, play, or poem (from beginning to middle to end) when discussing it in a critical essay. It is permissible, sometimes even desirable, to skip back and forth to different parts of the work. For some topics, however, following the chronology of the work is helpful.
3. Reference to the literary work should support a point, usually specified somewhere in the paragraph in a topic sentence.
4. When you are referring to the story, play, or poem to support an assertion, you need cite only pertinent details, not *all* the details in a particular scene or stanza.

The following paragraphs from an essay on the setting in John Cheever's "The Country Husband" (in Appendix) try to make the same point using topic sentences and similar evidence. However, the first paragraph summarizes, while the second uses evidence from the story selectively and more appropriately. Note the length of *discussion* and *interpretation* (underlined in the paragraphs) of the plot elements in the second paragraph compared with the lack of discussion in the first paragraph:

A. "The Country Husband" is set in a typical suburban town where everyone is happy and no one is supposed to have any problems. Every day the husbands are expected to take the train to work in the city, while the wives take care of the children at home. The husbands return by train; the families then have supper, and later the husbands and wives go out to a party. One day, while Francis is coming home by plane from a trip, he is almost killed in a plane crash. When he gets home, no one sympathizes or even takes notice of his near brush with death. He tries desperately to get a little recognition from his family, first telling his little son, then his oldest daughter, and finally the whole family including his wife, but he is ignored. His daughter prefers her magazine to talking with her father. The dinner scene that takes place is anything but sympathetic. When dinner is over, Francis goes out into the garden to think. In another scene, there is a party. Francis realizes that he recognizes the maid from his experience in the war. She is a French woman who had lived with a German officer when the Germans occupied France. The town punished her by publicly shaving her head and making her walk out of the town naked. Francis could not tell anyone at the party of this experience. But even worse, he couldn't trust his wife enough to tell her later either.

B. Shady Hill, the setting of "The Country Husband," is a superficially happy, very repressive suburban community. The more unpleasant aspects of life are never discussed in Shady Hill and, therefore, presumed not to exist. Social activities are what Shady Hill highlights. At dinner with his family, Francis has difficulty communicating about the plane crash and his brush with death, an unpleasant occurrence. At a subsequent dinner party which he attends, he cannot talk about his war experience or the maid's humiliation, but then a party may not be the appropriate place for such a discussion; however, he cannot trust Julia enough to tell her later either. There is never an appropriate place or moment for Francis to communicate his true feelings. He cannot, for instance, communicate his desire for the babysitter to his friend, Pinky Trabert. Julia best catches the attitude of Shady Hill when she reprimands Francis for his one moment of outspokenness. She says, "I don't know what makes you think that in a community like this you can indulge every impulse you have to be insulting, vulgar, and offensive." Unfortunately for Francis, most of what makes him feel intensely alive is either insulting, vulgar, or offensive, and, therefore, unacceptable to Shady Hill.

Paragraph A attempts to prove that Shady Hill is "a typical suburban town where everyone is happy and no one is supposed to have any problems." Some of the incidents cited, of course, show that this statement is not accurate and that, if the surface impression is that everyone in Shady Hill is happy, the reality is that Francis Weed is not. The first part of the paragraph presents the routine life of Shady Hill, but no connection is drawn between the routine presented and the topic sentence. There is no discussion of how this routine proves Shady Hill to be typical or happy. The dinner scene and Francis' war experience are both summarized in detail in this paragraph, but many of the details are not relevant to the discussion of the community of Shady Hill, and neither incident is related to the topic sentence through discussion. Compare the treatment of the war scene in both paragraphs. Paragraph A summarizes the whole history of the maid; paragraph B recognizes that the reader has read the story and will understand the reference. The whole story of the maid is not relevant to the point being made in this paragraph—that Shady Hill is repressive and that Francis cannot communicate his unpleasant experience. While paragraph A is full of references to the story, the references are not selective, nor are they discussed. This paragraph is defective and lapses into summary. Paragraph B uses evidence from the story appropriately.

- **EXERCISE**

13.1 The following paragraphs contain plot details which are unnecessary to the point of the paragraph. After reviewing the literary works in the Appendix, revise these paragraphs by identifying the main point, eliminating unnecessary details, and relating evidence from the work to the topic sentence of the paragraph through discussion.

On "The Jilting of Granny Weatherall" by Katherine Anne Porter:

A.   Granny Weatherall, as her name suggests, is a strong, active woman, who has weathered many adversities. She remembers the time she fenced in a hundred acres, digging the holes for the posts herself. The Negro boy helped her clamp the wires. She has changed, and her husband, if he were alive, would not recognize her. She used to be young and wear a comb in her hair and carry a fan. She used to help deliver babies and sit up with sick people, hardly ever losing one. The children looked to her for protection. When they'd come in from the dark, she would light the lamps and say a prayer. She would supervise the fruit-picking so that nothing was wasted. She only took little naps. She seemed never to tire.

On "The River-Merchant's Wife: A Letter" by Ezra Pound:

B.   Nature seems to reflect the narrator's sad feelings in the final stanzas of "The River-Merchant's Wife." The monkeys probably are making the same sound they always do, but the river-merchant's wife interprets the noise as "sorrowful" since she is feeling sorrowful because she misses her husband. She remembers how her husband dragged his feet when he left. The moss is overgrown. Autumn seems to be coming earlier. She notices the paired butterflies. She sees that she is growing older. She asks her husband in the conclusion of this letter to let her know if he will be traveling through "the narrows of the river Kiang" so that she can go out to meet him.

On "Snake" by D. H. Lawrence:

C. Using carefully selected images, Lawrence shows that the snake in his poem is much more than just a snake, something almost human, even godlike. Early in the poem, the snake is mostly a reptile: "trailed his yellow-brown slackness soft-bellied down" and "flickered his two-forked tongue." The day is hot, and the speaker and the snake are parched and thirsty. The snake comes from a hole in the wall, a "fissure," and probably from somewhere deep in the earth, as the speaker says, "from the burning bowels of the earth." There are references to the black snakes in Sicily being innocent and the gold ones as venomous. The snake in the poem is brownish gold and, therefore, a great danger to the speaker. At one point, the snake is compared with cattle, later as a quiet guest, and still later as a god and a king. So, one can see that the snake means something more than just a reptile who came for a drink.

Including All Relevant Details

In trying to support an interpretation of a literary work in an essay, the writer has an obligation not only to select details carefully and to sift out irrelevant material, but also to be honest to the literary work and to the audience. That is, the writer cannot ignore evidence in the story, play, or poem which contradicts the thesis of the essay. We're all familiar with tactics for "stretching the truth" by omitting pertinent details—like the child who, when asked by his teacher why his homework is not done, responds that there was a death in the family, knowing full well that it was his goldfish that died and that the teacher would assume a relative had died. The success of this tack depends upon the listener's ignorance.

In writing about literature, however, you cannot assume an ill-informed audience. The reader has the same access to information as the writer and will rightly call into question any interpretation which omits relevant details, whether deliberately or by oversight. Following are two paragraphs from different essays on Cheever's "The Country Husband." The first paragraph attempts to take appropriate account of the details which seem to contradict the main point—that Francis Weed is a loner. The second paragraph takes no account of evidence in the story which may question, if not contradict, the judgment that Francis Weed is insensitive.

A. Although he and his family are acclaimed in the social circle of his community and although he often goes to parties, Francis is still very much alone and probably doesn't have many friends. Julia seems to be the impetus behind their social life. Somehow it seems that Francis is not too pleased with the presence of too many people, and he openly admits it. He says to his wife,

"Julia, I do love you, and I would like to be as we were—sweet and bawdy and dark—but now there are so many people." Francis' wife points out how Francis is alone and doesn't have many friends. First she says, "You were alone when I met you, Francis Weed, and you'll be alone when I leave." Then Julia uses their wedding as an example. She reminds Francis of how only two people showed up for their wedding out of the fourteen invitations that he had sent out.

B.   Francis Weed is very insensitive to the needs of his family. He upsets both his wife, Julia, and his son, Toby, with his callousness when the family is at dinner in an early part of the story. He asks Julia "if the children couldn't have their dinner earlier," before he comes home. It is selfish of him not to want to dine with his children. After all, he hasn't seen them all day. Besides his lack of understanding for the children, Francis does not really appreciate all Julia has done—the cooking, the cleaning, and the laundry. Instead he picks a fight with her claiming that he doesn't like "to come home every night to a battlefield," as if it is Julia's fault that the children are fighting. Francis Weed only cares about himself, and he proves it by how he treats his family.

The writer of the second paragraph omits the fact that Francis has just been in a plane crash—not a normal everyday occurrence—and is himself in need of attention. His nearly fatal experience makes his short temper understandable, if not forgivable.

In writing or reading over your paper, if you discover details in the literary work which seem to challenge or contradict your interpretation, you have two alternatives. You can:

1. take account of these challenging details and show the reader that they have been considered and still do not make the thesis invalid;
2. modify or change the thesis to be more consistent with the new contradictory evidence.

• EXERCISE

13.2   The following prewriting guides take into account that not all details in a story, play, or poem may fit neatly into the writer's analysis. After reading Porter's "The Jilting of Granny Weatherall" (in Appendix) or another work assigned by your instructor, use Guide I to write a paragraph about the *main character*. After reading Williams' "The Widow's Lament in Springtime" (in Appendix) or another work assigned by your instructor, use Guide II to write one paragraph about the imagery used to convey the *setting*.

CHARACTER WORKSHEET
Prewriting Guide I

1. In one or two sentences, describe the character assigned. Use at least three personality traits in your description. Adjectives such as "kind," "bold," "stingy," "stubborn" are useful descriptive words. Underline the three qualities.

2. Choose one of the qualities you just mentioned. List briefly two or more incidents which prove that the character has this quality.

   Character trait:
   Incidents:

3. Are there any incidents in the story which would seem to disprove your character analysis? For example, if you see a character as brave, are there any incidents in the story where he or she may be perceived as cowardly? If such evidence exists, then briefly explain why it may not be inconsistent with your perception of the character.

4. Is there a quote in the story which is particularly appropriate in pointing out the characteristic you've chosen to develop? If so, cite the quotation here.

5. In a paragraph, develop one trait of the assigned character:

   a. In the topic sentence, mention the character and the quality you're about to develop.

   b. In the body of the paragraph, cite evidence for this quality, explaining how the incidents mentioned in No. 2 prove your point and how incidents mentioned in No. 3 do not disprove your point. You may incorporate the quote in No. 4 into your paragraph. Be sure to develop your points by relating details to the topic sentence with discussion, writing in full sentences with smooth transitions.

SETTING WORKSHEET
Prewriting Guide II

1. In one or two sentences, describe the setting in the assigned work. Use at least two descriptive words. Adjectives, such as "gloomy," "confining," or "cheerful," might help to characterize the mood created by the setting. Underline the descriptive qualities.

2. Choose one of the qualities you just mentioned above and list two or more details of the setting which bring out this quality.

   Quality:
   Details:

3. Are there any details in the story, play, or poem which would seem to prove the opposite of the quality you've chosen to develop? For example, if you say the setting is gloomy, is it consistently gloomy, or are there times when the setting is bright or cheerful? If the setting is not consistent throughout the work, is there a point to the inconsistency?

4. Does the setting tell you something about the character? The theme? Does it serve some other purpose? What is that purpose?

5. Is there a quote from the literary work which would be particularly appropriate in pointing out the characteristic of the setting which you've chosen to develop? If so, cite the lines here.

6. In a paragraph, develop one quality of the setting in the work assigned.

   a. In the topic sentence, mention the quality and its importance, its significance to the character, theme, or other elements. Consider your answers to questions 1, 3, and 4 in phrasing your main point.

   b. In the body of the paragraph, develop your topic sentence with evidence and discussion. Incorporate as much of sections 2, 3, 4, and 5 as possible into your paragraph.

RELIABLE INTERPRETATIONS

Sometimes you may feel hampered or restricted by the lack of information and the unanswered questions that stories, plays, and poems raise. In trying to strengthen an interpretation, a writer may be tempted to fill in the chinks in a literary work. However, if the essay is to prove a valid point about the work, you cannot change the work in any way. Just as you cannot ignore relevant details which may contradict or challenge an interpretation, you cannot create details which are not present in the literary work to support a point. You must interpret the work of literature *as it is written*, with all the questions and ambiguities it leaves unresolved.

Consider the evidence used in the following paragraph on Porter's "The Jilting of Granny Weatherall." Some of the evidence is drawn from the story; other portions are laden with speculations which fill in the holes Porter has deliberately left in the story.

> Although a strong woman in other respects, Granny Weatherall never really recovers from her loss of George. Sixty years later, on her deathbed, she still has not forgotten nor forgiven him. The emotional wound has not healed. She remembers the day he jilted her as the day that "The whole bottom dropped out of the world. . . ." He left her waiting at the altar. He did not love her. He ran off, and she never heard from him again. Perhaps he married someone else. He does not know that she is dying and is still thinking of him. She still loves George. Granny even named one of her children "George," not "John," after her husband. Although she still had a full life with a husband and children, Granny feels that George robbed her of something. Something is missing: "Something not given back." Maybe George was rich, and their life together would have been different from her hard life with John. Or maybe George had a great destiny she could have shared. George was her first love, and maybe she couldn't love anyone again as she loved him.

Since the story is told from Granny Weatherall's perspective, we know only as much about George as she reveals. Given her wandering state of mind, she provides us only with sporadic and spotty information which, when pieced together, certainly whets our appetites for the whole story. Yet the fact is that the whole story is never told; the reader is left with many unanswered questions, and to answer them would change the story. The writer of this paragraph speculates about Granny's relationship to George, about what their life together would have been like, and about what became of George. Such evidence is not in the story.

- ## EXERCISE

    13.3 Write a paragraph using appropriate evidence to support one of the following points. (All of the works are in the Appendix.)

    1. Granny Weatherall is a proud woman. ("The Jilting of Granny Weatherall")
    2. Julia Weed is a dependent woman. ("The Country Husband")
    3. The narrator fears and respects the snake. ("Snake")

4. The final paragraph of "The Country Husband" is a positive (or negative) ending.
5. The tone of "The Widow's Lament in Springtime" is melancholy.

TO QUOTE OR TO PARAPHRASE

Accurate interpretations and convincing critical essays are securely anchored to the work of literature through the frequent use of specific references to the story, play, or poem. These references are carefully selected to eliminate unnecessary summary. You can make reference to a literary work in a number of different ways. Consider the following three paragraphs, each of which presents a different form of literary evidence.

A. On Pound's "The River-Merchant's Wife: A Letter" and Williams' "The Widow's Lament in Springtime"

The narrators of the poems "The River-Merchant's Wife" and "The Widow's Lament in Springtime" are both women who miss their husbands. The river-merchant's wife is only 16 and has been married for only two years. She misses her husband who has been gone on a journey for the last five months. The widow had been married for 35 years. Her husband's departure is obviously permanent, and her grief is, therefore, more intense. The river-merchant's wife still has hope that her husband will return. This hope is made clear at the end of her letter where she offers to meet him on his journey home. The widow also wants to rejoin her husband. She no longer finds any joy in life and, at the end of the poem, expresses a desire to sink into the marsh and die.

B. On Cheever's "The Country Husband"

The first section of "The Country Husband" marks a change in Francis Weed which the reader can only appreciate later in the story. Francis is deeply affected by the plane crash. His senses seem to come alive. He watches the blackness outside the plane interrupted by the sparks from the engine, while the lights inside the plane flicker and go out. He feels the plane dropping; he feels his foot going to sleep; he notices the compartment is hot and stuffy; he is violently jolted by the landing, a physical sensation followed by the relief of being on the ground and still alive. During his ordeal, he hears a child crying, listens to the belated wishes of a fellow passenger, the warning of the stewardess, the song of the pilot, and the noticeable silence followed by the rumblings and squeals of an injured aircraft. After the landing, he is soothed by the sound and smell of rain. One noticeable item in the series of sensations Francis experiences might clue the reader into the fact that life has changed for Francis—the window curtains, those symbols of suburban civilization and isolation. Instead of finding the curtains a comforting sign, a reminder of home at a trying time, Francis observes that the curtains are misplaced in this atmosphere. Domesticity, tameness, has no place with the vivid sensations to which Francis has awakened. In this revitalized state, Francis returns to suburban Shady Hill.

C. On Pound's "The River-Merchant's Wife: A Letter"

The girl's feelings for her husband between the time of their marriage and the time of his departure have dramatically changed. As she so simply states, "At fourteen I married My Lord you." Her phrasing, especially her reference to her husband as "My Lord," would indicate a certain reverence for him, which is perhaps a cultural expectation which does not mesh with her actions, which indicate that she is not very happy in her new state. "Called to, a thousand times, I never looked back," she claims. She was not very obedient and did not respond readily to her husband's wishes. The next stanza, while also recording her change in feelings a year later, tells a bit more about her behavior in her first year of marriage. "At fifteen I stopped scowling," implies that at fourteen she must have scowled a lot. And when she questions, "Why should I climb the look out?" she indirectly admits that her previous dissatisfactions were frequently expressed by climbing the look out to gaze elsewhere, probably with unsaid hopes and desires. The most telling lines, however, indicating her change of feelings toward her husband are the lines: "I desired my dust to be mingled with yours / Forever and forever and forever." Her desire to be with him in death extends beyond the permanence familiarly expressed in Western marriage vows where the partners promise "till death do us part." Her endless devotion is emphasized by the careful repetition of "forever."

The writer of paragraph A makes *brief critical references* to the poems by mentioning details from the works to prove a point. The writer of paragraph B makes reference to the story by retelling a portion of the story, rephrasing it to prove his point. This technique is called *paraphrasing*. The writer of paragraph C uses *quotations*, the author's own words, as evidence to prove a point.

You'll probably use all three types of evidence in any literary essay— brief critical references to details in the literary work, more extensive paraphrasing of sections of the work, and selected quotations from the work. These sample paragraphs are deliberately limited to one type of evidence in order to illustrate each type. The writer of paragraph B, for example, might just as effectively have used quotations in combination with paraphrase to illustrate the topic sentence. While you're free to use a combination of evidence as appropriate, it may take some practice both to recognize what kind of reference would be most effective in a particular situation and to combine different kinds of evidence appropriately.

Brief critical references are probably the most common type of evidence, because they are concise and easily embedded in a discussion of the literary work. Citing a specific word or incident is especially effective when you're tracing patterns within the work, such as a pattern of images or a series of connected actions. Such references also serve to remind the reader of details discussed perhaps more fully in a previous section of the essay. Brief critical references are also common evidence in comparisons, as in sample paragraph A. They may also serve you well in an essay or sections of an essay where an in-depth analysis of the text is not required.

Sometimes, however, you will find that to make a point effectively in a literary essay, a detailed analysis of a section of a story, a scene in a play, or a line or stanza in a poem is called for, and a brief critical reference to an event, image, or character is not enough. You must cite the work more fully by either paraphrasing or quoting the author's own words, or by using a combination of these two methods. The decision should not be haphazard, but informed by the effect each method will have upon the essay and the reader. There are advantages and disadvantages to either method. Consider the following questions:

> How do you, as a reader, react when you come upon long and numerous quotations in an essay you are reading?

> What demands do quotations make upon a reader, especially if they are numerous and from different sources and, therefore, written in different styles? What effect do they have upon the essay?

> What advantages do you gain by using a quotation? by paraphrasing?

> Why and when should you use a direct quote?

The skillful use of *quotations* takes consideration and practice. A quotation provides the reader with the author's words *verbatim*. There is an advantage in citing the author's words when the way the words are phrased is particularly impressive or important, when you know that rephrasing the author's words would inevitably result in a loss of meaning or sense which is important to the point you're making. When you're calling attention to the words of the author, quotation, of course, is necessary. It is essential, for example, in discussions of style. Poetry, in particular, loses some of the original sense when paraphrased, and, therefore, you might find yourself quoting more frequently in critical writing on poetry.

One disadvantage of quotations, however, is that they are written in a style other than your own and thus tend to break up an essay. They cause the reader to stop and to readjust his or her inner reading voice to accommodate yet another person's words. Used in excess, quotations can make an essay very choppy, a stop-and-go trek for the reader. Here *paraphrasing* has an advantage. Since in paraphrasing you assimilate the thoughts and words of the source and rephrase them in your own words and style, the essay reads more smoothly. Quotations, however, do add variety to an essay and keep it from becoming monotonous. The goal, of course, is to find the appropriate proportion so that your essay is spiced with quotations without being overwhelmed. Even some experienced writers have difficulty keeping quotations in check.

Paraphrasing also has another advantage worth mentioning. In paraphrasing you are able to refocus a scene or segment of a story for the reader, not by changing the story, but by highlighting undercurrents present but not emphasized in the writer's words. Much the way a magazine photographer at a parade might view the whole panorama—the crowd, the bands, the floats—and then snap a picture of a little girl in the crowd smiling and eating cotton candy to capture the delight of the entire scene, so the essay writer, in retelling an event from a story, might emphasize a particular element in order to prove a point. That element may not have been emphasized by the author, whose subject is usually broader than the subject of any one literary analysis.

For example, consider paragraph B on page 213. This paragraph analyzes the first section of Cheever's "The Country Husband," using paraphrase. The writer, however, has reordered the details in Cheever's story to suit a purpose. Wishing to show that Francis is very much aware of the physical sensations around him, the writer has ordered the details according to the different senses of seeing, touching, hearing, and smelling. If you look back at the paragraph in the story from which these details are taken, you will note that the writer has highlighted what is present more subtly in Cheever's words.

As a general guideline:

1. Quote when the *author's words* are particularly important.
2. Quote in moderation.
3. Paraphrase with an eye toward proving the point you are making.

THE MISUSE OF QUOTATIONS

Paraphrasing without quoting is an acceptable way to provide evidence in a literary paper, as is quoting without paraphrasing. Even more effective is a combination of the two methods. But paraphrasing or quoting *without critical comment* does not advance the paper's discussion. Some writers mistake paraphrase for critical comment in a literary essay and thus repeat evidence instead of discussing and interpreting it. Compare this paragraph on "The River-Merchant's Wife" (in Appendix) to paragraph C on the same topic, page 214.

> The girl's feelings for her husband between the time of their marriage and the time of his departure have dramatically changed in "The River-Merchant's Wife." As she simply states, "At fourteen I married My Lord you." She married her husband, whom she considers her "Lord" when she was only fourteen. But she is not very happy in her new state. "I never laughed, being bashful. / Lowering my head, I looked at the wall. / Called to, a thousand times, I never looked back." She never laughs; she looks at the wall, and she doesn't even turn around when she is called. The next stanza records her change in feelings toward her husband. She says, "At fifteen I stopped scowling," indicating that she has stopped frowning. She asks, "Why should I climb the look out?" She doesn't see any reason to climb the look out. The most telling lines, however, indicating her change of feelings toward her husband are the lines: "I desired my dust to be mingled with yours / Forever and forever and forever." Her desire is to be with her husband even after death, with their dust mingling forever.

There is a difference between paraphrasing—repeating what is said in your own words—and commenting upon a quote. The above paragraph uses paraphrase simply to repeat the substance of each quotation. Critical comment or interpretation is virtually absent as compared to paragraph C on page 214, and the writer seems confused as to the purpose of quoting or paraphrasing. Both serve as evidence. The writer should either quote the lines and comment upon them—without paraphrasing them—or paraphrase (some of) the lines and omit the corresponding quotes. Omitting either the paraphrasing or the quotation and adding critical commentary will avoid the repetition.

Sometimes an insecure writer may fix upon quotations as a way to fill out an essay. When quotations are used in excess, the essay becomes a string of quotes loosely tied together by a sentence or two of transition. Like a collage, the essay is pieced together. In severe cases, if the quotations were eliminated from the essay, a mere paragraph or two of the writer's own words might be left. Compare the following paragraphs on Lawrence's "Snake" (in Appendix).

A. Since the devil in the form of a snake tempted Eve in the Garden of Eden and led her to disobey God and commit the first sin, the snake has been associated with evil in the Judaic-Christian world. Lawrence takes advantage of this cultural association, and through the netherworld images in "Snake," brings to mind the snake's evil nature. "He reached down from a fissure in the earth-wall in the gloom." He is described as "Being earth-brown, earth-golden from the burning bowels of the earth / On the day of Sicilian July, with Etna smoking." He departs again, "Into the burning bowels of this earth." He inspires fear in the narrator because he comes "From out the dark door of the secret earth," "withdrawing into that horrid black hole, / Deliberately going into the blackness. . . ." The snake is associated with blackness, "his tongue like a forked night on the air, so black. . . ." The narrator concludes that the snake was "Like a king in exile, uncrowned in the underworld. . . ."

B. Since the devil in the form of a snake tempted Eve in the Garden of Eden and led her to disobey God and commit the first sin, the snake has been associated with evil in the Judaic-Christian world. Lawrence takes advantage of this cultural association, and through the use of netherworld images in "Snake," he brings to mind the snake's evil nature. The "horrid, black hole," "dark door," "burning bowels of the earth," and "the blackness" suggest more than a snake hole; they remind the reader of the darkness and fires of hell. Hellfire is again suggested by the image of smouldering Mount Etna, a reminder of the regions from which the snake emerges, as well as a symbol of potential danger and destruction. The narrator finally associates the snake with a "king in exile, uncrowned in the underworld." With this simile, the narrator makes explicit the implicit associations made between the snake and the devil throughout the poem and unearths some reasons for man's fear and disdain of this creature.

Paragraph A misuses quotations; paragraph B uses quotations more appropriately. Note the lack of critical discussion (the underlined portions) in the first paragraph compared to the second. The writer of paragraph B interprets for the reader; the writer of paragraph A does not. The writer of paragraph A has carefully chosen the quotations for this paragraph but lets the quotations speak alone, providing little or no discussion after the first two sentences. Without guidance from the writer, the reader will wonder why a particular quotation is important. What exactly does the writer wish to convey by these quotations? What should the reader see? Remember: the reader can only read what is written and can only guess what is intended but unwritten. Unfortunately many fine thoughts are lost when a writer fails to discuss the quotations chosen to illustrate a point. If a line is important enough to quote, it is important enough to discuss.

THE MECHANICS OF QUOTATION

Incorporating quotations into your essay takes skill and knowledge. Skill is involved in introducing the quote in such a way that the transition between your words and the quotation is a smooth one. Knowledge of the conventions of punctuation will help you achieve a smooth transition. There are basically three ways to introduce a quotation, each one achieving a different transitional effect.

Quotation marks only. The smoothest transition between your own words and a quotation is achieved when the quotation becomes part of your sentence, and no pause or punctuation, other than quotation marks, breaks the flow of the sentence. For example, the following sentence smoothly incorporates Cheever's words into the text of the sentence without a pause; in speaking of Francis and Julia Weed, the writer states,

> He later goes on to tell her that "he doesn't like to come home every night to a battlefield."

Speaking verb, comma, quotation marks. Using a comma and quotation marks is a more common method of introducing a quote. The comma signals a brief pause, indicating a change of voice. This method is used when the speaker is present. Verbs such as "say," "question," "ask," "state," "admit," and others will introduce this direct quotation (without a "that"). In the following sentence Julia Weed is quoted.

> She says, "I don't know what makes you think that in a community like this you can indulge every impulse you have to be insulting, vulgar, and offensive."

Colon, quotation marks. The most abrupt and formal method of introducing a quotation calls for a colon (:) and quotation marks. This method is most common when lines of poetry are quoted. Colons are also sometimes used to introduce long prose quotations. The following example is taken from a paragraph on "Snake."

The voices challenge the narrator: ". . . If you were a man / You would take a stick and break him now, and finish him off."

Note also that when lines of poetry are quoted, a slash (/) is used to indicate the end of one line and the beginning of another. Capitalization remains as in the poem.

You should try to incorporate quotations into your paper as smoothly as possible. The punctuation within the quotation should remain the same as in the source from which the quotation is taken. At the end of a quote, commas and periods are always inside the quotation marks. If other punctuation marks are part of the quotation, they remain inside the quotation marks; if they are part of your sentence, they should be placed outside the quotation marks. *"Who knows when she will leave?"* and *Did she say, "I don't know when I will leave"?* are both questions, but in the first example the quotation is a question; in the second example, the quotation is not a question. The position of the question mark indicates whether the quotation itself is a question and thus whether the question mark is part of the original source.

If you leave out any words in the middle of a quotation, use an ellipsis (. . .) to alert the reader to the fact that you've edited the quotation. If you delete a portion of the quote in which one sentence ends and another begins before you resume with the author's words, an ellipsis with four dots is required (. . . .). Four dots are also required when an incomplete quotation occurs at the end of your sentence. You must excerpt with care; make sure that in omitting words you're not changing the author's meaning.

If you introduce material of your own into a quotation, you must do so with brackets [your words], not parentheses. Even if you underline a portion of a quote which is not underlined in the original, you must indicate that you have introduced a change by noting it within brackets: [underlining added].

Quotations longer than four lines should be single-spaced and centered in your essay. More than three lines of poetry should also be single-spaced and centered, but the spacing of the words should follow the original as closely as possible.

As a writer, you are obligated to cite the sources you use. Unless your instructor asks you to do otherwise, provide a footnote with bibliographical information for the first quotation from a particular work; for subsequent quotations, cite page numbers (or line numbers for poems) in parentheses at the end of the quote (see sample essay in Chapter 17 and the Appendix on The Research Paper for examples).

chapter 14

MIDDLE PARAGRAPHS: LOGIC

The word "logic" is the descendant of an ancient Greek word, *logos*, which means both "word" and "reason" or "thought." So closely did our ancestors see words and thoughts linked that they united them in one word. Today when we speak of logic, we refer to an orderly way of knowing or understanding our world, an activity that requires words.

Imagine a world without logic. Imagine suspending all your rational abilities. Imagine living in a dream where it is impossible to predict the outcome of any event. One moment may have little or no relation to the next, and the dreamer may be pleasantly surprised or terribly horrified by events seemingly out of his or her control. Our waking world is not so free, and by using our rational faculties, we begin to see patterns and rules. By engaging our reason, we can understand, we can share our knowledge with others, and we can change our world so that we're not simply victims of unpredictable events.

Philosophers have spent centuries bringing together the rules by which we reason and the fallacies or pitfalls which keep us from proper understanding. In this chapter we'll touch on only a small segment of this knowledge: the common errors which keep us from understanding literature and clearly presenting our insights in an essay.

UNITY AND DIGRESSION

A digression is an idea which seems irrelevant to the topic of a paragraph or the purpose of an essay. It's a detour from the main journey mapped out by a topic sentence or thesis. A digression doesn't further the discussion; it calls attention to itself, confuses the reader, and causes the audience to wonder why the point is included. In short, a digression causes a paragraph or an essay to lack *unity*. In Chapter 13 we discussed one specific type of digression which frequently causes beginning literary writers to stray—that is, plot summary. When a writer summarizes a story, paraphrases a whole poem, or quotes a long dialogue when only a specific incident, image, or line is needed, that writer is digressing. We spoke of being selective of textual details to keep the essay from wandering. In this section we'll consider three other common types of digressions:

1. change of stance,
2. points which stray from the topic sentence of a paragraph,
3. points which stray from the thesis of the essay.

Change of Stance

In Chapters 1 and 11 we acknowledged that there are many different approaches a writer can take when analyzing a work of literature—psychological, sociological, political, and personal, for example. What is important once you decide on your perspective is that you don't change it in the middle of the essay. We've been considering literature as a crafted work, with parts which, when analyzed, can help us understand and appreciate the whole. If in the middle paragraphs of an essay on the structure of Cheever's "The Country Husband," we suddenly note that the story exemplifies the lack of communication in American middle-class families, we have suddenly become sociological commentators. If in discussing the characterization of Francis Weed, we stray into an evaluation of the capitalistic values of Shady Hill, we've become political readers and commentators. In each of these cases we would have changed our stance, our relationship to literature, and would have created a digression. In the critical essay, we must treat a work of literature consistently from one perspective.

The following excerpt is a middle paragraph from an essay on Anne Sexton's poem "Cinderella." The main point of this paragraph is that Anne Sexton is making fun of the instant success stories, the rags to riches stories, so common in some popular magazines. The paragraph deals with the *tone* of the poem: Anne Sexton is being sarcastic. The paragraph makes a good critical point in the topic sentence (underlined), but instead of showing how Sexton achieves this tone and what effect it has on the poem, the writer launches into a comparison of the poem and real life.

<u>The poem "Cinderella" ridicules the desire for instant riches</u>. We all wish for some miracle of wealth to happen to us. Look at our TV game shows and the prizes all of us drool over. Look at our legalized gambling operations. There are some people who actually spend their families' food money betting on race horses because they believe they are going to win a million dollars this time. Because they are so obsessed with winning, they keep on betting, no matter how many times they lose.

The poem does not mention game shows or horse racing. The writer of this paragraph is no longer looking at the poem as a literary creation with a specific tone which contributes to making its point; instead, the writer is looking at the poem as a reflection of real life and judging it to be true to life. If the purpose of the paper were to compare the poem to life, this paragraph wouldn't be a digression. However, that was not the purpose. Like an art critic who begins to discuss the effectiveness of the dark and light shading in the Van Gogh painting "The Starry Night" and then decides to go outside to see if the shading is accurate, the focus of this writer's criticism has changed from the work of art to how the work compares with reality.

In Chapter 11 we mentioned that one way of beginning a critical essay is to discuss briefly how the work exemplifies real life. But once the writer states his or her thesis, the essay has moved from a discussion of life to literature, and the reader will expect the discussion which follows to be about literature. If the focus of the essay is a critical examination of a part or the parts which make up this whole we call a story, play, or poem, then we must be careful about introducing life experience into the middle paragraphs as evidence.

Digressing into personal or moral evaluations of a work is another common way writers can stray from their stance. While both these approaches to literature are valid stances in their own right—you can certainly write an essay about how a work relates to your personal experience, or you can judge a work for its moral values or lack of values—if these approaches are included in an essay which begins by looking at literature as a crafted work, they are digressions. One of the most important ways we react to literature is personally. A story or a poem may have a special meaning for each of us and a special way it relates to our lives, but including a discussion of how Francis Weed, for example, reminds you of Uncle Harry would not further an essay on characterization, nor would condemning Francis Weed for wanting an adulterous affair help us understand the author's skill in portraying the character.

Consider the following paragraphs. Both are from essays exploring characterization. Paragraph A is about "Tanhum" by Isaac Bashevis Singer; paragraph B is about "Bartleby the Scrivener" by Herman Melville. Both writers begin with a critical point about the character in the topic sentence (underlined) but digress from their discussion of how the authors portray the characters to personal and moral criticism.

A.   <u>Tanhum has unrealistic expectations of people</u>. Many people have high expectations of others. My father, for example, expects a great deal from me as a son. He wants me to be better than average in school. He does not even question the fact that I will graduate. He expects me to choose a professional school—like law or medicine—to continue my studies. I am sure I would displease him if I did not meet his standards, but I think we could talk it out, and he would understand if I chose a different career than he expected. He would not run off to a hermitage like Tanhum did. Tanhum expects everyone to be perfect. When he finds out his future father-in-law made a mistake and is not as honest as he expected, he will have nothing to do with him. He does not understand human nature.

This paragraph shows quite a bit of understanding of Tanhum's naïveté and a great deal of personal appreciation of this story, but instead of discussing the story, this writer is discussing his own experience. If the focus of the essay were his experience of the story, this paragraph would not be out of place (though it would need a different topic sentence). But the essay is about the characterization of Tanhum.

    B.   <u>Bartleby's withdrawal becomes more and more complete in this story until he dies</u>. He not only stops working, but he stops eating too. For all intents and purposes, Bartleby has committed suicide. He has thrown away one of God's truly magnificient gifts—life. Everyone is bound to come upon hard times in his life, but that doesn't mean he should give up living. He should find strength in family, friends, and God to go on. Even if Bartleby had no family, the lawyer, who was a good man, seemed willing to help, and God never deserts a child in need. But Bartleby doesn't seem to have any faith at all. He is pitiful, and he has sinned. Taking one's own life is immoral, but perhaps in Bartleby's case he will be forgiven because he seems to be not quite sane.

Bartleby's faith or lack of faith is not mentioned in this story. It is true that he withdraws and dies. It is true that he is without both family and friends. The writer has judged Bartleby for his withdrawal on moral or religious grounds. Such a judgment is not part of the story. The context of the criticism in this paragraph is not literary; that is, the paragraph is not concerned with how the character of Bartleby is portrayed in the story or why the portrayal takes this form. This paragraph would well suit an essay which measures the moral standards exhibited in the story, but it is a digression in an essay studying a literary element—characterization.

Paragraph Unity

A unified paragraph usually develops just one idea, which is frequently embodied within a single sentence—the *topic sentence*. Each sentence in the paragraph must then further this one idea by providing, interpreting, or analyzing evidence. If we introduce material which is not related to the main point of the paragraph, we have digressed and caused an additional problem—the paragraph now lacks *unity*. It is no longer about one idea.

The paragraphs on "Cinderella" and "Tanhum" in the previous section also exhibit this problem. The "Cinderella" paragraph begins by noting how the poem ridicules instant success stories. This topic sentence leads us to expect that the following sentences will provide us with evidence from the poem. The poem, however, is not mentioned again in this paragraph. The "Tanhum" paragraph seems to be about this character's unrealistic expectations of people. We expect to be told who Tanhum wants to be perfect, how he expects the person(s) to act, and why his expectations are unreasonable. The last two sentences make some attempt at providing us with this information; however, the largest part of this paragraph by far is devoted to the writer's relationship with *his* father.

Sometimes a detour from the topic sentence will not involve the more obvious digressions we saw in section one. Sometimes the writer misplaces a point that should be elsewhere in the essay. Consider the following middle paragraph taken from an essay comparing two works in the Appendix, Williams' "The Widow's Lament in Springtime" and Robinson's "The Mill." See if you can pick out the topic sentence and the digression in this paragraph.

> The women consider suicide at the end of both poems as a soothing union with nature. The widow of Williams' poem desires to "sink into the marsh" or to "fall into those flowers," the white flowers near the woods. The motion in these lines is downward, as into a grave. They also indicate a giving up, a yielding to nature which in its springtime bloom would cover her over. This desire is more obvious in the miller's wife of Robinson's poem. Not only does she see nature as providing a soothing method of suicide, she acts on her desire for oblivion. The weir she drowns herself in is pictured as smooth and black, like "starry velvet in the night," not horrifying but peaceful. The weir would "hide her" as she also intends to move downward under the water. The miller is present in part of Robinson's poem, however, unlike the widow's husband who is never portrayed as living. We don't know how long the miller's wife has been married to her husband, but she is just as close to him as the widow in Williams' poem was to her husband.

This paragraph is about the contemplated suicide of both widows, and how they both see themselves sinking into a peaceful oblivion in nature. The final two sentences in this paragraph are about the husbands and the length of their married lives, points which are not clearly related to the topic of this paragraph but which may belong elsewhere in the essay.

If you find a stray point in one of your paragraphs you should ask yourself: can I tie this point into the topic sentence? (Sometimes an additional sentence or two can make a connection the writer assumes is visible to the reader but, in fact, is not.) If the point truly does not belong in the paragraph, then you should ask: (1) does this point belong in my essay? (2) is it related to my thesis? If it is not, just leave it out. If it is, then you must decide where it belongs, either in a separate paragraph or perhaps as part of another paragraph which develops this idea.

● **EXERCISE**

14.1 Underline the topic sentence in the following paragraph. Decide which sentences belong in the paragraph and which do not. Revise the paragraph so that all details are related to the topic sentence, omitting those which you can't tie in. Nemerov's poem is in the Appendix of this text.

In the poem "The Vacuum" by Howard Nemerov, the narrator creates an angry tone. "I know now how life is cheap as dirt, / And still the hungry, angry heart / Hangs on and howls, biting at air" (ll. 13–15). He is angry that his "old woman" has died. He has a negative attitude toward life and will not accept this woman's death. He chooses a cold, mechanical object, the vacuum, and personifies it in order to represent his wife. He associates this vacuum with his "woman" because he was used to seeing her clean the house. He is unable to cope without her.

Essay Unity

In your prewriting activities, you're likely to generate more material than you can use in one essay. Some of your ideas may be very good indeed but may simply not fit the topic that you're writing about. For instance, if you were asked to discuss the light and dark imagery in Porter's "The Jilting of Granny Weatherall" and its relationship to life and death, and you noticed how the birth imagery is also ironically used when Granny is dying, you would probably have to leave this point out to preserve the unity of your essay. It's a great point, but unless it fits with your topic and your focus, it won't work in this particular essay. Each of your paragraphs must relate to your thesis, just as each of the sentences in individual paragraphs must develop the topic sentence. It's easier to see a digression when the essay is presented in skeletal form, outlining the thesis and the main points:

Introduction
Thesis: In the story "The Jilting of Granny Weatherall" by Katherine Anne Porter (in Appendix), the main character, an 80-year-old woman, faces at her death a trauma equal to the one she faced as a young woman who was jilted.

Middle Paragraph One
Topic Sentence: The deathbed scene with its religious trappings has many similarities to the wedding which ended in her jilting.

Middle Paragraph Two
Topic Sentence: Hapsy's appearance leads us to believe that Granny is dying.

Middle Paragraph Three
Topic Sentence: At her death Granny expects her savior, but she is jilted once more and again experiences anger and hostility.

Conclusion

As you can see, middle paragraph two does not tell us how the early jilting is related to the death scene. Hapsy, Granny's dead daughter, was not yet born when Granny was first jilted. Hapsy's appearance is important and a perceptive critical point, but it doesn't fit the thesis of this essay. It destroys the unity of the essay and should be left out.

Digressions from the thesis rarely occur in an outline. More frequently they will happen as you're trying to fill out your plan or if you've begun to write without a plan. Therefore, the only sure way to avoid digressions is to reread your entire first draft when it's complete to make sure that each point is tied into the thesis. You should then revise any questionable portions—revising the thesis if necessary, leaving out any irrelevant ideas, and making sure that pertinent ideas are seen as related to the thesis.

CONTRADICTIONS

When a writer says one thing and then the opposite, that writer has created a contradiction. Mathematically, a contradiction might be represented as $X = Y$ and $X \neq Y$ (X equals Y, and X does not equal Y). "John likes baseball; John does not like baseball" is a verbal example of a contradiction. You can see why contradictions are confusing. When they occur in an essay, they make the writer seem inconsistent, and they muddle the message.

Rarely do contradictions occur in forms as obvious as the foregoing example. Most of us would notice the inconsistency immediately if it were so readily recognizable. The contradictions that sneak into writing and speaking are usually more subtle. Take, for example, the politician who in a campaign speech one day says, "I am in favor of equal rights for women," and the next day proclaims that married women don't need to earn as much as men who are supporting a family. How can that politician say he favors equal rights for women while not accepting that women should receive equal pay for equal work? Newspaper reporters delight in pointing out these inconsistencies in campaign speeches, some of which the less critical listener might miss.

While most of us probably don't contradict ourselves deliberately in writing, unless we are self-critical thinkers and readers of our own essays, this type of inconsistency can easily occur. Maybe we wouldn't say that "Johnny likes baseball, and Johnny does not like baseball." More likely we would say in *paragraph two* that "Johnny plays baseball frequently and really enjoys it," and then in *paragraph ten* that "Johnny doesn't like sports." Here we have what seems to be a contradiction; after all, baseball is a sport. It might be true that, in general, Johnny does not like sports *with the exception of baseball*, but that's not what is said.

Contradictions of the type just cited are likely to occur when you lose track of the whole essay and concentrate on one point at a time, one paragraph or sentence, without seeing how the parts fit together. If you're writing ideas as they come to you, for instance, without a plan, chances are that you may not be tying those ideas together. That's why it is important to have a plan and to reread your entire essay to correct any inconsistencies between paragraphs. More often than not, these contradictions can be explained with a little qualification, like the example given in the previous paragraph. However, without that explanation all the reader sees is a writer who hasn't made up his or her mind and who can't keep track of the thoughts expressed in the essay. If you do find a contradiction in your essay, and you can't resolve it with some explanation, then you need to rethink your point carefully.

Consider the following examples. Each falls into a contradiction in a slightly different manner.

A. *Thesis:* Hamlet was disturbed by his father's death, but the appearance of the ghost caused Hamlet to become truly insane.

Paragraph Four: Hamlet is so determined to have his revenge that he feigns insanity.

Here we have what seems to be an obvious contradiction, separated by a few paragraphs. Hamlet cannot be truly insane if he is "feigning" madness. To feign means to pretend, to deceive deliberately. This writer may be misusing the word *feign*, or perhaps she means that Hamlet started out by faking madness and then really became insane. This explanation, however, is not given.

B. "The Dover Bitch" by Anthony Hecht is about the rather sleazy girl who was at Dover Beach with her boyfriend, Matthew Arnold. It seems that he really doesn't want to be with her. <u>He asks her to try to be true to him, and he will be true to her too.</u>

The evidence this writer introduces from the work (the underlined portion) seems to prove just the opposite of what he intends. Why would Matthew Arnold ask his girlfriend to be true to him and pledge to be true to her also if he really doesn't want to be with her? Either the writer has drawn a wrong conclusion from the evidence or has given the wrong evidence to support the conclusion. You must be certain that your evidence does not contradict, but supports your interpretation of the work.

BEGGING THE QUESTION

Begging the question, sometimes referred to as circular reasoning, occurs when the writer tries to prove a point just by saying it is true, assuming its validity and the reader's agreement. Saying something is true does not make it true—this is essentially what the question begger does. He or she begs, not earns, the reader's agreement. As suggested by the term, it's a less than respectable way of making a point.

For example, a writer who states that "Granny Weatherall is insecure and, therefore, gives up hope that her savior will appear at her death," has to establish two points—that Granny is insecure, and that Granny gives up hope. If the writer does not establish that Granny is insecure, and then uses "insecurity" as a reason for Granny's despair, that writer has begged the question.

To avoid begging the question, you shouldn't take for granted assumptions which can be challenged. Base your conclusions on proven statements. Back your interpretations up with evidence.

THE *NON SEQUITUR*

Non sequitur is Latin for "it does not follow." Two statements which are not logically connected but which follow one another as if they were meant to be connected constitute a *non sequitur*. A *non sequitur* hinders communication because the reader is distracted by more than one point and can't perceive their relationship. This type of writing is incoherent. Consider the following monologue:

> I like music. The sun can burn your skin if you let it. The rocker squeaks when you are lonely. My toes are stuffed into my shoes. There are missile sites in the desert. We must protect ourselves. Peach fuzz gives me the hives because I was born with stars in my eyes. Footsteps on the ceiling make me nervous. Mocha fudge is my favorite flavor ice cream, but caterpillars don't grow on trees. Even if I tried, I couldn't breathe. I left my heart on the Long Island Expressway. Fatimah is a person. I rode a chariot into the sky once.

If someone said this to you, how would you react? We usually expect a point or pattern in our verbal and written communication. In this monologue, there are only two sentences which seem connected: "There are missile sites in the desert. We must protect ourselves." The other sentences are isolated, and even clauses and phrases within sentences do not always relate to one another. The sentences are strung together in sequence as if they should proceed from one another, relating in some way. Instead, what we have here is a series of *non sequiturs*.

Non sequiturs are often used in poetry, drama, and fiction with startling effectiveness. Stream of consciousness writing, for example, which allows us to see the clutter inside a character's mind and challenges us to make sense of unrelated thoughts, can reveal a very coherent picture of a complex mind. But essays are rarely written in this style. They proceed from creative, but logical thought. *Non sequiturs* obstruct rather than advance the purpose of an essay.

You're probably saying that you would never write the kind of gibberish noted in the previous example. Few of us would write such extended pieces of unconnected thought, but many of us slip into a *non sequitur* without realizing it in the midst of some very coherent thoughts. Consider the following paragraph:

> In "Aunt Jennifer's Tigers," Adrienne Rich deals with a lady in her older days before she dies. In this poem, Aunt Jennifer seems to be doing needlepoint or making a tapestry. The figures she is working on are tigers. This is seen when Rich mentions how hard it is for Aunt Jennifer to pull the ivory needle through her material.

The sequencing of these sentences makes part of this paragraph illogical. The paragraph implies that we can tell Aunt Jennifer is making tigers because she has difficulty pulling the needle through the material. We do not have the ability to tell what a person is making by the ease or difficulty the sewer has with the needle. This passage makes no sense because the last sentence is a *non sequitur*. However, if the writer had moved the last sentence closer to the beginning of the paragraph and referred to Aunt Jennifer's clumsy or tired hands as being a result of her advanced age, then a logical connection would have been made.

Sometimes a *non sequitur* will result from the speaker's or writer's omitting an intermediate thought which the audience may or may not perceive. A child coming in from playing in the rain might say to her mother, "It's raining out. I need a new pair of shoes." The mother might mentally translate, "It's raining out. Her feet are all wet because her shoes have holes in them. She needs a new pair of shoes." Or, if the mother could not find the connection between the child's sentences, she might say, "You don't need a new pair of shoes just because it's raining."

Many of us assume that our readers are following our trend of thought when we've lost them by leaping ahead to a conclusion for which we have inadequately prepared. Without providing the middle steps, we create a *non sequitur*. Take, for example, the following selection from an essay on Cheever's "The Country Husband" (in Appendix).

> The scene in which Francis remembers the French maid's disgrace during World War II foreshadows what might happen to Francis. This scene is a warning. The French woman is disgraced and made to walk out of town with a shaven head and without any clothes. This World War II scene thus has tremendous significance. Francis' future in Shady Hill is in jeopardy.

Does the writer mean that Francis Weed will be marched out of Shady Hill without hair or clothes? Of course not. The writer has made a very perceptive connection here between the maid's circumstances and Francis' circumstances but has left part of the reasoning out of the essay, making it difficult for the reader to understand. The part that is left out is that Francis, like the French woman, is part of a small community (Shady Hill/small French town), and he, like the French woman, is thinking of consorting with an outsider whom the community despises (the babysitter/the Nazi). He may face banishment, like the French woman, but probably not physical abuse. These intermediate statements need to be made if the reader is to appreciate fully the conclusion drawn in the paragraph.

TRANSITIONS

We make connections between our written thoughts by using transitions. Transitions are words or phrases which form a bridge between one sentence and the next, one paragraph and the next. They show the relationship between one thought and the following thought. Without transitions, our sentences and paragraphs seem isolated and may even give the impression of being a series of *non sequiturs* or digressions.

Consider the following paragraph. Compare it with paragraph A on pp. 208–9. What differences do you see?

Francis Weed and his family are acclaimed in the social circle of Shady Hill. Francis Weed often goes to parties. Francis Weed is very much alone. Francis Weed doesn't have many friends. Julia seems to be the social impetus. Francis is not pleased with the presence of too many people. Francis makes an open admission. "Julia, I do love you and I would like to be as we were— sweet and bawdy and dark—but now there are so many people." "You were alone when I met you, Francis Weed, and you'll be alone when I leave." Julia refers to the wedding. Two people showed up for the wedding. Francis invited fourteen guests.

You probably noted the short, choppy sentences in this paragraph. Except for the quotations, all are simple sentences that contain no subordinate clauses or ideas. *Subordinating ideas* is one way of relating one idea to the next. The idea captured in the subordinate clause or in a phrase is less important than the idea in the main clause or sentence. Look at the first three sentences of this paragraph and the first sentence of the paragraph on pp. 208–9. Note how subordination clarifies the focus of the paragraph. Where else in the paragraph on pp. 208–9 can you find meaningful subordination?

By *coordinating ideas*, joining them with "and," "but," "or," and "nor," we also show relationship. Equally important ideas, closely related ideas, are joined by these "coordinating conjunctions." Where in the paragraph on pp. 208–9 does the writer use coordination to advantage? What elements are joined?

You also probably noted the lack of pronouns in the paragraph without transitions. *Pronouns* also signal relationships. By themselves, they have little meaning. They refer back to previous words and thus serve as a linking device. Underline the pronouns in the paragraph on pp. 208–9 and draw an arrow to the words to which they refer. Note how pronouns bridge sentences.

Note the sentences which *repeat key words and ideas* in the paragraph on pp. 208–9, such as, "Francis' wife points out how Francis is alone and *doesn't have any friends*." This sentence does not add a new idea, but it connects the first part of the paragraph about Francis' feelings and his preference for aloneness to the second part of the paragraph, Julia's evidence that Francis is alone. This sentence repeats the key words from the topic sentence.

Note the *transitional words and phrases*, devices used to show the relationship of one sentence to the next. Note how the paragraph on pp. 208–9 uses the word "example." Phrases like, "he says to his wife," and "she says," are used to introduce quotations smoothly. Words like "first" and "then" are used to indicate an orderly progression, a list.

The paragraph without transitions has all the essential information contained in the paragraph on pp. 208–9, but the information is unconnected. The writer needs to use transitional links to make the message clear. You can see how intricately we connect our thoughts, most of the time without giving transitions much conscious attention.

We have identified four ways to help you make smooth transitions from one sentence to the next. These methods can help unite paragraphs, as well as sentences, helping us achieve coherence. Let's look at each of them in more detail.

Subordinating and Coordinating Ideas

Writers *subordinate* ideas by making them less than a sentence. In addition, when writers subordinate ideas, they show the relationship between the major idea and the minor idea by using subordinating conjunctions. Consider the following four sentences which contain a main idea and a minor idea which is related to, but not as important as, the main idea.

A. Before it started to rain, she went bicycling.

Here we see a time sequence indicated: the main event—the bicycle ride—began before the rain.

B. She went bicycling because she needed the exercise.

The need for exercise, a subordinate idea, is the reason for the main event—the bicycle ride.

C. While she was bicycling, she ran over a groundhog.

D. She was bicycling when she ran over the groundhog.

While sentences C and D contain approximately the same information, the grammatical structures make the emphasis different in each. The fact that she ran over the groundhog is important in sentence C; that she was riding a bicycle (and not a car, for example) is emphasized in sentence D because this information is provided in the main clause.

Besides subordination, writers use *coordination* to relate ideas. Ideas joined by coordination are grammatically equal in importance.

E. She needed the exercise, so she went bicycling.

In this sentence, "so" joins two equal ideas, two main clauses (sentences in their own right). Other words which can act as coordinating conjunctions are *and, but, for, nor, or,* and *yet.* You should remember these words. They are the only ones which can be used to join two main clauses.

Following is a list of commonly used subordinating words, which will help you join thoughts, showing subtle relationships and degrees of importance. They can be used to subordinate a thought by introducing a clause attached to or embedded within a sentence:

after	because	if	that	until	where	while
although	before	once	though	what	whether	who
as	how	since	unless	when	which	why

Pronouns

By their very nature, pronouns serve to link ideas. A pronoun has little meaning in itself, but it refers to a previous word, the antecedent, for its meaning. The antecedent is usually a word, not a sentence or a phrase, and it should be close by the pronoun which represents it. Pronouns serve more often as a link between sentences in the same paragraph than as a link between paragraphs.

Following is a list of commonly used pronouns:

I	we	me	us	my	mine
our	ours	myself	ourselves		
you	your	yours	yourself	yourselves	
he	she	it	they	him	her	them
his	her	hers	its	their	theirs	
himself	herself	itself	themselves		
who	whom	whomever	which	what	
this	that	these	those		

Repeating Key Words and Ideas

Another way to unify a paragraph or an essay is to repeat key ideas. Simple repetition, of course, will not advance your essay, but relating new thoughts to previous ones by highlighting the idea which they share will not only advance your essay but provide coherence. In the paragraph on pp. 208–9, we find the key idea is that Francis is alone and doesn't have many friends. The word "alone" is repeated four times in different sentences in this paragraph. More important in holding together this paragraph are the many recurring words which focus on Francis' social life: "social circle," "community," "parties," "friends," "social life," "too many people," "so many people," "friends," "wedding," "only two people," "wedding," "fourteen invitations." This series of words forms a pattern which unifies the paragraph.

When you are using related words to tie sentences in a paragraph together, you need not repeat the same word over and over. An unobtrusive synonym can add variety, and a pronoun will call to mind the word it refers to without repeating the word. Synonyms and pronouns can help link ideas in a paragraph.

If you're trying to make a transition from one paragraph to a new paragraph, a frequently used method is to incorporate a key idea from the previous paragraph into the first sentence of the next paragraph to show the relationship between the two. For example, if you were to follow the paragraph on Francis Weed's lack of friends with a paragraph on his inability to communicate, you might make the following transition in your new paragraph:

One possible reason why Francis has so few friends is his inability to communicate.

This sentence mentions the main idea of the previous paragraph (Francis has so few friends), provides the idea for the new paragraph (Francis' inability to communicate), and shows the relationship between the previous paragraph and the new paragraph (the second paragraph provides a reason for the situation discussed in the first paragraph).

Transitional Words and Phrases

Transitional words and phrases are devices which a writer uses to give the reader signals for how an idea is related to the one before it. They serve as directional signs saying to the reader, "Here comes an example," "Now we are going to look at the opposite side," "Here we have a reason for . . . ," "Here we have a result of . . . ," "Here we have a comparison," and so on. But they provide these messages in only a word or two.

Transitional devices must be used with care. The meaning of the word must be appropriate to the relationship between your thoughts. If you start a sentence with "therefore," for example, the reader will expect a conclusion of some kind. If, instead, you provide an illustration, the reader will be confused. (Notice how we've used "for example" and "instead" in the last two sentences.) If you introduce a continuation of the same thought with "however," the reader will be puzzled because "however" indicates a change of direction in the discussion.

Try not to overuse these devices. They should be used in combination with the other methods we've talked about to make paragraphs coherent and to unify an essay. These transitional words and phrases can be used to link sentences within a paragraph as well as to provide a transition from one paragraph to the next.

In the following outline we've categorized the major transitional words and phrases. The heading in each case indicates the signal which the transitional device will send the reader. Some words fall into more than one category. Their meaning is determined by the context in which they are used.

To change direction in the discussion:
actually, although, but, despite, even though, however, instead, on the contrary, on the other hand, otherwise, yet

To present a choice:
either, neither, nor, or, rather, whether

To introduce a comparison or contrast:
by contrast, comparatively, in comparison, in the same way, just as, like, likewise, similarly, then, unlike, whereas

To show a consequence or a conclusion:

as a result, consequently, hence, in conclusion, therefore, thus

To show a continuation of the same discussion:

also, as well as, besides, furthermore, in addition, moreover, too

To emphasize a point:

certainly, especially, indeed, in fact, more importantly, still, to be sure

To enumerate:

first, second, third, etc., at last, finally, lastly

To give an example:

for example, for instance, in particular, like, more particularly, namely, specifically, such as, to illustrate

To show frequency:

always, hardly, infrequently, many times, never, occasionally, often, on occasion, sometimes, usually

To introduce a generality:

for the most part, in general, mostly, regardless, whatever the case, whatever the circumstance

To present a hypothetical situation or a possibility:

if, maybe, perhaps, possibly

To present a point taken for granted:

granted, granted that, obviously, of course, to be sure, true

To show relative position or place:

above, across, along, around, below, beneath, beside, between, beyond, close, close by, far, far away, here, in the distance, inside, near, on top, outside, opposite, toward, under, underneath

To indicate a reason:

because, since

To introduce a repetition or a summary:

again, as was stated before, as was previously stated, in brief, in other words, in short, in summary, once again, that is, to repeat, to review

To indicate sequence in time:

after, afterward, as, before, during, eventually, following, later, previously, since, subsequently, then, until, when, while

• **EXERCISE**

14.2 The following paragraphs lack coherence. There are no transitions between sentences. Try to smooth these paragraphs out by using subordination, coordination, pronouns, repeated key words and phrases (you can even create a transitional sentence or two), and transitional words or phrases. Don't omit any of the information in the paragraphs. All the works of literature on which these paragraphs are based are in the Appendix.

A. On "The Jilting of Granny Weatherall":

1. Granny Weatherall experiences feelings of hostility.
2. Granny Weatherall experiences feelings of disappointment.
3. Granny Weatherall believes too much.
4. Granny Weatherall believes in eternal salvation.
5. Granny Weatherall believed in marriage to George.
6. George jilted Granny.
7. Granny thinks of the jilting.
8. The hostility is apparent.
9. The anger is apparent.
10. Granny expresses a desire to see George.
11. Granny had a happy marriage with John.
12. Granny had five children.
13. Granny feels resentment toward George.
14. Granny feels resentment toward God.
15. Granny is dying.
16. Granny waits for the savior.
17. The savior does not come.
18. Granny feels cruelly cheated.

B. On "The River-Merchant's Wife: A Letter" and "The Widow's Lament in Springtime":

1. Both poems deal with a woman's extreme loneliness.
2. The husbands have left.
3. In Ezra Pound's "The River-Merchant Wife: A Letter," the husband is gone temporarily.
4. In Williams' work, the husband is gone forever.
5. The husband in Pound's poem went on a business trip.
6. "you have been gone five months. / The monkeys make sorrowful noise overhead."
7. The lines show a sad tone.
8. The wife hears sorrowful noise.
9. The wife feels sorrowful.
10. The husband has been gone a long time.
11. Williams' poem, "The Widow's Lament in Springtime," is straightforward.
12. The poem describes the woman's sorrow.

13. "but the grief in my heart / is stronger than they / for they were my joy formerly . . . ."
14. The masses of flowers no longer make the widow happy.
15. The flowers remind the widow of the lost husband.
16. The poem ends with sorrowful images.
17. "I feel that I would like / to go there / and fall into those flowers / and sink into the marsh near them."
18. The widow's loss has made life unbearable.

C. On "Snake":

1. The narrator experiences a conflict.
2. The snake represents evil in the eyes of society.
3. Society has influenced the narrator.
4. The narrator hears the "accursed" voices of education.
5. The narrator feels obligated.
6. His obligation is to kill the snake.
7. The narrator is enchanted by the snake.
8. "But must I confess how I liked him."
9. The narrator feels honored by the guest.
10. The guest is golden.
11. The snake has dignity.
12. The snake is seen as a god.
13. The snake is seen as a king.
14. The narrator is confused in feeling.

IMPROPER INFERENCES

We've spoken about inferences before. To review, an inference is a conclusion or judgment drawn by the reader from given information in the literary work. The inference is not stated in the written work, but implied. In reading literature, we draw inferences when we interpret character, setting, theme, and other literary elements; we base our conclusions on the words of the story, play, or poem. In order for the inference to be accurate, the reader-writer must be guided by some general rules.

Over 2,000 years ago, Confucius said that knowledge is knowing both what you know and what you don't know. His definition applies as well to the ability to draw proper inferences. None of us has unlimited information on any subject, and when we discuss literature, we're further limited in our understanding by what the author chooses to tell us. You remember in the previous chapter how we cautioned against filling in the gaps the author has deliberately created. As responsible readers, we have to base our judgments only on what we're given, not on any imagined extension of the author's words. Therefore, we learn to live with a lack of information, but we also make the most of what information we have, looking beyond the literal meaning to the implications of what we're told. We know a lot more about a literary work than is stated in the words of the story, play, or poem.

In the previous chapter we talked about the limitations in the evidence a literary work provides. In the chapters in the first part of this text, passages from various works allowed you to test your skill at drawing inferences about characters, setting, and other literary elements. In this section, we'll focus on two logical pitfalls which can cause a reader who is not careful to draw improper inferences. They are:

1. hasty generalizations,
2. oversimplification.

Hasty Generalizations

As the term suggests, a hasty generalization is one that is made too quickly on too little evidence. The more evidence you have for your conclusions, the more accurate your conclusions are likely to be. If, for example, you found your history course was unexciting, you'd be making a hasty generalization if you proclaimed: "All history courses are dull," or "History is a boring subject." You'd be basing your general statement on a very small sample—one course. Even if you took every history course at your school and still felt the same way, the most general *accurate* statement you could make would be: "I find the history courses taught at this school are dull."

Turning to literature, you should be wary of such sweeping statements as, " 'The Country Husband' shows what superficial lives the affluent American middle-class leads." "The Country Husband" is not about the entire American upper-middle class. It is about one community, Shady Hill, which may be like other communities, but cannot be taken to represent everyone in this class of people in an entire country. We should temper our generalizations to suit our sample. Use qualifying adjectives such as, "many," "some," "few," and so on. We frequently don't have enough information to generalize about "all," "everyone," "no one," and "none," and therefore we shouldn't.

We should also base our conclusions on *sufficient* evidence. What is sufficient evidence? That depends on the *type of evidence* and the *scope of the conclusion* we wish to draw from the evidence. If a drunken father beats his three-year-old son to death, we might rightly say that he is violent when he is drinking. The evidence, in this case, is so compelling and serious that it's likely to be convincing even though it's only one incident. However, if a drunken father shouts at his son and maybe breaks one of his toys, we couldn't build a strong case for a violent personality without showing some significant pattern of destructiveness. One incident in this case wouldn't be enough. We couldn't say in either case that all men who are intoxicated are violent. As the scope of our generalization broadens, as we include more people, so must our evidence increase.

We should apply the same rules in making literary judgments. Would you say that Francis Weed in "The Country Husband" is a physically violent man? True, he hits Julia. But we know of only one incident. He immediately repents, and we have no information that he's behaved this way before or after. Can you say that George, the man who jilted Granny Weatherall in "The Jilting of Granny Weatherall," is an unscrupulous louse? You might feel that way after seeing how Granny is affected by the jilting. But since we know nothing more about George, we really can't make a general assessment of his character. We need to be responsible in the conclusions we draw.

Oversimplification

If we ignore complex evidence in favor of an easy conclusion based on only part of the evidence, we've oversimplified. Oversimplification is related to hasty generalizations in that both are based on insufficient evidence, but whereas a person who makes a hasty generalization may not have sufficient evidence, the person who oversimplifies *ignores some evidence* in favor of other evidence. If a boy brings home a poor report card and his mother immediately concludes that the child is watching too much TV, she is possibly oversimplifying the situation. She may be ignoring other equally important factors. Maybe the child doesn't concentrate in school because he misses breakfast and is hungry. Maybe the child has a learning disability. Maybe he feels the teacher doesn't like him and is taking his revenge by not doing his work, or maybe the child lacks confidence. The easy answer isn't always an accurate one. Judgments should be made by weighing as much evidence as we have, even if it's contradictory, and then coming to a conclusion based on all the evidence. We may feel some evidence is less important or not as convincing as other evidence, but we shouldn't ignore any of it.

When interpreting literature, you'll find your interpretations frequently challenged if you base your judgments on only part of the evidence. (See "Including Relevant Details," Chapter 13.) Can you say without qualification, for example, that the narrator of Pound's "The River-Merchant's Wife: A Letter" is happily married? Not without ignoring the whole first part of the poem. She becomes happily married, but the obvious unhappiness of her fourteenth year can't be overlooked. Can you say that Granny has no weakness? Not without ignoring George and her reaction even years later to being jilted. This is not to say that you should favor complex explanations over simple explanations, or look for the exotic when faced with the obvious. Plan to face the work honestly, to give a simple conclusion when one is clear from the work, to deal with complexity when the work demands. As sensitive readers, we need to be attuned to the demands of the material.

- **EXERCISE**

  14.3 Test your skill at drawing inferences. Each of the following statements is based on works in the Appendix. Some of the statements are accurate; some are not. Mark each of the statements A (for accurate) or I (for inaccurate). Be prepared to state the evidence in the work which leads you to believe a statement is accurate or to explain why a statement is inaccurate:

Is it a hasty generalization?
Does it oversimplify?
Does it misread information provided?
Is it based on information the work does not provide?

A. "The River-Merchant's Wife: A Letter" by Ezra Pound

1. The river-merchant and his wife were close friends as children.
2. The river-merchant will never return.
3. The river-merchant's wife finds comfort in nature.
4. The river-merchant's wife misses her husband.
5. The river-merchant's wife wishes to take a trip.

B. "Snake" by D. H. Lawrence

1. The snake is a symbol of the devil.
2. The narrator doesn't like snakes.
3. The snake is portrayed as proud.
4. All men are afraid of snakes.
5. The narrator throws a log at the snake because the snake makes him wait for his turn at the watering trough.

C. "The Vacuum" by Howard Nemerov

1. The narrator doesn't love the dead woman.
2. The narrator is male.
3. The narrator doesn't want to live anymore.
4. The dead woman is the narrator's mother.
5. The narrator is a very sloppy person.

D. "The Widow's Lament in Springtime" by William Carlos Williams

1. This is the widow's first spring since her husband died.
2. The widow's son is trying to cheer her up.
3. The widow wishes to die.
4. The widow will never enjoy spring again.
5. The widow finds comfort in nature.

E. "The Jilting of Granny Weatherall" by Katherine Anne Porter

1. Hapsy is dead.
2. Cornelia is an inconsiderate pest.
3. Granny is a religious woman.
4. Granny never really loved her husband, John.
5. Granny expects her savior to appear at her death.

F.   "The Country Husband" by John Cheever

1.   The plane crash causes Francis to seek an affair with the babysitter.
2.   Francis Weed's evaluation of Clayton Thomas is unfair.
3.   We can conclude from the ending that Francis Weed lives happily ever after in Shady Hill.
4.   Anne Murchison loves Francis Weed.
5.   Pinky Trabert and Francis Weed are close friends.

chapter 15

WRITING THE CONCLUSION

Like the introduction of an essay, the conclusion has a special function. It does more than say that the essay has ended. First, the conclusion fulfills the reader's expectations, providing a sense of completion. In the conclusion the writer brings the essay full circle. Having investigated specific parts of a work in the middle paragraphs and having analyzed passages to prove a point, the writer once again has an opportunity to discuss the work in its entirety. Second, the conclusion provides an opportunity for the writer to make a strong restatement of the main point. Having provided and discussed all the supporting points and evidence in the middle paragraphs, the writer can now pull all these arguments together and show how valid the main point is. Also, since the conclusion is the last thing that the audience reads, it is strategically important. What is said in the conclusion will be freshest in the reader's mind, so the writer needs to aim for a strong ending.

The conclusion is in some ways like the introduction. Not only should it be *informative, relevant* and *coherent,* and *interesting,* but it is also limited in its content in ways that the middle paragraphs are not. Let's look at each of these qualities as it pertains to the conclusion.

Informative: The writer usually gives the reader a clue that the conclusion is beginning by bringing the essay back to its main point. The thesis of the literary essay, therefore, is usually reasserted in the conclusion, but not necessarily in the exact same words. It may be abbreviated, made stronger, or embellished, taking into account the discussion of the evidence presented in the essay. In short essays it may be especially important to vary the wording slightly so that the essay does not seem overly repetitious. The main points of the essay might also be briefly summarized in the conclusion, but you must use your discretion when deciding what and how much to summarize. A short essay would seem very repetitious if the main points were summarized in any detail since the reader has just finished going through them. In longer essays, there is more justification for summary. The conclusion of a two-page essay might restate only the thesis of the essay, whereas the conclusion of a ten-page essay might include the thesis and major points.

Relevant and coherent: Like all paragraphs in the essay, the conclusion should also be relevant and coherent. The ending of your essay should grow out of the discussion which precedes it. Introducing a new critical point into the conclusion of the essay is one of the most common ways that the conclusion of a literary essay can go astray. As we discussed previously, a critical observation needs proof, evidence. Statements which need supporting evidence belong in the middle paragraphs, not in the conclusion. The function of a conclusion is to bring the essay to a graceful, interesting close. Opening up new points for discussion is contrary to this aim.

The length of the conclusion should also be appropriate. Like the introduction, the length of the conclusion should suit the length of the essay. A short essay will usually have a one-paragraph conclusion; a longer essay may have several paragraphs; a book may require a whole chapter to conclude.

Interesting: A conclusion could hardly be called interesting if it were a simple restatement of the thesis and main points. Since the conclusion is the last thing your audience will read, try to engage their interest and leave them with something to think about. Finding that you have nothing more to say, you may overlook the chance to engage your readers once more. Because you might occasionally find yourself in this situation, in the next section we'd like to suggest some ways to conclude a literary essay that have worked for our students.

- **EXERCISE**

  15.1 Evaluate the following conclusions. Rate them using the following scale. Jot down the reasons for your evaluations.

	Not at All	Somewhat	Satisfactory	Good
Informative	1	2	3	4
Relevant and Coherent	1	2	3	4
Interesting	1	2	3	4

  A. This conclusion is from a 500-word essay examining the theme and imagery of Herrick's "To the Virgins, to Make Much of Time" (in Appendix).

  In conclusion, Herrick stresses that a woman should get married at a young age, and that time flies. I believe what he said about time going by so fast, but a woman can get married at any age. Reading this poem, a person could tell it was written a long time ago. Not many people get married at a young age anymore. Herrick's poem seems to be an insult to old people. Old people can find happiness in getting married just like young people.

B. This conclusion is also from a 500-word essay examining the theme and imagery of Herrick's "To the Virgins, to Make Much of Time."

Herrick advises young girls to marry at an early age before time withers them like the flower. Herrick only considers the virgin's beauty as a factor in making a match. He leaves unsaid the part which would probably offend modern readers: as women get older and uglier, they will be worth less and no one will want to marry them; then they will be without husbands! One would expect that when this poem was written, such a fate was thought worse than death. But that is not the case today. Herrick's light and playful tone perhaps lessens the unintentional affront to women, but the message of this poem seems to have lost some of its relevance to modern readers, though Herrick's artistry might still be appreciated.

C. This conclusion is from a 1000-word essay comparing Nemerov's "The Vacuum" to Williams' "The Widow's Lament in Springtime" (both in Appendix).

As I have tried to show, these two poems have many similarities and differences in the way they use death and in the way the characters react to it. There are many other ways to use the theme of death and sadness besides the ways Williams and Nemerov use it. This paper compares just the themes in these two poems.

D. This conclusion is also from a 1000-word essay comparing Nemerov's "The Vacuum" to Williams' "The Widow's Lament in Springtime."

Both Nemerov and Williams show how a person who loses a loved one suffers, as images from a familiar environment become a source of pain and a reminder of the loss. After their spouses die, these narrators both suffer, but they suffer differently. Nemerov's narrator feels anger, and the reader expects that he will survive despite his pain, but Williams' widow has given up on life. What makes one a survivor and one an emotional suicide is not totally clear. Is it a difference in their ages? Is it because Nemerov's narrator is likely a male and Williams' narrator is a female? Or is it a difference in each narrator's personality and relationship with the dead spouse? We can only guess at the answer in our attempt to understand further the human reaction to death.

SUGGESTIONS FOR CONCLUDING

There are many ways to end a literary essay. What is important is that you choose a way which fits the topic and purpose of your essay. We have found two types of conclusions are very common—the *evaluative* conclusion and the *speculative* conclusion. We'll discuss them further as suggested ways to conclude, but we hope that you'll go beyond our suggestions to discover a way that is appropriate for your essay.

The Evaluative Conclusion

When you evaluate something, you make a judgment about it. You might say it's good or bad, expensive or cheap, interesting or boring. You can evaluate a subject using many different criteria; some are personal, and others are more objective. For example, if you were to evaluate a movie, you might judge it upon the following bases:

Personal pleasure: Do you like it?

Personal agreement with the message or ideas: Do you agree with what it says?

Artistic merit: Is it well done?

Thematic merit: Does it contribute anything new to the world of ideas?

Rarely will the answers be totally positive or negative. For example, you may have liked the car chase in a movie, but found the rest of the film boring. Or the cinematography may have been brilliant, but the dialogue was flat and uninspired. A careful critic doesn't label works just "good" or "bad," but sees degrees in between.

Literary works can be evaluated in the same way. In the conclusion of an essay about literature, it's possible to interject carefully a personal opinion or an artistic judgment. We say "carefully" because you should always keep in mind the criteria we discussed in the previous section, especially *relevance*. The conclusion should not be a digression. If the essay is about the setting of Cheever's "The Country Husband," the conclusion should not evaluate the characters. If the essay is about the theme of Lawrence's "Snake," the conclusion should not evaluate the setting, and so on.

Let's look more closely at four types of evaluations one can make in the conclusion. While we discuss these categories as distinct, actually all four can be part of the same conclusion. Your choice should be governed by the appropriateness of the method; in short, it should suit your essay.

Personal evaluation.   The personal evaluation is the most subjective of the four types, although it can and should draw on artistic and thematic merits or faults of the literary works for substance. Too often writers fall into vague generalizations, resulting in very unconvincing and uninteresting opinions, such as:

> This poem was very interesting, and I enjoyed it very much. I like the image of the smoking volcano best. It was well done, and it made the work exciting. Lawrence is to be congratulated, I think, for "Snake" is truly a masterpiece and will be read for many years to come.

Such an evaluation is simplistic: it's all opinion without reasons. A personal evaluation should provide the *reason* for the judgment. It can answer either or both of the following sets of questions:

1. Do you like the work (or the aspect of the work under consideration in your essay)? Why or why not?
2. Do you agree with the ideas (situations, conclusions, solutions—whatever your essay is about) presented in the work? Why or why not?

Whether a work appeals to you or not, or whether you like one work better than another may ultimately be a question of personal taste, but in a literary essay you address an audience who should be able to understand, if not agree with, your personal preference. You must, therefore, explain your reasons. Try to avoid the mechanical response: "I like this work because," and don't forget that your evaluation usually follows from a restatement of the main point of your essay.

Consider the following conclusion to an essay comparing Robinson's "The Mill" to Williams' "The Widow's Lament in Springtime," both of which are in the Appendix. (The underlined portion is the reasserted thesis.)

> <u>Although both Robinson's and Williams' poems present women who are suicidal because they have lost their husbands, Robinson seems more interested in the story of the double suicide, while Williams focuses on the psychological state of the suffering widow.</u> "The Widow's Lament in Springtime" has more emotional impact than "The Mill." Although fewer facts are known about the widow in Williams' poem than about the miller and his wife, since Williams' widow narrates the poem, the reader feels closer to her experience and pain. We don't know how her husband died, but it doesn't matter. In comparison Robinson's narration seems cold. Feelings are necessarily lost because the narrator is outside of the action. Robinson tells us more about this couple than Williams does, and he tries to involve the reader in what the miller's wife is feeling, but Williams' widow's meditation on suicide seems more heartfelt than the stunned wife's drowning in "The Mill."

Another writer might have preferred the structure and emotional distance of "The Mill" to the freeness and emotional intensity of "The Widow's Lament in Springtime," feeling perhaps that the distilled emotion presented by the narrator of "The Mill" is preferable to the directness of Williams' poem. Either opinion is possible, but what is important is that the reasons for the opinion are explained so that the audience can understand *why* the writer prefers one work over another.

This type of conclusion works well in essays which compare two works, although it is possible to show why you like or dislike just one work. For example, this last paragraph could be rewritten to reveal the writer's opinion of "The Widow's Lament in Springtime." (The underlined portion is the reasserted thesis.)

> Williams' poem is a psychological study using imagery from nature to explore the suicidal feelings of a woman who has lost her husband. The poem is appealing because of its strong emotions. Although few facts are known about the widow, the reader feels close to her experience since she narrates the poem and tells us how she is feeling. We do not know how her husband died, but it does not matter. Her heartfelt meditation on suicide is convincing, making us aware of the degree of pain she feels over his loss.

A second type of personal evaluation involves a judgment about the ideas, actions, or conclusions expressed in the work. Do you agree with the theme? Do you like the conclusion and its implications? What do you think about the ideas expressed in the work? In this evaluation, you'll be measuring the author's ideas against your values and experiences and saying why you agree or disagree with his or her presentation. This type of conclusion works particularly well in essays focusing on theme, character, or setting. Again, the thesis of the essay is usually reasserted, and the evaluation grows out of the focus of the essay.

The following conclusion is from an essay on imagery and theme in Thomas' "Fern Hill" (in Appendix). The reasserted thesis is underlined.

> Using images of farm and forest, Thomas shows how the child is attuned to nature and oblivious of time. It is difficult to generalize about childhood from this poem, which obviously grew out of Thomas' time and place; however, I find his narrator's childhood strangely foreign to what I know of childhood. Modern city children know foxes and pheasants only from visits to a zoo, if at all, and some know more of pain than most of us like to think about. Perhaps Thomas would see the sad state of some of our children as the corruption caused by a very time-conscious civilization. In any case, childhood doesn't seem to be what it used to be, if indeed it were ever like the ideal which Thomas presents.

Notice how the thesis focuses on childhood, as does the rest of the conclusion. This writer found the romantic vision of childhood presented in the poem contrary to his experience. Notice how he does not say, therefore, that Thomas is "wrong" or that his poem is "bad." The writer realizes that Thomas' particular vision of childhood is not meant to be general; it is limited, and if it is not exactly "real," it still has a purpose in the context of the poem. The writer simply records that Thomas' experience of childhood differs from his own—a valid, personal reaction to the ideas presented in the poem.

Artistic evaluation.   Depending on the purpose and focus of your essay, you might have occasion to evaluate a work artistically. A conclusion which evaluates the artistic merit of a work explains why a work or the aspect of the work under consideration (character, setting, imagery, and so on) is well done or flawed, judging it according to some stated criteria. In writing such a conclusion, you'd consider the author's purpose in the work and whether that purpose was achieved through the characters, setting, imagery, or whatever the essay discusses. You might also consider if the author could have done better and how.

If your essay is a comparison–contrast essay, you might conclude by stating which work is better in a certain aspect, or weaker. Unlike a personal evaluation, which might discuss a preference for a work of equal merit to another work, the artistic evaluation distinguishes between works on the basis of some clearly stated standard which would make the work something good or worthy. In an artistic evaluation you'd try to explain why the work achieves its purpose well or fairly well or not so well, regardless of whether you liked it or not, or agreed with it or not (although a work's artistic merit does and should frequently influence our likes and dislikes).

Once again it's important to point out that unsupported generalities—such as "this work is well done," "this work is exquisitely executed," "this work is flawed"—will be unconvincing without an explanation of your reasons. Many of your reasons will probably refer to the earlier discussion of the work in your essay.

The following conclusion is from an essay which discusses the narrative perspective in Edgar Allan Poe's story, "The Pit and the Pendulum." Notice how the thesis is reaffirmed, and how the rest of the conclusion still focuses on the topic of the essay—the narrative perspective—and attempts to show why the writer believes it is imperfect. (Again, the reasserted thesis is underlined.)

> <u>Through the use of first-person narration, Poe is able to study and convey intense psychological terror, particularly the human fear of darkness and the unknown, of inescapable death, and of hell</u>. While his mode of narration allows Poe to investigate freely the thoughts and emotions of the victim, it also has a limitation. The victim must stay alive if the tale is to be believable. Poe, therefore, can only bring his victim to the brink of death. Some of the suspense is thus lost because the reader knows from the beginning that the narrator must survive the torture if he is to tell his tale. However, Poe seems to have forgotten that his narrator must survive until the last paragraph, when all of a sudden trumpets are heard; the French army has arrived in Toledo; the Inquisition is over. Poe's story comes to an abrupt and unexpected end. He could have prepared for the ending, but either he did not want to lessen the terror of the torture by holding forth the hope of rescue by the French army, or he simply forgot till the end and did not want to revise. In either case, the story is imperfect. The last paragraph changes the whole situation too quickly and too unexpectedly.

The artistic criterion this writer uses to evaluate the ending of Poe's story is that a good story prepares the reader for its conclusion. This writer has attempted to show that the conclusion of "The Pit and the Pendulum" is unprepared for, and, therefore, according to his criterion, the story is flawed.

Thematic evaluation.   In a thematic evaluation you would discuss the ideas in a work and compare them to similar or relevant ideas in other works. You would view the ideas from the literary work which you've discussed in light of what others have said on the topic. You would then decide if the literary work fits into a certain school of thought, if it adds something new to what people have said on this topic, or if it redoes an old theme. (Of course, a work may redo an old theme very well and still be interesting.) For example, if the subject of your essay were death as experienced by Granny Weatherall, you might consider how other authors have presented death and whether or not Katherine Anne Porter has made a new contribution. Or if your subject were Lawrence's use of the snake in "Snake," you might write a conclusion similar to this one (again, the reasserted thesis is underlined).

> Through the snake which arouses contrary feelings in the narrator, Lawrence successfully challenges the voices of our education and the values we mindlessly accept. He draws not only on the Biblical association of the snake with the devil, therefore suggesting evil, but he also brings out the godliness of the creature, familiar to other mythologies such as the Aztecs, who represented one of their gods as a feathered serpent. The snake's sexual symbolism also cannot be ignored. Freud would have approved of the primitive, natural power and the hidden life of the snake, as well as the narrator's irrational disgust which Lawrence focuses on this creature. Lawrence manages to transcend any one symbolic meaning by bringing together the contradictory associations snakes have had for humans since the beginning of time. He does this by showing the interaction between the narrator and the snake in his poem.

The writer of this conclusion shows how "Snake" draws on these somewhat contrary ideas human beings have associated with the snake: the Biblical representation of the snake as the devil in Genesis; the Aztec representation of the feathered snake as a god, Quetzalcoatl; and the Freudian association of the snake with sexuality. Lawrence's contribution is his ability to unite such diverse ideas in his poem.

Historical evaluation.   There are many types of historical evaluations you might make to conclude a literary essay. Again, you should choose the evaluation that best suits your purpose. We'll discuss two of the most common. The first considers how the work was received when it was first published or performed. The second considers whether a work has become dated, or how readers today might react to it. Of course, both these historical considerations might be useful in the same conclusion.

In order to discuss how a work was received when it was published or performed, you'll have to do a little research. Plays, novels, books of poetry, and collections of short stories are frequently reviewed in journals and literary magazines. You need to know the original date of the publication of a novel, or the date of the first performance of a play, before you can consult an index to locate a review. For a review of a poem or story, you'll need to know the name of the collection of poems or stories in which the work originally appeared, as well as the date of its publication, before you'll be able to locate reviews. (For copyrighted works, this information is usually included in the acknowledgments of most anthologies of literature.)

What might you discover by such research? If you were discussing the relationship between Nora and her husband, Helmer, in Ibsen's *A Doll's House*, you might be surprised to discover how shocked the audience of the late nineteenth century was by Nora's revolt. While Nora's struggle for an identity of her own may seem reasonable today, in Ibsen's time her actions were considered outrageous. Such information might be useful in concluding an essay about Ibsen's social criticism or the relationship between husband and wife in the play.

If you're discussing the ideas in a literary work which is not contemporary, you might discuss in your conclusion how readers today would react to these ideas. Shakespeare's sonnet "That Time of Year" (in Appendix), for example, is still as meaningful today as when it was written. Even though our lifespan may be longer, lovers still age and die as they did in Shakespeare's time. However, our attitudes toward women and marriage have changed since Herrick's time, and so perhaps has the reader's response to "To the Virgins, to Make Much of Time" (in Appendix). Not that the modern reader does not understand what Herrick is saying, but the poem may seem dated to some readers today. Such was the reaction of one writer who concluded an essay on the theme and imagery in Herrick's poem by evaluating Herrick's theme from the perspective of a late twentieth-century reader and disagreeing with urging young women to marry (see Exercise 15.1, B).

The Speculative Conclusion

The word "speculate" has a number of meanings. It can mean to think about and guess cautiously, to weigh what you know and to predict what will happen in the future. The word is derived from the Latin verb *speculare*, which means "to spy out," "to observe." It has come to be associated with risky financial ventures because it's difficult to look into the future and predict how investments will turn out, so "speculating" involves an element of risk.

When you write a speculative conclusion, you also enter into a risky business where caution is needed. A speculative conclusion is one which goes beyond the limits of the literary work to contemplate and guess about what happens next. Does Francis Weed in Cheever's "The Country Husband" live happily ever after? Does the widow in Williams' "The Widow's Lament in Springtime" recover? Does the narrator of Nemerov's "The Vacuum" recover? Are there more stages to the development of the relationship between the river-merchant and his wife in Pound's "The River-Merchant's Wife: A Letter"? None of these questions can be answered just by reading the literature. They're speculative questions which ask about a future that the works only hint at. While this type of consideration is usually inappropriate for the middle paragraphs in a literary essay, it can make an interesting conclusion. Of course, the question or speculation must be related to the subject of the essay.

Consider, for example, paragraph D in Exercise 15.1 (p. 243). This conclusion poses speculative questions but does not answer them. The following conclusion speculates on what happens to Francis Weed in "The Country Husband" (in Appendix) after the woodworking is over. (The reasserted thesis has been underlined.)

> <u>Francis Weed's brush with death kindles in him a desire to live more intensely, which we can see in Francis' fantasies about the baby-sitter and his treatment of Mrs. Wrightson and Julia.</u> However, Francis' desire is at odds with the values of his community, Shady Hill. The psychiatrist, instead of helping Francis constructively keep alive this zest for life, prescribes molding dead wood into coffee tables, more furniture for a Shady Hill social gathering. It is unlikely that Francis' desire for life can be extinguished so neatly. There are only so many coffee tables one can make. And what is to keep him from dreaming of Anne and the Alps while he is working? The plane crash brings to life a dissatisfaction that had been growing in Francis and will inevitably surface again unless the life he and Julia lead in Shady Hill changes dramatically, which is not going to happen.

This conclusion deals with what is likely to happen to Francis in the future, after the story ends. Note how the thesis is focused on the character, as is the speculation.

Another type of speculative conclusion involves imagining a hypothetical change in some aspect of the literary work and speculating on how the difference would affect the work. For example, what if another person narrated Granny's story in Porter's "The Jilting of Granny Weatherall"? How would such a change in narration affect the story? What if the structure of Cheever's "The Country Husband" were changed so that it was not episodic? What if the story were not told chronologically? What if Williams' "The Widow's Lament in Springtime" were changed to wintertime? A discussion of these questions would be appropriate in the conclusion of essays focusing on the narration of "The Jilting of Granny Weatherall," the structure of "The Country Husband," and the images of spring in "The Widow's Lament in Springtime," respectively. Such conclusions help us appreciate why the author chose the method he or she did.

Speculation is usually characterized by questions or words introducing conditional situations, such as "what if," "unless," or words indicating probability, such as "unlikely," "possible," "probable," or "likely." Speculative conclusions frequently involve one of the following questions:

> How would you have ended the story or play or poem?
> What do you think will happen to _____ in the future?
> What do you think happened to _____ in the past that was not mentioned in the work?
> If _____ were changed in the literary work, how would the work be affected?

The best speculative conclusions are implied by the literary works; they grow out of the evidence in the work but take the evidence one step further than the story, play, or poem does. Some speculative questions are not worth investigating because the work provides no clues or because the answer is unimportant. That woodworking is probably not a permanent solution to Francis Weed's problem is important in interpreting the conclusion of "The Country Husband" and in studying Francis as a character. However, a speculative conclusion based on the question—"How did the widow's husband die in "The Widow's Lament in Springtime"?—would probably be a poor conclusion because there is not enough evidence in the work to suggest an answer, and how he died is unimportant to the poem. It doesn't affect our interpretation or the way we picture the widow.

Other Conclusions

Of course, we can't hope to cover all possible ways to conclude a literary essay. Surely, some ways are yet to be discovered. We've presented just a few suggestions. We hope you'll add to them and consult our suggestions when you feel in need of an idea.

- **EXERCISES**

15.2 Explain at least two other ways to conclude an essay about literature which have not been mentioned.

15.3 Write an evaluative conclusion to an essay on Shapiro's "Auto Wreck" (in Appendix) or another poem of your choice.

15.4 Write an evaluative conclusion to an essay on two poems, stories, or plays, explaining why you think one is better than the other, or why you like one better than the other.

15.5 Write a speculative conclusion to an essay on "The Jilting of Granny Weatherall" (in Appendix) or another story of your choice.

15.6 Rewrite a conclusion from an essay you've already completed using a different method of development than the one which you originally used. Describe the methods you used originally and in the revision.

chapter 16

REVISING AND EDITING

Revision is a bridge between the first draft which grows out of the prewriting exercises and the more public form of the finished critical essay. Few of us are such skilled and gifted writers that the first draft of what we write is good enough to be the final draft. Most of us revise even as we write, crossing out words, changing phrases, moving words, adding phrases or sentences as new ideas come to us. Sometimes we write so quickly, trying to get our ideas down as they come to us, that we worry about organization, development, grammar, spelling, and style only after the first draft is complete. Then we go back and revise. We try to see if our sentences and paragraphs fit together; we make appropriate changes to improve the unity and coherence of our essay, as well as the clarity of our sentences. We use transitions and in other ways strive for a smoothness of style. We also clean up our grammar and our spelling, consulting a grammar handbook or a dictionary if necessary. Even experienced writers revise their work many times, sometimes after sharing their writing with another reader who might help them "to see again," to "re-vision" what they've written.

Revision, of course, takes time. Unless you leave yourself some time to go through your completed essay carefully at least once, you're missing the opportunity to polish and refine what is probably a rough first draft. After you've completed your first draft, put it aside (if you have the opportunity) for an hour or two, or a day or two if you have the time; then return to it refreshed and read it again. Try to be a critical reader of your own work. Read as a person who does not know the essay, or read as you think your audience or instructor will read. Go through your essay from beginning to end before you make any major revisions. Jot down your reactions in the margins. Perhaps you might read it aloud to hear how it sounds, listening to the way your words fit together in each sentence. After going through the essay in its entirety at least once, focus on its parts and revise. You might want to reread parts of it for a specific purpose. For example, you might want to read just the thesis and the topic sentences from each of the body paragraphs to see how they fit together. Or you might want to reread one or two of the middle paragraphs that look skimpy to see if you can add to the evidence and the discussion. Or perhaps you find yourself repeating the same point in two different places and want to reread those sections to see if they should be joined, or if one section should be deleted. After you've done all your revisions, read the essay in its entirety again and make whatever adjustments seem necessary. Of course, even after you've typed the final draft, you need to proofread your essay and correct any typographical errors.

In the following sections we'll suggest three methods of revision; all three might be used on the same essay, if there is time and opportunity. The first is a general checklist of questions focusing on parts of the essay. The second method involves knowing your writing habits and reading your essay specifically to correct problems you've experienced in the past that may easily recur without careful self-monitoring. For the third method, you'll need a friend or a class member—an audience to provide you with a reaction to your essay.

Before we discuss these methods of revision, we need to touch upon three stylistic conventions which writers of literary essays are usually expected to follow.

PERSONAL PRONOUNS AND VOICE

Like the writer of a story or poem, as an essay writer you must decide upon a voice for the essay. Are you going to be formal or friendly? Do you want to appear subjective or objective? Will you be serious or playful? You should choose a voice for your essay according to the purpose of your writing and your audience's expectations. Essays about literature can be playful. Mark Twain's essay, "Fenimore Cooper's Literary Offenses," for example, is a funny and satirical, as well as serious, outline of James Fenimore Cooper's faults in the Leatherstocking novels. The playful literary essay, however, is more the exception than the rule. Most of the time literary essays are serious.

Since you'll probably be writing your literary essay to fulfill a course requirement, your audience is usually your instructor and perhaps the other members of your class. Therefore, your voice should be suited to a formal presentation of your thoughts, and you'll want to strive for a more polished style than is probably evident in your journals, for example. This means that you'll be using the third-person pronoun, for the most part—he, she, it, they—and writing as objectively as possible. Does this mean that you can never interject an "I"? No. Depending on your instructor's preference, "I" may be used occasionally to interject a personal note. The overuse of the first person, however, as in "I think," "I feel," "in my opinion," and so on, lends a note of uncertainty to an essay, as if the writer were trying to justify his or her convictions by making them personal. A clear presentation of the evidence should be enough in itself to convince the reader and needs no further justification.

Can you use the second person "you" in a literary essay? Usually not. "You" is more rare than "I" in most literary writing. "You" is a direct address to the reader and, therefore, interjects a note of familiarity which is out of place in a formal essay. In addition, many times we slip into the second person when we're really not addressing anyone. We frequently use "you" in speech when we mean "I" or "he." This shift occurs much more visibly in writing when the writer forgets what pronoun he or she is using and thus confuses the reader by shifting.

Unlike the writer of a story or poem, who may experiment with different perspectives in the same work, speaking with different voices, the writer of an essay is usually *consistent in voice* throughout the essay. If you start the essay in the third person, talking about the "reader," you shouldn't shift to the second person and address the reader as "you." If you begin an essay in the third person, you probably will want to stay in the third person throughout.

If you have difficulty keeping your pronouns consistent, write down the pronoun voice you intend to use throughout the essay on an index card. Then look through your essay critically to locate any inconsistencies. If you find a shift, simply revise the sentence so that it's consistent with your chosen voice. Look especially for "you," a common pronoun shift.

LEVEL OF DICTION

An essay about literature is usually formal, but this fact shouldn't keep you from using everyday words and simple sentences to express your meaning. "Formal" does not refer to *complexity* but to a level of diction which includes a variety of sentence structures and most words in the dictionary not marked "slang," "colloquial," or "informal." In writing an essay about literature, we use a standard form of English. Words which are "colloquial" are used in conversation or informal writing. Words which are "slang" are used mainly in speaking, sometimes in writing, but only for a special effect. Slang words are not always found in a dictionary since they go in and out of fashion or change meaning so quickly. They're very limited words, often peculiar to one group or region of the country. Consider, for example, the following set of words which mean approximately the same thing:

Standard	*Informal or Colloquial*	*Slang*
girlfriend	girl	main squeeze

Only the standard form would be appropriate in formal writing. The other two are suitable in less formal circumstances.

VERB TENSE

It's conventional to write a literary essay in the *present tense.* The present tense conveys the idea that the work of art exists in the present, and not just in the reader's past experience of it. The literary work is not over when the reader has finished reading; therefore, the writer does not write about it in the past tense. If you were writing about Francis Weed's infatuation with the babysitter in John Cheever's "The Country Husband," you might say, "Francis *dreams* about Anne; thoughts of her *bring* some excitement into his dull life." If you were writing about Katherine Anne Porter's "The Jilting of Granny Weatherall," you might say, "Granny *is dying.* Her senses gradually *fail* her."

You may have reason to use the past tense in a literary essay if you write about an event that happened *in the past* in relation to other events in the story, play, or poem. For example, Francis Weed remembers (in the present) his experience in France during World War II (in the past): "Francis *remembers* how the French maid *walked* out of the town and *retained* her human dignity despite how the townspeople *treated* her." The verbs in the past tense indicate a past event in the story; World War II took place before Francis' life in Shady Hill (the present). The verb in the present tense refers to the present in the story. In "The Jilting of Granny Weatherall," any discussion of Granny's wedding and George's jilting her would also involve the past tense since the story takes place when her wedding is long over, and Granny is an old woman lying on her deathbed.

The important thing to remember is that you should write in the present tense unless you have a reason to shift to the past tense (or future tense, for that matter). Too often a writer will shift tense without thinking about it, making the verbs in the essay inconsistent and confusing. If you find yourself shifting tense without reason, you might find it helpful to proofread specifically for tense shifts, making sure that any verb not in the present tense is in a different tense for a reason.

REVISION METHOD ONE: GENERAL QUESTIONS

Following is a list of questions on organization, development, grammar, style, and manuscript form. After reading your essay completely, look again at your essay and its parts, and answer—mentally, at least—each of the questions on the checklist. Revise your essay when the answer to any of the questions indicates a need.

Organization: Essay

1. Does the essay have a thesis?
2. Is the thesis part of the introduction to the essay?
3. Is the thesis too broad or too limited for what is actually proven in this essay? Do the middle paragraphs fulfill the plan of the thesis?
4. Are there any words in the thesis which are vague? Can they be more precise?
5. Is each of the middle paragraphs related to the thesis of the essay?
6. Do any of the points in the middle paragraphs seem contradictory?
7. Are the paragraphs logically connected with smooth transitions?
8. Is the thesis reasserted in the conclusion?

Organization: Paragraph

1. Does each of the middle paragraphs have a topic sentence which makes a critical point?
2. Are any of the topic sentences merely plot summary and, therefore, in need of revision?
3. Does each paragraph develop only one idea?
4. Does each paragraph keep to the main idea, or does it digress from the point?

Development

1. Is the introduction relevant to the topic of the essay?
2. Is the introduction more than a summary or a statement of the thesis?
3. Does the introduction lead logically to the thesis?
4. Are the title(s) and author(s) of the work(s) identified in the introduction?
5. Is each of the middle paragraphs fully developed?
6. Are generalizations supported with details from the work(s) of literature?
7. Is each quotation discussed so that the reader understands its significance?
8. Are there too many quotations, making the essay choppy? (You have too many quotes if a large portion of the words in your essay are not your own.)
9. If there are too many quotes, can any of them be paraphrased?
10. Is the plot of the literary work summarized unnecessarily? Are there any plot details which are not needed to prove a critical point?
11. Do the quotes and plot details fit the points of the middle paragraphs?
12. Is there enough evidence to prove each point? Are any important details left out?
13. Are the conclusions justified from the evidence?
14. Is there a separate and adequately developed concluding paragraph?

Editing and Proofreading

1. Are all the sentences complete sentences?
2. Are sentences joined correctly so that there are no run-on sentences?

(Remember: sentences can be joined with a semicolon, or a comma *and* a conjunction such as "and," "but," "for," "nor," "or," "so." A comma alone should not be used to join sentences.)

3. Are all punctuation marks used correctly?
4. Do all subjects and verbs agree?
5. Do pronouns agree with their references?
6. Are there any vague pronouns (such as "this" or "it") which have no clear reference?
7. Are pronouns consistent in person (no "you" especially)?
8. Are verbs consistently in the present tense?
9. Is any shift in tense justified?
10. Are there any slang or colloquial words or phrases? Is there a standard word or phrase which can be substituted?
11. Are all words spelled correctly?
12. Is the meaning of any word unclear?
13. Are "there/their," "to/too/two" properly used?
14. Are quotations accurate, word-for-word representations for the author's words?
15. Do quotations begin and end with quotation marks, except for long quotes which are centered and single-spaced?
16. Do quoted lines of poetry which are not centered show line divisions?

Style

1. Are there any trite phrases or clichés?
2. Do you overuse the passive voice?
3. Can excess words which do not add to the meaning be trimmed?
4. Is there any needless repetition?
5. Are there any sentences which sound awkward? Can they be made clearer and smoother?
6. Are all lists or series in parallel form?
7. Is sentence structure varied or monotonous?
8. Read your essay out loud. How does it sound?

Manuscript Form

1. Is there a title?
2. Is there a title page (if required) with appropriate information (name, course, date, instructor's name)?
3. Are lines double-spaced?
4. Are any long quotes centered and single-spaced?
5. Are primary sources footnoted and noted in the bibliography (if required)?
6. Are secondary sources footnoted and noted in the bibliography?
7. Is there an inch margin around each page?

If you discover a mistake after your essay has been typed, and it's too late to retype the page or correct the error in type, you may correct the error by hand, preferably in black ink. You're responsible for the error even if someone else typed the essay. Many instructors would prefer a last-minute correction to your leaving an error uncorrected, although these kinds of corrections should be minimal. You should check with your instructor not only about his or her policy on corrections, but also about the form of the title page (if required), about using secondary sources, about the type of documentation preferred for primary and/or secondary sources, and also about the kind of typing paper that he or she prefers. Some instructors will discourage you from using erasable paper since the ink easily smears on these sheets.

REVISION METHOD TWO: REVISION CHARTS

Part of skillful revision is knowing what to look for. If you know your writing habits—your strengths and weaknesses—you'll be able to focus your attention on your likely weaknesses or problems after you've written your first draft. For example, if you know you've had difficulty making smooth transitions between sentences and paragraphs, it would be wise to read over the section on transitions in this text and then go back over your essay looking specifically at your transitions and making appropriate improvements. If you know you tend to leave out topic sentences, then take a close look at each of your middle paragraphs to be sure that you have a topic sentence.

How do you get to know your writing habits? By paying attention to responses to your writing from a trained reader, namely your instructor, and by analyzing your writing using both your instructor's guidance and the list of questions provided in Revision Method One. Once you've identified your strengths and weaknesses, review sections of this text or a writer's handbook which discuss problem areas, and concentrate on these areas during the process of revision.

We can all learn from past mistakes. For this reason we've provided a sample revision chart on which you can note your strengths and weaknesses in each essay as you understand them from your instructor's comments. Using such a chart to record and then to recall areas of concern *before* you write or revise your next essay can help you improve.

On the following pages you'll find three sample charts: one on organization, one on development, and one on grammar, style, and manuscript form. In each of the boxes, you can briefly note your strengths and weaknesses. You can use a "+" for strengths and a "−" for weaknesses, or perhaps it would be even more helpful if you could briefly describe your strengths and weaknesses. In the last box on each chart, you should note the pages you need to review in either this text or a handbook before you write your revision or your next essay.

REVISION CHART 1: ORGANIZATION

	Essay One	Essay Two	Essay Three	Essay Four
Thesis				
Middle Paragraphs and Thesis				
Introduction				
Topic Sentences				
Paragraph Coherence				
Transitions				
Conclusion				
Reading Assignment: Review Pages				

REVISION CHART 2: DEVELOPMENT

	Essay One	Essay Two	Essay Three	Essay Four
Introduction				
Middle Paragraphs' Use of Evidence				
Avoidance of Inappropriate Plot Summary				
Logic				
Conclusion				
Reading Assignment: Review Pages				

REVISION CHART 3: GRAMMAR / STYLE / FORM

	Essay One	Essay Two	Essay Three	Essay Four
Sentence Structure				
Punctuation				
Subject–Verb Agreement				
Verb Tense				
Pronouns				
Diction and Usage				
Style				
Manuscript Form				
Reading Assignment: Review Pages				

REVISION METHOD THREE:
ESSAY REACTION GUIDE

Professional writers frequently seek the reactions of fellow writers and friends before completing the final draft of an essay. In this way, they can anticipate their audience's reactions, and revise and clarify their writing before the more general audience ever reads the essay. You too may have the opportunity to seek help from and give help to fellow writers.

In reacting to another writer's essay, try to be both honest and helpful. You can't help a writer make his or her essay better by ignoring the problems you find or reacting with unfounded and insincere praise. Say what you find good about the essay and what you see as its strengths, of course, but also suggest what you see needs improvement. Sometimes you may not be sure what's wrong with an essay; perhaps you're confused by a sentence or a paragraph. Letting the writer know that you had difficulty with a passage will help the writer focus his or her revision. Try to be positive and helpful in your suggestions. Treat your fellow writer's essay the way you hope that he or she will treat yours.

ESSAY REACTION GUIDE

Writer_____   Title_____

Reviewer_____   Date_____

First Impressions: Read the paper through and jot down your general impressions.

Reread the essay, and comment briefly on each of the following categories:

Thesis Clarity: (No thesis at all; thesis is vague or unclear; thesis is adequate; thesis is quite clear)

Overall Thesis Development: (Does the essay develop the thesis adequately? Are there any digressions? omissions?)

Essay Organization: (Comment on introduction, order of middle paragraphs, any unnecessary repetition, the use of transitions, and the conclusion.)

Paragraph Control: (Comment on topic sentences and paragraph unity. Does each paragraph develop only one idea?)

Evidence: (Comment on whether evidence is sufficient, whether it is discussed, whether it is logical. Note any unnecessary plot summary or unsupported generalizations.)

Clarity/Grammar/Style: (Note any awkward or unclear passages, problems in punctuation, agreement, tense, pronouns, diction, usage, or spelling. If the essay is typed, note any problems with manuscript form.)

Suggestions for Improving:

You may find that some of the categories overlap, or that you don't have very much to say in a given category because everything seems fine. That's okay. The point is to try to make your comments constructive and specific so that the writer can recognize the problem and address it when revising. You'll not only be helping a fellow writer improve the essay, but you'll also become a better critical reader, not only of other people's essays, but of your own essays too.

What should you do with the reaction you get to your essay from one (or more) of your fellow writers? After you read their comments, try to look at your essay through their eyes, and see if you agree with their evaluations. If you do, of course, you should revise your work accordingly. If you don't understand their comments or if you disagree, perhaps discussing the points with your reviewers will help you decide whether to revise according to their suggestions or not. Remember, the Essay Reaction Guide is a useful tool and can provide you with helpful information if used properly, but the decision whether to revise according to the suggestions or another way or not at all is yours. You're the writer, the essay contains your views, and you decide how to use this revision tool in the most beneficial way.

• EXERCISES

16.1 Use Revision Method One on the first draft of an essay early in the course. Critique your own essay by answering each of the questions and write out a plan for revision. Then revise according to your plan.

16.2 Record your strengths and weaknesses as noted by your instructor and yourself on the Revision Charts (Revision Method Two). Assign yourself appropriate readings which address your problems (either from this text or a writer's handbook). Use your revision chart as a checklist for revising the first draft of your next essay.

16.3 Share your essay with another writer in class who has read the work you've written about. While he or she is filling out the Essay Reaction Guide for your essay, you should do the same for him or her. Exchange reactions. Discuss any unclear points. Write out a plan for revising your essay after considering the comments on the Essay Reaction Guide. If you disagree with any of the comments made, explain why.

chapter 17

THE WHOLE PROCESS

In this last chapter, we illustrate the complicated process of writing an entire critical essay by following an assignment through the prewriting stages to the first and final drafts. We've tried to record coherently initial inspirations and tentative plans, as well as revisions, which frequently occur not only between the first and final drafts, but even while the first draft is being composed and often while the final draft is being typed. In making the illustration understandable, we've been more formal than a writer would usually be, making sure each stage is written out completely. We've left out the natural jottings, false starts, and dead ends which would be intelligible only to the writer of this assignment. Only a first and a final draft appear, when actually an essay may involve more. We hope, however, that you'll see possibilities for relevant additions at many points, especially in the more personal phases of writing before the final draft.

The writer of this illustration was asked to read Thomas' "Fern Hill" (in Appendix). She knew that an essay topic would be provided later and began by keeping a journal on this poem, reading and writing daily. After a specific writing assignment was given, the writer tried a more formal prewriting strategy suited to the assignment before putting together a thesis and an outline and writing the first draft. Then she reviewed the draft using the revision questions provided in Chapter 16. The final draft shows the revisions made in response to these questions.

JOURNAL ON DYLAN THOMAS' "FERN HILL"

February 23rd

This poem seems very full to me, and I don't know if I understand most of it yet. Two parts definitely. There is a sad change by the last stanza. I like the final image of a man chained like the sea, but I'll have to think about that for a while. There is a lot of nature imagery in this poem too. About childhood.

February 24th

Looked up words I didn't know:

"lilting" means singing or playing cheerfully and lively

"dingle" means small, wooded valley

"hail" means to greet enthusiastically (at least I think this is the definition that fits the poem)

"windfall" is an apple which the wind knocked off the tree or an unexpected prize

"nightjars" are grayish brown nocturnal birds

"ricks" are haystacks

Thomas uses unusual words to describe things. The narrator says he was "young and easy." I understand "young," but what does he mean by "easy"? Maybe things were simple for him when he was a kid, maybe he was calm and had fun. It does seem he had fun when he was young. He says "once below a time." How can you be *below* time? He says "all the moon long" instead of "all night long" which I kind of like. He says "the heart was long." I don't know what that means yet. He says "sky blue trades." How can a trade have a color? Did he have a job as a young boy?

February 25th

I noticed that a lot of things seem to be alive in this poem that you usually don't think of as alive. The house is alive—lilting. Time gives him permission to do things and has eyes and leads him away at the end (personification?). The yard is happy, the sun is young, the hay is running, the chimney seems to be singing, the air is playing, the haystacks are flying, the farm is a wanderer, the stable is whinnying instead of the horses, the sea sings. The little boy seems to be very imaginative and maybe this is why. He sees himself as a prince, a huntsman, and a herdsman depending on where he is and what he's doing. His world seems almost magical which is true of a lot of children. I think children are a lot freer in their imaginings and there seem to be all kinds of possibilities in their world that adults don't have. Adults maybe know too much; anyway adults don't have as much fun. They see things as routine and following rules—haystacks don't fly. But to a kid they might because I think their dreams and imagination may be just as real as the real world, which sort of fit together in the poem. I can remember as a child playing princess, and the front yard was my palace and the backyard was my garden. Even city kids have fantasies, but the settings would be different and not have so much nature in them.

February 26th

I'm getting a little tired of Thomas though I know there's a lot I still don't understand. Today I thought about "Adam and the maiden." Since he speaks of "the birth of the simple light" in the next few lines, I get the feeling that this is Adam of Adam and Eve, which brings up Paradise. The little boy seems to be living in a paradise. He might be considered like Adam since he is the ruler (he thinks), the prince. I guess the apples might be important too, now that I think of it. This is an apple farm and there were apples in the Garden of Eden, but I don't think apples are the problem in this poem. Time seems to be the problem.

February 27th

Enough Thomas! I read this poem out loud to my roommate. She didn't understand it but said it sounds pretty, and I had to agree. I think I could write about the change in the narrator, I think I could write about the imagination of the little boy, and I think maybe I could say something about time. If I get pinned down to explain a line or two, I may still run into trouble.

These journal entries became the first writing in a prewriting portfolio which the writer started, adding to as ideas occurred to her. She now started to live with the poem and to record her reactions as she approached the assignment and the first draft.

TOPIC AND FORMAL PREWRITING

The following topic was assigned by the instructor:

Write an essay about the imagery and tone in "Fern Hill." Discuss how they help convey the theme.

Realizing that she wasn't sure of the tone, the writer decided to list the tone words and classify them, using the technique discussed under "Thought Patterns" in Chapter 3.

Stanza	Word	Tone
I	lilting	happy, joyful, good feeling
	happy	happy, joyful, good feeling
II	carefree	carefree
	happy	happy
	holy	feeling of reverence
III	lovely	positive, good feeling
	lovely	positive, good feeling
	blessed	feeling of reverence

Stanza	Word	Tone
IV	shining	bright, happy
	spellbound	mysterious
	fields of praise	joyful, reverence
V	happy	happy
	heedless	carefree
	out of grace	negative
VI	forever fled	sad, negative
	dying	sad
	sang in my chains	positive (sang), negative (chains), defiant

The writer noted that the tone changes from joyful, carefree, mysterious and reverential to sad and defiant. The shift occurs in stanza five.

Still not feeling ready to organize her thoughts, she decided to get more of her ideas down on paper by using another one of the formal prewriting methods—the Pentad (see Chapter 2). Always keeping the writing assignment in mind when formulating the questions, she proposed to answer the following:

1. Who are the principal characters? Who is the narrator?
2. What is the chief event in the poem? What is the theme? What are the images? What is the tone?
3. Where and when does the chief event occur?
4. How is the chief event accomplished?
5. Why does the chief event happen, and why does the work have the effect it does?

Here are the next entries, in response to the Pentad questions, which she added to the portfolio.

1. *Who.* The narrator is the principal character. A mature person looking back at his childhood and his early adulthood. The poem portrays him as both a child (first four stanzas) and an adult (last two stanzas). As a child he was imaginative and carefree. He felt in control of his world—princely. As an adult he is confined in a less pleasurable world.

   There is another character of sorts—Time. Time is personified as someone who is merciful to youth, allowing the child his carefree play, but then comes down hard on the adult. Time seems almost like a thief or a robber who takes the imaginative farm and setting away from the boy and leaves him in chains, an adult.

2. *What.* The chief event in the poem is the change caused by time, the change from childhood to adulthood. It is portrayed as the losing of the farm and childhood setting. The theme I think is that time causes the child to lose his gaiety, imagination, and carefreeness when he becomes an adult, but that he can retain something of the joy. The images are mostly

of nature: animals, grass, stars, green and gold colors. There is an image of Adam and Eve too. I think the child is "lord" of nature just like Adam until the apple. The tone seems to be happy, carefree, mysterious and reverential at first, and later sad and defiant as the narrator is chained by time. Robbed of his childhood fantasies, he still manages to sing.

3. *Where and When.*   The childhood events occur in an apple orchard and on a farm, and in the vicinity of the farm. The time seems to be the narrator's childhood and early adulthood—the changing point in his life.

4. *How.*   The chief event—the change—occurs without the narrator's being aware it's going to happen. And although the narrator doesn't like the results of the change, there's nothing he can do about it. Time is responsible for the change and takes the boy by the hand to a "childless land" and leaves him chained there; Time also flies away with the boy's fantasy farm and orchard.

5. *Why.*   The chief event happens because it's inevitable. People all grow up; we can't help it. The work has a sad effect because childhood is portrayed as so pleasant, a paradise that is lost when a person becomes an adult. But there is some joy in being able to remember so vividly.

At this point the writer decided to review the prewriting material on "Fern Hill" and highlight those parts which seemed to fit the assignment before organizing the essay. She found a great deal of material that could be worked into the essay.

THESIS AND OUTLINE

Having reviewed the prewriting material, the writer was ready to develop a tentative thesis in response to the assignment and to start organizing the essay. The topic assigned by the instructor had three elements which had to be identified: imagery, tone, and theme. In general the thesis should claim that the *imagery* and *tone* help convey the *theme*. Each element, however, had to be specified. The writer discovered that the specifics could be found in her answer to Pentad question 2 (the *What* question) and the classification exercise which preceded it. She formulates a tentative thesis from the prewriting material:

> Images of nature and paradise and a changing tone are used to show that time steals away the imagination and fantasies of childhood and leaves the narrator unwillingly trapped in the limited world of the adult.

This thesis is okay as a beginning, but it's a bit long; fantasy and imagination are redundant. Further revision is needed. The writer tried a two-step thesis which is specific and helped her to avoid an unwieldy sentence. Her new thesis looked like this:

Thomas shows how time steals the fantasies and freedom of childhood and leaves the youthful narrator unwillingly trapped in the limited world of the adult. The images of nature and the change in tone help show the change in the narrator.

Considering the possible organization of the essay, the student saw that this thesis was really the kernel of a cause-effect essay. Time is the cause, whose effects are the narrator's loss of childhood fantasies and freedom, and his change from carefree feelings to sad and defiant ones. Looking back at Chapter 10, she noted a possible organizational pattern for a cause-effect essay:

Introduction: Discussion of the cause (Time).
  Thesis: Time has A, B, C effects on Z (the boy and man).

Middle Section One: Time has effect A on the boy and man.

Middle Section Two: Time has effect B on the boy and man.

Middle Section Three: Time has effect C on the boy and man.

Conclusion

This basic pattern, however, didn't allow space for a discussion of what childhood is like for the narrator before time affects him, so the writer modified the structure to take into account this essential contrast. The detailed, revised structure looked like this:

Introduction: Discussion of time (the cause).
  Thesis: Thomas shows how time steals the fantasies and freedom of childhood and leaves the youthful narrator unwillingly trapped in the limited world of the adult. The images of nature and the change in tone help show the change in the narrator.

Middle Section One: Discussion of childhood before time's effects. The child lives in a world filled with fantasy and freedom (*focus on images*).

Middle Section Two: Discussion of childhood before time's effects. Child's world is filled with joy and reverence (*focus on tone*).

Middle Section Three: Discussion of time's effect on narrator. He loses his fantasies, his freedom (*focus on images*).

Middle Section Four: Discussion of time's effect on narrator. He feels sadness and defiance (*focus on tone*).

Conclusion: Reinforce the main idea and expand.

This outline provided both the thesis and the topic sentences for at least four middle paragraphs. Now the writer was ready to begin the rough

draft. (Remember, this is a first draft, and there are bound to be grammatical and stylistic errors which will later be corrected.)

FIRST DRAFT OF THE ESSAY

DYLAN THOMAS' "FERN HILL": A STUDY OF TIME'S EFFECTS

I.   Time has many different effects on people. We usually think of time as making us old and taking away our health and beauty but Dylan Thomas sees that we lose more than health and beauty, we lose a whole world. In "Fern Hill" Thomas shows how time steals the fantasies and freedom of childhood and leaves the youthful narrator unwillingly trapped in the limited world of the adult. The images of nature and the shift in tone shows the change in the narrator.

II.   In the first four stanzas, Thomas presents the childs world as full of fantasy and freedom. Inanimate things come alive from the childs perspective. The house was "lilting," the yard was "happy," "tunes" came out of the chimney; the air was "playing" and the stable was "whinnying." The childs fantasies extend to himself as well. The child sees himself as "prince of the apple towns," in command of the trees and leaves in the orchard; or again as "huntsman" or "herdsman" master of the calves and foxes. This childs world is filled with possibilities not bounded by logic. The world seemed magical—borne away by owls in the night, haystacks flying and "horses / Flashing into the night."

III.   The feelings that Thomas attaches to this childs world are feelings of joy and reverence. It's almost as if the child is high on nature. It was not hard to see that the house is not "lilting" all over nor the yard "happy," but the child is happy and sees these feelings in his surroundings as he sang and played. He is referred to as "lordly," "famous among the barns," "honored among the foxes and pheasants," almost as if he were royalty, something special. He seemed to be at once part of these natural surroundings and yet above them, as a master is part of the people whom he commands. Thomas used a Biblical metaphor for the child's world—"it was Adam and the maiden" refers to Genesis and Creation. Just like Adam in the Garden of Eden, this child is lord of what seems to be a paradise. His surroundings were referred to with reverence. The noise made by the stream trickling over pebbles is compared to bells ringing on the Sabbath in the lines: "And the Sabbath rang slowly / In the pebbles of the holy streams." The "nightjars" are described as "blessed among the stables." He speaks of the morning as of Creation, "Under the new made clouds . . . / In the sun born over and over," with a sense of awe.

IV.   The situation changes in the last half of stanza five. Time causes you to lose your fantasy world. Thomas does not go into detail in showing the situation of the new young adult, he merely pictures him as chained. You are, in a sense, forced into this situation. You have no choice and there is nothing you can do about it, Time is responsible for this change and all its limitations—your imaginative world is lost, you are limited in possibilities, and you will die.

V.   The farm is forever gone. The narrator finds himself in chains. Time takes off with the farm. When the boy goes to sleep.

VI.   Thomas seems to be saying in "Fern Hill" that childhood is brief and precious, "green" and "golden" are the colors he uses to convey this idea.

• EXERCISE

17.1 Review the preceding rough draft. Mark grammatical and stylistic errors. Make corrections on a separate sheet of paper. Make suggestions for revisions in organization and development.

REVISION

Next the writer used the "General Questions" from the previous chapter (pp. 256–257) to review critically the first draft and to revise the essay accordingly. She didn't actually write out the answers, as we've done, but rather made notes to herself in the margins and corrected mechanical errors, such as pronoun and tense shifts, directly on the copy. We've listed the answers only to the questions which showed a need for revision, rather than mark up the essay, to allow you the opportunity to review the rough draft yourself and to make your own suggestions for improvements.

General Questions

Essay Organization

3. Is the thesis too broad or too limited for what is actually proven in this essay? Do the middle paragraphs fulfill the plan of the thesis?
   Thesis is okay, but I really don't talk about the shift in tone. I need another paragraph to cover this topic.

4. Are there any words in the thesis which are vague? Can they be more precise?
   I could specify "images of nature" and "shift in tone" more.

5. Is each of the middle paragraphs related to the thesis of the essay?
   No, paragraph 5 is not.

7. Are the paragraphs logically connected with smooth transitions?
   Yes, but transition between paragraphs 3 and 4 could be better.

8. Is the thesis reasserted in the conclusion?
   Yes, but this can be fuller.

Paragraph Organization

1. Does each of the middle paragraphs have a topic sentence which makes a critical point?
   No, paragraph 5 retells part of the poem without a critical point.

2. Are any of the topic sentences merely plot summary and, therefore, in need of revision?

   Yes, paragraph 5.

3. Does each paragraph develop only one idea?

   Paragraph 2 does not develop freedom, the second idea mentioned in the topic sentence. It does develop the fantasy, which in a way is a type of freedom, but I think some revision is needed here. Maybe two paragraphs are needed.

Development

2. Is the introduction more than a summary or a statement of the thesis?

   Yes, but it's brief.

5. Is each of the middle paragraphs fully developed?

   Paragraphs 4 and 5 are too brief.

6. Are generalizations supported with details from the works of literature?

   Yes, except freedom is not discussed in paragraph 2, and change in tone mentioned in the thesis is not discussed in the essay.

10. Is the plot of the literary work summarized unnecessarily? Are there any plot details which are not needed to prove a critical point?

    Yes, paragraph 5.

12. Is there enough evidence to prove each point? Are any important details left out?

    Paragraph 2 needs evidence to prove the boy was free, and paragraph 4 needs more evidence.

14. Is there a separate and adequately developed conclusion?

    There is a separate conclusion, but it's not adequate.

Editing and Proofreading

1. Are all the sentences complete sentences?

   No, paragraph 5 has a fragment.

2. Are sentences joined correctly so that there are no run-on sentences?

   No, I'd better check each sentence.

3. Are all punctuation marks used correctly?

   No, check possessives and commas.

4. Do all subjects and verbs agree?

   No, the last sentence in the introduction has an agreement problem.

7. Are pronouns consistent in person (especially avoiding the use of *you*)?

   No, pronouns shift in paragraph 4.

8. Are verbs consistently in the present tense?

   No, verbs shift in paragraphs 2 and 3.

9. Is any shift in tense justified?

   No.

10. Are there any slang or colloquial words or phrases? Is there a standard word or phrase which can be substituted?

   Yes, "high on nature" in paragraph 3. I think I'll leave it out. Also "take off" in paragraph 5. "Leaves" would be a better word.

14. Are quotations accurate, word-for-word representations of the author's words?

   I think so, but I'll check again.

Style

1. Are there any trite phrases or clichés?

   Yes, "high on nature" in paragraph 3.

2. Do I overuse the passive voice?

   In paragraph 3: "His surroundings were referred to with reverence," and the sentence following this one.

3. Can excess words which do not add to the meaning be trimmed?

   Yes, "unwillingly" can be taken out of the thesis, since it's unlikely anyone would be willingly trapped; "feelings" is repeated in the topic sentence to paragraph 3; "all over" is unnecessary in the third sentence in paragraph 3; "almost" and "something special" are unnecessary in the fourth sentence of paragraph 3. "You have no choice and there is nothing you can do about it" repeats an idea from the previous sentence in paragraph 4.

Manuscript Form

1. Is there a title?

   Yes, but I don't like it. I'll think of another.

2. Is there a title page (if required)?

   No, but I'll do one.

5. Are primary sources footnoted and noted in the bibliography (if required)?

   Instructor asked for only line numbers, which I'll put in after each quote.

6. Are secondary sources footnoted and noted in the bibliography?

   I didn't use any.

FINAL DRAFT

After the revisions were made, the completed essay looked like this:

"FERN HILL": A LOST PARADISE

Rachel Green
February 22, 1983
English 102
Professor March

Time is an uncontrollable force that has many different effects on people. It governs and orders our lives as we punch time clocks and wait for the weekend. It takes away our health and beauty, making us old and less athletic. It brings us closer to death with each ticking of the clock. Few authors picture time as a kind force, and Dylan Thomas is no different. However, he sees that time robs us of more than health and beauty. Time robs us of a whole world. In "Fern Hill" Thomas shows how time steals the fantasies and freedom of childhood and leaves the youthful narrator trapped in the limited world of an adult. The images of nature, particularly of a lost paradise, and the shift in tone from joyful and reverent to sad and defiant show the change in the narrator.

In the first four stanzas, Thomas presents the child's world as full of fantasy. Inanimate things come alive from the child's perspective. The house is "lilting" (l. 2), the yard is "happy" (l. 11), "tunes" (l. 20) come out of the chimney, the air is "playing" (l. 21), and the stable is "whinnying" (l. 35). The child's fantasies extend to himself, as well. He sees himself as "prince of the apple towns" (l. 6), in command of the trees and leaves in the orchard; or again as "huntsman and herdsman" (l. 15), master of the calves and foxes. This child's world is filled with possibilities not bounded by logic. The world seems magical—borne away by owls in the night, and filled with haystacks flying and "horses / Flashing into the dark" (ll. 26–27).

The child has not only the freedom of his imagination, but also physical freedom and freedom from care. He roams freely from apple orchard to barn to field to house. He is pictured as running and singing. He is "happy as the grass was green" (l. 2), "carefree" (l. 10), and "heedless" (l. 40). He has no anxiety since he does not realize that his play will be cut short by time, and he does not care

> that time allows
> In all his tuneful turning so few and such morning songs
> Before the children green and golden
> Follow him out of grace.   (ll. 42–45)

The "morning song," the youthful part of the day, and by extension the childhood part of the narrator's life, is limited by time, which is personified as a kind of Pied Piper who leads children out of this blessed state.

The feelings that Thomas attaches to this child's world are joy and reverence. It is not hard to see that the house is not "lilting," nor the yard "happy," but the child is happy and sees these feelings in his surroundings as he sings and plays. He is referred to as "lordly" (l. 7), "famous among the barns" (l. 10), "honoured among foxes and pheasants" (l. 37), as if he were royalty. He seems at once to be part of the natural surroundings and yet feels he is above them, as a master is part of the people he governs, and yet apparently privileged and apart from them. Thomas uses a Biblical metaphor for the child's world—"it was Adam and the maiden" (l. 30) refers to Genesis and the Creation. Just like Adam, this child is lord of what seems to be a paradise. He speaks of his surroundings with reverence. The narrator compares the noise made by the stream trickling over pebbles to bells ringing on the Sabbath: "And the Sabbath rang slowly / In the pebbles of the holy streams" (ll. 17–

18). He describes the "nightjars" as "blessed among the stables" (l. 25). He speaks of the morning as of Creation with a sense of awe: "Under the new made clouds . . . / In the sun born over and over" (ll. 38–39).

Time permits the child his fantasies and joy only for a while. The situation changes in the last half of stanza five as time, who has passively allowed the child to play, now takes a more active role in limiting his future. Time causes the narrator to lose his fantasy world. The narrator says, "the children / Follow him [time] out of grace" (l. 45). Just like Adam and Eve, they are forced to leave paradise. They have left the state of grace and are subject to suffering, age, and death. The change occurs suddenly in stanza six when time flies away with the child's world while he is asleep. He awakens in a "childless land" (l. 51) with the farm gone forever. The narrator is no longer a child; paradise is no longer accessible to him. Thomas does not go into detail about the young adult; he merely pictures him as chained. He is, in a sense, forced into this situation. Time is responsible for this change and all its limitations— his imaginative world is lost, he is limited in his possibilities, and he will die.

The tone of the poem shifts as the narrator reflects on the change that time brings. A sad note is introduced for the first time in stanza five when the narrator notes how brief childhood is, as "time allows / In all his tuneful turning so few . . . morning songs" (ll. 42–43). It is also sad that there is no turning back once time leads the child to this more limited world—the farm is "forever fled" (l. 51). However, the last three lines make the loss most vivid as the narrator compares how he was as a child with how he sees himself now:

> Oh as I was young and easy in the mercy of his means,
> Time held me green and dying
> Though I sang in my chains like the sea.   (ll. 52–54)

The tragic part is that one so young and full of life, "green" as Thomas says, should be dying. But this, of course, is true of all men; each second after birth one is closer to death. The narrator does not become melancholy over this realization. The last line suggests that he lives fully even in his limited situation. Singing, as noted in the previous stanzas, is an activity associated with happiness in his childhood. In this final line, it seems to be a sign of defiance that he still engages in singing given his present circumstances. And he does not just sing a soft, mournful tune; he bellows, "like the sea," a powerful and noisy body of water. Ironically, this final simile is an image of strength in the face of inevitable defeat. Time will win, but the narrator will not have surrendered.

Thomas claims in "Fern Hill" that childhood is brief and precious. Even though there is nothing we can do about the march of time, Thomas shows us how the former child still has some control over how he spends the rest of his life, limited though it may be. With the memories of such an imaginative and vital childhood, Thomas' narrator does not succumb in spirit to time's power. The dauntless "prince of the apple towns" (l. 6) does not lose his daring even as a prisoner with no hope of reprieve.

The writer of this essay has come to understand "Fern Hill," to possess its meaning, to a degree probably not possible if she had only read and not written about the work. It's in the writing that we face our thoughts, organize them, test them, develop them in an expanded way. Literature lets us extend ourselves in reading, analyzing, and writing. Critical writing brings us closer to the ideas, experiences, and artistry of other minds, and allows us to add our explorations and discoveries to the understanding of the work.

appendix A

THE RESEARCH PAPER

The research paper is a special kind of essay. It involves all the activities that we've already discussed—that is, reading, prewriting, formulating a thesis, organizing, developing, and revising. In addition, it includes research, additional reading, and consideration of *what other writers have said* about the literary works being analyzed.

READING AND RESEARCH

Before you can write a research paper on a literary topic, you'll be doing two kinds of reading:

Primary sources: first, you'll have to read the works of literature you intend to write about. These are the *primary sources* for your paper.

Secondary sources: after you have read the literary works, then you'll read what other people have written about these works. These critical, biographical, historical, and other essays are the *secondary sources* for your essay.

It's important that you do the reading in order—primary sources first, secondary sources next—for two reasons. Unless you're familiar with the literary works, you're not likely to fully understand the essays about them. Also, you won't be able to agree or disagree with these other writers' opinions unless you form some opinions of your own first. Let's acknowledge from the start that student writers often approach a research or term paper under a great deal of pressure from work loads in other courses and deadlines. There may be the temptation to skip the focus of research—the primary literary sources—and go straight for summary pamphlets with research notes. If the research paper is to be a whole-hearted effort and commitment, more than a mechanical exercise, then you need to use the full time available to allow for both serious reading of the literature and critical reading of secondary sources.

Prewriting activities, such as keeping a journal, freewriting, and so on, if done before you read your secondary sources, can help you preserve your initial thoughts and reactions before you're influenced by other writers. Unfortunately, some beginning writers neglect this important initial stage. Because they haven't taken the time to think about the works and to jot down their ideas before they begin researching, they lose the opportunity for creative interaction with the thoughts of the critical writers whom they read. Their own ideas and voices become submerged in their research, and they merely echo other people's ideas. Ideally, a research essay should engage the ideas of other writers and show the reader that you've considered what they have to say and have come to your own conclusions, perhaps agreeing with some writers and disagreeing with others.

THE LIBRARY

Finding Information in Books

Libraries can be confusing until you learn the system of organization and where materials are kept. Once you've mastered some simple, key functions, centuries of knowledge and critical reaction will become available to you. The card catalogue or computerized information retrieval systems can help you locate information. Both work on the same principles. You can look up an *author* (last name first), and the catalogue or computer will provide the titles of all the works by the author which the library owns. The catalogue or computer will also give you either a Dewey Decimal number or a Library of Congress number for each title, so that you can locate the book in the library.

You can also look up a particular *title* in the catalogue or on the computer; you would then, again, get a number to locate the book. Finally, and most useful for doing initial research, you can look up a *subject* in the catalogue or on the computer to discover the authors, titles, and locating numbers of books which the library has on your subject.

For example, if you looked up "Shakespeare" as an author in the catalogue or on the computer, you would find cards or entries for each volume of plays or poems written by Shakespeare which the library owns. If you looked up the title, *Hamlet*, you would find a card or entry for each copy of *Hamlet* which the library owns. If you looked up the subject, "Hamlet," you would find entries for books written about Shakespeare's play by other authors. If you looked up the subject, "Shakespeare," you would find biographies, as well as works about Shakespeare's plays, poems, and times.

The card catalogue or computer can provide you with other useful information. Besides the author and title of the works, each entry contains the place of publication, the publisher, and the date of publication—useful information for your bibliography. In addition, the entry will tell you how many pages there are in the book, whether the book is illustrated, and what subject headings the book might be listed under—a clue to the book's contents. Also, some computer systems might tell you if the book is in the library or if someone has it out, and what date the book is due back, so you can have it put aside for you.

From the contents of the catalogue card or the computer entry, you can write your *bibliography cards*. A bibliography is a list of sources which you have consulted to write your essay. The bibliography card is an index card on which you write all the information needed for your bibliographical entry on one book.

Bibliography Card for a Book

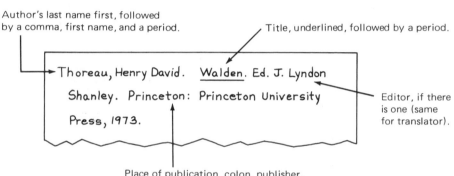

Author's last name first, followed by a comma, first name, and a period.

Title, underlined, followed by a period.

Thoreau, Henry David. Walden. Ed. J. Lyndon Shanley. Princeton: Princeton University Press, 1973.

Editor, if there is one (same for translator).

Place of publication, colon, publisher, comma, date of publication, period.

Sometimes many critical essays on one subject will be collected in a book. Each essay has a different author and title. For bibliographical purposes, you might list the whole book or one or more essays in the book, depending on how you use the book. If all, or most, of the essays were useful to you, then list the book with its editor (instead of author) in your bibliography (see Example A below). If only a few entries were useful, you may list each entry separately (see Example B below).

Example A

Mizener, Arthur, ed. *F. Scott Fitzgerald: A Collection of Critical Essays*. Englewood Cliffs, N.J.: Prentice-Hall, Inc., 1963.

Example B

Burnam, Tom. "The Eyes of Dr. Eckleburg: A Re-Examination of *The Great Gatsby*." In *F. Scott Fitzgerald: A Collection of Critical Essays*. Ed. Arthur Mizener. Englewood Cliffs, N.J.: Prentice-Hall, Inc., 1963, pp. 104–11.

Finding Information in Journals and Magazines

Besides books, libraries have collections of scholarly journals which will be useful to you in your literary research. In fact, the most contemporary criticism is usually found in journals, so you shouldn't overlook this important source. Journals such as *The Drama Review, Modern Poetry Studies, New England Quarterly, PMLA (Publications of the Modern Language Association of America), Southern Quarterly, Studies in Black Literature,* and many more provide essays on literary topics. To find these essays, you should consult an *index* which is usually divided into years, and under each year you can look up information about a particular author, title, or subject. Indexes are located in the reference sections of the library. If you're researching a contemporary topic, it's important to know in what year the book you're writing about was published, so that you know at what date to begin your research. For example, if you were writing about Robert Graves' novel *I, Claudius,* it would help to know that it was published in 1934, so that you wouldn't look at indexes dated before the publication of the primary source.

Some indexes which might be useful to you in your literary research are *MLA (Modern Language Association) International Bibliography,* an important source of information about critical essays; *New York Times Index,* a source of book reviews, play reviews, and literary articles; *The Reader's Guide to Periodical Literature,* a source of information about reviews and stories about contemporary people in popular magazines. Your librarian can help you locate these and suggest others which may be of help. Your library also has a master listing of the periodicals it owns, which are also noted by title in the card catalogue. So after you find the title, author, and source of an essay you want to read, it's helpful to consult either the master list or the card catalogue to find out whether the library owns the periodical and volume you're looking for, and where the periodical is located. Periodicals, like books, have call numbers.

Your bibliographical entry for an article should look like this:

Bibliography Card for an Article

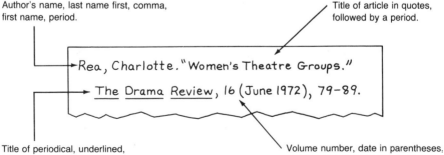

Author's name, last name first, comma, first name, period.

Title of article in quotes, followed by a period.

Rea, Charlotte. "Women's Theatre Groups."
The Drama Review, 16 (June 1972), 79–89.

Title of periodical, underlined, followed by a comma.

Volume number, date in parentheses, comma, and page numbers, period.

A Final Note on Looking Up Secondary Sources

Unless your topic is sufficiently narrowed, you're likely to be over-whelmed with secondary sources. Imagine how many books and articles have been written about Shakespeare or even about his play *Hamlet.* You'd have an easier time researching a paper on *Hamlet* if the topic were nar-rowed to Hamlet's or Ophelia's madness, or the relationship between par-ents and children in *Hamlet,* or the use of comedy in *Hamlet.* Then you could select among the books and articles only those which touch on your topic and thus focus and limit the readings on the topic. A key related skill that you'll develop the more research you do is the ability to scan tables of contents, indexes, and passages of texts to focus on the material relevant to your topic.

BIBLIOGRAPHY

The bibliography for your paper will list the books and essays you've con-sulted. This list occurs at the end of your essay and begins on a new sheet of paper with the heading "Bibliography" at the top of the page. You can list your primary sources separately, followed by your secondary sources, or both sources can form one list. Check for your instructor's preference.

If you've used bibliography cards, all you have to do is alphabetize them by the author's last name (or by the first word in the title if there is no author or editor) and make a bibliographical list from the cards. Each entry is double-spaced, with a double-space between entries also. The first line in an entry begins flush against the margin. If the entry takes more than one line, the subsequent lines are indented five spaces. Here are some examples.

> Alvarez, A. *The Savage God: A Study of Suicide.* New York: Random House, 1972.
>
> Meissner, William. "The Rise of the Angel: Life Through Death in the Poetry of Sylvia Plath." *Massachusetts Studies in English,* 3 (1971), 34–39.
>
> Newman, Charles, ed. *The Art of Sylvia Plath: A Symposium.* Bloomington: Indiana University Press, 1971.

Special Cases

Two or more works by the same author. List the works individually in alphabetical order, first by the author's last name, then by the title. The first entry should have the author's name; all following entries use a line (————) to indicate the author is the same as the one named above.

> Clemens, Samuel. *The Adventures of Huckleberry Finn.* Scranton: Chandler Publishing Co., 1962.
>
> ————. *The Innocents Abroad.* New York: New American Library, 1966.

More than one author   List the authors, noting the first author (last name first) and then the second (first name first), joined by a comma and an "and."

Grassi, Rosanna, and Peter DeBlois. *Composition and Literature.* Englewood
Cliffs, N.J.: Prentice-Hall, Inc., 1984.

If there are more than two authors, you can list them in a series (only the first name would appear reversed), or you can use *et al.*, or "and others" after the first author's name to indicate that there is more than one author.

NOTE TAKING

While reading your secondary sources, you'll want to take notes so that you can incorporate the author's words and ideas into your own work. Many writers find it helpful to use *notecards* to record important ideas and quotations. The notecards would also contain information about the source and the page numbers which you will need to do a footnote. The title may be abbreviated if you can retrieve the full title from your bibliography card. Here's a sample.

Duyckinck, Evert   "Melville's Moby Dick"   p. 403

Negative criticism from a contemporary of Melville

Compares Moby Dick to German melodrama in which
characters are concerned with the "problem of
the universe."

"We begin to have some faint idea of the association
of whaling and lamentation, and why blubber
is popularly synonymous with tears."

If the material on the notecard covers more than one page, you'll have to note the exact page changes in your notes in order to give proper credit in your footnotes.

You should be sure to record the source of ideas, as well as quotes, which you intend to use in your essay. *Plagiarism,* using another's *words or ideas* as your own without properly acknowledging that they belong to someone else, is stealing. Students have failed courses, or even been expelled from school, for deliberately trying to deceive their instructor by copying someone else's work.

FOOTNOTES

While the bibliography provides the reader with information about your research and sources, it doesn't tell which ideas or quotations come from which source. Footnotes provide this more specific information. They can occur at the bottom of the page which contains the quote or idea to be acknowledged, or they can be listed numerically at the end of the essay on a separate sheet(s) headed "Footnotes." Check for your instructor's preference.

In the text of your essay, a footnote is indicated by a raised number (^{1}) which refers the reader to the footnote with the corresponding number. Unless your essay is very long, you'll be using consecutive numbers (one through whatever number you need). The footnote for a book contains the author's name in normal order, title (underlined), place of publication, publisher, date, and page number(s). Note the punctuation in the following examples.

[6]Leslie A. Fiedler, *Love and Death in the American Novel,* rev. ed. (New York: Stein and Day, 1975), p. 93.

[7]Robert A. Heinlein, *Expanded Universe: The New Worlds of Robert A. Heinlein* (New York: Ace Books, 1980), p. 2.

A footnote for an article would list author, title of the essay, title of the journal or magazine (underlined), volume, number (if there is one), date, and page number. The page number in this case (unlike in the bibliography) would be just the page number referred to, not the pages for the whole article. For example,

[8]Katherine M. Jones Loheyde, "Freedom and Identity in *Invisible Man,*" *The English Record,* 23, no. 1 (1981), p. 7.

If you include any of the information from the footnote in your essay discussion, then you don't have to include that information in the footnote. For example, if in introducing a quote, you refer to the author and title of the book it came from, then you don't have to put the author and title in your footnote. You can begin the footnote with the place of publication.

You only have to footnote a work *fully* once. If you refer to a work again, all you need in your repeated note is the author's last name and the page number for the reference.

[2]Chopin, p. 67.

If you're using more than one work by the same author, to avoid confusion, you should use the title of the work and page number in a repeated footnote.

[3]*The Awakening,* p. 125.

Special Cases

Footnoting works from collections. In footnoting works from collections, you should include information about the work within the collection, as well as the entire collection. Your footnote would look like this:

[9]Stephen L. Mooney, "Poe's Gothic Wasteland," in *The Recognition of Edgar Allan Poe,* ed. Eric W. Carlson (Ann Arbor: The University of Michigan Press, 1970), p. 282.

Footnoting translations.   In footnoting a work which has been translated, you should note the translator, as well as the author. For example:

[1]Aristotle, *The Poetics,* trans. S. H. Butcher (New York: Hill and Wang, 1961), p. 61.

Footnoting works with more than one author.   In footnoting works with more than one author, you can list the authors in a series, or you can cite only the first author and use *et al.* or "and others" to indicate there is more than one author, just as in the bibliography.

Footnoting primary sources.   When you're writing a research paper on a literary topic, it's not unusual to include a number of quotes and references to your primary source(s)—the novel, story, play, or poem about which you're writing. Footnoting every reference can be cumbersome, so frequently authors of critical essays will footnote the primary sources *once,* and in the footnote, after the basic information, they note that "any additional references to this work will cite page numbers parenthetically in the text." In other words, after the first footnote, you refer to the primary source only by page numbers put in parentheses after each quote or reference. If there is more than one primary source, you might want to include the author and page number (Chopin, p. 72) or the title and page number (*The Awakening,* p. 72), whichever would be clearer.

Placing Footnotes

Footnotes placed at the bottom of the page should be triple-spaced from the last line of the text. There should also be a one-inch margin between the end of the footnote and the end of the paper. Indent the first line of the footnote five spaces; the second line is flush with the margin. Single-space material within a footnote but leave a double-space between successive footnotes.

If you place your footnotes at the end of your paper, you should follow the same format. The footnotes at the back are listed numerically, beginning with number one. There is one advantage to the footnote occurring at the foot of the page: the reader doesn't have to page back and forth to find the reference. Footnotes at the bottom of the page are more difficult to type, but they're more convenient for the reader.

Other uses of the footnote.   You can also use a footnote to provide additional or explanatory information which doesn't belong in the actual essay. This type of footnote should, however, be kept to a minimum.

WRITING THE RESEARCH PAPER

After you've done your reading and research, the steps to writing a research paper are identical to those we've discussed for the critical essay. You should try some formal prewriting, ask yourself a few questions, and try to formulate a thesis based on your notes and prewriting portfolio. You should then outline your essay, write a first draft, and revise. Referring often to your notecards should help you incorporate your research into the essay. You'll also want to make sure that your thesis and outline adequately reflect the research you've done. The section on quoting (Chapter 13) applies to quoting from critical essays, as well as from literature. Your format will be the same as that discussed in Chapter 17; however, you'll be adding footnotes and a bibliography. We haven't covered all the special circumstances for footnotes and bibliographical entries. For a thorough coverage, you should consult a handbook, such as the *MLA (Modern Language Association) Handbook*.

The principles of writing a good research paper are the same as those for writing any good essay. The main difference between the research paper and your other critical writing is that you're no longer the only critic being considered. In the research paper, you have the opportunity to enlarge your views, to engage and exchange ideas with others who have written on the topic. You have the opportunity to be critical not only of the literary work, but of what others have written about it, and to evaluate what others have said. As much as any other paper, you should view it as the product of your own composing skills applied over a wider breadth of material.

appendix B

LITERARY WORKS

The Country Husband
John Cheever

To begin at the beginning, the airplane from Minneapolis in which Francis Weed was traveling East ran into heavy weather. The sky had been a hazy blue, with the clouds below the plane lying so close together that nothing could be seen of the earth. Then mist began to form outside the windows, and they flew into a white cloud of such density that it reflected the exhaust fires. The color of the cloud darkened to gray, and the plane began to rock. Francis had been in heavy weather before, but he had never been shaken up so much. The man in the seat beside him pulled a flask out of his pocket and took a drink. Francis smiled at his neighbor, but the man looked away; he wasn't sharing his pain killer with anyone. The plane began to drop and flounder wildly. A child was crying. The air in the cabin was overheated and stale, and Francis' left foot went to sleep. He read a little from a paper book that he had bought at the airport, but the violence of the storm divided his attention. It was black outside the ports. The exhaust fires blazed and shed sparks in the dark, and, inside, the shaded lights, the stuffiness, and the window curtains gave the cabin an atmosphere of intense and misplaced domesticity. Then the lights flickered and went out. "You know what I've always wanted to do?" the man beside Francis said suddenly. "I've always wanted to buy a farm in New Hampshire and raise beef cattle." The stewardess announced that they were going to make an emergency landing. All but the children saw in their minds the spreading wings of the Angel of Death. The pilot could be heard singing faintly, "I've got sixpence, jolly, jolly sixpence. I've got sixpence to last me all my life . . ." There was no other sound.

The loud groaning of the hydraulic valves swallowed up the pilot's song, and there was a shrieking high in the air, like automobile brakes, and the plane hit flat on its belly in a cornfield and shook them so violently that an old man up forward howled, "Me kidneys! Me kidneys!" The stewardess flung open the door, and someone opened an emergency door at the back, letting in the sweet noise of their continuing mortality—the idle splash and smell of a heavy rain. Anxious for their lives, they filed out of the doors and scattered over the cornfield in all directions, praying that the thread would hold. It did. Nothing happened. When it was clear that the plane would not burn or explode, the crew and the stewardess gathered the passengers together and led them to the shelter of a barn. They were not far from Philadelphia, and in a little while a string of taxis took them into the city. "It's just like the Marne," someone said, but there was surprisingly little relaxation of that suspiciousness with which many Americans regard their fellow travelers.

In Philadelphia, Francis Weed got a train to New York. At the end of that journey, he crossed the city and caught just as it was about to pull out the commuting train that he took five nights a week to his home in Shady Hill.

He sat with Trace Bearden. "You know, I was in that plane that just crashed outside Philadelphia," he said. "We came down in a field . . ." He had traveled faster than the newspapers or the rain, and the weather in New York was sunny and mild. It was a day in late September, as fragrant and shapely as an apple. Trace listened to the story, but how could he get excited? Francis had no powers that would let him re-create a brush with death—particularly in the atmosphere of a commuting train, journeying through a sunny countryside where already, in the slum gardens, there were signs of harvest. Trace picked up his newspaper, and Francis was left alone with his thoughts. He said good night to Trace on the platform at Shady Hill and drove in his secondhand Volkswagen up to the Blenhollow neighborhood, where he lived.

The Weeds' Dutch Colonial house was larger than it appeared to be from the driveway. The living room was spacious and divided like Gaul into three parts. Around an ell to the left as one entered from the vestibule was the long table, laid for six, with candles and a bowl of fruit in the center. The sounds and smells that came from the open kitchen door were appetizing, for Julia Weed was a good cook. The largest part of the living room centered on a fireplace. On the right were some bookshelves and a piano. The room was polished and tranquil, and from the windows that opened to the west there was some late-summer sunlight, brilliant and as clear as water. Nothing here was neglected; nothing had not been burnished. It was not the kind of household where, after prying open a stuck cigarette box, you would find an old shirt button and a tarnished nickel. The hearth was swept, the roses on the piano were reflected in the polish of the broad top, and there was an album of Schubert waltzes on the rack. Louisa Weed, a pretty girl of nine, was looking out the western windows. Her younger brother Henry was standing beside her. Her still younger brother, Toby, was studying the figures of some tonsured monks drinking beer on the polished brass of the woodbox. Francis, taking off his hat and putting down his paper, was not consciously pleased with the scene; he was not that reflective. It was his element, his creation, and he returned to it with that sense of lightness and strength with which any creature returns to his home. "Hi, everybody," he said. "The plane from Minneapolis . . ."

Nine times out of ten, Francis would be greeted with affection, but tonight the children are absorbed in their own antagonisms. Francis had not finished his sentence about the plane crash before Henry plants a kick in Louisa's behind. Louisa swings around, saying, "*Damn* you!" Francis makes the mistake of scolding Louisa for bad language before he punishes Henry. Now Louisa turns on her father and accuses him of favoritism. Henry is always right; she is persecuted and lonely; her lot is hopeless. Francis turns to his son, but the boy has justification for the kick— she hit him first; she hit him on the ear, which is dangerous. Louisa agrees with this passionately. She hit him on the ear, and she *meant* to hit him on the ear, because he messed up her china collection. Henry says that this is a lie. Little Toby turns away from the woodbox to throw in some evidence for Louisa. Henry claps his hand over little Toby's mouth. Francis separates the two boys but accidentally pushes Toby into the woodbox. Toby begins to cry. Louisa is already crying. Just then, Julia Weed comes into that part of the room where the table is laid. She is a pretty, intelligent woman, and the white in her hair is premature. She does not seem to notice the fracas. "Hello, darling," she says serenely to Francis. "Wash your hands, everyone. Dinner is ready." She strikes a match and lights the six candles in this vale of tears.

This simple announcement, like the war cries of the Scottish chieftains, only refreshes the ferocity of the combatants. Louisa gives Henry a blow on the shoulder. Henry, although he seldom cries, has pitched nine innings and is tired. He bursts into tears. Little Toby discovers a splinter in his hand and begins to howl. Francis says loudly that he has been in a plane crash and that he is tired. Julia appears again from the kitchen and, still ignoring the chaos, asks Francis to go upstairs and tell Helen that everything is ready. Francis is happy to go; it is like getting back to headquarters company. He is planning to tell his oldest daughter about the airplane crash, but Helen is lying on her bed reading a *True Romance* magazine, and the first thing Francis does is to take the magazine from her hand and remind Helen that he has forbidden her to buy it. She did not buy it, Helen replies. It was given to her by her best friend, Bessie Black. Everybody reads *True Romance*. Bessie Black's father reads *True Romance*. There isn't a girl in Helen's class who doesn't read *True Romance*. Francis expresses his detestation of the magazine and then tells her that dinner is ready—although from the sounds downstairs it doesn't seem so. Helen follows him down the stairs. Julia has seated herself in the candlelight and spread a napkin over her lap. Neither Louisa nor Henry has come to the table. Little Toby is still howling, lying face down on the floor. Francis speaks to him gently: "Daddy was in a plane crash this afternoon, Toby. Don't you want to hear about it?" Toby goes on crying. "If you don't come to the table now, Toby," Francis says, "I'll have to send you to bed without any supper." The little boy rises, gives him a cutting look, flies up the stairs to his bedroom, and slams the door. "Oh dear," Julia says, and starts to go after him. Francis says that she will spoil him. Julia says that Toby is ten pounds underweight and has to be encouraged to eat. Winter is coming, and he will spend the cold months in bed unless he has his dinner. Julia goes upstairs. Francis sits down at the table with Helen. Helen is suffering from the dismal feeling of having read too intently on a fine day, and she gives her father and the room a jaded look. She doesn't understand about the plane crash, because there wasn't a drop of rain in Shady Hill.

Julia returns with Toby, and they all sit down and are served. "Do I have to look at that big, fat slob?" Henry says, of Louisa. Everybody but Toby enters into this skirmish, and it rages up and down the table for five minutes. Toward the end, Henry puts his napkin over his head and, trying to eat that way, spills spinach all over his shirt. Francis asks Julia if the children couldn't have their dinner earlier. Julia's guns are loaded for this. She can't cook two dinners and lay two tables. She paints with lightning strokes that panorama of drudgery in which her youth, her beauty, and her wit have been lost. Francis says that he must be understood; he was nearly killed in an airplane crash, and he doesn't like to come home every night to a battlefield. Now Julia is deeply concerned. Her voice trembles. He doesn't come home every night to a battlefield. The accusation is stupid and mean. Everything was tranquil until he arrived. She stops speaking, puts down her knife and fork, and looks into her plate as if it is a gulf. She begins to cry. "Poor Mummy!" Toby says, and when Julia gets up from the table, drying her tears with a napkin, Toby goes to her side. "Poor Mummy," he says. "Poor Mummy!" And they climb the stairs together. The other children drift away from the battlefield, and Francis goes into the back garden for a cigarette and some air.

It was a pleasant garden, with walks and flower beds and places to sit. The sunset had nearly burned out, but there was still plenty of light. Put into a thoughtful mood by the crash and the battle, Francis listened to the evening sounds of Shady Hill. "Varmints! Rascals!" old Mr. Nixon shouted to the squirrels in his bird-feeding station. "Avaunt and quit my sight!" A door slammed. Someone was cutting grass. Then Donald Goslin, who lived at the corner, began to play the "Moonlight Sonata." He did this nearly every night. He threw the tempo out the window and played it *rubato* from beginning to end, like an outpouring of tearful petulance, lonesomeness, and self-pity—of everything it was Beethoven's greatness not to know. The music rang up and down the street beneath the trees like an appeal for love, for tenderness, aimed at some lovely housemaid—some fresh-faced, homesick girl from Galway, looking at old snapshots in her third-floor room. "Here, Jupiter, here, Jupiter," Francis called to the Mercers' retriever. Jupiter crashed through the tomato vines with the remains of a felt hat in his mouth.

Jupiter was an anomaly. His retrieving instincts and his high spirits were out of place in Shady Hill. He was as black as coal, with a long, alert, intelligent, rakehell face. His eyes gleamed with mischief, and he held his head high. It was the fierce, heavily collared dog's head that appears in heraldry, in tapestry, and that used to appear on umbrella handles and walking sticks. Jupiter went where he pleased, ransacking wastebaskets, clotheslines, garbage pails, and shoe bags. He broke up garden parties and tennis matches, and got mixed up in the processional at Christ Church on Sunday, barking at the men in red dresses. He crashed through old Mr. Nixon's rose garden two or three times a day, cutting a wide swath through the Condesa de Sastagos, and as soon as Donald Goslin lighted his barbecue fire on Thursday nights, Jupiter would get the scent. Nothing the Goslins did could drive him away. Sticks and stones and rude commands only moved him to the edge of the terrace, where he remained, with his gallant and heraldic muzzle, waiting for Donald Goslin to turn his back and reach for the salt. Then he would spring onto the terrace, lift the steak lightly off the fire, and run away with the Goslins' dinner. Jupiter's days were numbered. The Wrightsons' German gardener or the Farquarsons' cook would soon poison him. Even old Mr. Nixon might put some arsenic in the garbage that Jupiter loved. "Here, Jupiter, Jupiter!" Francis called, but the dog pranced off, shaking the hat in his white teeth. Looking at the windows of his house, Francis saw that Julia had come down and was blowing out the candles.

Julia and Francis Weed went out a great deal. Julia was well liked and gregarious, and her love of parties sprang from a most natural dread of chaos and loneliness. She went through her morning mail with real anxiety, looking for invitations, and she usually found some, but she was insatiable, and if she had gone out seven nights a week, it would not have cured her of a reflective look—the look of someone who hears distant music—for she would always suppose that there was a more brilliant party somewhere else. Francis limited her to two week-night parties, putting a flexible interpretation on Friday, and rode through the weekend like a dory in a gale. The day after the airplane crash, the Weeds were to have dinner with the Farquarsons.

Francis got home late from town, and Julia got the sitter while he dressed, and then hurried him out of the house. The party was small and pleasant, and Francis settled down to enjoy himself. A new maid passed the drinks. Her hair was dark, and her face was round and pale and seemed familiar to Francis. He had not developed his memory as a sentimental faculty. Wood smoke, lilac, and other such perfumes did not stir him, and his memory was something like his appendix— a vestigial repository. It was not his limitation at all to be unable to escape the past; it was perhaps his limitation that he had escaped it so successfully. He might have seen the maid at other parties, he might have seen her taking a walk on Sunday afternoons, but in either case he would not be searching his memory now. Her face was, in a wonderful way, a moon face—Norman or Irish—but it was not beautiful enough to account for his feeling that he had seen her before, in circumstances that he ought to be able to remember. He asked Nellie Farquarson who she was. Nellie said that the maid had come through an agency, and that her home was Trenon, in Normandy—a small place with a church and a restaurant that Nellie had once visited. While Nellie talked on about her travels abroad, Francis realized where he had seen the woman before. It had been at the end of the war. He had left a replacement depot with some other men and taken a three-day pass in Trenon. On their second day, they had walked out to a crossroads to see the public chastisement of a young woman who had lived with the German commandant during the Occupation.

It was a cool morning in the fall. The sky was overcast, and poured down onto the dirt crossroads a very discouraging light. They were on high land and could see how like one another the shapes of the clouds and the hills were as they stretched off toward the sea. The prisoner arrived sitting on a three-legged stool in a farm cart. She stood by the cart while the Mayor read the accusation and the sentence. Her head was bent and her face was set in that empty half smile behind which the whipped soul is suspended. When the Mayor was finished, she undid her hair and let it fall across her back. A little man with a gray mustache cut off her hair with shears and dropped it on the ground. Then, with a bowl of soapy water and a straight razor, he shaved her skull clean. A woman approached and began to undo the fastenings of her clothes, but the prisoner pushed her aside and undressed herself. When she pulled her chemise over her head and threw it on the ground, she was naked. The women jeered; the men were still. There was no change in the falseness or the plaintiveness of the prisoner's smile. The cold wind made her white skin rough and hardened the nipples of her breasts. The jeering ended gradually, put down by the recognition of their common humanity. One woman spat on her, but some inviolable grandeur in her nakedness lasted through the ordeal. When the crowd was quiet, she turned—she had begun to cry—and, with nothing on but a pair of worn black shoes and stockings, walked down the dirt road alone away from the village. The round white face had aged a little, but there was no question but that the maid who passed his cocktails and later served Francis his dinner was the woman who had been punished at the crossroads.

The war seemed now so distant and that world where the cost of partisanship had been death or torture so long ago. Francis had lost track of the men who had been with him in Vesey. He could not count on Julia's discretion. He could not tell anyone. And if he had told the story now, at the dinner table, it would have been a social as well as a human error. The people in the Farquarsons' living room seemed united in their tacit claim that there had been no past, no war—that there was no danger or trouble in the world. In the recorded history of human arrangements, this extraordinary meeting would have fallen into place, but the atmosphere of Shady Hill made the memory unseemly and impolite. The prisoner withdrew after passing the coffee, but the encounter left Francis feeling languid; it had opened his memory and his senses, and left them dilated. Julia went into the house. Francis stayed in the car to take the sitter home.

Expecting to see Mrs. Henlein, the old lady who usually stayed with the children, he was surprised when a young girl opened the door and came out onto the lighted stoop. She stayed in the light to count her textbooks. She was frowning and beautiful. Now, the world is full of beautiful young girls, but Francis saw here the difference between beauty and perfection. All those endearing flaws, moles, birthmarks, and healed wounds were missing, and he experienced in his consciousness that moment when music breaks glass, and felt a pang of recognition as strange, deep, and wonderful as anything in his life. It hung from her frown, from an impalpable darkness in her face—a look that impressed him as a direct appeal for love. When she had counted her books, she came down the steps and opened the car door. In the light, he saw that her cheeks were wet. She got in and shut the door.

"You're new," Francis said.

"Yes. Mrs. Henlein is sick. I'm Anne Murchison."

"Did the children give you any trouble?"

"Oh, no, no." She turned and smiled at him unhappily in the dim dashboard light. Her light hair caught on the collar of her jacket, and she shook her head to set it loose.

"You've been crying."

"Yes."

"I hope it was nothing that happened in our house."

"No, no, it was nothing that happened in your house." Her voice was bleak. "It's no secret. Everybody in the village knows. Daddy's an alcoholic, and he just called me from some saloon and gave me a piece of his mind. He thinks I'm immoral. He called just before Mrs. Weed came back."

"I'm sorry."

"Oh, *Lord!*" She gasped and began to cry. She turned toward Francis, and he took her in his arms and let her cry on his shoulder. She shook in his embrace, and this movement accentuated his sense of the fineness of her flesh and bone. The layers of their clothing felt thin, and when her shuddering began to diminish, it was so much like a paroxysm of love that Francis lost his head and pulled her roughly against him. She drew away. "I live on Belleview Avenue," she said. "You go down Lansing Street to the railroad bridge."

"All right." He started the car.

"You turn left at that traffic light. . . . Now you turn right here and go straight on toward the tracks."

The road Francis took brought him out of his own neighborhood, across the tracks, and toward the river, to a street where the near-poor lived, in houses whose peaked gables and trimmings of wooden lace conveyed the purest feelings of pride and romance, although the houses themselves could not have offered much privacy or comfort, they were all so small. The street was dark, and, stirred by the grace and beauty of the troubled girl, he seemed, in turning into it, to have come into the deepest part of some submerged memory. In the distance, he saw a porch light burning. It was the only one, and she said that the house with the light was where she lived. When he stopped the car, he could see beyond the porch light into a dimly lighted hallway with an old-fashioned clothes tree. "Well, here we are," he said, conscious that a young man would have said something different.

She did not move her hands from the books, where they were folded, and she turned and faced him. There were tears of lust in his eyes. Determinedly—not sadly—he opened the door on his side and walked around to open hers. He took her free hand, letting his fingers in between hers, climbed at her side the two concrete steps, and went up a narrow walk through a front garden where dahlias, marigolds, and roses—things that had withstood the light frosts—still bloomed, and made a bittersweet smell in the night air. At the steps, she freed her hand and then turned and kissed him swiftly. Then she crossed the porch and shut the door. The porch light went out, then the light in the hall. A second later, a light went on upstairs at the side of the house, shining into a tree that was still covered with leaves. It took her only a few minutes to undress and get into bed, and then the house was dark.

Julia was asleep when Francis got home. He opened a second window and got into bed to shut his eyes on that night, but as soon as they were shut—as soon as he had dropped off to sleep—the girl entered his mind, moving with perfect freedom through its shut doors and filling chamber after chamber with her light, her perfume, and the music of her voice. He was crossing the Atlantic with her on the old *Mauretania* and, later, living with her in Paris. When he woke from his dream, he got up and smoked a cigarette at the open window. Getting back into bed, he cast around in his mind for something he desired to do that would injure no one, and he thought of skiing. Up through the dimness in his mind rose the image of a mountain deep in snow. It was late in the day. Wherever his eyes looked, he saw broad and heartening things. Over his shoulder, there was a snow-filled valley, rising into wooded hills where the trees dimmed the whiteness like a sparse coat of hair. The cold deadened all sound but the loud, iron clanking of the lift machinery. The light on the trails was blue, and it was harder than it had been a minute or two earlier to pick the turns, harder to judge—now that the snow was all deep blue—the crust, the ice, the bare spots, and the deep piles of dry powder. Down the mountain he swung, matching his speed against the contours of a slope that had been formed in the first ice age, seeking with ardor some simplicity of feeling and circumstance. Night fell then, and he drank a Martini with some old friend in a dirty country bar.

In the morning, Francis' snow-covered mountain was gone, and he was left with his vivid memories of Paris and the *Mauretania*. He had been bitten gravely. He washed his body, shaved his jaws, drank his coffee, and missed the seven-thirty-one. The train pulled out just as he brought his car to the station, and the longing he felt for the coaches as they drew stubbornly away from him reminded him of the humors of love. He waited for the eight-two, on what was now an empty platform. It was a clear morning; the morning seemed thrown like a gleaming bridge of light over his mixed affairs. His spirits were feverish and high. The image of the girl seemed to put him into a relationship to the world that was mysterious and enthralling. Cars were beginning to fill up the parking lot, and he noticed that those that had driven down from the high land above Shady Hill were white with hoarfrost. This first clear sign of autumn thrilled him. An express train—a night train from Buffalo or Albany—came down the tracks between the platforms, and he saw that the roofs of the foremost cars were covered with a skin of ice. Struck by the miraculous physicalness of everything, he smiled at the passengers in the dining car, who could be seen eating eggs and wiping their mouths with napkins as they traveled. The sleeping-car compartments, with their soiled bed linen, trailed through the fresh morning like a string of rooming-house windows. Then he saw an extraordinary thing; at one of the bedroom windows sat an unclothed woman of exceptional beauty, combing her golden hair. She passed like an apparition through Shady Hill, combing and combing her hair, and Francis followed her with his eyes until she was out of sight. Then old Mrs. Wrightson joined him on the platform and began to talk.

"Well, I guess you must be surprised to see me here the third morning in a row," she said, "but because of my window curtains I'm becoming a regular commuter. The curtains I bought on Monday I returned on Tuesday, and the curtains I bought Tuesday I'm returning today. On Monday, I got exactly what I wanted—it's a wool tapestry with roses and birds—but when I got them home, I found they were the wrong length. Well, I exchanged them yesterday, and when I got them home, I found they were still the wrong length. Now I'm praying to high heaven that the decorator will have them in the right length, because you know my house, you *know* my living-room windows, and you can imagine what a problem they present. I don't know what to do with them."

"I know what to do with them," Francis said.

"What?"

"Paint them black on the inside, and shut up."

There was a gasp from Mrs. Wrightson, and Francis looked down at her to be sure that she knew he meant to be rude. She turned and walked away from him, so damaged in spirit that she limped. A wonderful feeling enveloped him, as if light were being shaken about him, and he thought again of Venus combing and combing her hair as she drifted through the Bronx. The realization of how many years had passed since he had enjoyed being deliberately impolite sobered him. Among his friends and neighbors, there were brilliant and gifted people—he saw that—but many of them, also, were bores and fools, and he had made the mistake of listening to them all with equal attention. He had confused a lack of discrimination with Christian love, and the confusion seemed general and destructive. He was grateful to the girl for this bracing sensation of independence. Birds were singing—cardinals and the last of the robins. The sky shone like enamel. Even the smell of ink from his morning paper honed his appetite for life, and the world that was spread out around him was plainly a paradise.

If Francis had believed in some hierarchy of love—in spirits armed with hunting bows, in the capriciousness of Venus and Eros—or even in magical potions, philters, and stews, in scapulae and quarters of the moon, it might have explained his susceptibility and his feverish high spirits. The autumnal loves of middle age are well publicized, and he guessed that he was face to face with one of these, but there was not a trace of autumn in what he felt. He wanted to sport in the green woods, scratch where he itched, and drink from the same cup.

His secretary, Miss Rainey, was late that morning—she went to a psychiatrist three mornings a week—and when she came in, Francis wondered what advice a psychiatrist would have for him. But the girl promised to bring back into his life something like the sound of music. The realization that this music might lead him straight to a trial for statutory rape at the county courthouse collapsed his happiness. The photograph of his four children laughing into the camera on the beach at Gay Head reproached him. On the letterhead of his firm there was a drawing of the Laocoön, and the figure of the priest and his sons in the coils of the snake appeared to him to have the deepest meaning.

He had lunch with Pinky Trabert. At a conversational level, the mores of his friends were robust and elastic, but he knew that the moral card house would come down on them all—on Julia and the children as well—if he got caught taking advantage of a baby-sitter. Looking back over the recent history of Shady Hill for some precedent, he found there was none. There was no turpitude; there had not been a divorce since he lived there; there had not even been a breath of scandal. Things seemed arranged with more propriety even than in the Kingdom of Heaven. After leaving Pinky, Francis went to a jeweler's and bought the girl a bracelet. How happy this clandestine purchase made him, how stuffy and comical the jeweler's clerks seemed, how sweet the women who passed at his back smelled! On Fifth Avenue, passing Atlas with his shoulders bent under the weight of the world, Francis thought of the strenuousness of containing his physicalness within the patterns he had chosen.

He did not know when he would see the girl next. He had the bracelet in his inside pocket when he got home. Opening the door of his house, he found her in the hall. Her back was to him, and she turned when she heard the door close. Her smile was open and loving. Her perfection stunned him like a fine day—a day after a thunderstorm. He seized her and covered her lips with his, and she struggled but she did not have to struggle for long, because just then little Gertrude Flannery appeared from somewhere and said, "Oh, Mr. Weed . . ."

Gertrude was a stray. She had been born with a taste for exploration, and she did not have it in her to center her life with her affectionate parents. People who did not know the Flannerys concluded from Gertrude's behavior that she was the child of a bitterly divided family, where drunken quarrels were the rule. This was not true. The fact that little Gertrude's clothing was ragged and thin was her own triumph over her mother's struggle to dress her warmly and neatly. Garrulous, skinny, and unwashed, she drifted from house to house around the Blenhollow neighborhood, forming and breaking alliances based on an attachment to babies, animals, children her own age, adolescents, and sometimes adults. Opening your front door in the morning, you would find Gertrude sitting on your stoop. Going into the bathroom to shave, you would find Gertrude using the toilet. Looking into your son's crib, you would find it empty, and, looking further, you would find that Gertrude had pushed him in his baby carriage into the next village. She was helpful, pervasive, honest, hungry, and loyal. She never went home of her own choice. When the time to go arrived, she was indifferent to all its signs. "Go home, Gertrude," people could be heard saying in one house or another, night after night. "Go home, Gertrude. It's time for you to go home now, Gertrude." "You had better go home and get your supper, Gertrude." "I told you to go home twenty minutes ago, Gertrude." "Your mother will be worrying about you, Gertrude." "Go home, Gertrude, go home."

There are times when the lines around the human eye seem like shelves of eroded stone and when the staring eye itself strikes us with such a wilderness of animal feeling that we are at a loss. The look Francis gave the little girl was ugly and queer, and it frightened her. He reached into his pockets—his hands were shaking—and took out a quarter. "Go home, Gertrude, go home, and don't tell anyone, Gertrude. Don't—" He choked and ran into the living room as Julia called down to him from upstairs to hurry and dress.

The thought that he would drive Anne Murchison home later that night ran like a golden thread through the events of the party that Francis and Julia went to, and he laughed uproariously at dull jokes, dried a tear when Mabel Mercer told him about the death of her kitten, and stretched, yawned, sighed, and grunted like any other man with a rendezvous at the back of his mind. The bracelet was in his pocket. As he sat talking, the smell of grass was in his nose, and he was wondering where he would park the car. Nobody lived in the old Parker mansion, and the driveway was used as a lovers' lane. Townsend Street was a dead end, and he could park there, beyond the last house. The old lane that used to connect Elm Street to the riverbanks was overgrown, but he had walked there with his children, and he could drive his car deep enough into the brushwoods to be concealed.

The Weeds were the last to leave the party, and their host and hostess spoke of their own married happiness while they all four stood in the hallway saying good night. "She's my girl," their host said, squeezing his wife. "She's my blue sky. After sixteen years, I still bite her shoulders. She makes me feel like Hannibal crossing the Alps."

The Weeds drove home in silence. Francis brought the car up the driveway and sat still, with the motor running. "You can put the car in the garage," Julia said as she got out. "I told the Murchison girl she could leave at eleven. Someone drove her home." She shut the door, and Francis sat in the dark. He would be spared nothing then, it seemed, that a fool was not spared: ravening lewdness, jealousy, this hurt to his feelings that put tears in his eyes, even scorn—for he could see clearly the image he now presented, his arms spread over the steering wheel and his head buried in them for love.

Francis had been a dedicated Boy Scout when he was young, and, remembering the precepts of his youth, he left his office early the next afternoon and played some round-robin squash, but, with his body toned up by exercise and a shower, he realized that he might better have stayed at his desk. It was a frosty night when he got home. The air smelled sharply of change. When he stepped into the house, he sensed an unusual stir. The children were in their best clothes, and when Julia came down, she was wearing a lavender dress and her diamond sunburst. She explained the stir: Mr. Hubber was coming at seven to take their photograph for the Christmas card. She had put out Francis' blue suit and a tie with some color in it, because the picture was going to be in color this year. Julia was lighthearted at the thought of being photographed for Christmas. It was the kind of ceremony she enjoyed.

Francis went upstairs to change his clothes. He was tired from the day's work and tired with longing, and sitting on the edge of the bed had the effect of deepening his weariness. He thought of Anne Murchison, and the physical need to express himself, instead of being restrained by the pink lamps of Julia's dressing table, engulfed him. He went to Julia's desk, took a piece of writing paper, and began to write on it. "Dear Anne, I love you, I love you, I love you . . ." No one would see the letter, and he used no restraint. He used phrases like "heavenly bliss," and "love nest." He salivated, sighed, and trembled. When Julia called him to come down, the abyss between his fantasy and the practical world opened so wide that he felt it affected the muscles of his heart.

Julia and the children were on the stoop, and the photographer and his assistant had set up a double battery of floodlights to show the family and the architectural beauty of the entrance to their house. People who had come home on a late train slowed their cars to see the Weeds being photographed for their Christmas card. A few waved and called to the family. It took half an hour of smiling and wetting their lips before Mr. Hubber was satisfied. The heat of the lights made an unfresh smell in the frosty air, and when they were turned off, they lingered on the retina of Francis' eyes.

Later that night, while Francis and Julia were drinking their coffee in the living room, the doorbell rang. Julia answered the door and let in Clayton Thomas. He had come to pay for some theatre tickets that she had given his mother some time ago, and that Helen Thomas had scrupulously insisted on paying for, though Julia had asked her not to. Julia invited him in to have a cup of coffee. "I won't have any coffee," Clayton said, "but I will come in for a minute." He followed her into the living room, said good evening to Francis, and sat awkwardly in a chair.

Clayton's father had been killed in the war, and the young man's fatherlessness surrounded him like an element. This may have been conspicuous in Shady Hill because the Thomases were the only family that lacked a piece; all the other marriages were intact and productive. Clayton was in his second or third year of college, and he and his mother lived alone in a large house, which she hoped to sell. Clayton had once made some trouble. Years ago, he had stolen some money and run away; he had got to California before they caught up with him. He was tall and homely, wore horn-rimmed glasses, and spoke in a deep voice.

"When do you go back to college, Clayton?" Francis asked.

"I'm not going back," Clayton said. "Mother doesn't have the money, and there's no sense in all this pretense. I'm going to get a job, and if we sell the house, we'll take an apartment in New York."

"Won't you miss Shady Hill?" Julia asked.

"No," Clayton said. "I don't like it."

"Why not?" Francis asked.

"Well, there's a lot here I don't approve of," Clayton said gravely. "Things like the club dances. Last Saturday night, I looked in toward the end and saw Mr. Granner trying to put Mrs. Minot into the trophy case. They were both drunk. I disapprove of so much drinking."

"It was Saturday night," Francis said.

"And all the dovecotes are phony," Clayton said. "And the way people clutter up their lives. I've thought about it a lot, and what seems to me to be really wrong with Shady Hill is that it doesn't have any future. So much energy is spent in perpetuating the place—in keeping out undesirables, and so forth—that the only idea of the future anyone has is just more and more commuting trains and more parties. I don't think that's healthy. I think people ought to be able to dream big dreams about the future. I think people ought to be able to dream great dreams."

"It's too bad you couldn't continue with college," Julia said.

"I wanted to go to divinity school," Clayton said.

"What's your church?" Francis asked.

"Unitarian, Theosophist, Transcendentalist, Humanist," Clayton said.

"Wasn't Emerson a transcendentalist?" Julia asked.

"I mean the English transcendentalists," Clayton said. "All the American transcendentalists were goops."

"What kind of job do you expect to get?" Francis asked.

"Well, I'd like to work for a publisher," Clayton said, "but everyone tells me there's nothing doing. But it's the kind of thing I'm interested in. I'm writing a long verse play about good and evil. Uncle Charlie might get me into a bank, and that would be good for me. I need the discipline. I have a long way to go in forming my character. I have some terrible habits. I talk too much. I think I ought to take vows of silence. I ought to try not to speak for a week, and discipline myself. I've thought of making a retreat at one of the Episcopalian monasteries, but I don't like Trinitarianism."

"Do you have any girl friends?" Francis asked.

"I'm engaged to be married," Clayton said. "Of course, I'm not old enough or rich enough to have my engagement observed or respected or anything, but I bought a simulated emerald for Anne Murchison with the money I made cutting lawns this summer. We're going to be married as soon as she finishes school."

Francis recoiled at the mention of the girl's name. Then a dingy light seemed to emanate from his spirit, showing everything—Julia, the boy, the chairs—in their true colorlessness. It was like a bitter turn of the weather.

"We're going to have a large family," Clayton said. "Her father's a terrible rummy, and I've had my hard times, and we want to have lots of children. Oh, she's wonderful, Mr. and Mrs. Weed, and we have so much in common. We like all the same things. We sent out the same Christmas card last year without planning it, and we both have an allergy to tomatoes, and our eyebrows grow together in the middle. Well, goodnight."

Julia went to the door with him. When she returned, Francis said that Clayton was lazy, irresponsible, affected, and smelly. Julia said that Francis seemed to be getting intolerant; the Thomas boy was young and should be given a chance. Julia had noticed other cases where Francis had been short-tempered. "Mrs. Wrightson has asked everyone in Shady Hill to her anniversary party but us," she said.

"I'm sorry, Julia."

"Do you know why they didn't ask us?"

"Why?"

"Because you insulted Mrs. Wrightson."

"Then you know about it?"

"June Masterson told me. She was standing behind you."

Julia walked in front of the sofa with a small step that expressed, Francis knew, a feeling of anger.

"I did insult Mrs. Wrightson, Julia, and I meant to. I've never liked her parties, and I'm glad she's dropped us."

"What about Helen?"

"How does Helen come into this?"

"Mrs. Wrightson's the one who decides who goes to the assemblies."

"You mean she can keep Helen from going to the dances?"

"Yes."

"I hadn't thought of that."

"Oh. I knew you hadn't thought of it," Julia cried, thrusting hilt-deep into this chink of his armor. "And it makes me furious to see this kind of stupid thoughtlessness wreck everyone's happiness."

"I don't think I've wrecked anyone's happiness."

"Mrs. Wrightson runs Shady Hill and has run it for the last forty years. I don't know what makes you think that in a community like this you can indulge every impulse you have to be insulting, vulgar, and offensive."

"I have very good manners," Francis said, trying to give the evening a turn toward the light.

"Damn you, Francis Weed!" Julia cried, and the spit of her words struck him in the face. "I've worked hard for the social position we enjoy in this place, and I won't stand by and see you wreck it. You must have understood when you settled here that you couldn't expect to live like a bear in a cave."

"I've got to express my likes and dislikes."

"You can conceal your dislikes. You don't have to meet everything head on, like a child. Unless you're anxious to be a social leper. It's no accident that we get asked out a great deal! It's no accident that Helen has so many friends. How would you like to spend your Saturday nights at the movies? How would you like to spend your Sundays raking up dead leaves? How would you like it if your daughter spent the assembly nights sitting at her window, listening to the music from the club? How would you like it—" He did something then that was, after all, not so unaccountable, since her words seemed to raise up between them a wall so deadening that he gagged. He struck her full in the face. She staggered and then, a moment later, seemed composed. She went up the stairs to their room. She didn't slam the door. When Francis followed, a few minutes later, he found her packing a suitcase.

"Julia, I'm very sorry."

"It doesn't matter," she said. She was crying.

"Where do you think you're going?"

"I don't know. I just looked at a timetable. There's an eleven-sixteen into New York. I'll take that."

"You can't go, Julia."

"I can't stay. I know that."

"I'm sorry about Mrs. Wrightson, Julia, and I'm—"

"It doesn't matter about Mrs. Wrightson. That isn't the trouble."

"What is the trouble?"

"You don't love me."

"I do love you, Julia."

"No, you don't."

"Julia, I do love you, and I would like to be as we were—sweet and bawdy and dark—but now there are so many people."

"You hate me."

"I don't hate you, Julia."

"You have no idea of how much you hate me. I think it's subconscious. You don't realize the cruel things you've done."

"What cruel things, Julia?"

"The cruel acts your subconscious drives you to in order to express your hatred of me."

"What, Julia?"

"I've never complained."

"Tell me."

"You don't know what you're doing."

"Tell me."

"Your clothes."

"What do you mean?"

"I mean the way you leave your dirty clothes around in order to express your subconscious hatred of me."

"I don't understand."

"I mean your dirty socks and your dirty pajamas and your dirty underwear and your dirty shirts!" She rose from kneeling by the suitcase and faced him, her eyes blazing and her voice ringing with emotion. "I'm talking about the fact that you've never learned to hang up anything. You just leave your clothes all over the floor where they drop, in order to humiliate me. You do it on purpose!" She fell on the bed, sobbing.

"Julia, darling!" he said, but when she felt his hand on her shoulder she got up.

"Leave me alone," she said. "I have to go." She brushed past him to the closet and came back with a dress. "I'm not taking any of the things you've given me," she said. "I'm leaving my pearls and the fur jacket."

"Oh, Julia!" Her figure, so helpless in its self-deceptions, bent over the suitcase made him nearly sick with pity. She did not understand how desolate her life would be without him. She didn't understand the hours that working women have to keep. She didn't understand that most of her friendships existed within the framework of their marriage, and that without this she would find herself alone. She didn't understand about travel, about hotels, about money. "Julia, I can't let you go! What you don't understand, Julia, is that you've come to be dependent on me."

She tossed her head back and covered her face with her hands. "Did you say that *I* was dependent on *you?*" she asked. "Is that what you said? And who is it that tells you what time to get up in the morning and when to go to bed at night? Who is it that prepares your meals and picks up your dirty clothes and invites your friends to dinner? If it weren't for me, your neckties would be greasy and your clothing would be full of moth holes. You were alone when I met you, Francis Weed, and you'll be alone when I leave. When Mother asked you for a list to send out invitations to our wedding, how many names did you have to give her? Fourteen!"

"Cleveland wasn't my home, Julia."

"And how many of your friends came to the church? Two!"

"Cleveland wasn't my home, Julia."

"Since I'm not taking the fur jacket," she said quietly, "you'd better put it back into storage. There's an insurance policy on the pearls that comes due in January. The name of the laundry and the maid's telephone number—all those things are in my desk. I hope you won't drink too much, Francis. I hope that nothing bad will happen to you. If you do get into serious trouble, you can call me."

"Oh, my darling, I can't let you go!" Francis said. "I can't let you go, Julia!" He took her in his arms.

"I guess I'd better stay and take care of you for a little while longer," she said.

Riding to work in the morning, Francis saw the girl walk down the aisle of the coach. He was surprised; he hadn't realized that the school she went to was in the city, but she was carrying books, she seemed to be going to school. His surprise delayed his reaction, but then he got up clumsily and stepped into the aisle. Several people had come between them, but he could see her ahead of him, waiting for someone to open the car door, and then, as the train swerved, putting out her hand to support herself as she crossed the platform into the next car. He followed her through that car and halfway through another before calling her name—"Anne! Anne!"—but she didn't turn. He followed her into still another car, and she sat down in an aisle seat. Coming up to her, all his feelings warm and bent in her direction, he put his hand on the back of her seat—even this touch warmed him—and leaning down to speak to her, he saw that it was not Anne. It was an older woman wearing glasses. He went on deliberately into another car, his face red with embarrassment and the much deeper feeling of having his good sense challenged; for if he couldn't tell one person from another, what evidence was there that his life with Julia and the children had as much reality as his dreams of iniquity in Paris or the litter, the grass smell, and the cave-shaped trees in Lovers' Lane.

Late that afternoon, Julia called to remind Francis that they were going out for dinner. A few minutes later, Trace Bearden called. "Look, fellar," Trace said. "I'm calling for Mrs. Thomas. You know? Clayton, that boy of hers, doesn't seem able to get a job, and I wondered if you could help. If you'd call Charlie Bell—I know he's indebted to you—and say a good word for the kid, I think Charlie would—"

"Trace, I hate to say this," Francis said, "but I don't feel that I can do anything for that boy. The kid's worthless. I know it's a harsh thing to say, but it's a fact. Any kindness done for him would backfire in everybody's face. He's just a worthless kid, Trace, and there's nothing to be done about it. Even if we got him a job, he wouldn't be able to keep it for a week. I know that to be a fact. It's an awful thing, Trace, and I know it is, but instead of recommending that kid, I'd feel obligated to warn people against him—people who knew his father and would naturally want to step in and do something. I'd feel obliged to warn them. He's a thief . . ."

The moment this conversation was finished, Miss Rainey came in and stood by his desk. "I'm not going to be able to work for you any more, Mr. Weed," she said. "I can stay until the seventeenth if you need me, but I've been offered a whirlwind of a job, and I'd like to leave as soon as possible."

She went out, leaving him to face alone the wickedness of what he had done to the Thomas boy. His children in their photograph laughed and laughed, glazed with all the bright colors of summer, and he remembered that they had met a bagpiper on the beach that day and he had paid the piper a dollar to play them a battle song of the Black Watch. The girl would be at the house when he got home. He would spend another evening among his kind neighbors, picking and choosing dead-end streets, cart tracks, and the driveways of abandoned houses. There was nothing to mitigate his feeling—nothing that laughter or a game of softball with the children would change—and, thinking back over the plane crash, the Farquarsons' new maid, and Anne Murchison's difficulties with her drunken father, he wondered how he could have avoided arriving at just where he was. He was in trouble. He had been lost once in his life, coming back from a trout stream in the north woods, and he had now the same bleak realization that no amount of cheerfulness or hopefulness or valor or perseverance could help him find, in the gathering dark, the path that he'd lost. He smelled the forest. The feeling of bleakness was intolerable, and he saw clearly that he had reached the point where he would have to make a choice.

He could go to a psychiatrist, like Miss Rainey; he could go to church and confess his lusts; he could go to a Danish massage parlor in the West Seventies that had been recommended by a salesman; he could rape the girl or trust that he would somehow be prevented from doing this; or he could get drunk. It was his life, his boat, and, like every other man, he was made to be the father of thousands, and what harm could there be in a tryst that would make them both feel more kindly toward the world? This was the wrong train of thought, and he came back to the first, the psychiatrist. He had the telephone number of Miss Rainey's doctor, and he called and asked for an immediate appointment. He was insistent with the doctor's secretary—it was his manner in business—and when she said that the doctor's schedule was full for the next few weeks, Francis demanded an appointment that day and was told to come at five.

The psychiatrist's office was in a building that was used mostly by doctors and dentists, and the hallways were filled with the candy smell of mouthwash and memories of pain. Francis' character had been formed upon a series of private resolves—resolves about cleanliness, about going off the high diving board or repeating any other feat that challenged his courage, about punctuality, honesty, and virtue. To abdicate the perfect loneliness in which he had made his most vital decisions shattered his concept of character and left him now in a condition that felt like shock. He was stupefied. The scene for his *miserere mei Deus* was, like the waiting room of so many doctor's offices, a crude token gesture toward the sweets of domestic bliss: a place arranged with antiques, coffee tables, potted plants, and etchings of snow-covered bridges and geese in flight, although there were no children, no marriage bed, no stove, even, in this travesty of a house, where no one had ever spent the night and where the curtained windows looked straight onto a dark air shaft. Francis gave his name and address to a secretary and then saw, at the side of the room, a policeman moving toward him. "Hold it, hold it," the policeman said. "Don't move. Keep your hands where they are."

"I think it's all right, Officer," the secretary began. "I think it will be—"

"Let's make sure," the policeman said, and he began to slap Francis' clothes, looking for what—pistols, knives, an icepick? Finding nothing, he went off and the secretary began a nervous apology: "When you called on the telephone, Mr. Weed, you seemed very excited, and one of the doctor's patients has been threatening his life, and we have to be careful. If you want to go in now?" Francis pushed open a door connected to an electrical chime, and in the doctor's lair sat down heavily,blew his nose into a handkerchief, searched in his pockets for cigarettes, for matches, for something, and said hoarsely, with tears in his eyes, "I'm in love, Dr. Herzog."

It is a week or ten days later in Shady Hill. The seven-fourteen has come and gone, and here and there dinner is finished and the dishes are in the dish-washing machine. The village hangs, morally and economically, from a thread; but it hangs by its thread in the evening light. Donald Goslin has begun to worry the "Moonlight Sonata" again. *Marcato ma sempre pianissimo!* He seems to be wringing out a wet bath towel, but the housemaid does not heed him. She is writing a letter to Arthur Godfrey. In the cellar of his house, Francis Weed is building a coffee table. Dr. Herzog recommends woodwork as a therapy, and Francis finds some true consolation in the simple arithmetic involved and in the holy smell of new wood. Francis is happy. Upstairs, little Toby is crying, because he is tired. He puts off his cowboy hat, gloves, and fringed jacket, unbuckles the belt studded with gold and rubies, the silver bullets and holsters, slips off his suspenders, his checked shirt, and Levi's, and sits on the edge of his bed to pull off his high boots. Leaving this equipment in a heap, he goes to the closet and takes his space suit off a nail. It is a struggle for him to get into the long tights, but he succeeds. He loops the magic cape over his shoulders and, climbing onto the footboard of his bed, he spreads his arms and flies the short distance to the floor, landing with a thump that is audible to everyone in the house but himself.

"Go home, Gertrude, go home," Mrs. Masterson says. "I told you to go home an hour ago, Gertrude. It's way past your suppertime, and your mother will be worried. Go home!" A door on the Babcocks' terrace flies open, and out comes Mrs. Babcock without any clothes on, pursued by a naked husband. (Their children are away at boarding school, and their terrace is screened by a hedge.) Over the terrace they go and in at the kitchen door, as passionate and handsome a nymph and satyr as you will find on any wall in Venice. Cutting the last of the roses in her garden, Julia hears old Mr. Nixon shouting at the squirrels in his bird-feeding station. "Rapscallions! Varmints! Avaunt and quit my sight!" A miserable cat wanders into the garden, sunk in spiritual and physical discomfort. Tied to its head is a small straw hat—a doll's hat—and it is securely buttoned into a doll's dress, from the skirts of which protrudes its long, hairy tail. As it walks, it shakes its feet, as if it had fallen into water.

"Here, pussy, pussy, pussy!" Julia calls.

"Here, pussy, here, poor pussy!" But the cat gives her a skeptical look and stumbles away in its skirts. The last to come is Jupiter. He prances through the tomato vines, holding in his generous mouth the remains of an evening slipper. Then it is dark; it is a night where kings in golden suits ride elephants over the mountains.

The Jilting of Granny Weatherall
Katherine Anne Porter

She flicked her wrist neatly out of Doctor Harry's pudgy careful fingers and pulled the sheet up to her chin. The brat ought to be in knee breeches. Doctoring around the country with spectacles on his nose! "Get along now, take your schoolbooks and go. There's nothing wrong with me."

Doctor Harry spread a warm paw like a cushion on her forehead where the forked green vein danced and made her eyelids twitch. "Now, now, be a good girl, and we'll have you up in no time."

"That's no way to speak to a woman nearly eighty years old just because she's down. I'd have you respect your elders, young man."

"Well, Missy, excuse me." Doctor Harry patted her cheek. "But I've got to warn you, haven't I? You're a marvel, but you must be careful or you're going to be good and sorry."

"Don't tell me what I'm going to be. I'm on my feet now, morally speaking. It's Cornelia. I had to go to bed to get rid of her."

Her bones felt loose, and floated around in her skin, and Doctor Harry floated like a balloon around the foot of the bed. He floated and pulled down his waistcoat and swung his glasses on a cord. "Well, stay where you are, it certainly can't hurt you."

"Get along and doctor your sick," said Granny Weatherall. "Leave a well woman alone. I'll call for you when I want you. . . . Where were you forty years ago when I pulled through milk-leg and double pneumonia? You weren't even born. Don't let Cornelia lead you on," she shouted, because Doctor Harry appeared to float up to the ceiling and out. "I pay my own bills, and I don't throw my money away on nonsense!"

She meant to wave good-by, but it was too much trouble. Her eyes closed of themselves, it was like a dark curtain drawn around the bed. The pillow rose and floated under her, pleasant as a hammock in a light wind. She listened to the leaves rustling outside the window. No, somebody was swishing newspapers: no, Cornelia and Doctor Harry were whispering together. She leaped broad awake, thinking they whispered in her ear.

"She was never like this, *never* like this!" "Well, what can we expect?" "Yes, eighty years old. . . ."

Well, and what if she was? She still had ears. It was like Cornelia to whisper around doors. She always kept things secret in such a public way. She was always being tactful and kind. Cornelia was dutiful; that was the trouble with her. Dutiful and good: "So good and dutiful," said Granny, "that I'd like to spank her." She saw herself spanking Cornelia and making a fine job of it.

"What'd you say, Mother?"

Granny felt her face tying up in hard knots.

"Can't a body think, I'd like to know?"

"I thought you might want something."

"I do. I want a lot of things. First off, go away and don't whisper."

She lay and drowsed, hoping in her sleep that the children would keep out and let her rest a minute. It had been a long day. Not that she was tired. It was always pleasant to snatch a minute now and then. There was always so much to be done, let me see: tomorrow.

Tomorrow was far away and there was nothing to trouble about. Things were finished somehow when the time came; thank God there was always a little margin over for peace: then a person could spread out the plan of life and tuck in the edges orderly. It was good to have everything clean and folded away, with the hair brushes and tonic bottles sitting straight on the white embroidered linen: the day started without fuss and the pantry shelves laid out with rows of jelly glasses and brown jugs and white stone-china jars with blue whirligigs and words painted on them: coffee, tea, sugar, ginger, cinnamon, allspice: and the bronze clock with the lion on top nicely dusted off. The dust that lion could collect in twenty-four hours! The box in the attic with all those letters tied up, well, she'd have to go through that tomorrow. All those letters—George's letters and John's letters and her letters to them both—lying around for the children to find afterwards made her uneasy. Yes, that would be tomorrow's business. No use to let them know how silly she had been once.

While she was rummaging around she found death in her mind and it felt clammy and unfamiliar. She had spent so much time preparing for death there was no need for bringing it up again. Let it take care of itself now. When she was sixty she had felt very old, finished, and went around making farewell trips to see her children and grandchildren, with a secret in her mind: This is the very last of your mother, children! Then she made her will and came down with a long fever. That was all just a notion like a lot of other things, but it was lucky too, for she had once for all got over the idea of dying for a long time. Now she couldn't be worried. She hoped she had better sense now. Her father had lived to be one hundred and two years old and had drunk a noggin of strong hot toddy on his last birthday. He told the reporters it was his daily habit, and he owed his long life to that. He had made quite a scandal and was very pleased about it. She believed she'd just plague Cornelia a little.

"Cornelia! Cornelia!" No footsteps, but a sudden hand on her cheek. "Bless you, where have you been?"

"Here, mother."

"Well, Cornelia, I want a noggin of hot toddy."

"Are you cold, darling?"

"I'm chilly, Cornelia. Lying in bed stops the circulation. I must have told you that a thousand times."

Well, she could just hear Cornelia telling her husband that Mother was getting a little childish and they'd have to humor her. The thing that most annoyed her was that Cornelia thought she was deaf, dumb, and blind. Little hasty glances and tiny gestures tossed around her and over her head saying, "Don't cross her, let her have her way, she's eighty years old," and she sitting there as if she lived in a thin glass cage. Sometimes Granny almost made up her mind to pack up and move back to her own house where nobody could remind her every minute that she was old. Wait, wait, Cornelia, till your own children whisper behind your back!

In her day she had kept a better house and had got more work done. She wasn't too old yet for Lydia to be driving eighty miles for advice when one of the children jumped the track, and Jimmy still dropped in and talked things over:

"Now, Mammy, you've a good business head, I want to know what you think of this? . . ." Old. Cornelia couldn't change the furniture around without asking. Little things, little things! They had been so sweet when they were little. Granny wished the old days were back again with the children young and everything to be done over. It had been a hard pull, but not too much for her. When she thought of all the food she had cooked, and all the clothes she had cut and sewed, and all the gardens she had made—well, the children showed it. There they were, made out of her, and they couldn't get away from that. Sometimes she wanted to see John again and point to them and say, Well, I didn't do so badly, did I? But that would have to wait. That was for tomorrow. She used to think of him as a man, but now all the children were older than their father, and he would be a child beside her if she saw him now. It seemed strange and there was something wrong in the idea. Why, he couldn't possibly recognize her. She had fenced in a hundred acres once, digging the post holes herself and clamping the wires with just a negro boy to help. That changed a woman. John would be looking for a young woman with the peaked Spanish comb in her hair and the painted fan. Digging post holes changed a woman. Riding country roads in the winter when women had their babies was another thing: sitting up nights with sick horses and sick negroes and sick children and hardly ever losing one. John, I hardly ever lost one of them! John would see that in a minute, that would be something he could understand, she wouldn't have to explain anything!

It made her feel like rolling up her sleeves and putting the whole place to rights again. No matter if Cornelia was determined to be everywhere at once, there were a great many things left undone on this place. She would start tomorrow and do them. It was good to be strong enough for everything, even if all you made melted and changed and slipped under your hands, so that by the time you finished you almost forgot what you were working for. What was it I set out to do? she asked herself intently, but she could not remember. A fog rose over the valley, she saw it marching across the creek swallowing the trees and moving up the hill like an army of ghosts. Soon it would be at the near edge of the orchard, and then it was time to go in and light the lamps. Come in, children, don't stay out in the night air.

Lighting the lamps had been beautiful. The children huddled up to her and breathed like little calves waiting at the bars in the twilight. Their eyes followed the match and watched the flame rise and settle in a blue curve, then they moved away from her. The lamp was lit, they didn't have to be scared and hang on to mother any more. Never, never, never more. God, for all my life I thank Thee. Without Thee, my God, I could never have done it. Hail, Mary, full of grace.

I want you to pick all the fruit this year and see that nothing is wasted. There's always someone who can use it. Don't let good things rot for want of using. You waste life when you waste good food. Don't let things get lost. It's bitter to lose things. Now, don't let me get to thinking, not when I am tired and taking a little nap before supper. . . .

The pillow rose about her shoulders and pressed against her heart and the memory was being squeezed out of it: oh, push down the pillow, somebody: it would smother her if she tried to hold it. Such a fresh breeze blowing and such a green day with no threats in it. But he had not come, just the same. What does a woman do when she has put on the white veil and set out the white cake for a man and he doesn't come? She tried to remember. No, I swear he never harmed me but in that. He never harmed me but in that . . . and what if he did? There was the day, the day, but a whirl of dark smoke rose and covered it, crept up and over into the bright field where everything was planted so carefully in orderly rows. That was hell, she knew hell when she saw it. For sixty years she had prayed against remembering him and against losing her soul in the deep pit of hell, and now the two things were mingled in one and the thought of him was a smoky cloud from hell that moved and crept in her head when she had just got rid of Doctor Harry and was trying to rest a minute. Wounded vanity, Ellen, said a sharp voice in the top of her mind. Don't let your wounded vanity get the upper hand of you. Plenty of girls get jilted. You were jilted, weren't you? Then stand up to it. Her eyelids wavered and let in streamers of blue-gray light like tissue paper over her eyes. She must get up and pull the shades down or she'd never sleep. She was in bed again and the shades were not down. How could that happen? Better turn over, hide from the light, sleeping in the light gave you nightmares. "Mother, how do you feel now?" and a stinging wetness on her forehead. But I don't like having my face washed in cold water!

Hapsy? George? Lydia? Jimmy? No, Cornelia, and her features were swollen and full of little puddles. "They're coming, darling, they'll all be here soon." Go wash your face, child, you look funny.

Instead of obeying, Cornelia knelt down and put her head on the pillow. She seemed to be talking but there was no sound. "Well, are you tongue-tied? Whose birthday is it? Are you going to give a party?"

Cornelia's mouth moved urgently in strange shapes. "Don't do that, you bother me, daughter."

"Oh, no, Mother. Oh, no. . . ."

Nonsense. It was strange about children. They disputed your every word. "No what, Cornelia?"

"Here's Doctor Harry."

"I won't see that boy again. He just left five minutes ago."

"That was this morning, Mother. It's night now. Here's the nurse."

"This is Doctor Harry, Mrs. Weatherall. I never saw you look so young and happy!"

"Ah, I'll never be young again—but I'd be happy if they'd let me lie in peace and get rested."

She thought she spoke up loudly, but no one answered. A warm weight on her forehead, a warm bracelet on her wrist, and a breeze went on whispering, trying to tell her something. A shuffle of leaves in the everlasting hand of God, He blew on them and they danced and rattled. "Mother, don't mind, we're going to give you a little hypodermic." "Look here, daughter, how do ants get in this bed? I saw sugar ants yesterday." Did you send for Hapsy too?

It was Hapsy she really wanted. She had to go a long way back through a great many rooms to find Hapsy standing with a baby on her arm. She seemed to herself to be Hapsy also, and the baby on Hapsy's arm was Hapsy and himself and herself, all at once, and there was no surprise in the meeting. Then Hapsy melted from within and turned flimsy as gray gauze and the baby was a gauzy shadow, and Hapsy came up close and said, "I thought you'd never come," and looked at her very searchingly and said, "You haven't changed a bit!" They leaned forward to kiss, when Cornelia began whispering from a long way off, "Oh, is there anything you want to tell me? Is there anything I can do for you?"

Yes, she had changed her mind after sixty years and she would like to see George. I want you to find George. Find him and be sure to tell him I forgot him. I want him to know I had my husband just the same and my children and my house like any other woman. A good house too and a good husband that I loved and fine children out of him. Better than I hoped for even. Tell him I was given back everything he took away and more. Oh, no, oh, God, no, there was something else besides the house and the man and the children. Oh, surely they were not all? What was it? Something not given back. . . . Her breath crowded down under her ribs and grew into a monstrous frightening shape with cutting edges; it bored up into her head, and the agony was unbelievable: Yes, John, get the Doctor now, no more talk, my time has come.

When this one was born it should be the last. The last. It should have been born first, for it was the one she had truly wanted. Everything came in good time. Nothing left out, left over. She was strong, in three days she would be as well as ever. Better. A woman needed milk in her to have her full health.

"Mother, do you hear me?"

"I've been telling you—"

"Mother, Father Connolly's here."

"I went to Holy Communion only last week. Tell him I'm not so sinful as all that."

"Father just wants to speak to you."

He could speak as much as he pleased. It was like him to drop in and inquire about her soul as if it were a teething baby, and then stay on for a cup of tea and a round of cards and gossip. He always had a funny story of some sort, usually about an Irishman who made his little mistakes and confessed them, and the point lay in some absurd thing he would blurt out in the confessional showing his struggles between native piety and original sin. Granny felt easy about her soul. Cornelia, where are your manners? Give Father Connolly a chair. She had her secret comfortable understanding with a few favorite saints who cleared a straight road to God for her. All as surely signed and sealed as the papers for the new Forty Acres. Forever . . . heirs and assigns forever. Since the day the wedding cake was not cut, but thrown out and wasted. The whole bottom dropped out of the world, and there she was blind and sweating with nothing under her feet and the walls falling away. His hand had caught her under the breast, she had not fallen, there was the freshly polished floor with the green rug on it, just as before. He had cursed like a sailor's parrot and said, "I'll kill him for you." Don't lay a hand on him, for my sake leave something to God. "Now, Ellen, you must believe what I tell you. . . ."

So there was nothing, nothing to worry about any more, except sometimes in the night one of the children screamed in a nightmare, and they both hustled out shaking and hunting for the matches and calling, "There, wait a minute, here we are!" John, get the doctor now, Hapsy's time has come. But there was Hapsy standing by the bed in a white cap. "Cornelia, tell Hapsy to take off her cap. I can't see her plain."

Her eyes opened very wide and the room stood out like a picture she had seen somewhere. Dark colors with the shadows rising towards the ceiling in long angles. The tall black dresser gleamed with nothing on it but John's picture, enlarged from a little one, with John's eyes very black when they should have been blue. You never saw him, so how do you know how he looked? But the man insisted the copy was perfect, it was very rich and handsome. For a picture, yes, but it's not my husband. The table by the bed had a linen cover and a candle and a crucifix. The light was blue from Cornelia's silk lampshades. No sort of light at all, just frippery. You had to live forty years with kerosene lamps to appreciate honest electricity. She felt very strong and she saw Doctor Harry with a rosy nimbus around him.

"You look like a saint, Doctor Harry, and I vow that's as near as you'll ever come to it."

"She's saying something."

"I heard you, Cornelia. What's all this carrying-on?"

"Father Connolly's saying—"

Cornelia's voice staggered and bumped like a cart in a bad road. It rounded corners and turned back again and arrived nowhere. Granny stepped up in the cart very lightly and reached for the reins, but a man sat beside her and she knew him by his hands, driving the cart. She did not look in his face, for she knew without seeing, but looked instead down the road where the trees leaned over and bowed to each other and a thousand birds were singing a Mass. She felt like singing too, but she put her hand in the bosom of her dress and pulled out a rosary, and Father Connolly murmured Latin in a very solemn voice and tickled her feet. My God, will you stop that nonsense? I'm a married woman. What if he did run away and leave me to face the priest by myself? I found another a whole world better. I wouldn't have exchanged my husband for anybody except St. Michael himself, and you may tell him that for me with a thank you in the bargain.

Light flashed on her closed eyelids, and a deep roaring shook her. Cornelia, is that lightning? I hear thunder. There's going to be a storm. Close all the windows. Call the children in. . . . "Mother, here we are, all of us." "Is that you, Hapsy?" "Oh, no, I'm Lydia. We drove as fast as we could." Their faces drifted above her, drifted away. The rosary fell out of her hands and Lydia put it back. Jimmy tried to help, their hands fumbled together, and Granny closed two fingers around Jimmy's thumb. Beads wouldn't do, it must be something alive. She was so amazed her thoughts ran round and round. So, my dear Lord, this is my death and I wasn't even thinking about it. My children have come to see me die. But I can't, it's not time. Oh, I always hated surprises. I wanted to give Cornelia the amethyst set— Cornelia, you're to have the amethyst set, but Hapsy's to wear it when she wants, and, Doctor Harry, do shut up. Nobody sent for you. Oh, my dear Lord, do wait a minute. I meant to do something about the Forty Acres, Jimmy doesn't need it and Lydia will later on, with that worthless husband of hers. I meant to finish the altar cloth and send six bottles of wine to Sister Borgia for her dyspepsia. I want to send six bottles of wine to Sister Borgia, Father Connolly, now don't let me forget.

Cornelia's voice made short turns and tilted over and crashed. "Oh, Mother, oh, Mother, oh, Mother. . . ."

"I'm not going, Cornelia. I'm taken by surprise. I can't go."

You'll see Hapsy again. What about her? "I thought you'd never come." Granny made a long journey outward, looking for Hapsy. What if I don't find her? What then? Her heart sank down and down, there was no bottom to death, she couldn't come to the end of it. The blue light from Cornelia's lampshade drew into a tiny point in the center of her brain, it flickered and winked like an eye, quietly it fluttered and dwindled. Granny lay curled down within herself, amazed and watchful, staring at the point of light that was herself; her body was now only a deeper mass of shadow in an endless darkness and this darkness would curl around the light and swallow it up. God, give a sign!

For the second time there was no sign. Again no bridegroom and the priest in the house. She could not remember any other sorrow because this grief wiped them all away. Oh, no, there's nothing more cruel than this—I'll never forgive it. She stretched herself with a deep breath and blew out the light.

To the Virgins, to Make Much of Time

Robert Herrick

Gather ye rosebuds while ye may,
   Old time is still a-flying;
And this same flower that smiles today
   Tomorow will be dying.

The glorious lamp of heaven, the sun,   5
   The higher he's a-getting,
The sooner will his race be run,
   And nearer he's to setting.

That age is best which is the first,
   When youth and blood are warmer;   10
But being spent, the worse, and worst
   Times still succeed the former.

Then be not coy, but use your time,
   And, while ye may, go marry;
For, having lost but once your prime,   15
   You may forever tarry.

To The Stone-Cutters

Robinson Jeffers

Stone-cutters fighting time with marble, you foredefeated
Challengers of oblivion
Eat cynical earnings, knowing rock splits, records fall down,
The square-limbed Roman letters
Scale in the thaws, wear in the rain. The poet as well   5
Builds his monument mockingly;
For man will be blotted out, the blithe earth die, the brave sun
Die blind and blacken to the heart:
Yet stones have stood for a thousand years, and pained thoughts
    found
The honey of peace in old poems.   10

Snake

D. H. Lawrence

A snake came to my water-trough
On a hot, hot day, and I in pajamas for the heat,
To drink there.

In the deep, strange-scented shade of the great dark carob-tree
I came down the steps with my pitcher   5
And must wait, must stand and wait, for there he was at the trough
    before me.

He reached down from a fissure in the earth-wall in the gloom
And trailed his yellow-brown slackness soft-bellied down, over the
    edge of the stone trough
And rested his throat upon the stone bottom,
And where the water had dripped from the tap, in a small clearness,   10
He sipped with his straight mouth,
Softly drank through his straight gums, into his slack long body,
Silently.

Someone was before me at my water-trough,
And I, like a second comer, waiting.   15
He lifted his head from his drinking, as cattle do,
And looked at me vaguely, as drinking cattle do,
And flickered his two-forked tongue from his lips, and mused a
    moment,
And stooped and drank a little more,
Being earth-brown, earth-golden from the burning bowels of the
    earth   20
On the day of Sicilian July, with Etna smoking.

The voice of my education said to me
He must be killed,
For in Sicily the black, black snakes are innocent, the gold are
    venomous.

And voices in me said, If you were a man   25
You would take a stick and break him now, and finish him off.

But must I confess how I liked him,
How glad I was he had come like a guest in quiet, to drink at my
    water-trough
And depart peaceful, pacified, and thankless,
Into the burning bowels of this earth?   30

Was it cowardice, that I dared not kill him?
Was it perversity, that I longed to talk to him?
Was it humility, to feel so honored?
I felt so honored.

And yet those voices: 35
If you were not afraid, you would kill him!

And truly I was afraid, I was most afraid,
But even so, honored still more
That he should seek my hospitality
From out the dark door of the secret earth.   40

He drank enough
And lifted his head, dreamily, as one who has drunken,
And flickered his tongue like a forked night on the air, so black,
Seeming to lick his lips,
And looked around like a god, unseeing, into the air,   45
And slowly turned his head,
And slowly, very slowly, as if thrice adream,
Proceeded to draw his slow length curving round
And climb again the broken bank of my wall-face.

And as he put his head into that dreadful hole,   50
And as he slowly drew up, snake-easing his shoulders, and
    entered farther,
A sort of horror, a sort of protest against his withdrawing into that
    horrid black hole,
Deliberately going into the blackness, and slowly drawing himself
    after,
Overcame me now his back was turned.

I looked round, I put down my pitcher,   55
I picked up a clumsy log
And threw it at the water-trough with a clatter.

I think it did not hit him,
But suddenly that part of him that was left behind convulsed in
    undignified haste
Writhed like lightning, and was gone   60
Into the black hole, the earth-lipped fissure in the wall-front,
At which, in the intense still noon, I stared with fascination.

And immediately I regretted it.
I thought how paltry, how vulgar, what a mean act!
I despised myself and the voices of my accursed human education.   65

And I thought of the albatross
And I wished he would come back, my snake.

For he seemed to me again like a king,
Like a king in exile, uncrowned in the underworld,
Now due to be crowned again.   70

And so, I missed my chance with one of the lords
Of life.
And I have something to expiate;
A pettiness.

The Vacuum

Howard Nemerov

The house is so quiet now
The vacuum cleaner sulks in the corner closet,
Its bag limp as a stopped lung, its mouth
Grinning into the floor, maybe at my
Slovenly life, my dog-dead youth.

I've lived this way long enough,
But when my old woman died her soul
Went into that vacuum cleaner, and I can't bear
To see the bag swell like a belly, eating the dust
And the woolen mice, and begin to howl

Because there is old filth everywhere
She used to crawl, in the corner and under the stair.
I know now how life is cheap as dirt,
And still the hungry, angry heart
Hangs on and howls, biting at air.

From *New and Selected Poems* by Howard Nemerov. Copyright 1960 by the University of Chicago. Reprinted by permission of Howard Nemerov.

The River-Merchant's Wife: A Letter

Ezra Pound

While my hair was still cut straight across my forehead
I played about the front gate, pulling flowers.
You came by on bamboo stilts, playing horse,
You walked about my seat, playing with blue plums.
And we went on living in the village of Chokan:⠀⠀⠀⠀⠀⠀5
Two small people, without dislike or suspicion.

At fourteen I married My Lord you.
I never laughed, being bashful.
Lowering my head, I looked at the wall.
Called to, a thousand times, I never looked back.⠀⠀⠀⠀⠀⠀10

At fifteen I stopped scowling,
I desired my dust to be mingled with yours
Forever and forever and forever.
Why should I climb the look out?

At sixteen you departed,⠀⠀⠀⠀⠀⠀15
You went into far Ku-to-yen, by the river of swirling eddies,
And you have been gone five months.
The monkeys make sorrowful noise overhead.

You dragged your feet when you went out.
By the gate now, the moss is grown, the different mosses,⠀⠀⠀⠀⠀⠀20
Too deep to clear them away!
The leaves fall early this autumn, in wind.
The paired butterflies are already yellow with August
Over the grass in the West garden;
They hurt me. I grow older.⠀⠀⠀⠀⠀⠀25
If you are coming down through the narrows of the river Kiang,
Please let me know beforehand,
And I will come out to meet you
⠀⠀⠀⠀⠀⠀As far as Cho-fu-Sa.

By Rihaku

The Mill

Edwin Arlington Robinson

The miller's wife had waited long,
   The tea was cold, the fire was dead;
And there might yet be nothing wrong
   In how he went and what he said:
"There are no millers any more,"   5
   Was all that she had heard him say;
And he had lingered at the door
   So long that it seemed yesterday.

Sick with a fear that had no form
   She knew that she was there at last;   10
And in the mill there was a warm
   And mealy fragrance of the past.
What else there was would only seem
   To say again what he had meant;
And what was hanging from a beam   15
   Would not have heeded where she went.

And if she thought it followed her,
   She may have reasoned in the dark
That one way of the few there were
   Would hide her and would leave no mark: 20
Black water, smooth above the weir
   Like starry velvet in the night,
Though ruffled once, would soon appear
   The same as ever to the sight.

That Time of Year

William Shakespeare

That time of year thou mayst in me behold
When yellow leaves, or none, or few, do hang
Upon those boughs which shake against the cold,
Bare ruined choirs, where late the sweet birds sang.
In me thou see'st the twilight of such day   5
As after sunset fadeth in the west;
Which by and by black night doth take away,
Death's second self, that seals up all in rest.
In me thou see'st the glowing of such fire,
That on the ashes of his youth doth lie,   10
As the deathbed whereon it must expire,
Consumed with that which it was nourished by.
    This thou perceiv'st, which makes thy love more strong,
    To love that well which thou must leave ere long.

Auto Wreck
Karl Shapiro

Its quick soft silver bell beating, beating,
And down the dark one ruby flare
Pulsing out red light like an artery,
The ambulance at top speed floating down
Past beacons and illuminated clocks   5
Wings in a heavy curve, dips down,
And brakes speed, entering the crowd.
The doors leap open, emptying light;
Stretchers are laid out, the mangled lifted
And stowed into the little hospital.   10
Then the bell, breaking the hush, tolls once,
And the ambulance with its terrible cargo
Rocking, slightly rocking, moves away,
As the doors, an afterthought, are closed.

We are deranged, walking among the cops   15
Who sweep glass and are large and composed.
One is still making notes under the light.
One with a bucket douches ponds of blood
Into the street and gutter.
One hangs lanterns on the wrecks that cling,   20
Empty husks of locusts, to iron poles.

Our throats were tight as tourniquets,
Our feet were bound with splints, but now,
Like convalescents intimate and gauche,
We speak through sickly smiles and warn   25
With the stubborn saw of common sense,
The grim joke and the banal resolution.
The traffic moves around with care,
But we remain, touching a wound
That opens to our richest horror.   30
Already old, the question Who shall die?
Becomes unspoken Who is innocent?

For death in war is done by hands;
Suicide has cause and stillbirth, logic;
And cancer, simple as a flower, blooms.   35
But this invites the occult mind,
Cancels our physics with a sneer,
And spatters all we knew of denouement
Across the expedient and wicked stones.

Fern Hill

Dylan Thomas

Now as I was young and easy under the apple boughs
About the lilting house and happy as the grass was green,
   The night above the dingle starry,
    Time let me hail and climb
   Golden in the heydays of his eyes,   5
And honoured among wagons I was prince of the apple towns
And once below a time I lordly had the trees and leaves
    Trail with daisies and barley
   Down the rivers of the windfall light.

And as I was green and carefree, famous among the barns   10
About the happy yard and singing as the farm was home,
   In the sun that is young once only,
    Time let me play and be
   Golden in the mercy of his means,
And green and golden I was huntsman and herdsman, the calves   15
Sang to my horn, the foxes on the hills barked clear and cold,
    And the sabbath rang slowly
   In the pebbles of the holy streams.

All the sun long it was running, it was lovely, the hay
Fields high as the house, the tunes from the chimneys, it was air   20
   And playing, lovely and watery
    And fire green as grass.
   And nightly under the simple stars
As I rode to sleep the owls were bearing the farm away,
All the moon long I heard, blessed among stables, the nightjars   25
   Flying with the ricks, and the horses
    Flashing into the dark.

And then to awake, and the farm, like a wanderer white
With the dew, come back, the cock on his shoulder: it was all
   Shining, it was Adam and maiden,   30
    The sky gathered again
   And the sun grew round that very day.
So it must have been after the birth of the simple light
In the first, spinning place, the spellbound horses walking warm
   Out of the whinnying green stable   35
    On to the fields of praise.

And honoured among foxes and pheasants by the gay house
Under the new made clouds and happy as the heart was long,
   In the sun born over and over,
      I ran my heedless ways,   40
   My wishes raced through the house high hay
And nothing I cared, at my sky blue trades, that time allows
In all his tuneful turning so few and such morning songs
   Before the children green and golden
      Follow him out of grace,   45

Nothing I cared, in the lamb white days, that time would take me
Up to the swallow thronged loft by the shadow of my hand,
   In the moon that is always rising,
      Nor that riding to sleep
I should hear him fly with the high fields   50
And wake to the farm forever fled from the childless land.
Oh as I was young and easy in the mercy of his means,
    Time held me green and dying
   Though I sang in my chains like the sea.

The Widow's Lament in Springtime

William Carlos Williams

Sorrow is my own yard
where the new grass
flames as it has flamed
often before but not
with the cold fire   5
that closes round me this year.
Thirtyfive years
I lived with my husband.
The plumtree is white today
with masses of flowers.   10
Masses of flowers
load the cherry branches
and color some bushes
yellow and some red
but the grief in my heart   15
is stronger than they
for though they were my joy
formerly, today I notice them
and turned away forgetting.
Today my son told me   20
that in the meadows,
at the edge of the heavy woods
in the distance, he saw
trees of white flowers.
I feel that I would like   25
to go there
and fall into those flowers
and sink into the marsh near them.

INDEX